Kaplan Publishing are constantly finding ways to make a difference to your studie exciting online resources really do offer something different to students looking for exam success.

D0997684

This book comes with free MyKaplan online resources so that you can study anytime, anywhere. This free online resource is not sold separately and is included in the price of the book.

Having purchased this book, you have access to the following online study materials:

CONTENT	ACCA (including FFA,FAB,FMA)		FIA (excluding FFA,FAB,FMA)	
	Text	Kit	Text	Kit
Eletronic version of the book	✓	✓	✓	✓
Check Your Understanding Test with instant answers	✓			
Material updates	✓	✓	✓	✓
Latest official ACCA exam questions*		✓		
Extra question assistance using the signpost icon**		✓		
Question debriefs using clock icon***		✓		
Consolidation Test including questions and answers	✓			

*   Excludes AB, MA, FA, LW, FAB, FMA and FFA; for all other subjects includes a selection of questions, as released by ACCA

**   For ACCA SBR, AFM, APM, AAA only

*** Excludes AB, MA, FA, LW, FAB, FMA and FFA

How to access your online resources

Kaplan Financial students will already have a MyKaplan account and these extra resources will be available to you online. You do not need to register again, as this process was completed when you enrolled. If you are having problems accessing online materials, please ask your course administrator.

If you are not studying with Kaplan and did not purchase your book via a Kaplan website, to unlock your extra online resources please go to www.mykaplan.co.uk/addabook (even if you have set up an account and registered books previously). You will then need to enter the ISBN number (on the title page and back cover) and the unique pass key number contained in the scratch panel below to gain access.

You will also be required to enter additional information during this process to set up or confirm your account details.

If you purchased through Kaplan Flexible Learning or via the Kaplan Publishing website you will automatically receive an e-mail invitation to MyKaplan. Please register your details using this email to gain access to your content. If you do not receive the e-mail or book content, please contact Kaplan Publishing.

Your Code and Information

This code can only be used once for the registration of one book online. This registration and your online content will expire when the final sittings for the examinations covered by this book have taken place. Please allow one hour from the time you submit your book details for us to process your request.

Please scratch the film to access your MyKaplan code.

Please be aware that this code is case-sensitive and you will need to include the dashes within the passcode, but not when entering the ISBN. For further technical support, please visit www.MyKaplan.co.uk

ACCA

Applied Knowledge

Diploma in Accountin
and Business

Accountant in Business (AB/F

Study Text

British library cataloguing-in-publication data

A catalogue record for this book is available from the British Library.

Published by:

Kaplan Publishing UK
Unit 2 The Business Centre
Molly Millars Lane
Wokingham
Berkshire
RG41 2QZ

ISBN 978-1-78740-077-1

© Kaplan Financial Limited, 2018

Acknowledgements

We are grateful to the Association of Chartered Certified Accountants and the Chartered Institute of Management Accountants for permission to reproduce past examination questions. The answers have been prepared by Kaplan Publishing.

These materials are reviewed by the ACCA examining team. The objective of the review is to ensure that the material properly covers the syllabus and study guide outcomes, used by the examining team in setting the exams, in the appropriate breadth and depth. The review does not ensure that every eventuality, combination or application of examinable topics is addressed by the ACCA Approved Content. Nor does the review comprise a detailed technical check of the content as the Approved Content Provider has its own quality assurance processes in place in this respect.

Contents

KAPLAN PUBLISHIN

Introduction

How to Use the Materials

These Kaplan Publishing learning materials have been carefully designed to make your learning experience as easy as possible and to give you the best chances of success in your examinations.

The product range contains a number of features to help you in the study process. They include:

1   Detailed study guide and syllabus objectives

2   Description of the examination

3   Study skills and revision guidance

4   Study text

5   Question practice

The sections on the study guide, the syllabus objectives, the examination and study skills should all be read before you commence your studies. They are designed to familiarise you with the nature and content of the examination and give you tips on how to best to approach your learning.

The **Study Text** comprises the main learning materials and gives guidance as to the importance of topics and where other related resources can be found. Each chapter includes:

- The **learning objectives** contained in each chapter, which have been carefully mapped to the examining body's own syllabus learning objectives or outcomes. You should use these to check you have a clear understanding of all the topics on which you might be assessed in the examination.

- The **chapter diagram** provides a visual reference for the content in the chapter, giving an overview of the topics and how they link together.

- The **content** for each topic area commences with a brief explanation or definition to put the topic into context before covering the topic in detail. You should follow your studying of the content with a review of the illustration/s. These are worked examples which will help you to understand better how to apply the content for the topic.

- **Test your understanding** sections provide an opportunity to assess your understanding of the key topics by applying what you have learned to short questions. Answers can be found at the back of each chapter.

- **Summary diagrams** complete each chapter to show the important links between topics and the overall content of the paper. These diagrams should be used to check that you have covered and understood the core topics before moving on.

Quality and accuracy are of the utmost importance to us so if you spot an error in any of our products, please send an email to mykaplanreporting@kaplan.com with full details, or follow the link to the feedback form in MyKaplan.

Our Quality Co-ordinator will work with our technical team to verify the error and take action to ensure it is corrected in future editions.

Icon Explanations (Header C)

 Definition – Key definitions that you will need to learn from the core content.

 Key point – Identifies topics that are key to success and are often examined.

 New – Identifies topics that are brand new in papers that build on, and therefore also contain, learning covered in earlier papers.

 Tricky topic – When reviewing these areas care should be taken and all illustrations and Test your understanding exercises should be completed to ensure that the topic is understood.

 Supplementary reading – These sections will help to provide a deeper understanding of core areas. The supplementary reading is **NOT** optional reading. It is vital to provide you with the breadth of knowledge you will need to address the wide range of topics within your syllabus that could feature in an exam question. **Reference to this text is vital when self-studying**.

 Test your understanding – Exercises for you to complete to ensure that you have understood the topics just learned.

 Illustration – Worked examples help you understand the core content better.

 Tutorial note – Included to explain some of the technical points in more detail.

 Footsteps – Helpful tutor tips.

On-line subscribers

Our on-line resources are designed to increase the flexibility of your learning materials and provide you with immediate feedback on how your studies are progressing.

If you are subscribed to our on-line resources you will find:

1   On-line reference ware: reproduces your Study text on-line, giving you anytime, anywhere access.

2   On-line testing: provides you with additional on-line objective testing so you can practice what you have learned further.

3   On-line performance management: immediate access to your on-line testing results. Review your performance by key topics and chart your achievement through the course relative to your peer group.

Syllabus introduction

Syllabus background

The aim of ACCA **Accountant in Business**/FIA Diploma in Accounting and Business, **Accountant in Business**, is to introduce knowledge and understanding of the business and its environment and the influence this has on how organisations are structured and on the role of the accounting and other key business functions in contributing to the efficient, effective and ethical management and development of an organisation and its people and systems.

Objectives of the syllabus

- Understand the purpose and types of business and how they interact with the key stakeholders and the external environment.

- Understand business organisation structure, functions and the role of corporate governance.

- Recognise the function of accountancy and audit in communicating, reporting and assuring financial information and in effective financial control and compliance.

- Recognise the principles of authority and leadership and how teams and individuals are recruited, managed, motivated and developed.

- Understand the importance of personal effectiveness as the basis for effective team and organisational behaviour.

- Recognise that all aspects of business and finance should be conducted in a manner which complies with and is in the spirit of accepted professional ethics and professional values.

Core areas of the syllabus

- The business organisation, its stakeholders and the external environment.
- Business organisational structure, functions and governance.
- Accounting and reporting systems, controls and compliance.
- Leading and managing individuals and teams.
- Personal effectiveness and communication.
- Professional ethics in accounting and business.

Syllabus objectives

We have reproduced the ACCA's syllabus below, showing where the objectives are explored within this book. Within the chapters, we have broken down the extensive information found in the syllabus into easily digestible and relevant sections, called Content Objectives. These correspond to the objectives at the beginning of each chapter.

Syllabus learning objective	Chapter reference

A   THE BUSINESS ORGANISATION, ITS STAKEHOLDERS AND THE EXTERNAL ENVIRONMENT

1   The purpose and types of business organisation

   (a) Define business organisations and explain why they are formed.   1

   (b) Describe common features of business organisations.

   (c) Outline how business organisations differ.

   (d) List the industrial and commercial sectors in which business organisations operate.

   (e) Identify the different types of business organisation and their main characteristics

      (i)   Commercial

      (ii) Not-for-profit and cooperatives

      (iii) Public sector

      (iv) Non-governmental organisations and cooperatives.

2   Stakeholders in business organisations   5

   (a) Define stakeholders and explain the agency relationship in business and how it may vary in different types of business organisation.

   (b) Define internal, connected and external stakeholders and explain their impact on the organisation.

Syllabus learning objective	Chapter reference

Syllabus learning objective   **Chapter reference**

(c)   Identify the main stakeholder groups and the objectives of each group.

(d)   Explain how the different stakeholder groups interact with each other and how their objectives may conflict with each other.

(e)   Compare the power and influence of various stakeholder groups and how their needs should be accounted for, such as under the Mendelow framework.

3   **Political and legal factors affecting business**   **6**

(a)   Explain how the political system and government policy affects the organisation.

(b)   Describe the sources of legal authority, including supra-national bodies, national and regional governments.

(c)   Explain how the law protects the employee and the implications of employment legislation for the manager and the organisation.

(d)   Identify the principles of data protection and security.

(e)   Explain how the law promotes and protects health and safety in the workplace.

(f)   Recognise the responsibility of the individual and organisation for compliance with laws on data protection, security and health and safety.

(g)   Outline principles of consumer protection such as sale of goods and simple contract.

4   **Macro-economic factors**   **7**

(a)   Define macro-economic policy and explain its objectives.

(b)   Explain the main determinants of the level of business activity in the economy and how variations in the level of business activity affect individuals, households and businesses.

(c)   Explain the impact of economic issues on the individual, the household and the business:

     (i)   inflation

     (ii)   unemployment

     (iii)   stagnation

     (iv)   international payments disequilibrium.

KAPLAN PUBLISHING

Syllabus learning objective	Chapter reference

(d) Describe the main types of economic policy that may be implemented by government and supra-national bodies to maximise economic welfare.

(e) Recognise the impact of fiscal and monetary policy measures on the individual, the household and businesses.

5 Micro economic factors 7

(a) Define the concept of demand and supply for goods and services.

(b) Explain elasticity of demand and the impact of substitute and complementary goods.

(c) Explain the economic behaviour of costs in the short and long term.

(d) Define perfect competition, oligopoly, monopolistic competition and monopoly.

6 Social and demographic factors 8

(a) Explain the medium and long-term effects of social and demographic trends on business outcomes and the economy.

(b) Describe the impact of changes in social structure, values, attitudes and tastes on the organisation.

(c) Identify and explain the measures that governments may take in response to the medium and long-term impact of demographic change.

7 Technological factors 8

(a) Explain the effects of technological change on the organisation structure and strategy

   (i) Downsizing

   (ii) Delayering

   (iii) Outsourcing.

(b) Describe the impact of information technology and information systems development on business processes.

Syllabus learning objective		Chapter reference

8 Environmental factors   8

(a) List ways in which the business can affect or be affected by its physical environment.

(b) Describe ways in which businesses can operate more efficiently and effectively to limit damage to the environment.

(c) Identify the benefits of economic sustainability to a range of stakeholders.

9 Competitive factors   9

(a) Identify a business's strengths, weaknesses, opportunities and threats (SWOT) in a market and the main sources of competitive advantage.

(b) Describe the activities of an organisation that affect its competitiveness: purchasing, production, marketing and service.

(c) Explain the factors or forces that influence the level of competitiveness in an industry or sector using Porter's five forces model.

(d) Identify the main elements within Porter's value chain and explain the meaning of a value network.

B BUSINESS ORGANISATION STRUCTURE, FUNCTIONS AND GOVERNANCE

1 The formal and informal business   3

(a) Explain the informal organisation and its relationship with the formal organisation.

(b) Describe the impact of the formal organisation on the business.

2 Business organisation, structure and design   2

(a) Describe Mintzberg's components of the organisation and explain the different ways in which formal organisations may be structured: entrepreneurial, functional, matrix, divisional (geographical, by product, or by customer type), boundaryless (virtual, hollow or modular).

(b) Explain basic organisational structure concepts:

(i) separation of ownership and management

(ii) separation of direction and management

(iii) span of control and scalar chain

Syllabus learning objective	Chapter reference

    (iv)   tall and flat organisations

    (v)   outsourcing and offshoring

    (vi)   shared services approach.

(c)   Explain the characteristics of the strategic, tactical and operational levels in the organisation in the context of the Anthony hierarchy.

(d)   Explain centralisation and decentralisation and list their advantages and disadvantages.

(e)   Describe the roles and functions of the main departments in a business organisation:

    (i)   research and development

    (ii)   purchasing

    (iii)   production and direct service provision

    (iv)   marketing

    (v)   administration

    (vi)   finance.

(f)   Explain the role of marketing in an organisation

    (i)   the definition of marketing

    (ii)   the marketing mix

    (iii)   the relationship of the marketing plan to the strategic plan.

3   Organisational culture in business   3

(a)   Define organisational culture.

(b)   Describe the factors that shape the culture of the organisation.

(c)   Explain the contribution made by writers on culture: Schein, Handy and Hofstede.

4   Committees in business organisations   11

(a)   Explain the purposes of committees.

(b)   Describe the types of committee used by business organisations.

(c)   List the advantages and disadvantages of committees.

(d)   Explain the role of the Chair and Secretary of a committee.

Syllabus learning objective			Chapter reference

5 Governance and social responsibility in business — 11

(a) Explain the agency concept in relation to corporate governance.

(b) Define corporate governance and social responsibility and explain their importance in contemporary organisations.

(c) Explain the responsibility of organisations to maintain appropriate standards of corporate governance and corporate social responsibility.

(d) Briefly explain the main recommendations of best practice in effective corporate governance: executive and non-executive directors, remuneration committees, audit committees and public oversight.

(e) Explain how organisations take account of their social responsibility objectives through analysis of the needs of internal, connected and external stakeholders.

(f) Identify the social and environmental responsibilities of business organisations to internal, external and connected stakeholders.

C ACCOUNTING AND REPORTING SYSTEMS, CONTROLS AND COMPLIANCE

1 The relationship between accounting and other business functions — 15

(a) Explain the relationship between accounting and other key functions within the business such as procurement, production and marketing.

(b) Explain financial considerations in production and production planning.

(c) Identify the financial issues associated with marketing.

(d) Identify the financial costs and benefits of effective service provision.

2 Accounting and finance functions within business — 13

(a) Explain the contribution of the accounting function to the formulation, implementation and control of the organisation's policies, procedures and performance.

(b) Identify and describe the main financial accounting functions in business: recording financial information, codifying and processing financial information and preparing financial statements.

Syllabus learning objective	Chapter reference

(c) Identify and describe the main management accounting and performance management functions in business: recording and analysing costs and revenues, providing management accounting information for decision-making and planning and preparing budgets and exercising budgetary control.

(d) Identify and describe the main finance and treasury functions: calculating and mitigating business tax liabilities, evaluating and obtaining finance, managing working capital and treasury and risk management.

(e) Identify and describe the main audit and assurance roles in business: internal and external audit. — 16

(f) Explain the main functions of the internal auditor and the external auditor and how they differ. — 16

3 Principles of law and regulation governing accounting and audit — 12

(a) Explain basic legal requirements in relation to retaining and submitting proper records and preparing and auditing financial statements.

(b) Explain the broad consequences of failing to comply with the legal requirements for maintaining and filing accounting records.

(c) Explain how the international accountancy profession regulates itself through the establishment of reporting standards and their monitoring.

4 The sources and purpose of internal and external financial information, provided by business — 13

(a) Explain the various business purposes for which the following financial information is required: the income statement, the statement of cash flows and the statement of financial position.

(b) Describe the main purposes of the following types of management accounting reports:

(i) Cost schedules

(ii) Budgets

(iii) Variance reports.

Syllabus learning objective			Chapter reference
5	**Financial systems, procedures and related IT applications**		
	(a)	Identify an organisation's system requirements in relation to the objectives and policies of the organisation.	14
	(b)	Describe the main financial systems used within an organisation:	
		(i) purchases and sales invoicing	
		(ii) payroll and credit control	
		(iii) cash and working capital management.	
	(c)	Explain why it is important to adhere to policies and procedures for handling clients' money.	
	(d)	Identify weaknesses, potential for error and inefficiencies in accounting systems.	
	(e)	Recommend improvements to accounting systems to prevent error and fraud and to improve overall efficiency.	
	(f)	Explain why appropriate controls are necessary in relation to business and IT systems and procedures.	
	(g)	Identify business uses of computers and IT software applications: Spreadsheet applications, database systems and accounting packages. Describe the relative benefits and limitations of manual and automated financial systems that may be used within an organisation.	4
6	**Internal controls, authorisation, security and compliance within business**		16
	(a)	Explain internal control and internal check.	
	(b)	Explain the importance of internal financial controls in an organisation.	
	(c)	Describe the responsibilities of management for internal financial control.	
	(d)	Describe the features of effective internal financial control procedures in an organisation, including authorisation.	
	(e)	Identify and describe the types of information technology and information systems used by the business organisation for internal control.	

KAPLAN PUBLISHING

Syllabus learning objective	Chapter reference

(f) Identify and describe features for protecting the security of IT systems and software within businesses.

(g) Describe general and application systems controls in business.

7 Fraud and fraudulent behaviour and their prevention in business   17

(a) Explain the circumstances under which fraud is likely to arise.

(b) Identify different types of fraud in the organisation.

(c) Explain the implications of fraud for the organisation.

(d) Explain the role and duties of individual managers in the fraud detection and prevention process.

(e) Define the term 'money laundering'.

(f) Give examples of recognised offences under typical money laundering regulation.

(g) Identify methods for detecting and preventing money laundering and explain how suspicions of money laundering should be reported to the appropriate authorities.

D LEADING AND MANAGING INDIVIDUALS AND TEAMS

1 Leadership, management and supervision

(a) Define leadership, management and supervision and explain the distinction between these terms.   18

(b) Explain the nature of management:

    (i) scientific/classical theories of management – Fayol, Taylor

    (ii) the human relations school – Mayo

    (iii) the functions of a manager – Mintzberg, Drucker.

(c) Explain the areas of managerial authority and responsibility.

(d) Explain the situational, functional and contingency approaches to leadership with reference to the theories of Adair, Fiedler, Bennis, Kotter and Heifetz.

(e) Describe leadership styles and contexts: using the models of Ashridge and Blake and Mouton.

Syllabus learning objective			Chapter reference
2	**Recruitment and selection of employees**		19
	(a)	Explain the importance of effective recruitment and selection to the organisation.	
	(b)	Describe the recruitment and selection process and explain the stages in this process.	
	(c)	Describe the roles of those involved in the recruitment and selection processes.	
	(d)	Describe the methods through which organisations seek to meet their recruitment needs.	
	(e)	Explain the advantages and disadvantages of different recruitment and selection methods.	
	(f)	Explain the purposes of a diversity policy within the human resources plan.	
	(g)	Explain the purposes and benefits of an equal opportunities policy within human resource planning and the practical steps that an organisation may take to ensure the effectiveness of its diversity and equal opportunities policy.	
3	**Individual and group behaviour in business organisations**		20
	(a)	Describe the main characteristics of individual and group behaviour.	
	(b)	Outline the contributions of individuals and teams to organisational success.	
	(c)	Identify individual and team approaches to work.	
4	**Team formation, development and management**		20
	(a)	Explain the differences between a group and a team.	
	(b)	Define the purposes of a team.	
	(c)	Explain the role of the manager in building the team and developing individuals within the team. Belbin's team role theories and Tuckman's theory of team development.	
	(d)	List the characteristics of effective and ineffective teams.	
	(e)	Describe tools and techniques that can be used to build the team and improve team effectiveness.	

Syllabus learning objective	Chapter reference

5   Motivating teams and individuals   21

   (a) Define motivation and explain its importance to the organisation, teams and individuals.

   (b) Explain content and process theories of motivation: Maslow, Herzberg, McGregor and Vroom.

   (c) Explain and identify types of intrinsic and extrinsic rewards.

   (d) Explain how reward systems can be designed and implemented to motivate teams and individuals.

6   Learning and training at work   22

   (a) Explain the importance of learning and development in the workplace.

   (b) Describe the learning process: Honey and Mumford, Kolb.

   (c) Describe the role of the human resources department and individual managers in the learning process.

   (d) Describe the training and development process: identifying needs, setting objectives, programme design, delivery and validation.

   (e) Explain the terms 'training', 'development' and 'education' and the characteristics of each.

   (f) List the benefits of effective training and development in the workplace.

7   Review and appraisal of individual performance   23

   (a) Explain the importance of performance assessment.

   (b) Explain how organisations assess the performance of human resources.

   (c) Define performance appraisal and describe its purposes.

   (d) Describe the performance appraisal process.

   (e) Explain the benefits of effective appraisal.

   (f) Identify the barriers to effective appraisal and how these may be overcome.

   (g) Explain how the effectiveness of performance appraisal may be evaluated.

Syllabus learning objective	Chapter reference

E PERSONAL EFFECTIVENESS AND COMMUNICATION IN BUSINESS

1 Personal effectiveness techniques

(a) Explain the importance of time management.	24

(b) Describe the barriers to effective time management and how they may be overcome.

(c) Describe the role of information technology in improving personal effectiveness.

2 Consequences of ineffectiveness at work	24

(a) Identify the main ways in which people and teams can be ineffective at work.

(b) Explain how individual or team ineffectiveness can affect organisational performance.

3 Competence frameworks and personal development

(a) Describe the features of a competence framework.	24

(b) Explain how a competence framework underpins professional development needs.

(c) Explain how personal and continuous professional development can increase personal effectiveness at work.

(d) Explain the purpose and benefits of coaching, mentoring and counselling in promoting employee effectiveness.

(e) Describe how a personal development plan should be formulated, implemented, monitored and reviewed by the individual.

4 Sources of conflict and techniques for conflict resolution and referral	24

(a) Identify situations where conflict at work can arise.

(b) Describe how conflict can affect personal and organisational performance.

(c) Explain how conflict can be avoided.

(d) Identify ways in which conflict can be resolved or referred.

KAPLAN PUBLISHING

Syllabus learning objective			Chapter reference
5	**Communicating in business**		25
	(a)	Define communications and identify methods of communication used in the organisation and how they are used.	
	(b)	Explain how the type of information differs and the purposes for which it is applied at different levels of the organisation: strategic, tactical and operational.	
	(c)	List the attributes of good quality information.	4
	(d)	Explain a simple communication model: sender, message, receiver, feedback, noise.	25
	(e)	Explain formal and informal communication and their importance in the workplace and identify the consequences of ineffective communication.	
	(f)	Describe the attributes of effective communication, the barriers to effective communication and identify practical steps that may be taken to overcome them.	
	(g)	Describe the main methods and patterns of communication.	
F	**PROFESSIONAL ETHICS IN ACCOUNTING AND BUSINESS**		
1	**Fundamental principles of ethical behaviour**		10
	(a)	Define business ethics and explain the importance of ethics to the organisation and to the individual.	
	(b)	Describe and demonstrate the following principles from the IFAC code of ethics, using examples: Integrity, Objectivity, Professional competence, Confidentiality and Professional behaviour.	
	(c)	Describe organisational values which promote ethical behaviour using examples: Openness, Trust, Honesty, Respect, Empowerment and Accountability.	
	(d)	Explain the concept of acting in the public interest.	

Syllabus learning objective	Chapter reference
2 **The role of regulatory and professional bodies in promoting ethical and professional standards in the accountancy profession**	10

(a) Recognise the purpose of international and organisational codes of ethics and codes of conduct, I FAC, ACCA, etc.

(b) Describe how professional bodies and regulators promote ethical awareness and prevent or punish illegal or unethical behaviour.

(c) Identify the factors that distinguish a profession from other types of occupation.

(d) Explain the role of the accountant in promoting ethical behaviour.

(e) Recognise when and to whom illegal, or unethical conduct by anyone within the organisation should be reported.

3 **Corporate codes of ethics**	10

(a) Define corporate codes of ethics.

(b) Describe the typical contents of a corporate code of ethics.

(c) Explain the benefits of a corporate code of ethics to the organisation and its employees.

4 **Ethical conflicts and dilemmas**	10

(a) Describe situations where ethical conflicts can arise.

(b) Identify the main threats to ethical behaviour.

(c) Outline situations at work where ethical dilemmas may be faced.

(d) List the main safeguards against ethical threats and dilemmas.

KAPLAN PUBLISHING

The examination

Examination format

The syllabus is assessed by computer-based examination (CBE). Questions will assess all parts of the syllabus and will test knowledge and some comprehension or application of this knowledge. The examination will consist of:

	Number of marks
Thirty 2-mark questions	60
Sixteen 1-mark question	16
Six 4-mark questions	24
	———
Total time allowed: 2 hours	100

Examination tips

Spend the first few minutes of the examination reviewing the format and content so that you understand what you need to do.

Divide the time you spend on questions in proportion to the marks on offer. One suggestion **for this exam** is to allocate 1.2 minutes to each mark available.

Objective test questions: Read the questions carefully and work through any calculations required. If you don't know the answer, eliminate those options you know are incorrect and see if the answer becomes more obvious.

Guess your final answer rather than leave it blank if necessary.

Computer-based examination (CBE) – Tips

Be sure you understand how to use the software before you start the exam. If in doubt, ask the assessment centre staff to explain it to you.

Questions are **displayed on the screen** and answers are entered using keyboard and mouse. At the end of the exam, you are given a certificate showing the result you have achieved.

The CBE exam will not only examine multiple choice questions but could include questions that require data entry or a multiple response.

Do not attempt a CBE until you have **completed all study material** relating to it. **Do not skip any of the material** in the syllabus.

Read each question very carefully.

Double-check your answer before committing yourself to it.

Answer every question – if you do not know an answer, you don't lose anything by guessing. Think carefully before you **guess.**

The CBE question types are as follows:

- Multiple choice – where you are required to choose one answer from a list of options provided by clicking on the appropriate 'radio button'

- Multiple response – where you are required to select more than one response from the options provided by clicking on the appropriate tick boxes (typically choose two options from the available list)

- Multiple response matching – where you are required to indicate a response to a number of related statements by clicking on the 'radio button' which corresponds to the appropriate response for each statement

- Number entry – where you are required to key in a response to a question shown on the screen.

With an objective test question, it may be possible to eliminate first those answers that you know are wrong. Then choose the most appropriate answer(s) as required from those that are left. This could be a single answer (e.g. multiple choice) or more than one response (e.g. multiple response and multiple response – matching).

After you have eliminated the ones that you know to be wrong, if you are still unsure, guess. But only do so after you have double-checked that you have only eliminated answers that are definitely wrong.

Don't panic if you realise you've answered a question incorrectly. Try to remain calm, continue to apply examination technique and answer all questions required within the time available.

Study skills and revision guidance

This section aims to give guidance on how to study for your exams and to give ideas on how to improve your existing study techniques.

Preparing to study

Set your objectives

Before starting to study decide what you want to achieve – the type of pass you wish to obtain. This will decide the level of commitment and time you need to dedicate to your studies.

Devise a study plan

Determine which times of the week you will study.

Split these times into sessions of at least one hour for study of new material. Any shorter periods could be used for revision or practice.

Put the times you plan to study onto a study plan for the weeks from now until the exam and set yourself targets for each period of study – in your sessions make sure you cover the course, course assignments and revision.

If you are studying for more than one exam at a time, try to vary your subjects as this can help you to keep interested and see subjects as part of wider knowledge.

When working through your course, compare your progress with your plan and, if necessary, re-plan your work (perhaps including extra sessions) or, if you are ahead, do some extra revision/practice questions.

KAPLAN PUBLISHING

Effective studying

Active reading

You are not expected to learn the text by rote, rather, you must understand what you are reading and be able to use it to pass the exam and develop good practice. A good technique to use is SQ3Rs – Survey, Question, Read, Recall, Review:

1 **Survey the chapter**– look at the headings and read the introduction, summary and objectives, so as to get an overview of what the chapter deals with.

2 **Question** – whilst undertaking the survey, ask yourself the questions that you hope the chapter will answer for you.

3 **Read** through the chapter thoroughly, answering the questions and making sure you can meet the objectives. Attempt the exercises and activities in the text, and work through all the examples.

4 **Recall** – at the end of each section and at the end of the chapter, try to recall the main ideas of the section/chapter without referring to the text. This is best done after a short break of a couple of minutes after the reading stage.

5 **Review** – check that your recall notes are correct.

You may also find it helpful to re-read the chapter to try to see the topic(s) it deals with as a whole.

Note-taking

Taking notes is a useful way of learning, but do not simply copy out the text. The notes must:

- be in your own words
- be concise
- cover the key points
- be well organised.
- be modified as you study further chapters in this text or in related ones.

Trying to summarise a chapter without referring to the text can be a useful way of determining which areas you know and which you don't.

Three ways of taking notes:

Summarise the key points of a chapter.

Make linear notes – a list of headings, divided up with subheadings listing the key points. If you use linear notes, you can use different colours to highlight key points and keep topic areas together. Use plenty of space to make your notes easy to use.

Try a diagrammatic form – the most common of which is a mind-map. To make a mind-map, put the main heading in the centre of the paper and put a circle around it. Then draw short lines radiating from this to the main sub-headings, which again have circles around them. Then continue the process from the sub-headings to sub-sub-headings, advantages, disadvantages, etc.

Highlighting and underlining

You may find it useful to underline or highlight key points in your study text - but do be selective. You may also wish to make notes in the margins.

Revision

The best approach to revision is to revise the course as you work through it. Also try to leave four to six weeks before the exam for final revision. Make sure you cover the whole syllabus and pay special attention to those areas where your knowledge is weak. Here are some recommendations:

Read through the text and your notes again and condense your notes into key phrases. It may help to put key revision points onto index cards to look at when you have a few minutes to spare.

Review any assignments you have completed and look at where you lost marks – put more work into those areas where you were weak.

Practise exam standard questions under timed conditions. If you are short of time, list the points that you would cover in your answer and then read the model answer, but do try to complete at least a few questions under exam conditions.

Also practise producing answer plans and comparing them to the model answer.

If you are stuck on a topic find somebody (a tutor) to explain it to you.

Read good newspapers and professional journals, especially ACCA's Student Accountant – this can give you an advantage in the exam.

Ensure you know the structure of the exam – how many questions and of what type you will be expected to answer. During your revision attempt all the different styles of questions you may be asked.

Further reading

You can find further reading and technical articles under the student section of ACCA's website.

Technical update

This text has been updated to reflect Examinable Documents September 2018 to June 2019 issued by ACCA.

The business organisation

Chapter learning objectives

Upon completion of this chapter you will be able to:

- define 'business organisations' and explain why they are formed

- describe common features of business organisations

- outline how business organisations differ

- list the industrial and commercial sectors in which business organisations operate

- identify the different types of business organisation: commercial, not-for-profit, public sector, non-governmental organisations, co-operatives.

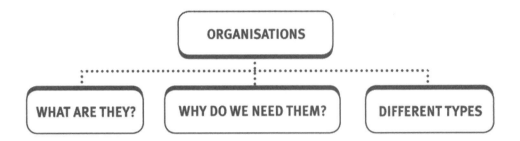

1 Business organisations and the reason they are formed

1.1 What is a business organisation?

Defining an organisation is difficult as there are many types of organisations which are set up to meet a variety of needs, such as clubs, schools companies, charities and hospitals.

What they all have in common is summarised in the definition produced by

Buchanan and Huczynski.

 'Organisations are social arrangements for the controlled performance of collective goals.'

Note the three key aspects of this definition:

- collective goals

- social arrangements

- controlled performance

What is an organisation?

Consider the three aspects of Buchanan and Huczynski's definition in more detail:

(a) 'Collective goals' – organisations are defined by their goals. The main goal of a school is to educate pupils. It will therefore be organised differently to a company that aims to make profits.

(b) 'Social arrangements' – someone working alone cannot be classed as an organisation. Organisations are structured to allow people to work together towards a common goal. Usually, the larger the organisation, the more formal its structures.

(c) 'Controlled performance' – an organisation will have systems and procedures in place to ensure that group goals are achieved. For a company this could involve setting sales targets, or periodically assessing the performance of staff members.

It is worth noting that a major similarity between most organisations is that they are mainly concerned with taking inputs and transforming them into outputs.

For a manufacturing company, this could involve taking raw materials and transforming them into a finished product that can be sold onto its customers.

An accountancy training firm will also take inputs (students and syllabuses) and transform them into outputs (qualified accountants).

Illustration 1 – Football team

A football team can be described as an organisation because:

- It has a number of players who have come together to play a game.

- The team has an objective (to score more goals than its opponent).

- To do their job properly, the members have to maintain an internal system of control to get the team to work together. In training they work out tactics so that in play they can rely on the ball being passed to those who can score goals.

- Each member of the team is part of the organisational structure and is skilled in a different task: the goalkeeper has more experience in stopping goals being scored than those in the forward line of the team.

- In addition, there must be team spirit, so that everyone works together. Players are encouraged to do their best, both on and off the field.

Test your understanding 1

Which of the following would be considered to be an organisation according to the definition produced by Buchanan and Huczynski?

(i)   A sole trader

(ii)   A tennis club

(iii) A hospital

A   (i), (ii) and (iii)

B   (i) and (ii) only

C   (ii) and (iii) only

D   (i) and (iii) only

1.2 Why do we need organisations?

Organisations enable people to:

- **Share skills and knowledge** – this can enable people to perform tasks that they would be unable to achieve on their own. Knowledge can also be shared between all the people within the organisation.

- **Specialise** – individual workers can concentrate on a limited type of activity. This allows them to build up a greater level of skill and knowledge than they would have if they attempted to be good at everything.

- **Pool resources** – whether money or time.

This results in **synergy** where organisations can achieve more than the individuals could on their own.

Test your understanding 2

Jared is organising a social event. Which of the following would be benefits of him forming a committee to manage the planning process and the event itself?

(i)   It would help to overcome his limitations, by bringing on board other people with different skills to him.

(ii) It would save time through the joint efforts of everyone on the committee.

(iii) It would help to satisfy Jared's social needs.

(iv) All members of the committee would have to be skilled in all aspects of managing the social event.

A   (i), (ii) and (iii) only

B   (i), (iii) and (iv) only

C   All of the above

D   None of the above

2 Different types of organisation

As we have discussed, different organisations have different goals. We can therefore classify them into several different categories.

2.1 Commercial versus not-for-profit

Commercial organisations

Commercial (or profit-seeking) organisations see their main objective as maximising the wealth of their owners.

There are three common forms that a commercial company can take:

- **Sole traders** – the organisation is owned and run by one person. In this type of organisation the owner is not legally separate from the business itself. If a sole trader's business is sued by a customer, the customer is actually suing the owner themselves.

- **Partnerships** – the organisation is owned and run by two or more individuals. Traditionally, partnerships (like sole traders) do not have a separate legal identity from their owners. However in recent years many countries have created alternative partnership structures (such as Limited Liability Partnerships (LLPs) in the UK) which mean that the business exists as a separate legal entity and the owners' liability is limited to the amount they have invested into the partnership.

- **Limited liability companies** – a company has a separate legal identity to its owners (who are known as shareholders). The owner's liability is limited to the amount they have invested into the company.

  In the UK, there are two types of limited company:

  Private limited companies (with 'Ltd' after their name) – these tend to

  be smaller businesses, often owned by a few shareholders. Shares cannot be offered to the general public.

  Public limited companies (with 'plc' after their name) – these can be much larger businesses. Shares can be offered to the general public, meaning that there can be millions of different shareholders. This makes it easier for the company to raise finance, enabling further growth.

Not for profit organisations

Not-for-profit organisations (NFPs or NPOs) do not see profitability as their main objective. Instead, they seek to satisfy the particular needs of their members or the sectors of society that they have been set up to benefit.

Illustration 2 – NFP examples
NFPs include the following: • government departments and agencies (such as HM Revenue and Customs)   • schools   • hospitals   • charities (such as the Red Cross, Oxfam and Doctors Without Borders)   • clubs.

The objectives of different NFPs will vary significantly:

- Hospitals exist to treat patients.

- Councils may see their mission as caring for their communities.

- Government organisations usually exist to implement government policy.

- A charity may have 'provision of relief to victims of disasters' as its main objective.

2.2 Public versus private sector organisations

Public sector organisations

The public sector is the part of the economy that is concerned with providing basic government services and is controlled by government organisations.

Illustration 3 – Public sector organisations

The organisations that make up the public sector vary from country to country, but generally include:

- police

- military

- public transport

- primary education

- healthcare for the poor

Private sector organisations

The private sector consists of organisations that are run by private individuals and groups rather than the government.

Illustration 4 – Private sector

The private sector will therefore normally include:

- businesses

- charities and

- clubs.

Within these will be both profit-seeking and not-for-profit organisations.

Test your understanding 3

Many schools run fund-raising events such as fêtes, where the intention is to make a profit. This makes them 'profit-seeking'.

Is this statement:

A   True

B   False

Non-governmental organisations (NGOs)

A non-governmental organisation is one which does not have profit as its primary goal and is not directly linked to the national government.

NGOs often promote political, social or environmental change within the countries they operate.

Illustration 5 – NGOs

NGOs include:

- the Red Cross
- Doctors Without Borders
- Greenpeace
- Amnesty International.

2.3 Co-operatives

Co-operatives are organisations that are owned and democratically controlled by their members – the people who buy their goods or services. Each member usually gets a single vote on key decisions – unlike companies where shareholders get one vote for each share that they own.

They are organised solely to meet the needs of the member-owners, who usually share any profits.

Illustration 6 – Co-operatives

In the UK, the largest example of a co-operative is the Co-operative Group, which has over 5.5 million members and operates in diverse markets, such as banking, travel and groceries.

Test your understanding 4

Which of the following are usually seen as the primary objectives of companies?

(i)   To maximise the wealth of shareholders

(ii)   To protect the environment

(iii)   To make a profit

A   (i), (ii) and (iii)

B   (i) and (ii) only

C   (ii) and (iii) only

D   (i) and (iii) only

Test your understanding 5

Which of the following organisations is most likely to be classified as part of the public sector?

A   A charity

B   A social club

C   A school

D   A public limited company

3   Sectors in which organisations operate

A further difference between organisations is the market in which they operate. There are a large number of different sectors, which include:

- **Agriculture** – production, processing and packaging of foodstuffs.

- **Mining** – extraction and processing of minerals.

- **Finance** – this includes banks and other companies that profit through investments and the lending of money to others.

- **Retailers** – sale of goods produced by manufacturers to consumers.

- **Service** – production of intangible goods and services.

- **Transportation** – movement of goods between locations.

This is not an exhaustive list, but it should give you some idea of the wide range of activities that support organisations.

4 Summary

In summary, there are a number of key differences between the various types of organisations. These include (but are not limited to):

- **Ownership** – private sector organisations are likely to be owned by individual owners or shareholders (depending on the type of organisation). Public sector organisations will be controlled by the government, while co-operatives will be owned by their members.

- **Objectives** – as mentioned, each organisation has very different goals. This can range from the provision of social services (for charities and public sector organisations) to the maximisation of owner wealth (for profit-seeking organisations).

- **Activities** – the activities of an organisation will be designed to support its objectives. This means that organisational activities are as varied as the organisations themselves!

- **Sources of funding** – public sector organisations will tend to raise money from the central government. Private sector organisations, such as companies and co-operatives, will most likely have to raise funds from their owners. Charities are usually funded by donations.

- **Size** – organisations vary in size from large, multinational companies to sole traders consisting of only one person.

- **Liability** – the owners of sole traders or partnerships are liable for any losses their businesses make. Owners of companies enjoy **limited liability**.

In spite of these differences, the different types of organisations often face similar issues to each other. For instance, most will have employees that need to be motivated. Many organisations will need to design strategies for the future, or will need to consider what systems should be put in place to ensure the accurate recording of transactions.

It is these common issues that we are going to examine in more detail in the coming chapters.

5 Chapter summary

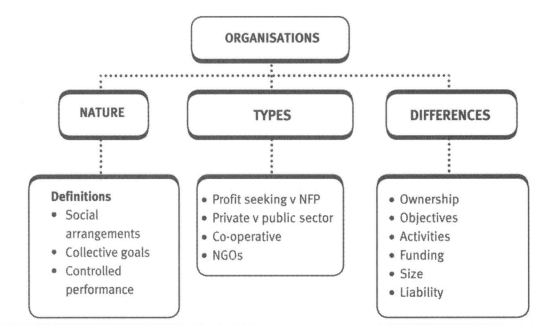

6 Practice questions

Test your understanding 6

Which of the following is NOT a benefit that organisations have over individuals?

A   They allow the sharing skills and knowledge

B   They enable people to perform tasks they would be unable to achieve on their own

C   They enable synergy to be achieved

D   They speed up the time taken to make decisions

Test your understanding 7

GreenWatch is an independent environmental charity set up to lobby the government for improved environmental regulation on business. What type of organisation is GreenWatch most likely to be classed as?

A   Public sector

B   Co-operative

C   Non-governmental

D   Commercial

Test your understanding 8

Which of the following statements regarding types of business is correct?

A   Partnerships are owned and run by one or more people

B   Private limited companies can sell shares to the public

C   Shareholders in companies typically have limited liability

D   The owners of sole traders typically have limited liability

Test your understanding 9

Which of the following statements regarding organisations are correct?

(i)   Companies tend to raise money from central government.

(ii)   Most sole traders and partnerships have the aim of maximising owner wealth.

(iii)   Public sector organisations are controlled by the central government.

(iv)   Charities form part of the public sector.

A   (i) and (ii) only

B   (iii) and (iv) only

C   (ii) and (iii) only

D   (ii) and (iv) only

Test your understanding 10

Here are four statements relating to the features of different types of organisation:

A   This type of organisation can sell its shares to the public.

B   This type of organisation is owned and run by two or more people who are legally indistinguishable from the organisation itself.

C   This type of organisation is controlled by the government.

D   This type of organisation is owned and democratically controlled by its members.

Required:

(a)   Identify the description above which is associated with each of the following types of organisation, by selecting A, B, C, D or none.

    (i)   Private limited company

    (ii)   Partnership

    (iii)   Public limited company

    (iv)   Co-operative

    (v)   Public sector organisation

    (vi)   Sole trader

(0.5 marks each, total = 3 marks)

(b) Below are four types of organisation:

A   Charities

B   Schools

C   Limited companies

D   Police forces

Required:

Write down which two of the above are most likely to be classified as part of the private sector by selecting TWO of the letters from (A, B, C, D).

(0.5 marks each, total = 1 mark)

(Total: 4 marks)

Test your understanding answers

Test your understanding 1

The correct answer is C

There would be no **collective** goals for a sole trader, so this does not satisfy the definition given.

Test your understanding 2

The correct answer is A

Statement (iv) would not be true, as organisations (which this committee could be classified as) allow for specialisation. Not all of the members would have to be skilled at performing all of the necessary tasks.

Test your understanding 3

The correct answer is B – False

Schools run fund-raising activities to help pay for extra books, e.g. to improve the quality of education given to pupils. The primary objective is educational, not profit. The money made at the fête is thus a means not an end.

Test your understanding 4

The correct answer is D

While protecting the environment is to be encouraged and is reinforced within statute to some degree, it is not a primary objective of the company. Companies exist primarily to maximise the return to their owners.

Test your understanding 5

The correct answer is C

Public sector organisations will be controlled by the central government. This is unlikely to be a charity, a company or a social club – which are typical examples of the private sector.

Note that a privately owned and operated school could be part of the private sector, but schools are still the most likely from the list to be public.

Test your understanding 6

The correct answer is C

Sole traders do not enjoy limited liability as, legally, they are not separate from their owners. Only public limited companies can issue shares to the public and partnerships cannot be owned by one person!

Test your understanding 7

The correct answer is C

As a charity, GreenWatch is not commercial as it does not have a profit-making objective. It is not obviously controlled by the central government, meaning that it is not in the public sector. It also clearly does not meet the definition of a co-operative, which is an organisation that is controlled by the people who buy its goods.

Test your understanding 8

The correct answer is D

Forming an organisation means that people work collectively. Typically this will mean that decision-making will become slower, as more people (with potentially differing ideas) are involved in the decision-making process.

Test your understanding 9

The correct answer is C

Companies usually raise money from sources other than the central government and charities are part of the private sector, rather than the public sector.

Test your understanding 10

(a)   The correct answers are:

(i)   **None**

(ii)   **B**

(iii)   **A**

(iv)   **D**

(v)   **C**

(vi)   **None**

(b)   The private sector refers to organisations that are run by private individuals and groups rather than the government. Therefore, the correct answers are **A** and **C**.

Business organisation and structure

Chapter learning objectives

Upon completion of this chapter you will be able to:

- describe the different ways in which formal organisations may be structured: entrepreneurial, matrix, functional, divisional (by geographical area, by product or by customer type), boundaryless (virtual, hollow or modular)

- explain basic organisational structure concepts: separation of ownership and control, separation of direction and management, span of control and scalar chain, tall and flat organisations, outsourcing and offshoring, shared services approach

- explain the characteristics of the strategic, tactical and operational levels in the organisation in the context of the Anthony hierarchy

- explain centralisation and decentralisation and list their advantages and disadvantages

- describe the roles and functions of the main departments in a business organisation: research and development, purchasing, production, direct service provision, marketing, administration and finance

- explain the role of marketing in an organisation:
    - the definition of marketing
    - the marketing mix
    - the relationship of the marketing plan to the strategic plan.

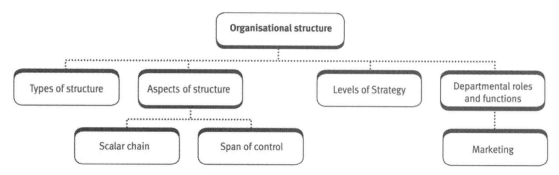

 ## 1 Organisational structure

Organisational structure is concerned with the way in which work is divided up and allocated.

It outlines the roles and responsibilities of individuals and groups within the organisation.

There are several possible ways in which an organisation can be structured. For this exam you need to be familiar with each of them, as well as being able to weigh up their advantages and disadvantages.

The structure of most organisations will change over time as the company grows. A typical pattern of structural change would be as follows:

 ### 1.1 Entrepreneurial structure

This structure is built around the owner manager and is **typical of small businesses** in the early stages of their development.

It is also often found where the entrepreneur has specialist knowledge of the product or service that the organisation offers.

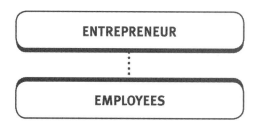

Advantages	Disadvantages
• Fast decision making. • More responsive to market. • Goal congruence. • Good control. • Close bond to workforce.	• Lack of career structure. • Dependent on the capabilities of the manager/owner. • Cannot cope with diversification/growth.

Advantages and disadvantages of entrepreneurial structures

Advantages

- There is only one person making decisions – this should lead to decisions being made quickly.

- As soon as an element of the market alters, the entrepreneur should recognise it and act quickly.

- A lack of a chain of command and the small size of the organisation should mean that the entrepreneur has control over the workforce and all decisions within the organisation, leading to better goal congruence.

Disadvantages

- This type of structure is usually suited to small companies where due to the size there is no career path for the employees.

- If the organisation grows, one person will not be able to cope with the increased volume of decisions etc.

1.2 Functional/departmental structure

Functional organisations group together employees that undertake similar tasks into **departments**.

This type of structure is often found in organisations that have outgrown the entrepreneurial structure.

It is most appropriate for small organisations which have relatively few products or locations and which exist in a relatively stable environment.

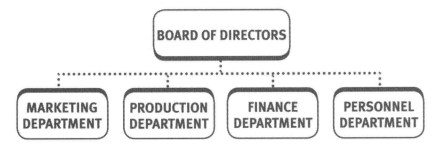

Advantages	Disadvantages
• Economies of scale.	• Empire building.
• Standardisation.	• Slow.
• Specialists more comfortable.	• Conflicts between functions.
• Career opportunities.	• Cannot cope with diversification.

Advantages and disadvantages of functional structures

Advantages

- Rather than duplicating roles in different parts of the company, similar activities are grouped together, leading to:
    - lower costs
    - standardisation of output/systems, etc.
    - people with similar skills being grouped together and so not feeling isolated.

- Due to the larger size of the organisation and the grouping into functions, there is a career path for employees – they can work their way up through the function.

Disadvantages

- Managers of the functions may try to make decisions to increase their own power or are just in the best interests of their function, rather that working in the best interest of the company overall. This leads to empire building and conflicts between the functions.

- Due to the longer chain of command, decisions will be made more slowly.

- This style of structure is not suited to an organisation which is rapidly growing and diversifying. For example, the specialists in one organisation's production function may not be able to cope with making, say, gas fires and radios.

1.3 Divisional/product structure

This structure occurs where an organisation is split into several **divisions** – each one autonomously overseeing a product (i.e. separate divisions for cars and motor bikes), a geographic section (i.e. separate divisions for US and Europe) or even by customer (i.e. separate divisions that look after corporate clients and private clients).

Each division is likely to have a functional structure, with all the departments it needs in order to operate in its particular market segment.

Divisions are likely to be run as profit centres, with their own revenues, expenditure and capital investments. Each division is a separately identifiable part of the overall organisation, which is often referred to as a **strategic business unit** (SBU).

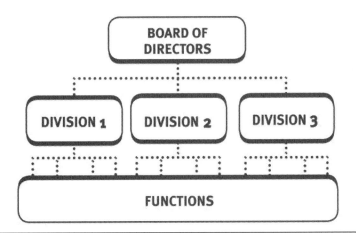

 Illustration 1 – Divisional structure

A Ltd is a company that manufactures two different products – toasters and televisions. The products require different components and require different advertising and sales.

A Ltd therefore operates a divisional structure, with a toasters division and a television division. Each division has its own sales, purchasing, HR and advertising divisions.

The finance department, however, is still operated centrally.

Advantages	Disadvantages
• Enables growth.	• Potential loss of control.
• Clear responsibility for products/divisions.	• Lack of goal congruence. Duplication.
• Training of general managers.	• Specialists may feel isolated.
• Easily adapted for further diversification.	• Allocation of central costs can be a problem.
• Top management free to concentrate on strategic matters.	

Advantages and disadvantages of divisional structures

Advantages

- If an organisation wants to grow and diversify, the functional structure cannot cope, so instead the divisional structure should be adopted. Should the company want to diversify further, it is easy to 'bolt on' another division.

- It encourages growth and diversity of products, e.g. by adding additional flavours etc. to capture other segments of the market. This in turn promotes the use of specialised equipment and facilities.

- Due to the breakdown of the company's activities into the divisions, it should mean that the divisional managers can clearly see where their area of responsibility lies and it should leave the top management free to concentrate on strategic matters, rather than to get involved in the day to day operations of each division – although this can lead to a lack of control over the activities of the division and possible lack of goal congruence.

- The focus of attention is on product performance and profitability. By placing responsibility for product profitability at the division level, they are able to react and make decisions quickly on a day to day basis.

- The role of the general manager has less concentration upon specialisation. This promotes a wider view of the company's operations.

Disadvantages

- In most divisionalised companies, some functions, e.g. accounting or human resources will be provided centrally. If this is the case, the cost of the centralised function could be recharged to those divisions using e.g. the human resource function. There are different ways of calculating the recharge and divisional managers may complain if the profitability of their division is reduced by an amount that they perceive as being arbitrary.

1.4 Geographically structured

This is similar to the divisional structure, but involves each division covering a specific location.

For example, a global company may be split into different divisions based on geographic areas. There may be a division that looks after the organisation's Asian operations, one that covers Europe and another division for America.

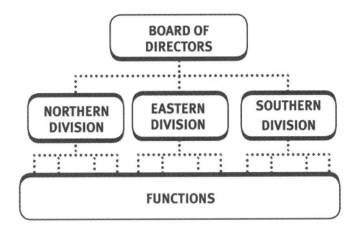

Advantages	Disadvantages
• Enables geographic growth. • Allows local decision-making. • Clear responsibility for areas. • Training of general managers. • Top management free to concentrate on strategic	• As for divisional structure above.

Product v geographic divisional structure

Product divisionalisation is generally preferred over say geographic divisionalisation when the product is relatively complex and requires a high cost of capital equipment, skilled operators, etc., e.g. the car industry.

1.5 Matrix structure

Matrix structures are a combination of the functional and divisional structures.

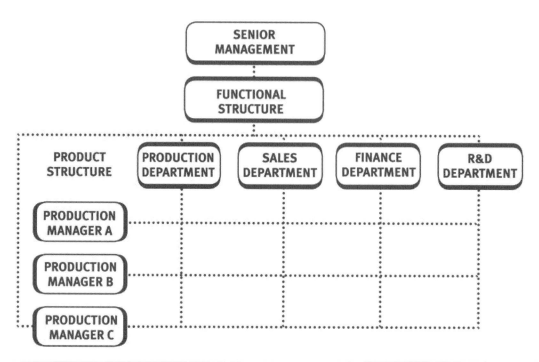

The matrix requires dual reporting to two different managers. For example, looking at the diagram above, an employee manufacturing product A would have to report to the manager of the production department **and** the manager in charge of product A.

The aim of the matrix structure is to combine the benefits of both the divisional and functional structures.

Advantages	Disadvantages
• Advantages of both functional and divisional structures.	• Dual command and conflict.
• Flexibility.	• Dilution of functional authority.
• Customer orientation.	• Time-consuming meetings.
• Encourage teamwork and the exchange of opinions and expertise.	• Higher admin costs.

Advantages and disadvantages of matrix structures

Advantages

- In today's rapidly changing environment, there is a need for effective coordination in very complex situations. If a car manufacturer wants to design, produce and market a new model, the process involves most parts of the organisation and a flexible system is needed to achieve the objectives. The more rigid structure experienced in a divisional company would not have the flexibility to be able to coordinate the tasks and the people, whereas the matrix structure can cope.

- The production managers could be replaced with customer managers, in which case the whole team will be focussed on meeting the needs of the customer.

Disadvantages

- Where the matrix structure can cause difficulty is in the lines of control. These may become ambiguous and conflict with each other. A team member may be answerable to the product manager and to a functional head, and this may cause confusion and stress. Time consuming meetings may be required to resolve the conflict, so resulting in higher administration costs.

Test your understanding 1

Consider the following statements:

(i)   Under the functional structure, each department operates as a strategic business unit.

(ii) The matrix structure will enable rapid decision-making within the organisation.

Which of the statements is/are correct?

A   (i) only

B   (ii) only

C   Both

D   Neither

Test your understanding 2

M plc is a large company that operates in country G. It manufactures several different products, each of which is highly complex and extremely specialised. Its sales have grown significantly over the last several years, with each of its products producing a roughly equal amount of M's overall revenue.

Which organisational structure is most likely to be appropriate for M?

A   Geographic

B   Divisional

C   Functional

D   Entrepreneurial

1.6 Boundaryless structure

This is a contemporary model of organisational design, which adopts a more flexible approach to structure.

Boundaryless organisations are, essentially, an unstructured design that is not constrained by having a chain of command or formal departments, with the focus instead being on flexibility.

There are a number of different types of boundaryless organisations that you need to be aware of – hollow, virtual and modular.

Hollow organisations

Hollow organisations split their functions into core (i.e. strategically important) and non-core activities. Anything which is classified as non-core is outsourced to other organisations.

Outsourcing refers to the contracting out of aspects of the organisation's work to specialist providers. We will look at outsourcing in more detail in chapter 8.

For example, an accountancy training organisation might outsource less important functions (such as payroll) to a third party organisation specialising in payroll processing. Core functions, such as training students, would be kept in house and undertaken by employees of the company.

Virtual organisations

This occurs where an organisation outsources many of its functions to other organisations and simply exists as a network of contracts, with very few, if any, functions being kept in-house.

For example, many internet retailers could be seen as virtual companies. Their products are bought in from manufacturers, sales are delivered to customers by third-party couriers and even their websites may be maintained and hosted by external IT specialists.

There is typically only a small central staff within a virtual business, who coordinate all of these different third parties and ensure that their customers' needs are therefore met.

Modular organisations

These are examples of boundaryless manufacturing companies. Rather than simply making their own product, they break the manufacturing process down into modules or components. Each component can then be made by the company or outsourced to an external supplier.

For example, a mobile phone manufacturer may pay external manufacturers to make some key components for its handsets – such as processors and screens. These are then assembled by the manufacturer along with other components it has manufactured itself.

In extreme cases, the manufacturing of all components can be outsourced, meaning that the company simply assembles them to create its final product.

1.7 Mintzberg's Organisational Configurations

Management theorist Henry Mintzberg (The Structuring of Organisations and Structures in 5's: Designing Effective Organisations) argued that organisations are made up of five key 'building blocks'.

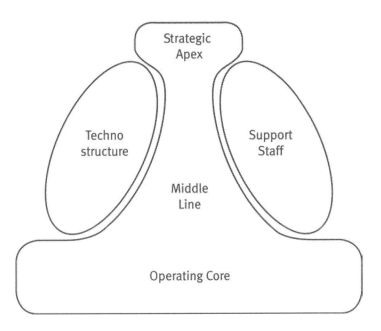

Each 'building block' corresponds to a specific group of people within the organisation:

- **Strategic apex** – senior levels of management.

- **Middle line** – middle management.

- **Operating core** – workers involved in producing or creating the core product or service offered by the organisation.

- **Technostructure** – provide technical input that is not part of the organisation's core activities (typically relating to standardisation of organisational procedures). They are analysts who plan and control the work of others.

- **Support staff** – administrative support and indirect services.

Ideology is the organisation's beliefs and values (culture) and can be discerned by examining norms or observable behaviour in the workplace.

Illustration 2 – Mintzberg's building blocks

Scenario

Q plc runs five factories that assemble childrens toys, each of which is run by its own Production Manager. The five Production Managers report directly to the Board of Directors of Q. All assembly staff in the factories report directly to the Production Managers.

Q's directors have recently stated that the company 'must cut costs to maximise profits for investors'.

Q has recently hired a job design specialist, who has started investigating how assembly workers' jobs should be organised and what the most effective shift patterns would be to maximise Q's productivity.

Q's Strategic Accountant has recently created a set of guidelines on the claiming of expenses by staff which the company hopes will reduce costs.

Q's factories also have a number of administrative staff – including canteen workers and secretarial employees.

Application to Mintzberg's Organisational Configurations

The Board of Directors of Q will make all of the major strategic decision for the company and would therefore be classified as the **strategic apex**.

The Production Managers are the main interface between the Board of Directors and the assembly staff, indicating that they are middle management – or the **middle line**.

The assembly staff are involved in the actual production of Q's product and would therefore form the **operating core**.

> The Strategic Accountant and the job design specialist would both be part of the **technostructure** as they have technical input into the design of Q's operations and are attempting to standardise operations within the company.
>
> The other administrative staff (canteen workers and secretarial staff) would be non-core, indirect support and would therefore be considered **support staff**.
>
> The directors have stated a desire for the company to be more profitable and cut costs – a desire which is backed up by the actions of the technostructure. This would appear to form the core of Q's **ideology**.

Mintzberg argued that any one of these building blocks could dominate within the organisation, leading to a variety of possible structures.

- **The simple structure** (strategic apex dominates)

    This is also known as the entrepreneurial structure. It tends to occur in newer organisations with one or a few top managers who control the rest of the workforce by way of direct supervision. While this is a fast, flexible structure, its reliance on just a few main managers means it will struggle to handle significant growth.

- **Machine bureaucracy** (technostructure dominates)

    This structure tends to occur in large, established organisations. Work becomes very formalised, with large numbers of rules and procedures. Jobs and roles will be clearly defined and there will be a large number of plans and budgets. Standardisation is seen as crucially important.

    Many large manufacturing organisations and government agencies tend towards this structure.

- **Professional bureaucracy** (operating core dominates)

    This occurs in organisations that rely on highly skilled members of staff, such as in the medical and legal industries. These organisations are often still bureaucratic, with large numbers of rules and procedures, but decision making is decentralised, with each individual staff member having significant independence and power. It can be very difficult for senior management to effectively control this sort of organisation.

- **Divisionalised** (middle line dominates)

    This closely matches the divisional structure mentioned above in section 1.3. The heads of each division (the middle line managers) will have a great deal of control over the day to day operations and strategy of their part of the business, with the directors (the strategic apex) will focus on 'big-picture' strategic planning.

- **Adhocracy** (support staff/operating core dominate)

  The focus within an adhocracy is on innovation – making it more suitable than the other, more formal, structures for fast-moving, dynamic industries (such as high-tech or pharmaceuticals). Such organisations tend to create teams of experts from different fields and decisions are decentralised, with power being allocated where it is needed within the organisation. Standardisation is not usually encouraged.

- **Missionary** (ideology dominates)

  The mission and beliefs of the organisation are dominant, with all employee actions having to tie in to this. Behaviour (or norms) become standardised.

 Test your understanding 3

F is a supervisor at a factory which manufactures steel girders. His role is to train new employees in how to use the machinery, as well as monitor staff to ensure that they are performing their work in the most efficient manner possible. F does not undertake any manufacturing work himself.

According to Mintzberg's organisational configurations model, which organisational building block would F be included within?

A   Support staff

B   Operating core

C   Strategic apex

D   Technostructure

---

2   Other basic organisational concepts

As well as the different types of organisation structure, you need to be aware of six other key structural concepts.

2.1 Separation of direction and management

Ownership and management of larger organisations are often separated. This is especially common in larger companies, where the owners (shareholders) elect directors to run the company on their behalf.

In order to ensure that directors are running the business in the best interests of the owners, many safeguards and controls are put in place. These will be dealt with in more detail in chapter 11.

Note that direction and management may also be separated in larger organisations. Directors may lack the time to deal with every issue that arises in the day-to-day running of the organisation. They will therefore appoint managers to undertake these tasks for them.

This leaves the directors free to focus on creating and managing the high-level strategies for the organisation, while the managers focus on the day-to-day operational issues. For example, the directors may decide that the organisation is going to launch a new product, or will open a chain of new stores. The managers will be in charge of decisions such as hiring and firing junior staff and dealing with customer complaints.

Test your understanding 4

In a small company there is usually a divorce of ownership and control. Is this statement:

A   True

B   False

2.2 Scalar chain

This is the line of authority which can be traced up or down the chain of command, from the most senior member of staff to the most junior. It therefore relates to the number of levels of management within an organisation.

2.3 Span of control

A manager's span of control is the number of people for whom he or she is directly responsible.

The factors that influence the span of control include:

- **the nature of the work** – the more repetitive or simple the work, the wider the span of control can be.

- **the type of personnel** – the more skilled and motivated the managers and other staff members are, the wider the span of control can be.

- **the location of personnel** – if personnel are all located locally, it takes relatively little time and effort to supervise them. This allows the span of control to become wider.

Test your understanding 5

Consider the following statements:

(I)   The scalar chain relates to the number of people over whom a manager has authority.

(II)   A business with highly skilled, motivated members of staff will tend to have a wider span of control than a business with demotivated employees.

Which of these statements is/are correct?

A (i) only

B (ii) only

C Both

D Neither

2.4 Tall and flat organisations

A 'tall' organisation has many levels of management (a long scalar chain) and a narrow span of control.

A 'flat' organisation has few levels of management (a short scalar chain) and a wide span of control.

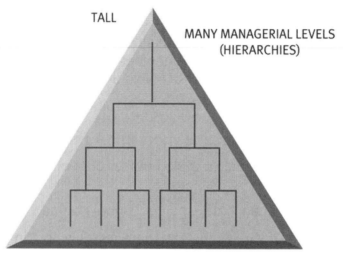

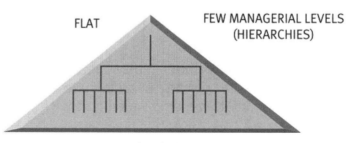

It is worth noting that tall organisations tend to be more bureaucratic and take longer to make decisions, due to the large number of levels of management that need to be involved.

Flat organisations tend to have weaker control and fewer chances for employees to progress or be promoted within the organisation.

Test your understanding 6

If a managerial structure has many levels of management, is it likely to have a narrow or wide span of control at each level of management?

2.5 Offshoring

Offshoring refers to the process of outsourcing or relocating some of an organisation's functions from one country to another, usually in an effort to reduce costs.

For example, many companies in the UK have moved their customer call centres to other countries, such as India and the Philippines. These countries have significantly lower wage rates than the UK, making the call centres cheaper for the offshoring company to operate.

While the cost savings can be significant, offshoring can create additional problems for the organisation, including problems with cultural differences and language barriers.

2.6 Shared Services Approach

This approach involves restructuring the provision of certain services within the organisation so that instead of the service being found in several different parts of the organisation it is centralised into one specific part of the organisation.

For example, a medium-sized business may have a couple of staff in each department (i.e. sales, production) that deal with IT for that part of the organisation.

A shared services approach would be to form a distinct IT department that all the IT staff were transferred into. This IT department would then offer IT services to the entire organisation.

This approach has several advantages, including:

- improved quality of service provision

- improved consistency of service

- cost savings through greater efficiency and reduced duplication of roles

Note that a shared services approach is more than simply centralising the function into one place. Shared services often involves running the service, for example IT, like a separate business within the organisation and charging the rest of the organisation for the use of the service.

3 Centralisation and decentralisation

Another method of analysing structures is by reference to the level at which decisions are made.

- In a centralised structure, the upper levels of an organisation's hierarchy retain the authority to make decisions.

- In a decentralised structure the authority to take decisions is passed down to units and people at lower levels.

The factors that will affect the amount of decentralisation are:

- management style

- ability of management/employees

- geographic spread

- size of the organisation/scale of activities.

The advantages and disadvantages of decentralisation are:

Advantages	Disadvantages
• Senior management free to concentrate on strategy.	• Loss of control by senior management.
• Better local decisions due to local expertise.	• Dysfunctional decisions due to a lack of goal congruence.
• Better motivation due to increased training and career path.	• Poor decisions made by inexperienced managers.
	• Training costs.
• Quicker responses/flexibility, due to smaller chain of command.	• Duplication of roles within the organisation.
	• Extra costs in obtaining information.

Test your understanding 7

Which of the following is **NOT** a likely additional cost to an organisation caused by decentralisation?

A   Additional training costs are often required in a decentralised organisation

B   Duplication of roles, leading to higher personnel costs

C   Extra costs of gathering information from various sources and locations

D   Lost sales due to lack of local knowledge and expertise

Test your understanding 8

How does the ability of the employees affect the level of decentralisation?

4 Levels of strategy

Within an organisation, each level of management will have different roles and responsibilities. This is especially the case when it comes to developing a strategy, or plan for the future, for the organisation.

The Anthony Triangle is a model that can be used to illustrate the types of strategic planning that will be made at each level of the organisation's hierarchy.

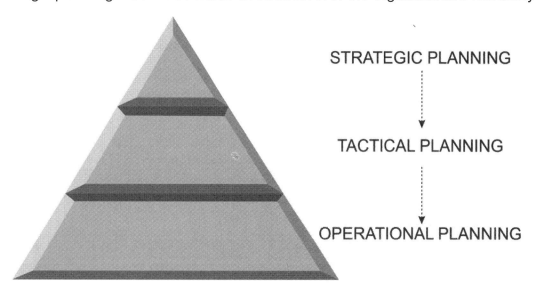

Different levels of planning

- **Strategic planning** is undertaken by senior managers. It involves making long-term decisions for the entire organisation.

- **Tactical planning** is undertaken by middle management. It tends to look at plans for specific divisions or departments and specifies how to use resources.

- **Operational planning** is undertaken by junior managers and supervisors. It is short-term, detailed and practical.

Illustration 3 – Strategic, tactical and operational planning

The above planning levels could be applied to a supermarket as follows:

- Strategic planning would involve making plans for the whole business. This could involve which locations to open or close stores and whether to raise cash from investors.

- Tactical planning would be the creation of strategies for a particular supermarket. For example decisions about special offers, local advertising and which products should be stocked.

- Operational planning involve practical, day-to-day strategies, such as organising shift patterns, deciding when to stock the shelves and advertising for and selecting new employees.

Note that in order to be successful, the levels of strategy must support each other. If a strategic decision is made to improve customer service, this must be supported by appropriate tactical decisions being made in each store, such as allocating more of the store's budget to hiring additional customer services employees. Even then, this will only be a success if the operational strategies select the most appropriate candidates for the new role.

Test your understanding 8

H is a retail store selling electronics. It is currently deciding how many units of its products it will need to order next month in order to meet customer demand.

Which level of strategic planning does this relate to?

A   Strategic

B   Functional

C   Tactical

D   Operational

5 The roles and functions of the main departments in a business organisation

In spite of their structural differences, organisations usually have many similarities. One of these is that many organisations operate similar basic departments to each other, with the same roles and concerns.

Some of the most common departments are listed below.

Department	Role	Key concerns
Research and development	• Improving existing products • Developing new products	• Anticipating customer needs • Generating new ideas • Testing • Cost
Purchasing	• Acquiring the goods and services necessary for the business	• Price and payment terms • Quality • Stock levels/delivery schedules

Department	Role	Key concerns
Production	• Converting raw materials into finished goods	• Quality (of materials and finished goods) • Costs • Wastage/efficiency • Stock levels/production schedules
Direct service provision	• Providing services to clients (e.g. accountancy firm)	• Quality • Time sheets/scheduling
Marketing	• Identifying customer needs • Market research • Product design • Pricing • Promotion • Distribution	• Customer needs • Quality • Promotional strategy • Distribution channel strategy • Pricing strategy
Administration	• Administrative support • Processing transactions	• Efficiency • Information processing
Finance	• Bookkeeping • Financial reporting • Financial controls • Budgeting • The raising of capital	• Accuracy and completeness of record keeping • Monthly management reporting • Annual financial reporting

 Test your understanding 10

Which of the following is not part of the responsibility of a research and development department?

A   Improving existing products

B   Developing new products

C   Researching new technologies for application to future products

D   Researching market demand for products

6   Marketing

6.1 What is meant by 'marketing'?

Marketing is defined by the Chartered Institute of Marketing as 'the management process that identifies, anticipates and supplies customer needs efficiently and profitably.'

The key emphasis is thus on customer needs:

*   Identifying and anticipating needs – market research.

*   Supplying customer needs – product design and development.

*   Efficiency – distribution.

*   Profitability – pricing decisions and promotion (informing customers about your product so they buy it).

 Marketing involves much more than just advertising!

Marketing versus product orientation

Marketing orientation

The emphasis in marketing on pre-empting and meeting customers' needs gives rise to a belief system that places the customer at the centre of organisational activity. This marketing orientation is a philosophy of business that permeates all areas focusing attention towards the customer and believing, deep within corporate culture, that to meet the customers' needs better than competitors is the path to corporate success.

Product orientation

Management view is that success is achieved through producing goods and services of optimum quality. The major task is to pursue improved research and development and extensive quality control services.

While customers will generally welcome a better product, this approach has the following dangers:

*   costs escalate in the pursuit of the 'perfect product' and customers are no longer willing to pay the resulting price

*   the product may include features that customers do not want or value.

Test your understanding 7

Marketing is mainly concerned with which of the following?

A   Increasing sales revenue

B   Streamlining production

C   Anticipating and meeting customer needs

D   Maximising profit

6.2 The marketing mix

The marketing mix is the set of controllable variables that a firm blends to produce desired results from its chosen target market.

There are four basic elements (the '4Ps'), which must be managed to satisfy customers' needs at a profit.

Product	This includes product features, durability, design, brand name, packaging, range, after-sales service, warranties and guarantees.
Place	Choice of distribution channels, transportation, outlet management, stocks and warehouses.
Promotion (distribution)	Advertising, personal selling, publicity, sales promotion techniques.
Price	Price levels, discounts, allowances, payment terms, credit policy.

The marketing mix – additional detail

According to **Kotler et al.** (1999) 'the marketing mix is a set of controllable tactical marketing tools ... that the firm blends to produce the response it wants in the target market'. Hence, in an effective marketing programme all of those elements are 'mixed' to successfully achieve the company's marketing objectives.

The marketing mix is concerned with how to influence consumer demand and is primarily the responsibility of the marketing department. As outlined above, the mix is made up of:

- **Price** – an organisation may attack competitors by reducing price or increasing the size for the same money. The question of price policy in terms of competitors may be stated as Jet petrol's statement, 'We will always sell at 1–2p below the market leaders'.

- **Promotion** – advertising, money-back coupons, special prizes are all means of boosting sales without cutting price. Whereas a price cut may lead to a retaliatory war from competitors, a money-off coupon is seen as a temporary initiative and competitors may ignore it.

- **Place** – refers to the outlets, geographic areas and distribution channels. Some manufacturers have specified that only their goods can be sold in an outlet, e.g. most car manufacturers stipulate this requirement. Others choose a competition strategy involving vertical integration by which they take over distribution outlets and block a competitor's products. An example of this is the retail shoe industry.

- **Product** – refers to anything offered for attention, acquisition, use or consumption that might satisfy a want or need. Products can be physical objects, services, persons, places, organisations and ideas. An organisation may choose to lead the competition by being the best performer in those areas that it believes customers count as important and competitors can be outscored.

Beyond the 4Ps other elements of the marketing mix have come to light through the work of **Kotler** amongst others:

- **People** – this relates to both staff and the need to understand customer needs.

- **Processes** – these are the systems through which the service is delivered.

- **Physical evidence** – testimonials and references regarding proposed service.

6.3 Product issues

There are two main product issues to consider:

- Product definition – The main issue regarding product is to define exactly what the product should be. This can be done on three levels:

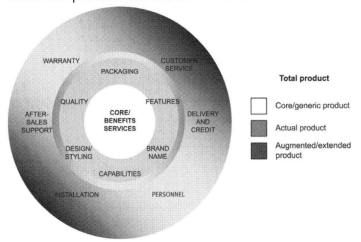

- Product positioning – With all of these factors the question of product positioning is critical – how does our product compare with the offerings of competitors? Is our product better? If so, in what way?

Illustration 4 – Marketing

A new car could be specified as follows:

- Core/generic product – personal transportation.

- Actual product – range of engine sizes, different body shapes offered, etc.

- Augmented product – manufacturer's warranty or dealer's discounted service contract.

Product – further considerations

The **core product** – what is the buyer really buying? The core product refers to the use, benefit or problem-solving service that the consumer is really buying when purchasing the product, i.e. the need that is being fulfilled.

The **actual product** is the tangible product or intangible service that serves as the medium for receiving core product benefits.

The **augmented product** consists of the measures taken to help the consumer put the actual product to sustained use, including installation, delivery and credit, warranties, and after-sales service.

A product, therefore, is more than a simple set of tangible features. Consumers tend to see products as complex bundles of benefits that satisfy their needs. Most important is how the customer perceives the product. They are looking at factors such as aesthetics and styling, durability, brand image, packaging, service and warranty, any of which might be enough to set the product apart from its competitors.

6.4 Pricing issues

There are four key considerations (the '4Cs') when deciding the price of a product:

- **Cost** – the price must be high enough to make a profit.

- **Customers** – what are they willing to pay?

- **Competition** – is our price higher than competitors?

- **Corporate objectives** – e.g. the price could be set low to gain market share.

These issues can be blended to give a range of pricing tactics, including the following:

- Cost plus pricing – the cost per unit is calculated and then a mark-up added.

- Penetration pricing – a low price is set to gain market share.

- Perceived quality pricing – a high price is set to reflect/create an image of high quality.

- Price discrimination – different prices are set for the same product in different markets, e.g. peak/off-peak rail fares.

- Going rate pricing – prices are set to match competitors.

- Price skimming – high prices are set when a new product is launched. Later the price is dropped to increase demand once the customers who are willing to pay more have been 'skimmed off.

- Loss leaders – one product may be sold at a loss with the expectation that customers will then go on and buy other more profitable products.

- Captive product pricing – this is used where customers must buy two products. The first is cheap to attract customers but the second is expensive, once they are captive.

6.5 Promotional issues

Promotion is essentially about market communication. The primary aim is to encourage customers to buy the products by moving them along the **AIDA** sequence:

$$\text{Awareness} \boxtimes \text{Interest} \boxtimes \text{Desire} \boxtimes \text{Action}$$

Towards this firms will use a combination of different promotional techniques as part of their 'promotional mix', including:

- Advertising – e.g. placing adverts on TV, in newspapers, on billboards, etc.

- Sales promotion techniques – e.g. 'Buy one get one free'.

- Personal selling – e.g. door-to-door salesmen.

- Public relations (PR) – e.g. sponsoring sports events.

6.6 Place (distribution) issues

The key decision under 'place' is between:

- **Selling direct** – here the manufacturer sells directly to the ultimate consumer without using any middlemen, e.g. accountancy firms deal directly with their clients without recourse to brokers or other middlemen.

- **Selling indirect** – here the channel strategy could comprise a mixture of retailer, distributors, wholesalers and shipping agents, e.g. food distribution will often involve distributors and retailers to get the product from farmer to consumer.

Variations in marketing mix settings

Different companies put different emphasis on each of the four components of the marketing mix.

For example, some companies place all the focus on making a good quality product; other companies place the emphasis on making it at a cheap price or emphasise the promotion and advertising to sell it. A manufacturer of desks might wish to sell to both the consumer market and the industrial market for office furniture. The marketing mix selected for the consumer market might be low prices with attractive dealer discounts, sales largely through discount warehouses, modern design but fairly low quality and sales promotion relying on advertising by the retail outlets, together with personal selling by the manufacturing firm to the reseller. For the industrial market, the firm might develop a durable, robust product that sells at a higher price; selling may be by means of direct mail-shots, backed by personal visits from salespeople.

An interesting comparison can be made between different firms in the same industry; for example, Avon and Elizabeth Arden both sell cosmetics but, whereas Avon relies on personal selling in the consumer's own home, Elizabeth Arden relies on an extensive dealer network and heavy advertising expenditure.

Test your understanding 12

Nile is an online retailer of games, DVDs and books. It is currently planning an upgrade to its website to make it easier for customers to find the items that they are looking for.

Which one of the 4Ps of marketing does this relate to?

A   Price

B   Place

C   Promotion

D   Product

6.7 The strategic marketing process

The marketing process impacts the strategic planning process of an organisation as follows:

Strategic analysis of the firm and its business environment

Marketing analysis will include:

- analysis of brand strength, product quality, reputation, etc.
- analysis of competition
- market research to determine market attractiveness
- detailed analysis of customer expectations and power.

Strategic choice

Marketing decisions will include:

- decisions regarding which products to sell
- segmenting potential markets (e.g. by age) and then targeting attractive segments
- developing strategies for each of the marketing mix variables.

Strategy implementation

Implementing marketing strategies will include:

- setting budgets for advertising, etc.
- setting targets for sales revenue, market share, brand awareness, etc.
- monitoring and control.

Strategic marketing – further analysis

Strategic analysis

Market research can be carried out as follows:

(a) **Desk research**

Here use is made of information which already exists, e.g. government statistics can provide demographic data; trade associations can provide more specialised data about market sizes and trends; the organisation's own systems should be able to provide information such as sales trends, sales per region, sales per product and stock turnover.

(b) **Field research**

This is normally conducted by asking people, ideally chosen at random, for their views on different products. Sometimes individuals are asked to try out products and they are then asked for detailed reactions.

(c) **Test marketing**

Before a new product is launched, a test marketing campaign may be mounted in an area which is relatively small, typical, with a stable population, and which possesses the required promotional facilities. This can be regarded as the refinement of the marketing mix and campaign before a full national and international launch is approved.

Strategic choice

Markets can be segmented in many different ways:

- Geographic – The EU could be split into different countries or viewed as one market. Television advertising regions.

- Demographic – Age, sex, income – e.g. Saga Holidays targets the over 50s. Family lifecycle models – e.g. 'empty nesters'.

- Psychological – Older people are more security conscious.

- Socio-economic – Class based systems e.g. A, B, C1, etc.

Attractive segments can be selected using a range of criteria including:

- Size

- Growth prospects

- Intensity of competition. Targeting strategies can include:

- Differentiated, where each segment is approached with a different marketing mix e.g. Ford offering a range of different cars at different prices to meet varying customer needs.

- Undifferentiated, where all segments are approached with the same basic marketing mix e.g. originally Ford only offered one colour – black.

- Concentrated, where only one segment is targeted.

Test your understanding 13

Analysis of brand strength would come under which part of the strategic planning process?

A   Strategic analysis

B   Strategic choice

C   Strategic implementation

7 Chapter summary

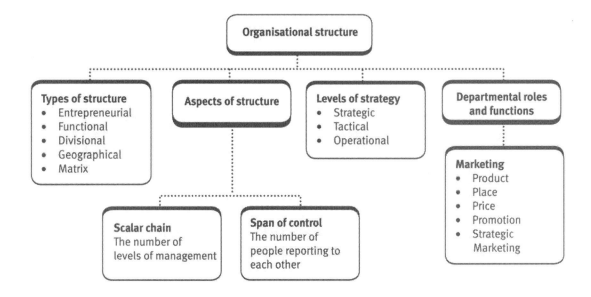

8   Practice questions

Test your understanding 14

The following four statements relate to either the functional or divisional structures.

(i)   Enables access to economies of scale

(ii)   Tends to cause duplication of roles

(iii)   Does not usually cope well with diversification

(iv)   Specialists may feel isolated

Which of the statements relate to a functional structure?

A   (i) and (ii)

B   (i) and (iii)

C   (ii) and (iii)

D   (ii) and (iv)

Test your understanding 15

Conflicting demands over allocation of resources is most likely to be a disadvantage for which type of organisational structure?

A   Entrepreneurial

B   Matrix

C   Divisional

D   Geographical

Test your understanding 16

P runs a small business making and selling garden ornaments. He has identified what he states is the 'best and most effective method' of making the ornaments and forces his staff to use this process. P has also designed a number of rigid processes that staff have to follow relating to a range of issues, such as taking annual leave and recording the number of hours they work for each day.

Which of the following of Mintzberg's structural configurations most closely matches P's business?

A   Machine bureaucracy

B   Divisionalised

C   Missionary

D   Professional bureaucracy

Test your understanding 17

H Ltd is a manufacturing company. The work undertaken is simple, meaning that each manager looks after a large number of employees. Because of this, there are relatively few levels of management within the company.

Which of the following is correct with regards to the structure of H Ltd?

A   Wide span of control, short scalar chain

B   Narrow span of control, short scalar chain

C   Wide span of control, long scalar chain

D   Narrow span of control, long scalar chain

Test your understanding 18

Which of the following would be a typical feature of a flat organisation?

A   Easy career progression for employees

B   Close supervision of employees by managers

C   Faster decision making

D   High levels of bureaucracy

Test your understanding 19

Which of the following is an advantage of centralised decision-making?

A   Allows senior management to focus on high level strategic decisions

B   Better motivation for more junior staff

C   Improved local decisions

D   Avoidance of dysfunctional decision-making

Test your understanding 20

G Ltd is a supermarket. It has three strategies in place:

1   To hire fifty new checkout operators within the next five weeks to help reduce customer queue times

2   To begin the sale of electronics in all stores within the next two years

3   To relocate one of its stores in town A to a new, more suitable site, located by the store manager.

Using the Anthony triangle model, what would each of these strategies be classified as?

	Strategy 1	Strategy 2	Strategy 3
A	Strategic	Tactical	Operational
B	Operational	Strategic	Tactical
C	Tactical	Operational	Strategic
D	Operational	Tactical	Strategic

Test your understanding 21

Pear plc has created a new type of mobile phone. It took a number of years of research and development and Pear are concerned that the company's rivals will quickly copy the phone and sell their own versions. Pear have therefore decided to sell the phone at a very high initial price per unit in order to quickly recoup the development costs. Once rival products are launched, Pear will drop the price in order to compete more effectively.

What type of pricing strategy is Pear using?

A   Penetration pricing

B   Going rate

C   Perceived quality

D   Price skimming

Test your understanding 22

Consider the following statements.

(i)   Promotion involves the use of the AIDA sequence, which stands for Advertise, Interest, Desire and Action.

(ii)   When looking at strategic marketing, setting budgets for adverts would occur at the strategic implementation stage.

Which of these statements is/are correct?

A   (i) only

B   (ii) only

C   Both

D   Neither

Test your understanding 23

J plc wishes to change its corporate structure. It has decided to outsource all of its non-core functions to external third-parties.

Which of the following boundaryless structures is J plc planning to adopt?

A   Informal

B   Virtual

C   Modular

D   Hollow

Test your understanding 24

(a) A Ltd is considering changing its organisational structure. However, it is concerned about the possible drawbacks of whichever structure is selected.

The two organisational structures that are being considered are:

A   Functional

B   Matrix

Required:

Classify the following disadvantages as primarily relating to either A (Functional) or B (Matrix):

(i)   Large numbers of time-consuming meetings

(ii)   Dual command, leading to conflict

(iii) Difficulty coping with diversification

(iv) Overlap of authority between managers

(0.5 marks each = 2 marks in total)

(b) A Ltd is also concerned about its marketing process, which it believes is currently ineffective. It is aware that there are four key aspects to the marketing function, which are:

A   Product

B   Place

C   Promotion

D   Price

The following sentences contain gaps which specify the relevant aspect of the marketing function.

A Ltd feels it is important to consider the cost, customers, competition and its own corporate objectives when thinking about **1**.

Required:

(i)   **Select the aspect of the marketing function which appropriately fills gap 1 above; i.e. select A, B, C or D.**

A Ltd is concerned that it is failing to communicate with the market, meaning that customers are simply not interested in buying A's products. This indicates a weakness in A's **2**.

Required:

(ii) **Select the aspect of the marketing function which appropriately fills gap 2 above; i.e. select A, B, C or D.**

(1 mark each, total = 2 marks in total)

(Total: 4 marks)

Test your understanding answers

Test your understanding 1

The correct answer is D

The separate parts of the organisation operate as SBUs in a divisional structure – not a functional structure.

The matrix structure tends to require time-consuming meetings and has significant overlap of authority between managers. This tends to slow the decision-making process down.

Test your understanding 2

The correct answer is B

As M has several complex products, a structure that creates a separate division to look after each one seems the most logical. Functional and geographical structures would struggle to cope with the differing needs of the products. The level of work needed to run a large, complex organisation would also probably be beyond the capabilities of an entrepreneurial structure.

Test your understanding 3

The correct answer is D

F does not undertake any manufacturing work himself, so he cannot be part of the operating core. As he does have direct input into the operating core's role, he is not part of the support staff, as this relates to administrative and indirect services.

Note that he does not appear to be in charge of the factory, suggesting that he is not part of the strategic apex.

F does, however, train up staff members and ensure standardisation of their work. This would indicate that he is part of the factory technostructure.

Test your understanding 4

The correct answer is B – False

They tend to be owner managed.

Test your understanding 5

The correct answer is B

The scalar chain relates to the number of levels of management within the organisation.

Test your understanding 6

Narrow

Test your understanding 7

The correct answer is D

A decentralised business delegates decision-making down to employees at a lower, or more local, level. This should allow for better local decisions to be made, hopefully maximising sales.

Note that another cost of decentralisation could be poor decisions or goal congruence leading to increased costs.

Test your understanding 8

The more able the employees, the more decisions they can be entrusted with, and the greater the level of decentralisation.

Test your understanding 9

The correct answer is D

This strategy is very detailed and practical. Note that functional strategy is another name for tactical strategy.

Test your understanding 10

The correct answer is D

Demand would be assessed by a market research function within the marketing department.

Test your understanding 11

The correct answer is C

The key focus of marketing is customer needs.

Test your understanding 12

The correct answer is B

Given that the website is the main location that Nile transacts business, making the site it easier to use will be improving Niles place of business.

Test your understanding 13

The correct answer is A

Strategic analysis would include an assessment of the firm's strengths and weaknesses, including brand name.

Test your understanding 14

The correct answer is B

Make sure you remember the relative advantages and disadvantages of each organisational structure.

Test your understanding 15

The correct answer is B

The main difficulty with matrix organisations is conflicts over the lines of control which can lead to conflicting demands over allocation of resources.

Test your understanding 16

The correct answer is A

The business is highly standardised with emphasis on rules and procedures. This is typical of a bureaucratic environment – suggesting either answer A or D. However, professional bureaucracies occur when staff are highly skilled and are given a great degree of autonomy in decision-making, which clearly is not happening in P's business.

KAPLAN PUBLISHING

Test your understanding 17

The correct answer is A

There are few levels of management, meaning the scalar chain is short. The fact that each manager has a large number of subordinates would indicate a wide span of control.

Test your understanding 18

The correct answer is C

Flat organisations have wide spans of control and a short scalar chain. This means that there will be relatively few management positions for staff to be promoted into. A wide span of control will also mean that it is difficult for managers to monitor the activities of all staff. However, fewer managers tends to mean faster decisions can be made.

Test your understanding 19

The correct answer is D

Centralisation involves decisions being made by senior management, rather than by junior or regional staff. Options A, B and C are advantages of decentralisation. Centralisation does, however, ensure that all the decisions are made by the same team of managers, improving goal congruence.

Test your understanding 20

The correct answer is B

Strategy one is practical and short-term, making it an operational strategy. Strategy 2 affects the whole business and is long-term, indicating a strategic plan. Strategy three affects a specific section of the business (in this case, a particular store) and is made by middle management (the store manager), indicating a tactical plan.

Test your understanding 21

The correct answer is D

This is a classic example of price skimming.

Test your understanding 22

The correct answer is B

AIDA stands for **awareness**, interest desire and action, so statement (i) is wrong. Statement (ii) is correct.

Test your understanding 23

The correct answer is D

Remember that outsourcing non-core activities refers to a hollow organisation. Virtual organisations outsource all functions (including core), while modular organisations have some components of their product made by other organisations.

Test your understanding 24

(a) The correct answers are:

  (i)   **B**

  (ii) **B**

  (iii) **A**

  (iv) **B**

  Remember that the matrix structure has both functional and divisional management in place. While this can be an advantage when diversifying, it means having two sets of management, which can lead to conflict, disagreement and additional expense.

(b) The correct answers are:

  (i)   **D** – you are provided with the 4Cs in the statement, which relate to pricing.

  (ii) **C** – by definition, this refers to promotion.

Organisational culture in business

Chapter learning objectives

Upon completion of this chapter you will be able to:

- define organisational culture
- describe the factors that shape the culture of the organisation
- explain the contribution made by writers on culture:
    - Schein – determinants of organisational culture
    - Handy – four cultural stereotypes
    - Hofstede – international perspectives on culture
- explain the informal organisation and its relationship with the formal organisation
- describe the impact of the informal organisation on the business.

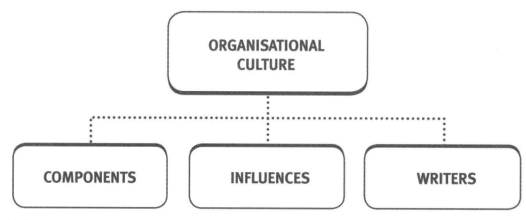

 1 Defining organisational culture

1.1 Definition

There are many definitions of corporate culture. These include:

'The specific collection of values and norms that are shared by people and groups in an organisation and that control the way they interact with each other and with stakeholders outside the organisation.' **Hill & Jones**

'The way we do things around here'. **Handy**

Ultimately, culture means the sum total of all the beliefs, attitudes, norms and customs that prevail within an organisation.

Each organisation will have its own distinctive cultures, and behaviour acceptable in one organisational culture may be inappropriate in another. For example, some companies will expect staff to undertake additional work in their own time, while other organisations will not.

Also cultures develop over time or can change instantly as a result of a single major event, e.g. death of company founder, threatened takeover, etc.

1.2 Components of culture

There are three key elements to any organisation's culture.

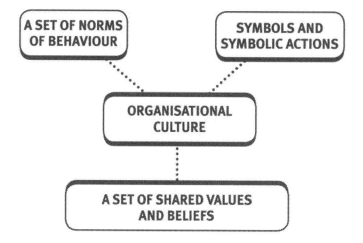

- Norms guide people's behaviour, suggesting what is or is not appropriate (the 'done thing') – e.g. informal dress codes.

- Symbols or symbolic action – e.g. rituals such as buying the office a cake on your birthday.

- Shared values and beliefs underlie the culture by identifying what is important – e.g. a belief in the importance of people as individuals.

2 The factors that shape the culture of the organisation

The six major influences on the culture of an organisation are as follows:

- Size
- Technology
- Diversity
- Age
- History
- Ownership

The main factors that shape culture

- **Size** – How large is the organisation – in terms of turnover, physical size, employee numbers?

- **Technology** – How technologically advanced is the organisation – either in terms of its product, or its productive processes?

- **Diversity** – How diverse is the company – either in terms of product range, geographical spread or cultural make-up of its stakeholders?

- **Age** – How old is the business or the managers of the business – do its strategic level decision makers have experience to draw upon?

- **History** – What worked in the past? Do decision makers have past successes to draw upon; are they willing to learn from their mistakes?

- **Ownership** – Is the organisation owned by a sole trader? Are there a small number of institutional shareholders or are there large numbers of small shareholders?

Other influences on culture

There are other, more subtle influences.

- The degree of individual initiative – is it encouraged or are decisions always referred upwards?

- The degree of risk tolerance – are managers only allowed to follow low-risk strategies?

- Clarity of direction – is there a clear focus; are these clear objectives and performance expectations?

- The degree of integration between groups – are different units encouraged to work together? Are management aloof or approachable; is communication clear to lower level staff?

- The reward system – are individuals rewarded for succeeding, i.e. are rewards based on performance criteria?

- Conflict tolerance – are employees encouraged to air grievances?

- Communication patterns – is there a formal hierarchy or an informal network?

- Formalisation of clothing and office layout – are there strict rules over this?

- The kind of people employed (graduates, young, old, etc.).

3 Writers on culture

There are three writers you need to have knowledge of: **Schein, Handy** and **Hofstede**.

3.1 Schein

Schein argues that the first leaders of a company create its culture. Future leaders will only be selected if they support this original culture. Thus the link between culture and leadership is very strong and it can be very difficult to change.

Schein further commented that it if leaders are to lead, it is essential that they understand the culture of the organisation. In order to try and define culture, Schein described three levels:

- **Artefacts** – these are the aspects of culture that can be easily seen, e.g. the way that people dress.

- **Espoused values** – these are the strategies and goals of an organisation, including company slogans etc.

- **Basic assumptions and values** – these are difficult to identify as they are unseen, and exist mainly at the unconscious level.

New employees find the last level of culture the most difficult to understand, and lack of understanding of the basic values is one of the main contributors to failure when trying to implement change.

Test your understanding 1

Which of the following would **NOT** be classified by Schein as an artefact?

A   Dress codes in the organisation

B   Design of the organisation's premises

C   Stated aim of the organisation to improve customer service

D   Office facilities provided by the organisation

3.2 Handy

Handy popularised four cultural types.

- **Power** culture (denoted by the Greek god Zeus) – Here there is **one major source of power** and influence. For example, in a small owner-managed business the owner may strive to maintain absolute control over subordinates. There may be few procedures and rules of a formal kind as staff take direction directly from the owner.

  Note that this is often found in organisations with an entrepreneurial structure, as outlined in the last chapter.

- **Role** culture (denoted by the Greek god Apollo) – In this version of culture, people describe their job by its duties, not by its purpose, so job descriptions dictate 'the way we do things around here'. This would be seen in a **bureaucratic** organisation, where the structure determines the authority and responsibility of individuals and there is a strong emphasis on hierarchy and status.

  This tends to be most effective in stable environments, where the work performed by employees rarely changes.

- **Task** culture (denoted by the Greek god Athena) – The emphasis here is on **achieving the particular task at hand** and staff may need to be flexible to ensure deadlines are met. People therefore describe their positions in terms of the results they are achieving. Nothing is allowed to get in the way of task accomplishment. This is best seen in project teams that exist for a specific task.

- **Person** culture (denoted by the Greek god Dionysius) – This is characterised by the fact it exists to **satisfy the requirements of the particular individual(s)** involved in the organisation. The person culture is to be found in a small, highly participatory organisation where individuals undertake all the duties themselves, for example, a barrister in chambers.

Test your understanding 2

Identify the correct statement regarding Handy's cultural types from the following:

A   Role cultures tend to focus on the needs of the individuals working in the organisation

B   Power cultures tend to be bureaucratic organisations with large numbers of powerful managers

C   Person cultures tend to develop in small, highly participatory organisations

D   Role cultures normally require staff to be flexible in order to ensure deadlines are met

Test your understanding 3

Identify two disadvantages that a task culture could create for an organisation.

3.3 Hofstede

Hofstede looked for national differences between over 100,000 of IBM's employees in different parts of the world, in an attempt to find aspects of culture that might influence business behaviour.

He found four traits or 'cultural dimensions':

- **Individualism (vs. collectivism)** – looks at the extent to which people are integrated into groups. Some cultures are more cohesive than others. e.g. Anglo Saxon cultures are generally more individualistic than the collectivist cultures of South America.

  High individualism indicates that staff expect to be assessed on their own achievements and performance.

  Low individualism (or collectivism) would mean that staff expect to be assessed on a group basis and prefer the organisation to set group goals.

- **Uncertainty avoidance (UA) index** – deals with a society's tolerance for uncertainty and ambiguity – e.g. France and Japan use bureaucracy to reduce uncertainty because they dislike it.

  High UA cultures will not like to act outside their normal job descriptions or roles. They prefer to be directed by management and like formal rules and guidelines.

  Low UA cultures will be prepared to take more risks and go beyond their 'comfort zones'. They tend to dislike bureaucracy as it stifles initiative.

- **Power distance (PD) index** – the extent to which the less powerful members of organisations and institutions accept and expect that power is distributed unequally – e.g. in South American societies, differences in power were tolerated more than in North European cultures.

  High PD cultures expect to answer to powerful managers and do not expect to have any democratic input into decisions that are made.

  Low PD cultures expect to be involved with the decision-making process and want less direct supervision by managers.

- **Masculinity (vs. femininity)** – a masculine culture is one where the distinction between the roles and values of the genders is large and the males focus on work, power and success (e.g. in Japanese culture) whereas in feminine cultures such as Finland, the differences between the gender roles is much smaller.

  Employees in masculine cultures can be motivated by offering them job titles, increased status and pay rises, as this is what the culture values.

  Staff in feminine cultures will be motivated more by work life balance, quality of life and relationships at work.

More recently, two additional dimensions have been added to Hofstede's model:

- **Long-term orientation (vs. short-term orientation)** – societies with a long-term orientation focus on future rewards, with a particular focus on saving, persistence and the ability to adapt to changing circumstances.

  Short-term oriented cultures focus on past and present concerns, such as respect for tradition, social obligations and saving 'face'.

- **Indulgence vs. restraint** – indulgent societies allow relatively free gratification of basic and natural human drives related to enjoying life and having fun. More restrained societies suppress gratification of needs and regulate it by means of strict social norms.

Test your understanding 4
Looking at the **Hofstede** traits, choose the classification that most closely fits Great Britain.

Individualistic or collective?

Large power distance or small?

Masculine or feminine roles?

Test your understanding 5

Jane has recently moved to country A to head up a newly created research team.

She quickly discovers that her staff seems unwilling to make major decisions for themselves and expect her to monitor their work closely.

Which of the following features of Hofstede's cultural dimensions are Jane's staff demonstrating?

A   High individualism

B   Low power-distance index

C   High uncertainty avoidance

D   Femininity

4   The informal organisation and its relationship with the formal organisation

In the last chapter, we looked at the concept of the formal structures of an organisation. These have been designed by management to try and ensure that the organisation meets its goals.

Now we need to look at the **informal** organisation.

The informal organisation is the network of relationships that exist within an organisation.

This network evolves over time and tends to arise through common interests and friendships between members of staff. These relationships are often across divisions.

An informal organisation will be present to some degree within all formal organisations.

Think of the informal organisation as being an aspect of the organisation's culture.

The advantages and disadvantages of informal organisation are:

Advantages	Disadvantages
• better motivation • better communication • provision of social control	• inefficient organisations • opposition to change can be intensified • the 'grapevine effect', where potentially inaccurate information or rumours spread through the informal organisation • conformity

Advantages and disadvantages of the informal organisation

Advantages

- If managers can work with the informal groups within their department, there should be higher levels of motivation and productivity.

- Interdivisional communication should be better through the informal network. This could lead to increased innovation which should help the company succeed.

- The informal organisation may also help maintain conformity in the organisation. For example, employees will be unlikely to dress too casually if others in the company are likely to disapprove.

Disadvantages

- If the formal structure is in conflict with the informal structure, the organisation may end up being inefficient at meeting its objectives. This can arise due to, e.g. formal lines of communication being blocked as informal lines of communication are more efficient and become more important.

- If managers try to implement change, they may find opposition from not only the formal but also the informal organisation e.g. change in one division, may lead to companywide unrest as word of the changes spread through the informal network, and other divisions start to be concerned that 'they will be next' (the grapevine effect).

- The informal organisation may also encourage conformity. This means that employees may be unwilling to perform too well in case it 'shows up' less productive members of staff. This will harm the efficiency of the organisation.

Test your understanding 6

Which of the following statements is/are correct?

(i)   Informal relationships are shown on organisational charts.

(ii)   Informal relationships within an organisation can be across divisions.

A   (i) only

B   (ii) only

C   Both

D   Neither

The informal organisation can either enhance or hold back the business.

Managers need to be aware of the informal structure and ensure that they:

- adapt the formal structure to complement the informal one

- maintain a looser formal structure so that the informal structure can thrive.

- at the very least take account of the informal structure in decision making.

Informal groups

If a manufacturing department has split itself into two informal groups and output is in decline, the declining output could have nothing to do with the formal structure, but be due to lack of integration of the whole division due to the opposing groups. Rather than changing the formal structure, management could for example mix members of the two 'cliques' on training courses, and so try and reduce the impact of the informal organisation.

5 Chapter summary

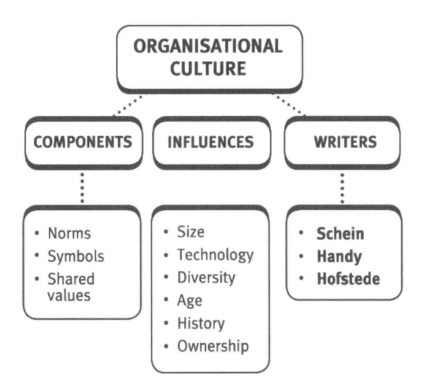

6 Practice questions

Test your understanding 7

According to Schein, there is a strong link between culture and

_____ .

Which word or words best fill the blank?

A   Management style

B   Leadership

C Diversity

D   The size of the organisation

Test your understanding 8

H company is analysing its corporate culture. It has found that many of its staff believe that the main purpose of the company is to simply earn as much profit as possible and therefore they are failing to provide high quality service to customers.

According to Schein, what level of culture has H company identified?

A   Espoused values

B   Artefacts

C   Basic assumptions and values

D   Power

Test your understanding 9

Country V has a standing army of ten thousand soldiers. Each soldier has a series of closely defined duties and tasks that they are expected to fulfil on a regular basis. The accomplishment of these tasks is monitored by a highly bureaucratic administration function. Non-compliance with the rules is punished and soldiers are not expected to go beyond the duties they have been set.

According to Charles Handy, what type of culture does country V's army demonstrate?

A   Role

B   Task

C   Power

D   Person

Test your understanding 10

Staff in country G dislike their managers interfering in their work. According to Hofstede, this means that the culture is:

A   Masculine

B   High uncertainty avoidance

C   Low power-distance

D   Collective

Test your understanding 11

B owns a chain of stores in country H. It is aware that its staff dislike using new technology as it conflicts with their long-held working practices.

According to Hofstede's model, this indicates that the culture in country B has a:

A   Long-term orientation

B   Short-term orientation

Test your understanding 12

Information may be passed informally between individuals within an organisation, sometimes leading to the spread of inaccurate rumour. This is known as the .

Which word or words best fill the gap?

A   Informal organisation

B   Formal organisation

C   Corporate culture

D   Grapevine effect

Test your understanding 13

Company R is a manufacturing company where most workers are part of the same union. Employees prefer to negotiate pay and conditions as a group, rather than it being negotiated on a one-to-one basis with management.

Company S operates a large call centre. Staff members have stated their preference to have detailed scripts provided by management. These scripts can help the employees to deal with any unexpected queries or objections that may arise when talking to customers.

Company T has relatively few managers, as most staff members are felt to be self-motivated and trustworthy. When decisions are made by managers, employees expect to have a chance to state their opinions and have these taken into account by their managers.

Company U has recently been involved in pay negotiations with members of its workforce. Its managers have discovered that most employees simply wish to be paid more or be given new job titles. They seem uninterested in additional holidays or the offer of flexible working arrangements.

The following are dimensions used by Hofstede to classify different types of organisational culture:

		1 High	2 Low
A	Power distance	A1	A2
B	Uncertainty avoidance	B1	B2
C	Individualism	C1	C2
D	Masculinity	D1	D2

Required:

(i) For Company R, select which combination of dimensions apply from the grid above (i.e. A1).

(ii) For company S, select which combination of dimensions apply from the grid above (i.e. A1).

(iii) For Company T, select which combination of dimensions apply from the grid above (i.e. A1).

(iv) For Company U, select which combination of dimensions apply from the grid above (i.e. A1).

(1 mark each, total = 4 marks)

Test your understanding answers

Test your understanding 1

The correct answer is C

This would be classified as one of the organisation's espoused values.

Test your understanding 2

The correct answer is C

A is a definition of the person culture, not the role culture.

B is incorrect as a power culture tends to only have one major source of power. Bureaucracy tends to be found in a role culture.

D is also incorrect as this describes a task culture.

Test your understanding 3

A task culture is one where nothing is allowed to get in the way of completing the task.

Disadvantages could be:

- high levels of stress

- quality compromised in an effort to get the job finished on time

- people feeling that their individual needs are surpassed by the needs of the task, e.g. feeling pressurised to work late.

Test your understanding 4

Although the points can be debated, and the culture is changing, Great Britain is probably:

Individualistic

Small power distance

Masculine roles

Test your understanding 5

The correct answer is C

The workers are demonstrating a dislike of uncertainty. Note that if they had low power-distance, they would not want Jane to supervise their work closely.

There is insufficient information available to conclude on the masculinity or individualism of the culture.

Test your understanding 6

The correct answer is B

Test your understanding 7

The correct answer is B

While the others are factors that may affect culture, Schein believed in a strong link between leadership and culture.

Test your understanding 8

The correct answer is C

Basic assumptions and values are often difficult to identify and exist mainly at an unconscious level. In this case, it relates to what staff believe their function is and what they think the organisation expects of them. This can be quite different to the organisation's stated goals (espoused values).

Test your understanding 9

The correct answer is A

Role cultures value the performance of an individual's duties - no more, no less. Armed forces are a common real-world example of this.

Test your understanding 10

The correct answer is C

By definition.

Test your understanding 11

The correct answer is B

A culture with a short-term orientation is concerned with maintaining tradition. A long-term oriented culture is willing to adapt to changing circumstances.

Test your understanding 12

The correct answer is D

The grapevine effect relates to informal communication between individuals within the organisation. Don't get confused between this and informal organisation itself, which describes the relationships between individuals in the organisation. In reality, the grapevine often follows the same routes as the informal organisation.

Test your understanding 13

The correct answers are:

(i)   **C2** – workers prefer to negotiate and be judged collectively, rather than as individuals.

(ii) **B1** – employees clearly dislike dealing with the unexpected, indicating high UA.

(iii) **A2** – employees expect to have a say in management activities, indicating a low power distance.

(iv) **D1** – employees are motivated by money and status, rather than work-life balance. This indicates a masculine culture.

Information technology and information systems in business

Chapter learning objectives

Upon completion of this chapter you will be able to:

- identify an organisation's system requirements in relation to the objectives and policies of the organisation

- identify business uses of computers and IT software applications: spreadsheets, databases and accounting packages

- describe and compare the relative benefits and limitations of manual and automated financial systems that may be used in an organisation

- explain how the type of information differs and the purposes for which it is applied at different levels of the organisation: strategic, tactical and operational

- list the attributes of good quality information.

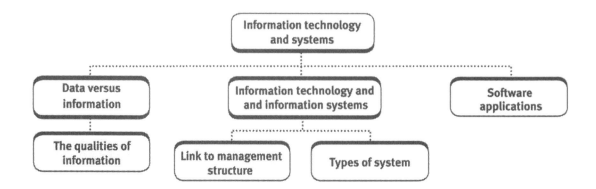

1 Data and information

Information and data are two different things.

Data consists of numbers, letters, symbols, raw facts, events and transactions, which have been recorded but not yet processed into a form that is suitable for making decisions.

Types of data

There are several types of data that an organisation may gather.

Quantitative data is that which is capable of being measured numerically, e.g. the standard labour hours required to produce one unit of output.

Qualitative data is not capable of being measured numerically but may reflect distinguishing characteristics, e.g. the grade of labour used to produce the unit of output.

Data is said to be **discrete** when it can only take on specific fixed values, e.g. the actual number of vehicles through a car wash per day could be 35 but not 35.3. Whereas **continuous** data takes on any numerical value and we could, in an eight hour day, measure the throughput of cars as 4.375 per hour, i.e. 35 cars/8 hours.

Data needs to be collected and summarised in the form required by the user.

Primary data is collected for a particular enquiry, for example by observation, employees would be observed performing a 'value adding' activity when establishing a standard time for the activity.

Data collected by a trade association from a number of firms and comprising trade association statistics would become secondary data when used by a firm in the sector making an enquiry of its own.

Information is data that has been processed in such a way that it has meaning to the person that receives it, who may then use it to improve the quality of their decision-making.

Information is vital to an organisation and is required both internally and externally. Management requires information:

- to provide records, both current and historical

- to analyse what is happening in the business

- to provide the basis for decision-making in the short- and long-term

- to monitor the performance of the business by comparing actual results with plans and forecasts.

This information will be used by various third parties, including:

- the shareholders or owners – who will want to know how their investment is performing

- customers and suppliers – who will want to know how stable the business is and therefore whether it will be a reliable trading partner

- employees – who will have an interest in the performance of the organisation and how it impacts on the job security and pay

- government agencies – such as tax authorities.

Illustration 1 – Turning data into information

Twenty five employees from the finance department of a large organisation took an introductory course in Computing. The test at the end of the course resulted in the marks shown below. The marks were out of 50 and the pass mark was 20 out of 50.

12	19	8	21	32
25	34	22	30	20
43	21	16	45	32
27	38	39	21	18
33	11	28	26	27

At the moment, this data is simply not useful. To give it meaning, we need to process it and turn it into information.

There are actually many ways that this data can be turned into information.

For example, we could simply calculate the percentage of students who passed the assessment. In this case, 19 employees out of 25 passed – or 76%.

Alternatively, for more detail we could create a frequency distribution.

Marks obtained	Frequency
0–9	1
10–19	5
20–29	10
30–39	7
40+	2

This chart shows that the 19 employees that pass the test (achieve 20+) are in the top 3 class intervals and those that fail – 6 employees – are in the bottom two intervals.

However the data is processed, we can use it to make key decisions. For instance, we could compare these results to those of other classes and identify whether there were any problems with it.

As information is so important to the business, it is vital that the business only relies on good information.

'Good' information helps in the decision-making process, is useful to the recipient and can be relied upon.

To be 'good', information should have the following characteristics (which you can remember using the acronym **ACCURATE**).

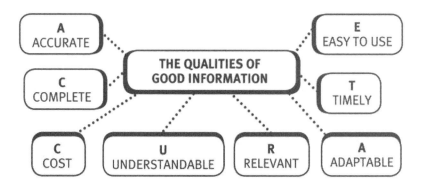

- **A**ccurate – information should be sufficiently accurate for its intended purpose and the decision-maker should be able to rely on the information.

- **C**omplete – the more complete information is, the more reliable it will be.

- **C**ost – the information should not cost more to obtain than the benefit derived from it.

- **U**nderstandable and user friendly information is much more readily acted upon.

- **R**elevant – the information provided should concentrate on the essentials and ignore trivia.

- **A**daptable – information should be tailored to the needs and level of understanding of its intended recipients.

- **T**imely – information that is out-of-date is a waste of time, effort and money.

- **E**asy to use – information should be clearly presented and sent using the right medium and communication channel.

Test your understanding 1

Consider the following statements:

(i)   Good information must be obtained cheaply.

(ii) Information consists of raw facts and figures which have been recorded but not yet processed into a useful form.

Which of the above statements is/are correct?

A   (i) only

B   (ii) only

C   Both

D   Neither

2   Information technology and information systems

In the modern business world, many organisations hold and process vast amounts of data and information. This would not be practical to do manually, so they rely on automated systems to perform the handling and storage required.

Information systems (IS) refer to the management and provision of information to support the running of the organisation.

There are five major types of information system that you need to be aware of for your exam, which we will examine in detail shortly.

Information technology (IT) describes any equipment concerned with the capture, storage, transmission or presentation of data.

Put simply, IT is the hardware infrastructure that runs the information systems.

This will include desktop computers, laptops, servers, printers and hard drives used by the organisation.

3 Types of information system

3.1 Management structure and information requirements

As outlined in chapter 2, there are three levels of management – strategic, tactical and operational.

Each level creates different types of strategy within the organisation and therefore needs different types of information, as outlined by the following chart:

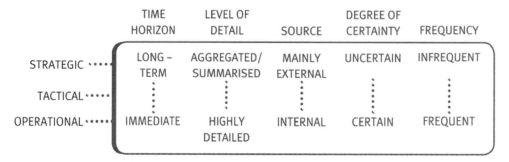

	TIME HORIZON	LEVEL OF DETAIL	SOURCE	DEGREE OF CERTAINTY	FREQUENCY
STRATEGIC ····	LONG – TERM	AGGREGATED/ SUMMARISED	MAINLY EXTERNAL	UNCERTAIN	INFREQUENT
TACTICAL ····					
OPERATIONAL ····	IMMEDIATE	HIGHLY DETAILED	INTERNAL	CERTAIN	FREQUENT

- The strategic level of management requires information from internal and external sources in order to plan the long-term strategies of the organisation. Internal information – both quantitative and qualitative – is usually supplied in a summarised form, often on an ad-hoc basis.

- The tactical level of management requires information and instructions from the strategic level of management, together with routine and regular quantitative information from the operational level of management. The information would be in a summarised form, but detailed enough to allow tactical planning of resources and manpower.

- The operational level of management requires information and instructions from the tactical level of management. The operational level is primarily concerned with the day-to-day performance of tasks and most of the information is obtained from internal sources. The information must be detailed and precise.

Illustration 2 – Management structure and information

This example refers to capital equipment use in an organisation:

Operational information would include a current week's report for a cost centre on the percentage capacity of the plant used in the period.

Tactical information could include the short-term budget for 12 months and would show the budgeted machine use in terms of machine hours for each item of plant. The total machine hours being predetermined from the production budget for the period.

Strategic information would relate to the longer-term strategy on the company's market share, which in turn informs the production plan. This plan would be used to predetermine the level of investment required in capital equipment in the longer term. This process would also lead to investigating new methods and technology.

Test your understanding 2

Operational level managers need information that is _____ term and comes mainly from _____ sources.

Which words correctly complete the sentence above?

(1)   Long

(2)   Short

(3)   Internal

(4)   External

A   (1) and (4)

B   (2) and (3)

C   (1) and (3)

D   (2) and (4)

As each level of manager needs different types of information, they will need different information systems to provide them with this.

INFORMATION SYSTEMS TO SUPPORT DECISION MAKING

Operational

Programmable decisions with specific inputs and outputs.
Transaction processing system (TPS) used.

Tactical

Use variety of data from different sources – emphasis on exception reporting.
Management information system (MIS) used.

Strategic

Varied information needs –sometimes difficult to predict.
MIS and Executive information systems (EIS) used.

3.2 Transaction processing system (TPS)

A TPS records all the daily transactions of the organisation and summarises them so they can be reported on a routine basis.

Transaction processing systems are used mainly by operational managers to make basic decisions.

Examples include:

- Sales/marketing systems – recording sales transactions and providing details on marketing and promotional activities

- Manufacturing production systems – recording details of purchases, production and shipping of goods

- Finance and accounting systems – maintenance of financial data in an organisation.

Illustration 3 – TPS

A TPS could be used to record the sales for a bookstore. At the end of each day, it will produce a summary of how many of each type of book has been sold.

This will allow the operational managers to decide which books they need to order from their suppliers and how many books they need to buy in order to replenish their stocks.

3.3 Management information systems (MIS)

Management information systems convert data from the TPS into information for tactical managers. This information will be designed to help them monitor performance, maintain co-ordination and provide background information about the organisation's operations.

The MIS will be used for both historic and current analysis of business performance, as well as to make predictions about future operations.

Illustration 4 – MIS

A company that operates a national chain of car showrooms could use an MIS for performance measurement.

The MIS could use the information from the sales TPS to generate reports such as:

- total sales for each type of car

- total sales made by each salesperson

- total sales by showroom or by geographic area

This information could be extremely useful for control and performance appraisal purposes.

3.4 Decision support systems (DSS)

A DSS is a computer system that helps decision-makers deal with semi- or unstructured decisions, where there is a high degree of uncertainty, or unknown factors that may affect the decision.

The DSS draws on both internal information about the organisation (from the TPS) and external information (about the market, economic growth, etc).

A DSS will be tailor-made to the requirements of the organisation.

Illustration 5 – DSS

A supermarket chain is planning to start selling its goods online, but is uncertain of whether it is appropriate for the organisation.

A DSS would gather information about the company itself – does it have the resources to start selling online?

It will also provide information about the online groceries market, such as the size of the market and who the competitors are.

The DSS will then present this information in a way that is easy to understand, helping the management to make the decision.

 3.5 Executive information systems (EIS)

These systems provide strategic managers with flexible access to information from the entire business, as well as relevant information from the external environment.

The EIS enables senior management to easily model the entire business by turning its data into useful, summarised reports.

This information can then easily be distributed to key staff members.

 Illustration 6 – EIS

A typical report from an EIS would combine many types of data on the same screen and make it easier for executives to understand the performance of the business.

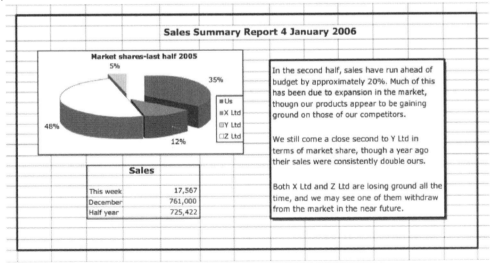

3.6 Expert systems (ES)

Expert systems hold specialist (expert) knowledge and allow non-experts to interrogate the system for information, advice and recommended decisions.

This is not part of the normal hierarchy of information systems and will be used by employees at all levels of the organisation.

Expert systems are widely used in technical or complex areas, such as:

- law (e.g. conveyancing)
- taxation (e.g. personal tax calculations)
- banking (e.g. granting credit)
- medicine (e.g. diagnosis of symptoms).

Illustration 7 – ES

An accountant could use an ES to calculate a client's personal tax liability.

The accountant will input the relevant information about the client's circumstances. The ES will then access its database of rules and regulations about personal tax, decide which rules apply to the client and then use them to calculate a tax liability.

Test your understanding 3

AFT plc is considering setting up a new IT system. It needs the system to provide both internal and external information to help the strategic managers monitor the performance of the entire business quickly and easily.

Which type of information system is AFT planning on setting up?

A   TPS

B   EIS

C   DSS

D   MIS

Test your understanding 4

Consider the following statements:

(i)   Expert systems tend to be very expensive, meaning that their use is restricted to strategic level staff only.

(ii)   Each decision support system tends to be tailored to the organisation that operates it.

Which of these statements is/are correct?

A   (i) only

B   (ii) only

C   Both

D   Neither

4   Software applications

For your exam, you need to be able to discuss three specific software applications.

Software applications are computer programmes that are designed to help users with certain tasks.

It is important that organisations are aware of the advantages and disadvantages of common software applications to ensure that they choose the right application for the right task.

4.1 Spreadsheets

Spreadsheets are designed to analyse data and sort lists of items, not for long-term storage of raw data. A spreadsheet should be used for 'crunching' numbers and storage of single lists of items. They also include graphing functions that allow for quick reporting and analysis of data.

Advantages	Disadvantages
• Relatively easy to use. • Require little training to get started. • Most data managers are familiar with them.	• Data must be re-copied over and over again to maintain it in separate data files. • They are unable to efficiently identify data errors. • Lack of detailed sorting and querying abilities. • There can be sharing violations among users wishing to view or change data at the same time. • They are often restricted to a finite number of records, and can require a large amount of hard-drive space for data storage.

4.2 Databases

To store large amounts of raw data, it is best to use a database. This is especially true in circumstances where two or more users share the information.

Advantages	Disadvantages
• The most important benefit gained by using a database is the ease of reporting and sharing data. • Databases require little or no duplication of data between information tables. • Changes made to the data do not corrupt the programming (e.g. at the cell level of a spreadsheet where calculations are running). • Databases offer better security to restrict users from accessing privileged information, and from changing coded information in the programming.	• Requires the user to learn a new system. • Requires a greater investment in training and software. • The initial time and cost of migrating all of the data into a new database system is significant.

4.3 Accountancy packages

Many businesses choose to utilise specialised software packages that record and process the individual transactions within the business, rather than relying on manual records.

These accounting packages are often designed to automatically produce year-end accounts and management reports when requested.

Advantages	Disadvantages
• Rapid recording of transactions, when compared to a manual system. • Lower likelihood of mistakes. • Rapid production of reports and financial statements.	• Usually requires training before use. • Packages can be expensive to purchase and install. • May be unnecessary for a small business with low numbers of transactions.

Test your understanding 5

Which of the following is not an advantage that databases have over spreadsheets:

A   Less training required

B   Better security

C   Less duplication of information

D   Greater ease of sharing information

5   The advantages of computerisation

Most aspects of the economy, from the music industry to manufacturing, banking, retailing and defence, are now totally dependent on modern information processing systems. Developments in information technology provide companies with new opportunities, e.g.:

- internet

- access to corporate databases

- mobile computing

- improved telecommunication structure.

The value of computer systems in handling and processing business data cannot be underestimated.

Computers have revolutionised information systems for the following reasons:

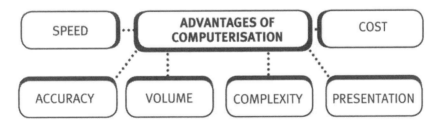

Advantages of computerisation

The advantages of computerisation include the following:

- **Speed** – Computers are ideal for dealing with repetitive processes. The limiting factors, for example, in processing a payroll by computer are not the speed of calculation by the computer, but the speed with which data can be input and the speed of the printer at the output.

- **Accuracy** – In general, computers do not suffer from errors, or lapses of concentration but process data perfectly. Any mistakes that computers make nowadays are not caused by electronic error, but by human error, for example at the input stage, or in designing and programming software.

- **Volume** – Not only do computers work fast, but they do not need to rest. They can work twenty-four hour days when required. They are therefore able to handle vast volumes of data.

- **Complexity** – Once subsystems are computerised they can generally function more reliably than human beings. This makes it easier to integrate various subsystems. Computers are therefore able to handle complex information systems efficiently. However, one of the problems with this is that when the computer does fail, there is often a major breakdown in the system, with many personnel unable to perform their work functions.

- **Cost** – All the above advantages mean that computers have become highly cost-effective providers of information. The process of substituting computers for human beings has revolutionised information-oriented industries such as accountancy, banking and insurance and this process is continuing.

- **Presentation** – More recently, emphasis has been placed on displaying information in as 'user-friendly' a way as possible. Modern packages containing sophisticated word processors, spreadsheets and graphics combined with the development of colour printers now enable boring reports to be presented in new and exciting ways!

Note – It is necessary, however, to remember the advantages that people have as providers of information. Chief amongst these is judgement of reasonableness. People can usually see when an item of information looks unreasonable. Although it is possible to program limited reasonableness tests into computer systems, it is still very difficult to program judgement. The computer remains a highly trained idiot, which is particularly apparent when a programming error is made or it is subject to a computer virus.

6 Chapter summary

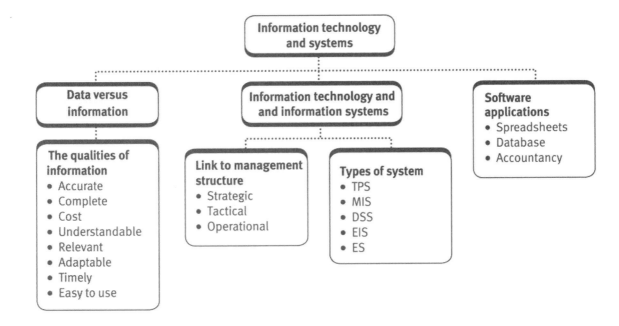

7 Practice questions

Test your understanding 6

Consider the following two statements:

(i) A transaction processing system (TPS) would normally be used by operational-level managers.

(ii) Data is facts and figures that have been processed in such a way that it has meaning to the user.

Which of these statements is/are correct?

A   (i) only

B   (ii) only

C   Both

D   Neither

Test your understanding 7

A business has recently installed an information system that allows historic analysis of the business results as well as creation of budgets and predictions about future operations.

What type of information system has the business installed?

A   A transaction processing system

B   An expert system

C   A management information system

D   An executive information system

Test your understanding 8

JNB plc is a multinational retailer which is considering opening its first ever store in country B. JNB has no experience of trading in country B and is unsure whether consumers will choose to shop in its store or what the reaction of existing retailers in country B will be to its entry.

What type of information system could JNB use to help it choose whether to open the new store or not?

A   Management information system

B   Executive information system

C   Expert system

D   Decision support system

Test your understanding 9

Jay has to analyse the historic results for his business over the last ten years. He wishes to represent the information using a series of graphs that he can show to potential investors.

Which software application would be most appropriate for Jay to use?

A   Database

B   Accountancy package

C   Spreadsheet

D   Desktop publishing

Test your understanding 10

There are a number of different information systems that may be used within organisations. These include:

A   Decision-support systems

B   Transaction processing systems

C   Executive information systems

D   Management information systems

Required:

(a)   Identify which of the above systems is associated with each of the following descriptions, by selecting A, B, C or D.

   (i)   Converts information about basic transactions into information that will help tactical managers control the organisation.

   (ii)   Records all the daily transactions within the organisation and summarises them periodically.

   (iii)   A tailor-made system that will draw on internal and external information to help deal with unstructured or semi-structured problems.

   (iv)   Provides internal and external information to strategic managers, enabling modelling of the entire business.

(0.5 marks each = 2 marks in total)

(b) Below is a list of characteristics:

A   Cost free

B   Easy to use

C   Rapid

D   Adaptable

E   Perfect

F   Cautious

G   Factual

Required:

Which TWO of these are characteristics of 'good' information? Select TWO from A, B, C, D, E, F, G.

(1 mark each = 2 marks in total)

(Total: 4 marks)

Test your understanding answers

Test your understanding 1

The correct answer is D

While information should not cost more to obtain than the benefit derived from it, this does not mean it will always be cheap to obtain.

The definition in (ii) is of data – not information.

Test your understanding 2

The correct answer is B – they need short-term information from internal sources.

Test your understanding 3

The correct answer is B

Test your understanding 4

The correct answer is B – (i) is incorrect – expert systems are commonly expensive to buy, but their use is not restricted to senior managers, as they will be useful throughout the organisation.

Test your understanding 5

The correct answer is A – Database systems are generally considered to be more complex than spreadsheets.

Test your understanding 6

The correct answer is A – A TPS is a low-level system that summarises internal information, such as transactions. This would be used by either junior or operational level managers. The definition given for data is actually that of information. Be careful not to get the two confused!

Test your understanding 7

The correct answer is C – This is the definition of a management information system.

Test your understanding 8

The correct answer is D – A decision support system helps users deal with semi- or un-structured decisions where some factors are unknown. This would be ideal for JNB.

Test your understanding 9

The correct answer is C – This would be a typical use of a spreadsheet application, which is designed for 'number-crunching' and graphical analysis of information.

Test your understanding 10

(a) The correct answers by definition are:

    (i) **D**

    (ii) **B**

    (iii) **A**

    (iv) **C**

(b) The correct characteristics are **B** and **D**. The other characteristics are: accurate, complete, cost effective, understandable, relevant and timely.

Stakeholders in business organisations

Chapter learning objectives

Upon completion of this chapter you will be able to:

- define stakeholders

- define internal, external and connected stakeholders and explain their impact on the organisation

- identify the main stakeholder groups and the objectives of each group

- explain how the different stakeholder groups interact and how their objectives may conflict with one another

- compare the power and influence of various stakeholder groups and how their needs should be accounted for, such as under the Mendelow framework.

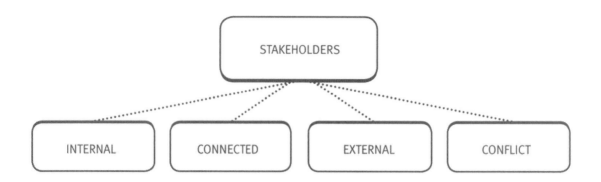

1 What are stakeholders?

 A stakeholder is an individual or group who has an interest in what the organisation does, or who affects, or can be affected by, the organisation's actions.

It is vital for managers to understand the varying needs of the different stakeholders in their organisation. Failure to do so could mean that important stakeholders do not have their needs met, which could be disastrous for the company.

Stakeholders can be broadly categorised into three groups: internal, external and connected.

2 Types of stakeholder

2.1 Internal stakeholders

 These are any stakeholders that are within the organisation itself. Their objectives are likely to have a strong influence on how it is run.

Internal stakeholders include:

Stakeholder	Need/expectation	Example
Employees	Pay, working conditions and job security	If workers are to be given more responsibility, they will expect increased pay.
Managers/directors	Status, pay, bonus, job security	If growth is going to occur, the managers will want increased profits, leading to increased bonuses.

KAPLAN PUBLISHING

Test your understanding 1

Which of the following statements is/are correct?

(i)   Internal stakeholders have little influence over the way an organisation is run.

(ii)   The needs and expectations of managers and employees will always tend to be the same as they are both internal stakeholders.

A   (i) only

B   (ii) only

C   Neither

D   Both

2.2 Connected stakeholders

Connected stakeholders either invest in or have dealings with the firm.

They tend to have varied objectives.

Stakeholder	Need/expectation	Example
Shareholders	Steady flow of income, possible capital growth and the continuation of the business.	If capital is required for growth, the shareholders will expect a rise in the dividend stream.
Customers	Satisfaction of customers' needs will be achieved through providing value-for-money products and services.	Any attempt to, for example, increase the quality and the price, may lead to customer dissatisfaction.
Suppliers	Paid promptly.	If a decision is made to delay payment to suppliers to ease cash flow, existing suppliers may cease supplying goods.
Finance providers	Ability to repay the finance including interest, security of investment.	The firm's ability to generate cash.

2.3 External stakeholders

 These stakeholders tend to not have a direct link to the organisation but can influence or be influenced by its activities.

As with connected stakeholders, they will have very diverse objectives for the organisation to take account of.

Stakeholder	Need/expectation	Example
Community at large	The general public can be a stakeholder, especially if their lives are affected by an organisation's decisions.	E.g. local residents' attitude towards out-oftown shopping centres.
Environmental pressure groups	The organisation does not harm the external environment.	If an airport wants to build a new runway, the pressure groups may stage a 'sit in'.
Government	Company activities are central to the success of the economy (providing jobs and paying taxes). Legislation (e.g. health and safety) must be met by the company.	Actions by companies could break the law, or damage the environment, and governments therefore control what organisations can do.
Trade unions	Taking an active part in the decision-making process.	If a department is to be closed the union will want to be consulted, and there should be a scheme in place to help employees find alternative employment.

 Test your understanding 2

Which of the following would NOT be described as a connected stakeholder?

A   Customers

B   Suppliers

C   Employees

D   Shareholders

2.4 Primary and secondary

This is a different method of categorising stakeholders, which is based on whether or not they have a contractual relationship with the organisation.

 Primary stakeholders are those that have a contractual relationship, for instance employees, directors, shareholders – in fact any stakeholder who falls into the 'connected' or 'internal' categories which are examined above.

 Secondary stakeholders are parties that have an interest in the organisation, but have no contractual link, such as the public. Any stakeholders in the 'external' category would fall into this group.

3 Stakeholder conflict

An organisation can have many different stakeholders, all with different needs. Inevitably, these needs of some stakeholders will come into conflict with the needs of others.

Some of the most common conflicts include:

Stakeholders	Conflict
Employees versus managers	Jobs/wages versus bonus (cost efficiency)
Customers versus shareholders	Product quality/service levels versus profits/dividends
General public versus shareholders	Effect on the environment versus profit/dividends
Managers versus shareholders	Growth versus independence

 Test your understanding 3

How could a conflict arise between shareholders and bankers?

In the event of conflict, an organisation will need to decide which stakeholder's needs are more important. This will commonly be the most dominant stakeholder (in other words, the one with the most power).

If an organisation is having difficulty deciding who the dominant stakeholder is, they can use **Mendelow's power-interest matrix**.

Level of interest

		Low	High
	Low	Minimal effort	Keep informed
Level of power	**High**	Keep satisfied	Key players

By plotting each stakeholder according to the power they have over the organisation and the interest they have in a particular decision, the dominant stakeholder(s), i.e. the key players can be identified. The needs of the key players must be considered during the formulation and evaluation of new strategies.

Further issues with Mendelow's matrix

Although the other stakeholders may be fairly passive, the managers must be aware that stakeholder groups can emerge and move from quadrant to quadrant as a result of specific events, so changing their position in the matrix.

Sources of stakeholder power

Sources of stakeholder power include:

Hierarchy – provides people or groups with formal power over others. Influence – may arise from personal qualities (leadership).

Control of the environment – knowledge, contact and influence of the environment can be a source of power if they are able to reduce the uncertainty experienced by others.

 It should be noted that, in reality, managers need to consider the needs of as many stakeholders as possible. This means that nearly every decision becomes a compromise. For example, a business will have to earn a satisfactory return for its shareholders whilst paying reasonable wages.

Test your understanding 4

Chop Ltd is a forestry business which leases several large woodlands from the central government of country Z. It currently employs 2,000 members of staff across the country.

Chop supplies over three hundred small businesses with wood across country Z. However, recently its profitability has been poor and it has been struggling to pay any dividends.

This has angered the company's three shareholders, who each own around twenty percent of Chop's share capital. The remainder is owned by the public, with no one investor owning more than one percent of the total share capital.

The three main shareholders have asked the Board of Directors to consider making 200 employees redundant. The employees are not heavily unionised.

State the appropriate strategy from Mendelow's matrix for each of the following stakeholders:

A   Chop's customers

B   Major shareholders

C   Employees

D   Government of country Z

4 Chapter summary

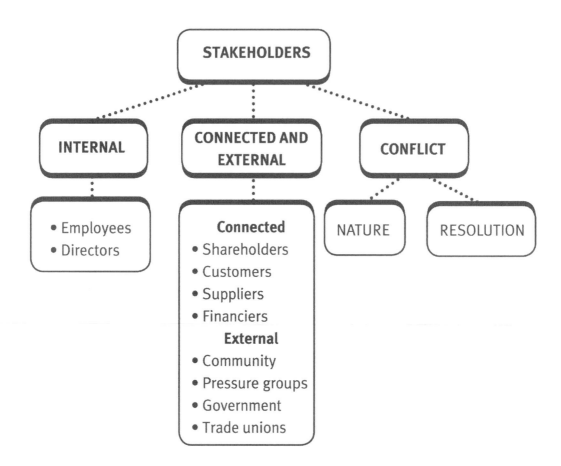

5 Practice questions

Test your understanding 5

Which of the following would be classified as an internal stakeholder?

A   Shareholders

B   Customers

C   Directors

D   Finance providers

Test your understanding 6

There are a number of different ways of classifying stakeholders, including:

(i)   Internal

(ii)   Connected

(iii)   Primary

(iv)   Secondary

Which **two** of the above categories would suppliers fall into?

A   (i) and (iii)

B   (i) and (iv)

C   (ii) and (iii)

D   (ii) and (iv)

Test your understanding 7

A plc has a large number of shareholders. The largest is H, a pension company. H owns 35% of A's share capital. None of the other shareholders own more than 10% of the share capital each. H has stated that it is happy with A's strategy and dividends and has no intention of intervening in A.

If A prepares Mendelow's matrix, which quadrant would H fall into?

A   Minimal effort

B   Keep informed

C   Keep satisfied

D   Key player

Test your understanding 8

A stakeholder has a high level of interest, but has little influence over the organisation. According to Mendelow's matrix, the strategy that should be adopted for this stakeholder is:

A   Minimal effort

B   Keep satisfied

C   Keep informed

D   Key player

Test your understanding 9

Consider the following statements regarding stakeholders:

(i)   Managers only need to consider those stakeholders who are 'key players' on Mendelow's matrix.

(ii)   Employees and managers are both internal stakeholders, meaning that they have the same objectives as each other.

Which of these statements is/are correct?

A   (i) only

B   (ii) only

C   Both

D   Neither

Test your understanding answers

Test your understanding 1

The correct answer is C

Neither are correct. Internal stakeholders have a huge amount of influence over the running of an organisation.

In addition, just because they are in the same category of stakeholder does not mean that managers and employees have the same goals. For instance, managers will want to keep profits high to ensure they maximise their bonuses. This may encourage them to keep staff wages low, which is clearly not in the interests of employees!

Test your understanding 2

The correct answer is C

Employees are internal stakeholders.

Test your understanding 3

The shareholders may be willing to take more risks in return for higher profits/returns, whereas the bankers will be more concerned with low risk/security.

Test your understanding 4

A   **Minimal effort.** Chop's customers are likely to have little interest in the staffing of their suppliers as long as it does not affect the service or products they receive. They will individually have little power as they do not form a significant part of Chop's revenue.

B   **Key players.** The board will see the three major shareholders as having high power due to their high proportion of voting rights in the business. They are clearly highly interested in their investment in Chop.

C   **Keep informed.** Employees are not heavily unionised, so have little collective power. They will be highly interested, however, as many of their jobs are at risk.

D   **Keep satisfied.** The government of country Z would have significant power over Chop, if it chooses to exercise it, as it owns the forests that Chop leases. However, as long as Chop obeys the law, it is unlikely to take an active interest in the reduction of its workforce.

Test your understanding 5

The correct answer is C

Internal stakeholders are within the organisation itself. The other three are all connected stakeholders.

Test your understanding 6

The correct answer is C

Suppliers have a contractual relationship with the company, meaning that they are both connected and primary.

Test your understanding 7

The correct answer is C

H has comparatively high power due to its large number of shares. However, it has expressed a low level of interest in the running of A. This means that A's directors should work to keep H from taking an active interest in the future.

Test your understanding 8

The correct answer is C

According to Mendelow, these stakeholders have to be kept informed about the organisation's plans.

Test your understanding 9

The correct answer is D

Managers need to consider the needs of all stakeholders. However, in practice, the needs of more powerful stakeholders usually takes priority. In addition, just because two stakeholders are in the same classification, it does not mean that they have the same needs, goals or desires.

External analysis – political and legal factors

Upon completion of this chapter you will be able to:

- Explain how the political system and government policy affect the organisation

- Describe the sources of legal authority, including supra-national bodies, national bodies and regional governments

- Explain how the law protects the employee and the implications of employment legislation for the manager and the organisation

- Identify the principles of data protection and security

- Explain how the law promotes and protects health and safety in the workplace

- Recognise the responsibility of the individual and the organisation for compliance with laws on data protection, security and health and safety

- Outline principles of consumer protection such as sale of goods and simple contract.

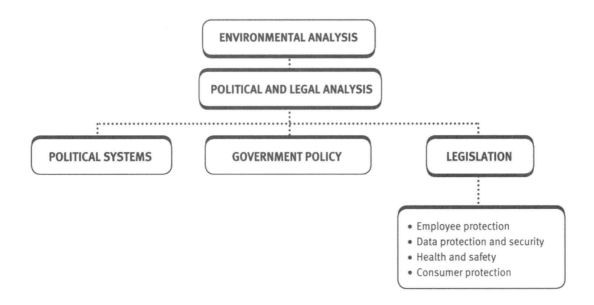

1   Introduction

In order to fully understand an organisation, we need to examine the environment that it operates in – essentially, we need to earn about the world around it.

This analysis should include the following factors:

- **P**olitical/legal factors – covered in this chapter

- **E**conomic factors – covered in chapter 7

- **S**ocial/demographic factors – covered in chapter 8

- **T**echnological factors – covered in chapter 8

Reviewing these factors is often referred to as PEST analysis.

In addition, we will need to examine the organisation's competitors, which we will do in chapter 9.

 PEST analysis

This same categorisation of environmental factors is sometimes referred to as

- PESTL analysis – where legal is separated from political.

- STEP analysis – PEST reordered!

- PESTLE analysis – political, economic, social, technical, legal and ecological/environmental.

Illustration 1 – Introduction to PEST analysis

For example, a haulage firm might monitor the following factors:

Political

- Fuel tax

- Government steps to reduce pollution from lorries

- Congestion charges in cities

- Plans to build new roads

- Road blockades due to strikes (e.g. in France)

Economic

- State of the economy – a downturn would result in less trade

- Fuel is a major cost so oil price movements will be seen as significant

- Most hauliers borrow to purchase trucks, so a rise in interest rates would increase costs

Social

- Predicted car numbers and usage would affect likelihood of traffic jams and hence journey times

- Public concerns over safety could result in lorries being banned from certain routes or/and reductions in speed limits

Technological

- Developments in route planning software

- Anti-theft devices

- Tracking systems to monitor driver hours

- Developments in tyre technology

Competitive

- Competitive rivalry from other hauliers

- Threat from substitutes – e.g. haulage by rail

- Threat of new firms entering the market

2 Political systems and government policy

 A political system is:

- a set of institutions, political organisations and interest groups (such as lobby groups); and

- the relationship between them; and

- the rules and norms that govern their functions (such as constitutions and election law).

There are three levels of political systems that organisations have to take account of.

- Global – such as the World Trade Organisation (WTO), European Union (EU) legislation.

- National – national government policy (see below).

- Local – local government departments, councils.

Sources of legal authority include the following:

Supra-national

- UN resolutions.

- International Court of Justice.

- European Parliament.

- European Courts.

National

- National Governments through Acts of Parliament.

- Senior Courts (such as the Supreme Court in the UK and USA).

- Other major courts through the principles of case law and the setting of precedents.

Regional

- Regional/Federal Government (e.g. Welsh Assembly in the UK, State Government in the USA).

- Local councils through the use of bye-laws.

2.1 How can the government affect an organisation?

Governments can affect organisations in two major ways.

The first is **government policy**.

Illustration 2 – Political systems and government policy

Housing

- New housing developments can give opportunities to house building firms and will create new communities that will demand shops, leisure facilities, etc., giving opportunities for firms in these industries.

Crime

- Crime policy can affect firms that specialise in security.

Education

- Education policy can affect the availability of suitable potential employees for firms.

Defence

- Defence policy will primarily affect arms manufacturers.

- Closure of a military base could have serious implications for local suppliers.

Healthcare

- Healthcare policy has obvious implications for drugs and equipment manufacturers and private hospitals.

Energy

- Policy regarding choice of energy sources (e.g. nuclear) will be critical to power generators.

Environmental

- Targets on greenhouse gas emissions will affect major manufacturers.

Farming

- Government support through subsidies is critical for many farmers.

Town planning

- National plans to build new roads could influence business location.

- On a local level firms need to obtain planning permission for a new factory or to open new shops or build new houses.

Domestic

- A government may use regional development grants to attract new employers to areas of high unemployment.

Foreign

- Protectionism.

- Trade relations with other countries, e.g. a ban of the sale of arms to Iran.

The other way that governments can affect organisations is by **direct legislation.**

Organisations must comply with appropriate legislation. Failure to do so could result in fines, closure, bad publicity and/or loss of customers.

Most industries have specific legislation that they have to comply with – e.g. food labelling in the food industry.

However, there are a number of pieces of legislation that apply to most or all organisations. These include:

- employee protection
- data protection
- health and safety
- consumer protection

These are covered in detail below.

Test your understanding 1

Consider the following statements:

(i)   Senior courts are a source of supra-national authority.

(ii) Legislation and policy can both be used by government to affect organisations.

Which of these statements is/are correct?

A   (i) only

B   (ii) only

C   Both

D   Neither

3   Employee protection

Within many countries, the national governments have passed legislation which protects employees from unfair treatment by their employers.

This type of legislation is often designed specifically to cover termination of the employment of a worker.

3.1 Dismissal

Organisations usually dismiss workers by terminating their contract.

Sometimes employees may resign because their employer has breached the terms of their contract of employment. This is known as **constructive dismissal**. Examples of constructive dismissal include employees resigning due to their employer:

- reducing their wages without agreement
- allowing them to be bullied or harassed in the workplace.

In either case, there is normally a statutory minimum notice period that must be given by either the employee or the employer to terminate the contract. Employees are usually entitled to a written statement of the reasons for their dismissal.

Under the Employment Rights Act in the UK, to be 'fair', an employee must have been dismissed for one of the following reasons:

- They lacked the capability or qualifications for the job.

- They were guilty of misconduct (such as dishonesty or theft).

- The job was redundant (the organisation no longer needed them).

- They were dismissed for legal reasons (for example some jobs require employees to have no criminal record).

If an organisation is unable to prove that a dismissal was fair, they may be accused of **unfair dismissal** by the employee whose contract has been terminated.

Unfair dismissal occurs when an employee has been dismissed for an 'unfair' reason (i.e. one that is not on the above list of 'fair' reasons). In the UK, unfair reasons could include:

- Pregnancy or parental leave

- Joining a trade union

- Discrimination over an employee's religion, ethnicity, gender or sexuality

Note that unfair dismissal is not the same as **wrongful dismissal**. Wrongful dismissal occurs when an employer breaks the terms of the employee's contract during the dismissal – for instance by not giving the proper notice period for dismissal.

It is important that the organisation follows its internal disciplinary policies in the run up to any dismissal. Failure to do so can lead to expensive and time-consuming legal action being brought by ex-employees of the company.

3.2 Redundancy

Redundancy is a form of dismissal which occurs when an employer needs to reduce the size of their workforce.

Legislation in this area gives several typical rights to the employee being made redundant, including:

- the right to consultation

- the right to a fair notice period

- the right to redundancy pay (which will vary depending on the circumstances)

- the right for redundancy selection to be carried out fairly.

Again, failure to provide these rights may open the organisation up to legal claims from any employees who have been made redundant.

4 The principles of data protection

As the business world becomes more complex, organisations are holding increasing amounts of data about individuals.

 Data protection is concerned with protecting individuals against the misuse of this information.

Under the UK Data Protection Act 1998, the main principles of data protection are:

(1) Personal data shall be obtained and processed fairly and lawfully, and in particular shall not be processed unless at least one of the following is met:

– The data subject has given his or her consent; or, processing is necessary; or

– For the performance of a contract to which the data subject is party (or to take steps to enter into a contract at the request of the data subject); or

– To comply with any legal obligation of the data controller; or – For the administration of justice; or

– For the exercise of any function conferred by or under enactment; or for any other function in the public interest.

– For the processing of 'sensitive personal data', data controllers have to meet additional requirements including:

– The data subject has given explicit consent; or

– The data relates to ethnic origin and the processing relates to the company's maintenance of equal opportunity standards.

(2) Personal data shall be obtained for one or more specified and lawful purposes, and shall not be further processed in any manner incompatible with those purposes.

(3) Personal data shall be adequate, relevant and not excessive in relation to the purpose or purposes for which it is processed.

(4) Personal data shall be accurate and kept up-to-date.

(5) Personal data should not be kept for longer than is necessary.

(6) Personal data shall be processed in accordance with the rights of data subjects.

(7) A data user is responsible for the security and protection of data against unauthorised access, alteration, destruction, disclosure or accidental loss.

(8) Personal data should not be transferred to another country outside the European Economic Area unless that country ensures an adequate level of protection for the rights and freedoms of data subjects in relation to the processing of personal data.

The rights of data subjects

In the UK the Data Protection Act sets out seven rights of individuals with respect to information stored about them:

(1) Right of subject access – upon making a written request and paying a fee, individuals are entitled to be told whether the data controller or someone on their behalf, holds personal data about them and if so to be given:

- A description of the personal data;

- The purposes for which they are being processed; and

- Those to whom they may be disclosed.

(b) Right to prevent processing likely to cause damage or distress.

(c) Right to prevent processing for the purposes of direct marketing.

(d) Rights in relation to automated decision making (no decision is taken against an individual by purely automated means – the individual has 21 days to require the data controller to reconsider the decision or to take the decision on a different basis).

(e) Right to take action for compensation for damages caused by the data controller.

(f) Right to take action to rectify, block, erase or destroy personal data – through application by an individual to the Courts.

(g) Right to request that the Commissioner assesses whether any contravention of the Act has occurred.

5 Data security

Data security is concerned with keeping data safe from various hazards that could destroy or compromise it.

These include:

- **Physical risks** – impact on the physical environment in which the system exists (e.g. fire or flood).

- **Human risks** – access is gained to the system by an unauthorised user, either physically or remotely (e.g. hacking, virus infection or fraud).

Illustration 3

In April 2011, hackers gained access to over 77 million PlayStation user accounts held by Sony. These accounts included personal information and credit card details for many customers.

This security failure led to significant loss of reputation and sales to Sony, who estimated the cost of the breach to be around £109m, excluding the costs of compensating customers whose details were stolen.

Test your understanding 2

Joe has found that a utility supplier has sold information about him to a market research company. Is this an issue of data protection or data security?

The main risks to computer systems and the data they contain include the following:

Potential threats	Counter measures
Physical damage, due to • fire • flooding • terrorist acts power failures • other environmental – heat, cold, humidity, dust.	• Well documented fire procedures. • Staff training. • Provide fire extinguishers and smoke/heat detectors, fire-doors. • Computer equipment might be located in a segregated area in which air conditioning and dust controls operate effectively. • Back-up generators. • Off-site facilities to cater for the possibility of total destruction of the in-house computer equipment. • Off-site back-up copies of data files.
Human Damage caused by human interference, such as unauthorised access resulting in theft, piracy, vandalism.	• Restricted access to the computer room (e.g. PIN codes). • Closed circuit TV and security guards. • Hardware can be physically or electronically tagged to sound an alarm if it is removed from the building. • Hardware can be locked down.
Operational problems, such as program bugs and user operational errors.	• Thorough testing of new programs. • strict operating procedures. • adequate training of all staff members.
Data corruption, e.g. viruses, hackers.	• Anti-virus and firewall software. • passwords and user number limits. • off-site back-up copies of data files.
Data theft, e.g. fraud, industrial espionage, loss of confidentiality.	• Data encryption techniques. • passwords and user numbers. • physical access controls.

KAPLAN PUBLISHING

Test your understanding 3

Ragu Ltd holds data about many of its customers. It has recently set up an off-site backup of this data to improve its data security.

Which potential data security threat will this measure most likely reduce?

A   Hacking

B   Data theft

C   Viruses

D   Fire or flood

6 Health and safety in the workplace

There are a number of potential hazards in any workplace.

Some examples include:

- unsafe electrics
- torn carpets
- poor lighting
- wet floors
- top-heavy filing cabinets

To deal with this, many countries have created detailed legislation covering health and safety in the workplace.

 The law typically puts the responsibility for health and safety on **both** the employer and the employee.

6.1 Employer's responsibilities

The employer has a duty, amongst other things, to:

- provide a safe working environment
- prevent risks to health
- ensure that plant and machinery is safe to use and that safe working practices are set up and followed
- inform staff of any potential hazards
- provide adequate first aid facilities
- check that the right equipment is used and that is regularly maintained
- set up emergency plans.

6.2 Employee's responsibilities

The employee has, amongst other things, a duty to:

- take reasonable care of their own health and safety

- take reasonable care not to put other people at risk

- co-operate with their employer to ensure they have adequate training and are familiar with their employer's health and safety policies

- report any injuries suffered as a result of performing their job

- inform their employer if anything affects their ability to work safely.

6.3 Breaches of health and safety

If employers fail to provide a safe and healthy working environment, they may be in breach of common law, enabling employees to make a civil claim against them.

In addition, they may be guilty of a criminal offence and be open to prosecution.

Test your understanding 4

'Health and safety law is concerned with eliminating risks.'

Is this statement:

A   True

B   False

Test your understanding 5

While Dave was running down a staircase at work, he tripped and injured himself. Who is responsible for this accident?

A   Dave

B   His employer

7   Consumer protection

Many countries have legislation which attempts to protect consumers from falling victim to unscrupulous or unethical businesses.

These laws are often very complex and will vary from country to country. However, for the purposes of your exam, only a basic understanding of the common principles found in such legislation is required.

7.1 Sale of goods

Many countries have legislation designed to protect consumers when they purchase goods from other individuals or from businesses. In the UK, this is dealt with by the Sale of Goods Act (1979).

This has many features, but there are several key principles built into the Act. These include:

*   The seller must have legal title to, or ownership of, the item they are selling.

*   The goods sold must be of satisfactory quality and fit for their intended purpose.

*   When a buyer makes a purchase based on the description of an item, the goods must correspond with this description.

In addition, legislation also often extends to the provision of services – not just goods. In the UK this is covered by the Supply of Goods and Services Act (1982).

This requires services provided to be:

*   Carried out with reasonable skill and care.

*   Completed within a reasonable length of time.

*   Completed at a reasonable price.

Illustration 4 – Service provision

The provision of accountancy services would fall under sale of goods and services legislation. Should the accounts contain errors or be prepared too late for filing deadlines due to the firm of accountants preparing them, the customer may well have recourse against the firm.

Test your understanding 6

Jane buys a television from After plc, an online retailer of homewares. When the television arrives, she discovers that it is a different model and size to the one she ordered. She also finds that the screen image is blurred and the remote control is faulty and does not work.

Why is After plc likely to have breached local sale of goods legislation?

7.2 Simple contracts

Generally

A contract is a legally enforceable agreement between two or more parties. Such a contract is known as 'simple' if it is not required to be in any particular form.

 It is a commonly held misconception that all contracts must be written in order to be legally binding. In fact, many contracts can be in other forms, such as verbal contracts. However, in the event of disputes between the parties, non-written contracts can be difficult to prove or enforce.

Features of a simple contract

Simple contracts must have the following features in order to be valid:

*   **Agreement** – the parties must have agreed on the terms of the contract. Normally this means that one party has made an offer that has been accepted by the other.

*   **Consideration** – in many countries, both parties usually have to get some value from the contract. Each party must offer some consideration to the other.

*   **Intention to create legal relations** – both parties must clearly intend their relationship to be legally binding. For example, an informal arrangement to go shopping with a friend would not normally constitute a legally binding contract.

*   **Capacity and legality** – each party to the contract must have the capability to enter the contract. In many countries, individuals under the age of 16 cannot enter a legally binding contract. In addition, contracts cannot be formed for the purposes of an illegal act. For instance, a contract to commit murder cannot be legally enforced.

By creating legislation surrounding simple contracts, the government can protect consumers from being taken advantage of by businesses or other individuals. For example, children will be unable to sign binding contracts, as they are unlikely to be fully aware of the consequences.

 Test your understanding 7

John has agreed with Eric that he will pay him $200 if Eric maintains his garden for the next year. At the end of the year, John refuses to pay Eric, in spite of Eric having undertaken the work agreed. John has told Eric that because the contract was not written and signed by both parties, he has no obligation to pay for the work done.

Is John correct?

Chapter summary

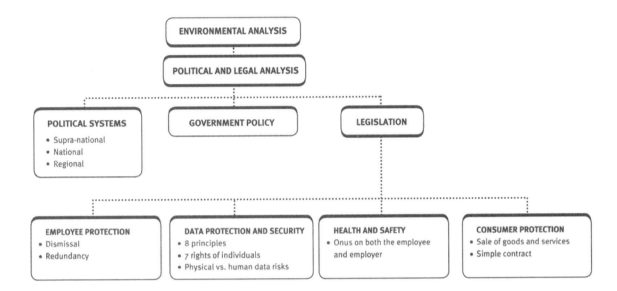

8 Practice questions

Test your understanding 8

Governments may create _____. If an organisation fails to comply with this, it will lead to prosecution, fines and even closure.

What phrase best fits the gap?

A   Direct legislation

B   Government policy

C   Charitable objectives

D   National targets

Test your understanding 9

Which of the following is **not** a typical 'fair' reason for dismissal?

A   Lack of qualifications

B   Gross misconduct

C   High salary

D   Redundancy

Test your understanding 10

Which of the following is one of the rights of individuals under typical data protection legislation?

A   Immediate access to personal data at any time

B   The right to erase personal information through an application to the data holder

C   No decisions should be taken against an individual on a purely automated basis

D   The right to prevent data being processed for the profit of others

Test your understanding 11

_____ _____ is concerned with keeping data safe from various hazards that could destroy or compromise it.

Which two words complete this definition?

A   Data protection

B   Data security

C   Physical risk

D   Human risk

Test your understanding 12

Consider the following statements:

(i)   Employers have the sole responsibility for the health and safety of their employees.

(ii)   As long as employers have adequately trained their staff about the potential hazards they will face in the workplace, they have discharged the health and safety responsibilities.

Which of these statements is/are correct?

A   (i) only

B   (ii) only

C   Both

D   Neither

Test your understanding 13

John is a manager at V company. As part of his contract with V, he is not supposed to hire any employees who are female or over the age of thirty-five. This contract is subsequently found to be unenforceable.

Which of the features of a simple contract is missing from this agreement?

A   Agreement

B   Legality

C   Consideration

D   Capacity

Test your understanding 14

Which of the following is a requirement of typical consumer protection legislation?

A   All goods and services must be reasonably priced

B   Goods should be of good quality

C   The seller must have legal title to the goods being sold

D   Buyers do not have to make payment until after receipt of the goods

Test your understanding 15

(a)   Sources of legal authority may be supra-national, national or regional. Within the UK, for example, these sources include:

A   National Government through Acts of Parliament

B   United Nations resolutions

C   Local council bye-laws

D   UK Supreme Court judgements

E   European Parliament

F   International Court of Justice judgements

G   European Court of Justice judgements

H   UK Crown Court judgements

Required:

Write down which of the FOUR boxes from A – H contain sources of supra-national legal authority.

(0.5 marks each, total = 2 marks)

(b)   Redundancy is a form of dismissal which occurs when an employer needs to reduce the size of their workforce. Consider the following employee rights:

A   The right to refuse redundancy

B   The right to consultation regarding the redundancy process

C   The right to be redeployed elsewhere within the organisation where possible

D   The right to be offered redundancy pay (dependant on the circumstances)

E   The right to a fair notice period

F   The right to a fair redundancy selection process

G   The right to retraining to aid in securing a new job

H   The right to time off work to search for a new job

Required:

Select FOUR of the above rights (A – H) which are typically included in redundancy legislation.

(0.5 marks each, total = 2 marks)

(Total: 4 marks)

Test your understanding answers

Test your understanding 1

The correct answer is B

Courts are sources of national authority.

Test your understanding 2

Data protection – there is no indication of the market research firm obtaining the information through hacking or other underhand means.

Test your understanding 3

The correct answer is D

Off-site backups will not help prevent the theft of data!

Test your understanding 4

The correct answer is B – False

While the media can sometimes give this impression, health and safety is about taking practical actions to control real risks, not about trying to eliminate risk altogether. It is impossible to eliminate all risk.

Test your understanding 5

The correct answer is A – Dave

Dave's employer is responsible for ensuring that there are safe ways in and out of the place of work and that Dave has a safe working environment. Unless there was a problem with the staircase (e.g. poorly lit, uneven steps), which is not indicated, then it would appear that the employer has fulfilled their responsibility.

Dave is also responsible for his own safety and shouldn't have been running.

Test your understanding 6

There are two probable reasons why Jane could argue that After plc has breached sale of goods legislation.

Firstly, she has bought the television based on the description given on After plc's website. As the television she has received is of a different model and size to the one she ordered, the description given by After plc is inaccurate.

In addition, the television appears to be faulty or damaged. The goods cannot be said to be either of satisfactory quality or fit for the purpose of viewing television programmes.

Jane should be able to return the item for a replacement or full refund.

Test your understanding 7

No – John is not correct. Simple contracts do not have to be written. Given that Eric has undertaken the work, he is likely to have a case against John due to their verbal contract.

Test your understanding 8

The correct answer is A

Government legislation must be complied with. Government policy refers to any course of action that the government wishes to take in order to change a certain situation within the country. Until it is backed up by legislation, organisations would not be bound to follow it.

Test your understanding 9

The correct answer is C

The fourth reason is for an employee to be dismissed for legal reasons.

Test your understanding 10

The correct answer is C

While individuals have the right to access their personal data, this may involve a written request being made and the payment of a fee – this is unlikely to happen instantly. Application for the erasure of data may have to be through the courts.

Data processing can only be prevented if it will cause damage or distress to the individual or is for the purposes of direct marketing.

Test your understanding 11

The correct answer is B

By definition. Options C and D are both types of data security risk.

Test your understanding 12

The correct answer is D

Employees also have responsibilities under health and safety legislation. Employers also have to provide a safe working environment for employees – not just train them about the hazards.

Test your understanding 13

The correct answer is B

This contract involves discriminating against some potential employees, which is illegal in most jurisdictions. Remember that a contract is not valid if it requires one or more parties to break the law.

Test your understanding 14

The correct answer is C

While services should be completed at a reasonable price, goods and services do not, in themselves, have to be reasonably priced. Goods have to be fit for purpose (or of satisfactory quality), rather than good quality. Finally, there is no requirement for buyers to pay in advance.

Test your understanding 15

(a) Supra-national sources of authority are those that are above national governmental level. The correct answers would therefore be: **B, E, F and G**. A, D and H are national, while C is regional.

(b) The correct answers are: **B, D, E, F**. Note that some businesses may offer staff some of the other options given (i.e. time off to find new work) but this is not typically legislated for.

External analysis – economic factors

Chapter learning objectives

Upon completion of this chapter you will be able to:

- define the concept of demand and supply for goods and services

- explain elasticity of demand and the impact of substitute and complementary goods

- explain the economic behaviour of costs in the short and long term

- define perfect competition, oligopoly, monopolistic competition and monopoly

- define macro-economic policy and explain its objectives

- explain the main determinants of the level of business activity in the economy and how variations in the level of business affect individuals, households and businesses

- explain the impact of economic issues on the individual, the household and businesses: inflation, stagnation, unemployment, international payments disequilibrium

- describe the main types of economic policy that may be implemented by government and supra-national bodies to maximise economic welfare

- recognise the impact of fiscal and monetary policy measures on the individual, the household and businesses.

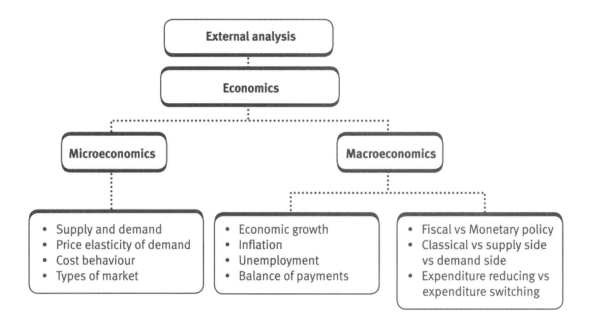

1 Introduction

Part of an organisation's external PEST analysis will involve assessing the economic factors which will affect its industry. The key issue is to identify potential opportunities and threats.

 Economics can be defined in various ways, including:

- 'the study of how society allocates scarce resources, which have alternative uses, between competing ends'

- 'the study of wealth creation'.

It is useful to distinguish between two aspects of economics:

- **Microeconomics** is the study of the economic behaviour of individual consumers, firms, and industries.

- **Macroeconomics** considers aggregate behaviour, and the study of the sum of individual economic decisions – in other words, the workings of the economy as a whole.

We will consider macroeconomics later in the chapter.

2 Microeconomics

2.1 Defining microeconomics

 Microeconomics focuses on how the individual parts of an economy make decisions about how to allocate scarce resources. As mentioned, these individual parts include consumers, firms and industries.

Microeconomics attempts to examine how supply and demand decisions made by these individuals affect the selling prices of goods and services within an industry or market.

2.2 Demand

2.2.1 Individual demand

 Individual demand shows how much of a good or service someone intends to buy at different prices. This demand needs to be effective, in that consumers need to have the cash available to buy the goods or services, rather than just generally desiring them. When considering the level of demand at a given price, we assume that the 'conditions of demand' (i.e. other variables) are held constant.

- Demand tends to be higher at a low price and lower at a high price for most goods and services.

- When the demand for a good or service changes in response to a change in its price, the change is referred to as:

  - an **expansion** in demand as demand rises when the price falls

  - a **contraction** in demand as demand falls when the price rises.

- Thus in the diagram below the demand curve D illustrates a normal downward-sloping demand curve and movements along this curve as the price changes would be called a contraction in demand (price is rising) or an expansion in demand (price is falling).

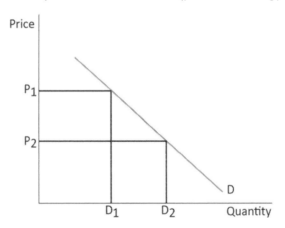

- For most goods, the lower the price, the higher will be its demand. This is the result of two processes.

  - There is a *substitution* effect. This is where a consumer buys more of one good and less of another because of relative price changes. Thus if two goods are substitutes, a fall in the price of the first will lead consumers to switch some demand to the lower-price good, substituting the first good for the second.

  - There is an *income* effect. This is where a change in the price of a good affects the purchasing power of the consumers' income (a change in their real income). If the price of a good falls, the consumer experiences a rise in their real income and, as a result, tends to buy more of all normal goods and services.

Individual demand

K plc is a motor car manufacturer. It may find that if it raises the price it sells its cars for, the demand for the vehicles, and therefore the number of cars the company sells, will fall.

This could be due to the **substitution effect**. There are a large number of car manufacturers that customers can choose between. If K raises its prices, it may become more expensive than its rivals, leading customers to switch to lower-priced alternatives.

K's sales may also suffer because of the **income effect**. Cars are normally relatively expensive, costing a high proportion of a consumer's income. If K prices its cars at too high a price, many of its customers may simply become unable to afford the product, leading to a drop in demand.

- In most cases the income effect is relatively weak. However, if expenditure on the good is a large proportion of consumer income, e.g. in the case of a house purchase, the effect will be relatively large.

  Tastes, of course, can be manipulated by advertising and producers to try to 'create' markets, particularly for ostentatious goods, for example, air conditioners which our ancestors survived perfectly well without. Some goods are in seasonal demand (e.g. cooked meat) even though they are available all year round, because tastes change (i.e. more salads are consumed in the summer).

2.2.2 Market demand

Market demand shows the total amount of effective demand from all the consumers in a market. Market demand is usually shortened to **demand** and represented by a straight-line curve on a graph. The demand curve for most normal goods is negatively inclined, sloping downwards from left to right for the reasons explained in the previous section.

2.2.3 Conditions of demand

Individual and market demand consider exclusively the influence of price on the quantity demanded, assuming other factors to be constant. These factors, termed the conditions of demand, will now be considered, with price held constant.

Any change in one or more of the conditions of demand will create shifts in the demand curve itself.

- If the shift in the demand curve is outward, to the right, such a shift is called an **increase** in demand.

- If the shift in the demand curve is inward, to the left, such a shift is called a **decrease** in demand.

It is important to distinguish such increases and decreases in demand that result from a shift in the demand curve as a whole from **expansions** and **contractions** in demand that result from price changes leading to movements along the demand curve itself.

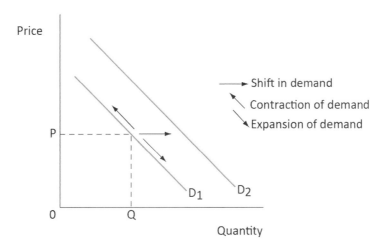

The main conditions that affect demand are:

- **Income**

  Changes in income often affect demand. Lower direct taxes raise disposable incomes and, other things being equal, make consumers better off. This might cause less demand for necessities and more demand for luxuries. In recent years, improvements in the standard of living have led to greater spending on services and leisure activities. Furthermore, if average wage increases exceed the rate of inflation, consumers will become better off in real terms and thus have greater flexibility and scope in the use of their income.

  There are also **inferior** goods. In these cases, a rise in income leads to a lower demand for the product as consumers, now being richer, substitute better quality and preferred goods and services for the original ('inferior') good or service. An example of this is public transport. Here, as incomes rise, the demand for public transport falls as consumers substitute private transport such as cars.

- **Tastes**

  Tastes, in particular fashions, change frequently and it may make the demand for certain goods volatile. For instance, concerns about health have increased the demand for brown bread and vegetable oil at the expense of white bread and animal fats.

  Tastes, of course, can be manipulated by advertising and producers to try to 'create' markets. Some goods are in seasonal demand (e.g. cooked meat) even though they are available all year round, because tastes change (i.e. more salads are consumed in the summer).

- **The prices of other goods**

  Goods may be unrelated, or they may be complements or substitutes for each other. The former have no effect but the latter two are significant. If goods are in joint demand (i.e. complements such as cars and tyres) a change in the price of one will affect the other also. Therefore, if the price of cars falls demand for them will rise, meaning there is likely to be an increase in demand for tyres. Where goods are substitutes (e.g. Quality Street chocolates and Roses chocolates), a rise in the price of one will cause an increase in demand for the other (and thus the demand curve will shift to the right). Sometimes, technological breakthroughs mean that new products come into the market. For instance, the advent of ink cartridge pens reduced the demand for fountain pens, because the former became a cheaper (and less messy) substitute.

- **Population**

  An increase in population creates a larger market for most goods, thereby shifting demand outwards. For instance, an influx of immigrant workers will raise the demand for most essential goods. Changes in population distribution will also affect demand patterns. If the proportion of old people relative to young people increases, then the demand for products such as wheelchairs and care homes will increase while cots and nappies would be expected to decline.

In the analysis of how the demand and supply model works, the distinctions between increase/decrease in demand and expansion/contraction in demand are very important. Remember:

- If a *price change* occurs, there will be a movement along the demand curve and the result will be either an expansion or a contraction in demand

- If the *conditions of demand* change, there will be a shift in the demand curve and the result will be either an increase or a decrease in demand.

Test your understanding 1

Which one of the following would NOT lead to a shift in the demand curve for overseas holidays?

A   An advertising campaign by holiday-tour operators

B   A fall in the disposable income of consumers

C   A rise in the price of domestic holidays

D   A rise in the exchange rate for the domestic currency

2.3 Elasticity of demand

Elasticity, generally, refers to the relationship between two variables and measures the responsiveness of one (dependent) variable to a change in another (independent) variable: There are several types which are useful to economists.

2.3.1 Price elasticity of demand (PED)

 This concept explains the relationship between changes in quantity demanded and changes in price.

- Price elasticity of demand explains the responsiveness of demand to changes in price.

- The co-efficient of price elasticity of demand (PED) is calculated by:

$$\frac{\text{Percentage change in quantity demanded}}{\text{Percentage change in price}}$$

It is critical that percentage or proportional changes are used rather than absolute ones (i.e. we need to use the percentage movements in quantity demanded and price, rather than the change in the number of units demanded or actual selling price movement). Note that if a percentage change is negative, the minus sign is typically ignored.

A summary of price elasticity is given below:

Description	PED	Actual examples
Relatively inelastic	<1	Tea, salt
Unit elasticity	=1	–
Relatively elastic	>1	Cameras, air travel

Illustration 1 – PED

Suppose we are currently selling a product at a price of $20 with a resulting demand of 500,000 units per annum. A marketing manager has suggested dropping the price to $19 and claims that demand will rise to 550,000 units.

Calculate the PED.

Solution

- Percentage change in price = –5%

- Percentage change in demand = +10%

- PED = (10)/(5) = 2

Test your understanding 2

F plc produces a popular product, the F1200. Currently it sells 15,000 units of this product each year at a price of £55 per unit. The company is now looking at whether it could make higher profits by increasing the sales price. Market research has indicated that if it increases the sales price of the F1200 to £60 per unit, demand would fall to 12,000 units.

Calculate the price elasticity of demand for the F1200 and comment on your results.

2.3.2 The link between PED and total revenue

The PED can also be calculated by examining **total revenue**. This method is most useful to business people.

- If total revenue increases following a price cut, then demand is price elastic.

- If total revenue increases following a price rise, then demand is price inelastic.

Conversely, if total revenue falls after a price cut, then the demand is inelastic; and after a price rise it is elastic. If total revenue remains unchanged, then the demand is of unitary elasticity.

2.3.3 Factors that influence PED

There are several factors which determine the price elasticity of demand:

- **Proportion of income spent on the good**

  Where a good constitutes a small proportion of consumers' income spent, then a small price change will be unlikely to have much impact. Therefore, the demand for unimportant items such as shoe polish, matches and pencils is likely to be very inelastic. Conversely, the demand for quality clothing will probably be elastic.

- **Substitutes**

  If there are close and available substitutes for a product, then an increase in its price is likely to cause a much greater fall in the quantity demanded as consumers buy suitable alternatives. Thus, the demand for a specific variety box of chocolates may be fairly elastic because there are many competing brands in the market. In contrast, the demand for a unique product such as the Timeform Racehorses Annual for racing enthusiasts will tend to be inelastic.

- **Necessities**

  The demand for vital goods such as sugar, milk and bread tends to be stable and inelastic; conversely luxury items such as foreign skiing holidays are likely to be fairly elastic in demand. It is interesting to note that improvements in living standards push certain commodities such as televisions from the luxury to the necessity category.

- **Habit**

  When goods are purchased automatically, without customers perhaps being fully aware of their price, for example, newspapers, the demand is inelastic. This also applies to addictive products such as cigarettes and drugs.

- **Time**

  In the short run, consumers may be ignorant of possible alternative goods in many markets, so they may continue to buy certain goods when their prices rise. Such inelasticity may be lessened in the long run as consumers acquire greater knowledge of markets.

- **Definition of market**

  If a market is defined widely (e.g. food), there are likely to be fewer alternatives and so demand will tend to be inelastic. In contrast, if a market is specified narrowly (e.g. orange drinks) there will probably be many brands available, thereby creating elasticity in the demand for these brands.

Illustration 2 – PED

Would a computer games manufacturer expect to see a high or low PED for its products?

- **Availability of substitutes** – there are a number of other computer games manufacturers in the market. This would tend to increase PED as it means that if the games manufacturer raises their prices, their customers can easily switch to a lower priced competitor. However, if the company has a strong reputation in the market, or produces an innovative game, it will reduce the PED as customers may be willing to pay higher prices to buy what they perceive as a superior product.

- **Proportion of income spent on items** – the higher the proportion of their income that a customer spends on a games console, the higher the PED. If buying a computer game uses a large proportion of a customer's income, price rises will increase the chance that they will be unable to afford the product, reducing demand. Customers will also be more likely to scrutinise high-price purchases to see if they represent value for money.

- **Necessity** – necessities, such as bread or petrol, are normally inelastic, as customers will be forced to purchase them regardless of whether the price increases or not. Games are not necessities, so this will tend to make them more elastic. If the price becomes too high, customers can simply choose not to purchase them.

- **Time** – the longer a price change lasts, the more likely the product is to become elastic. A rise in prices for a games console may not reduce demand in the short term. However, the longer the price remains high, the more time customers have to shop around for cheaper substitutes.

Overall, the games consoles are likely to be at least somewhat elastic due to the high price and lack of necessity. This effect may be reduced if the manufacturer has a powerful brand name, or produces an innovative computer game – at least in the short term.

Test your understanding 3

The government of country C provides free medical treatment to all its citizens. However, for more affluent citizens, a small charge is made if they need medication. The government has recently decided to increase this charge by a moderate amount to reflect the increasing cost of the medicines.

What effect is this likely to have on the demand for medicine within country C?

Cross elasticity of demand (XED)

Definition

Cross elasticity of demand (XED) measures the sensitivity of demand for one good to changes in the price of **another** good.

The formula for cross elasticity of demand (XED) is given below.

XED = (percentage change in quantity demanded of Good A)/ (percentage change in price of Good B)

For example, suppose the XED of butter with respect to margarine is +1.5 and the price of margarine falls by 6%. We can estimate that demand for butter will decrease by 1.5 × 6% = 9%.

The sign of cross elasticity of demand

When looking at PED earlier, a key consideration was whether the figure was greater or smaller than one. With XED the key issue is the sign - whether the elasticity is positive or negative.

In the preceding activity, the XED between butter and margarine was positive. This is because butter and margarine are substitutes. When the price of margarine went down, demand for margarine rose and demand for butter fell – consumers switched to buying more cheaper margarine **instead** of butter. In other words, the price of margarine and demand for butter move in the same direction, so XED is positive.

Conversely, the XED between complements is negative. Consider gas central heating and gas. If the price of gas central heating fell, demand for gas central heating would rise. Gas central heating and gas are complementary, so demand for gas is also likely to rise. The price of gas central heating and demand for gas move in opposite directions, so the XED of complements is negative.

The XED of substitutes is positive, while that for complements is negative.

2.4 Supply

2.4.1 The supply curve of a firm

A supply curve shows how many units producers would be willing to offer for sale, at different prices, over a given period of time.

The supply curve of a firm is underpinned by the desire to make profit. It demonstrates what a firm will provide to the market at certain prices. If the prices that goods can be sold at increases, each unit will make more profit for the supplier, meaning that they will wish to manufacture, or supply, more units for the market. This means that supply curves tend to slope upwards.

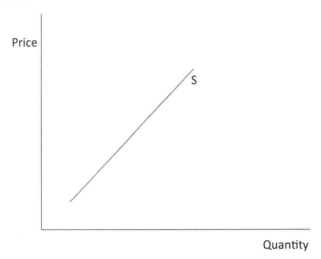

2.4.2 Conditions of supply

A change in factors other than the price will move the supply curve itself.

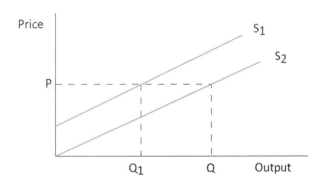

An upward shift of supply

This means that the cost of supply has increased. At existing prices less will now be supplied, as shown on the upward-sloping, elastic supply curve. At price P, the quantity supplied falls from Q to Q1 as the supply curve shifts from S_2 to S_1.

This results from:

- **Higher production costs.** The costs of production may increase because the factors of production become expensive. Thus conditions such as higher wage costs per unit, higher input prices and increased interest rates will lead to reductions in supply.

- **Indirect taxes.** The imposition of an indirect tax, such as VAT, makes supply at existing prices less profitable. With an indirect tax, the costs of production are raised directly because the tax must be paid on each item sold. The profit margin is reduced (by some varying amount) as an indirect effect.

A downward shift of supply

For example, a shift in the supply curve from S1 to S2 illustrates an increase in supply with more being supplied at each price, showing that the cost of production has fallen or lower profits are being taken.

Lower unit costs may arise from:

- **technological innovations**, for example, the advance of microchip technology lowered the cost of computers and led to large increases in supply

- more **efficient use of existing factors of production**, for example, introduction of a shift system of working might mean fuller use of productive capacity, leading to lower unit costs. Improvements in productivity may be secured by maintaining output but with fewer workers

- **lower input prices**, such as, cheaper raw material imports and lower-priced components could bring down production costs

- a reduction or abolition of an **indirect tax** or the application or increase in subsidies.

2.5 Equilibrium

Now we have looked at demand and supply in detail, let us consider how the price mechanism sets a price.

The way to see how market forces achieve equilibrium is to consider what happens if the price is too high or too low:

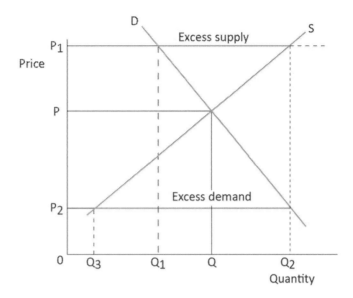

The graph shows the **intended demand and planned supply** at a set of prices. It is only at price P where demand and supply are the same. If the demand of consumers and the supply plans of sellers correspond, then the market is deemed to be in **equilibrium**. Only at output Q and price P are the plans of both sellers and buyers realised. Thus Q is the **equilibrium quantity** and P is the **equilibrium price** in this market.

There is only one equilibrium position in a market. At this point, there is no tendency for change in the market, because the plans of both buyers and sellers are satisfied. At prices and outputs other than the equilibrium (P, Q) either demand or supply aspirations could be fulfilled but not both simultaneously.

- For instance at price P_1, consumers only want Q_1 output but producers are making Q_2 output available. There is a surplus, the excess supply being Q_1 Q_2 output.

    Assuming the conditions of demand and supply remain unchanged, it is likely that the buyers and sellers will reassess their intentions.

    This will be reflected in the short term by retailers having unwanted goods, returns made to manufacturers, reduced orders and some products being thrown away and so suppliers may be prepared to accept lower prices than P1 for their goods.

    This reduction in price will lead to a **contraction** in supply and an **expansion** in demand until equilibrium is reached at price P.

- Conversely, at a price of P_2, the quantity demanded, Q_2, will exceed the quantity supplied, Q_3. There will be a **shortage** ($Q_2 - Q_3$), demonstrating the **excess demand**.

    This will be reflected in the short term by retailers having empty shelves, queues and increased orders. Furthermore there may be high second-hand values, for example on eBay. The supplier will respond by increasing prices to reduce the shortage.

This excess demand will thus lead to a rise in the market price, and demand will **contract** and supply will **expand** until equilibrium is reached at price P.

> ### Test your understanding 4
>
> When the price of a good is held above the equilibrium price, the result will be:
>
> A   excess demand
>
> B   a shortage of the good
>
> C   a surplus of the good
>
> D   an increase in demand

2.5.1 Shifts in supply and/or demand

As well as signalling information in a market, price acts as a stimulant. The price information may provide incentives for buyers and sellers. For instance, a price rise may encourage firms to shift resources into one industry in order to obtain a better reward for their use.

- For example, suppose the equilibrium is disturbed when the conditions of demand change. Consumers' tastes have moved positively in favour of the good and a new curve D_1 shows customers' intentions.

- Supply is initially Q, at the equilibrium, and it is momentarily fixed, so the market price is bid up to P_1.

- However, producers will respond to this stimulus by expanding the quantity supplied, perhaps by running down their stocks.

- This expansion in supply to Q_2 reduces some of the shortage, bringing price down to P_2, a new equilibrium position, which is above the old equilibrium P.

Note that if we had drawn the diagram with steeper supply (and demand curves), then the price fluctuations would have been greater. Thus more inelastic supply tends to give rise to greater price volatility in a particular market over the longer term.

The longer-term effects of these changes in the market depend upon the reactions of the consumers and producers. The consumers may adjust their preferences and producers may reconsider their production plans. The impact of the latter on supply depends upon the length of the production period. Generally the longer the production period, and the more inelastic the supply is, the more unstable price will tend to be.

- Price acts as a signal to sellers on what to produce.

- Price rises, with all other market conditions unchanged, will act as a stimulus to extra supply.

- Equilibrium price is where the plans of both buyers and sellers are satisfied.

2.6 Minimum and maximum prices

There may be occasions when the equilibrium price established by the market forces of demand and supply may not be the most desirable price. With such cases the government might wish to set prices above or below the market equilibrium price.

2.6.1 Minimum price

In certain markets government may seek to ensure a minimum price for different goods and services. It can do this in a number of ways such as providing subsidies direct to producers (e.g. the Common Agricultural Policy in Europe). Alternatively, it can set a legal minimum price (e.g. a statutory minimum wage). To be effective, legal minimum prices must be above the current market price.

If the government sets a minimum price above the equilibrium price (often called a price floor), there will be a surplus of supply created.

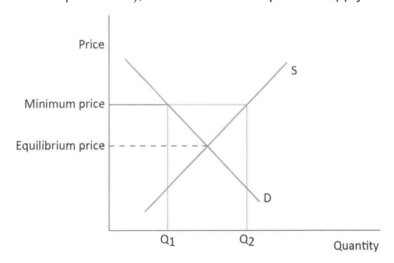

In the diagram this surplus is Q_1Q_2.

If this minimum price was applied in the labour market, it would be known as a minimum wage and the surplus would be the equivalent of unemployment, which would be a waste of a factor of production.

If applied to physical goods, then price floors cause surpluses of products which have to be stored or destroyed. With the EU Common Agricultural Policy (CAP) this has, over the years, resulted in the EU storing large quantities of food ("butter mountains"), selling the surplus to countries outside the EU (such as Russia) and even paying farmers not to grow the product in the first place but to remove land from agricultural use (so called "set aside" conditions).

Another way of looking at the same problem is to state that it leads to a misallocation of resources both in the product and/or the factor market which causes lower economic growth. There also may be the temptation for firms to attempt to ignore the price floor, for example, by informal arrangements with workers, which would lead to a further waste of resources in implementing such arrangements as well as raising issues of fair treatment for the workers involved.

In summary government-imposed minimum prices cause:

- Excess supply
- Misallocation of resources
- Waste of resources.

2.6.2 Maximum price

Governments may seek to impose maximum price controls or price ceilings on certain goods or services, either to

- benefit consumers on low incomes, so that they can afford the particular good, or to
- control inflation.

If the government sets a maximum price below the equilibrium price (often called a price ceiling), there will be a shortage of supply created.

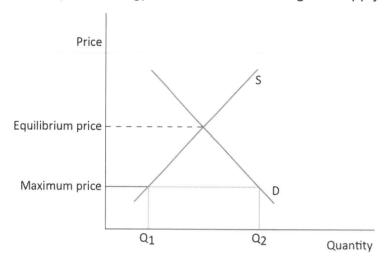

This shortage is Q_1 Q_2. If the shortages of supply persist then problems can arise. The limited supply has to be allocated by some means other than by price.

This can be done by queuing, by rationing or by some form of favouritism, for example, by giving preference to regular customers. The difficulty with any of these alternative mechanisms is that they can be considered arbitrary and unfair by those who fail to secure the product. A consequence of the shortage can be the emergence of black markets. This is where buyers and sellers agree upon an illegal price which is higher than that which has been officially sanctioned at the maximum price.

Maximum prices can also lead to a misallocation of resources. Producers will reduce output of those products subject to price controls as these products are now relatively less profitable than those products where no price controls exist. In the housing market this may lead to fewer apartments for rent as landowners develop office blocks rather than residential houses. Alternatively the quality of the product may be allowed to drop as a way of reducing costs when profits are constrained by price controls. This failure to maintain property can mean that apartments fall into disrepair.

In summary, government-imposed maximum prices cause:

- Shortages of supply

- Arbitrary ways of allocating a product

- Misallocation of resources.

Test your understanding 5

The government of country F has decided to impose a minimum wage for all workers, which is above the current average market labour rate. Which of the following is a potential consequence of this?

A   Rising employment within country F

B   Falling costs of manufacturing in country F

C   Lower selling prices, leading to higher demand

D   Surplus of labour created within country F

2.7 The economic behaviour of costs

The relationship between selling price and the quantity supplied or demanded is not the only relationship explored by microeconomics. It also examines how costs tend to vary over time.

Short term cost behaviour

In the short term, micro economists believe that costs follow the **law of diminishing returns**.

As equal quantities of one variable factor of input (such as labour or materials) are added to a fixed factor, output initially increases by a greater proportion, increasing returns and causing the average cost per unit to fall. However, beyond a certain point, the addition to output will begin to decrease and the average cost per unit will start to rise again.

Illustration 3 – Short-term cost behaviour

Suppose we increase the number of workers while keeping the number of machines constant. Initially the extra workers will allow specialisation and increased efficiency. This will cause average costs to fall.

As we keep adding staff, however, they will eventually start getting in each other's way and having to wait to access machines. The system therefore becomes less efficient and the average production costs will begin to rise.

The short-run average total cost curve (SRATC) tends to therefore be 'U'–shaped, following the **law of diminishing returns**.

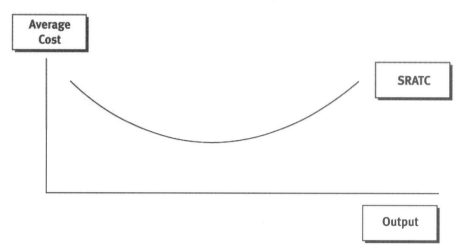

Long term cost behaviour

In the long term, all costs tend to be variable in nature. This is because it is now possible to vary the quantities of any factors that were fixed in the short term.

Eventually, however, as the business expands, it will tend to become less efficient at controlling costs due to poor management and pressure on supplies. This effect is sometimes referred to as **diseconomies of scale** and results in the average cost of production increasing.

Illustration 4 – Long-term cost behaviour

As a business grows, the number of units it produces will increase. This means that in the short term, the average cost of factory rent per unit will fall, as the fixed costs will be spread over a larger number of units. Therefore as production increases, the total cost per unit falls.

If the company continues to grow, it will eventually need to rent more and more factory space. As factory space becomes scarce, it will become more expensive to rent. This will push rent costs upwards and will force the cost per unit back up.

This gives rise to a long-run average total cost curve (LRATC) which is broadly similar to the SRATC.

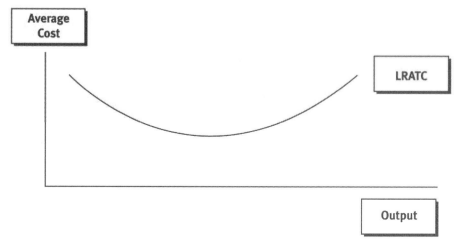

2.8 Types of market

Micro-economic models make certain assumptions about how the market operates. There are three types of market that you need to be able to demonstrate knowledge of in the exam.

Perfect and imperfect markets

A perfect market exists when the following criteria are met:

- Large numbers of customers and suppliers – none of whom have the power to dominate the market.

- The products or services sold by all suppliers are identical (homogenous).

- There is perfect information – all customers and suppliers have complete information on the prices that goods and services are being sold at elsewhere in the market.

- No barriers to entry to, or exit from, the market – that is, competitors can easily enter and exit the market.

This is seen as being the 'ideal' market position. If any of the factors above do not hold true, the market is described as **imperfect**. In the real world, most markets are imperfect.

Perfect markets tend to be assumed when looking at price elasticity of demand. Equilibrium is only likely to happen in a perfect market.

You need to be aware of three specific forms of imperfect market: monopolies, monopolistic competition and oligopolies.

Each of these forms depend on how organisations compete within the market.

Competition is an important concept in economics and refers to the rivalry amongst sellers as they try to increase their profits, sales volume or market share by varying their marketing mix (such as price, product, promotion or place).

Monopoly

Monopolies occur when one company controls all or nearly all of the market for a particular product or service and no major competitors.

The key features include:

- Only one major supplier in the market

- No close substitutes are available for this supplier's products

- The supplier is therefore free to set prices due to the lack of competition.

This situation is often caused by high barriers to entry for the market, or due to government legislation.

Monopolistic competition

This type of market occurs when a business has many different competitors, but each offers a somewhat differentiated product. For example, restaurants exist in such a market. Each restaurant is trying to attract the same customers, but each one offers different menu options cooked in a different way.

Monopolistic competition typically has the following features:

- each business makes independent decisions about the products it offers and the price it charges

- there are no major barriers to entering or leaving the market

- products are differentiated between each business, meaning that they can charge more or less than their competitors – customers will be willing to spend more if they feel that one business has a product that is 'better' than those sold by its rivals

- due to the large amount of competition in the market, there is typically significant advertising expenditure by all the businesses in the market.

Oligopolies

Oligopolies are another form of imperfect market where the market is controlled by a small number of organisations. While there is no precise number typically the market must be dominated by between two and six different firms for it to be classed as an oligopoly.

If only two firms dominate the market, this is referred to as a **duopoly**.

The dominant position of the businesses in an oligopoly will tend to:

- make it difficult for new firms to enter the market; and

- give them significant influence over the prices of the goods and services that they sell.

Illustration 5 – Monopolies

Many pharmaceutical companies enjoy monopolies in the provision of certain medicines. This is due to the high costs of research, development and testing which create barriers to other companies developing similar drugs.

In addition, as new medicines are usually protected by patents, it may be impossible for competitors to provide legal versions of the same drugs.

This allows pharmaceutical companies to charge relatively high prices for their products.

Test your understanding 6

Consider the following statements.

(i)   Not all items being bought and sold in a market have to be identical for it to be perfect.

(ii) Monopolies are a form of equilibrium.

Which of these statements is/are correct?

A   (i) only

B   (ii) only

C   Both

D   Neither

3   Macroeconomics

3.1 Defining macroeconomics

Rather than examining the behaviour of individual firms and individuals, macroeconomics focuses on the workings of the economy as a whole, including:

- the overall ('aggregate') demand for goods and services

- the output of goods and services ('national output' or 'national product')

- the supply of factors of production

- total incomes earned by providers of factors of production ('national income')

Factor	Income
Labour	Wages
Land	Rent
Capital	Interest
Entrepreneurship	Profit

- money spent in purchasing the national product ('national expenditure')

- government policy – see below.

The problem of scarce resources

Given that resources are limited ('scarce'), it is not possible to make everything everyone would want ('unlimited wants'). All societies are thus faced with a fundamental economic problem:

- What goods and services should be produced?
- In what quantities?
- Who should make them?
- Who gets the output?

The market economy is one approach to dealing with this problem.

In a market economy, interaction between supply and demand (market forces) determines what is made, in what quantity, and who gets the output. Patterns of economic activity are determined by the decisions made by individual consumers and producers.

In its purest form, this would imply no government intervention in the economy. In reality, most modern economies are a mix of free markets and government intervention to provide public services such as health and education.

3.2 Macroeconomic policy

While some economists advocate a free market (one without government interference), in reality most governments intervene through various macroeconomic policies in an attempt to improve the performance of the economy.

Their main objectives are typically:

- **Economic growth** – increasing the productive capacity of the economy
- **Low inflation** – ensuring that prices remain stable and sustainable
- **High employment** – getting as many people into work as possible
- **Sustainable balance of payments** – managing trade with other countries

We will look at these objectives in more detail below.

Test your understanding 7

Which of the following is NOT an objective of macroeconomic policy?

A   Economic growth

B   Control of Inflation

C   Lower levels of taxation

D   A balanced balance of payments

3.3 The level of business activity in the economy

While the level of activity within a particular industry will depend on specific PEST issues, the overall level of activity in an economy (and therefore its growth) can be predicted by reference to several key factors.

Aggregate demand

- This is the total demand for a country's output.

- It is given by the formula:

$$AD = C + I + G + X - M$$

- This means: Aggregate demand (AD) = Consumer spending (C) + Investment by firms (I) + Government spending (G) + Demand from exports (X) – Imports (M).

- Higher demand can result in firms increasing output (e.g. by hiring more staff) to meet the demand, leading to growth in the economy.

Consumer confidence

- This is the degree of optimism that consumers or businesses feel about the state of the economy and their own personal financial state.

- Higher consumer confidence means that they are willing to spend more on goods and services, normally leading to growth in aggregate demand.

- Higher business confidence will result in increased levels of investment in new factories and machinery (for example), also increasing aggregate demand.

- Confidence can be reduced by a number of factors, such as high unemployment, high inflation, or even natural disasters.

Capital

- Greater availability of finance will allow businesses to raise the funds that they need to expand. This will therefore tend to increase aggregate demand.

- Lower interest rates will make capital cheaper, also tending to boost investment by businesses.

Government policy

- Governments can increase or decrease the level of aggregate demand in the economy by adjusting their fiscal policies (governmental spending and taxation).

- For instance, increased tax rates may harm consumer confidence, leading to a fall in aggregate demand.

Exchange rate movements

- A strengthening currency will make a country's exports more expensive, but imports will become cheaper.

- This would tend to reduce the aggregate demand in the economy.

Use of resources

- New technology and more efficient working practices can improve business productivity and lower costs, thereby increasing business output.

- Higher levels of education can also improve the efficiency and effectiveness of the workforce.

Illustration 6 – Factors that influence the level of business activity

2008 global recession

VAT reductions

During the global recession of 2008, the UK government temporarily reduced the level of VAT to 15%. This had the effect of making consumer's purchases cheaper, increasing their confidence and meaning that their wages were able to buy more goods.

This was used as a way of stimulating the economy and boosting aggregate demand in a period when the UK economy was struggling.

Interest rates

Meanwhile, the Bank of England started significantly reducing interest rates. This was an attempt to make it cheaper for businesses to borrow funds.

The additional investment by businesses that this caused was also designed to boost aggregate demand.

Test your understanding 7

Consider the following two statements:

(i) Changing the level of taxation is the only way that a government can affect aggregate demand.

(ii) A weakening currency could provide a boost to the aggregate demand of a country.

Which of these statements is/are correct?

A   (i) only

B   (ii) only

C   Both

D   Neither

3.4 Trade cycles

Many economies exhibit fluctuations in economic activity over time with an underlying trend of output growth.

Some economists argue that one role of governments is to smooth out this pattern to avoid 'boom and bust' years.

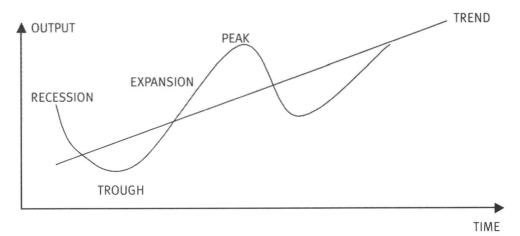

Boom and bust

- A recession starts when demand begins to fall. Firms respond to the fall in demand by reducing their output, causing a decline in purchases of raw materials and an increase in unemployment, as workers are laid off.

- The reduction in demand will feed through into households' incomes, causing these to fall too, resulting in a further reduction in demand.

- The economy will quickly move into a slump, with low business confidence and little incentive to carry out investment.

- Once in the slump, it can take a long time before the economy begins to recover. One of the most difficult things to restore is business and consumer confidence.

- Eventually, though, economic activity begins to pick up. It may be a new invention that tempts entrepreneurs to invest, it may be that replacement investment can be put off no longer or a war may force the government to inject expenditure into the economy.

- The extra investment will push up incomes, which will persuade consumers to spend and this will induce yet more investment, reducing unemployment.

- The economy will expand, pushing upwards into a boom. After some time, however, full capacity will be reached and demand will become stable. The reduction in investment starts off the downward spiral once again.

The main implications of 'boom and bust' are:

	Boom	**Bust**
Individuals and households	On the whole a boom time will be good for households: • low unemployment • rising house prices • high levels of confidence • increasing consumer spending. But: • People may be tempted to over-stretch borrowings. • Possible inflation, the main problem with 'boom and bust'.	The main problem with 'boom and bust' is the 'bust': • job losses • people losing their homes when unable to pay mortgages • fall in labour mobility due to negative equity • bankruptcy • low confidence.
Firms	• Growth in profitability • Extra competition as new firms are established.	• Corporate failures • Fall in profits • Excess capacity.

Most people and firms would prefer steady growth without the high risks associated with the extremes of 'boom and bust'.

Illustration 7 – Trade cycles

The Great Depression

The Great Depression was a worldwide economic downturn that lasted through most of the 1930s. It was focused on North America and Europe, but had knock-on effects around the world.

• Construction virtually stopped in many countries as demand fell sharply.

• Unemployment and homelessness soared.

• Cities based on heavy industry suffered particularly badly.

• Rural areas and farmers suffered as prices for crops fell by 40-60%.

• Mining and logging areas were also hit hard as there was little alternative economic activity.

3.5 The effect of key economic issues

For this exam, you need to be understand the four key economic issues and the effect that they can have on consumers and businesses.

3.5.1 Stagnation and economic growth

As outlined above, most governments try to encourage economic growth. This should have several **benefits** for the country, including:

- more goods being demanded and produced, which means:

- more jobs in the economy, meaning that more people will be employed, leading to:

- people earning more and being able to afford more goods and a higher standard of living

In reality, though, economic growth is not without its **problems**. These include:

- the gap between rich and poor may widen, as the benefits of growth may not be evenly distributed

- growth may be in de-merit goods, such as illegal drugs

- growth may be at the expense of the environment or through exploitation of the poor

- rapid growth means rising incomes, often leading to increased demand for imports. This can significantly worsen aggregate demand in the economy

- if demand for goods rises faster than production capacity within the country, goods will become scarce. This will often lead to rapid rises in prices – significantly increasing inflation.

Governments therefore have a delicate balancing act. They need to ensure that the country enjoys the benefits of economic growth while attempting to minimise the risks.

 ### 3.5.2 Inflation

Inflation is the rise in the prices of goods and services within an economy over time. It reduces the purchasing power of money, meaning that each unit of currency (each pound or dollar, for example) buys fewer goods and services.

Most governments want stable prices and low inflation. This is because high levels of inflation tend to have the following **problems**:

- As prices rise, consumers may purchase fewer goods, reducing growth in the economy.

- Employees will push for higher pay rises, in order to match price rises. This can lead to problems for businesses.

- Other costs (such as raw materials) will also rise for businesses, possibly leading to reductions in investment and production.

- Consumer confidence may be damaged due to uncertainty in the future prices of goods and services.

- People on fixed incomes (such as students or pensioners) may find themselves worse off, as their income will not rise even though the cost of goods has increased.

- High inflation in one country can make cheaper imported goods more attractive to consumers and businesses. This can adversely affect the level of aggregate demand in the economy.

Note that high inflation can have different effects on individual savers:

- People who save to spend later (**a 'transactions motive'**) will save less in order to avoid the purchasing power of their saving being eroded.

- People who save in case of future emergencies (**a 'precautionary motive'**) will save more as they will be uncertain how much money they may need in the future due to rapid price rises.

 In some cases, inflation may rise rapidly while economic growth slows. This is referred to as **stagflation**. Stagflation goes against traditional views of economics, which (as outlined above) tend to suggest that inflation can often be caused by significant economic growth. This can cause a dilemma for governments as the actions needed to bring down inflation often lead to reductions in the level of economic growth in the economy.

 ### 3.5.3 Unemployment

Unemployment occurs when people are willing and able to work, but cannot find a job. Note that whether they are claiming unemployment benefits or not is irrelevant.

There is always likely to be some unemployment within any economy as people change jobs. However, most governments try to keep unemployment low. This is because high levels of unemployment cause the following **problems**:

- The government will suffer a loss of income from income tax and VAT, as well as increased unemployment benefits payments.

- This may lead to increased taxes on other workers, reducing their spending power. Workers may also worry about their own job security, damaging consumer confidence.

- Unemployed individuals will suffer a significant reduction in their income and this may affect their self-image.

It should be noted that businesses may **benefit** from high levels of unemployment.

- High unemployment makes it easy for a business to find employees as there is a ready pool of labour to draw on.

- It may reduce the amount of wages that need to be offered to attract new members of staff.

- Existing staff may be more willing to take lower pay increases as it will be difficult for them to find alternative work.

However, these benefits will need to be weighed against the decreased demand for goods and services within the economy at high levels of unemployment.

 ### 3.5.4 Balance of payments

A country's balance of payments (BOP) records all financial transactions made between individuals, businesses and its government with foreign consumers and organisations.

The balance of payments is split into three parts:

- current account (import and export of goods and services)

- capital account (net change in ownership of foreign assets, such as loans between the government and other countries)

- financial account (cash flows).

Often when people talk about the balance of payments, they are just referring to the surplus or deficit on imports and exports – i.e. the current account.

If the country's imports exceed exports, this is known as a **trade deficit**. If exports exceed imports, this is a **trade surplus**.

Generally, governments would like to avoid long-term balance of payment surpluses or deficits. This is because there are problems with both.

Trade deficits mean that there is a net outflow of cash from the country. In the long-term this is clearly not supportable. The country will drain its reserves and damage its international credit rating. This will make it difficult for the country to raise further finance.

Trade surpluses mean that there is a net inflow of money into the country. This will increase the wealth of the country. This in turn increases demand for goods and services and can lead to significant rates of inflation and the problems that go along with this.

Test your understanding 9
Which of the following statements is true?
A   Economic growth always brings benefits to all members of a society
B   Economic growth can lead to an increase in imports
C   Inflation does not affect those on fixed incomes as much as those in employment
D   Inflation encourages investment in a national economy

Test your understanding 10

Which of the following are consequences of unemployment?

(i)   There is less pressure for the government to increase taxes.

(ii)   There is reduced economic output.

(iii) There is greater inflationary pressure in the economy.

A   (i) only

B   (ii) only

C   (i) and (ii) only

D   (ii) and (iii) only

---

4   Economic policy options

So far we have identified that governments tend to have several major economic objectives. For instance, most governments want to encourage steady economic growth, low inflation and unemployment as well as running a balance of payments that is in equilibrium.

How can a government accomplish this?

Governments have two main ways of affecting the economy.

Fiscal policy refers to the government's taxation and spending plans.

Monetary policy refers to the management of the money supply (the total amount of money including currency in circulation and deposited in banks and building societies) in the economy.

In particular, monetary policy involves the changing of interest rates or varying of the amount of money that banks need to keep in reserve.

We will look at each of these types of policy option in turn.

4.1 Fiscal policy options

The two key elements that governments must plan for each year are:

- **Income** – this is primarily the money the government raises from direct and indirect taxes on individuals and businesses.

- **Expenditure** – this is the total amount the government will need to spend to provide services for the population. These may include the costs of the police and army, road and rail building as well as the wages of civil servants.

In the medium- to long-term, most governments would prefer to run a **balanced budget**. This occurs when government income and expenditure are exactly matched.

Don't get confused between a balanced budget and the balance of payments. The former refers to the relationship between government income (from taxation) and spending, while the latter refers to the flow of funds into and out of a country.

However, rather than having a balanced budget, a government may decide to run either a budget surplus or budget deficit.

- **Budget deficit**

  - This occurs when government spending is higher than government income.

  - To fund a deficit, the government will need to borrow money. This borrowing is referred to as the **Public Sector Net Cash Requirement (PSNCR)**.

  - By running a budget deficit, the government is injecting more money into the economy than it is taking out. This will help boost aggregate demand and reduce unemployment.

  - Because of this, running a deficit is known as an 'expansionary' strategy.

  - It is often used when a **'deflationary gap'** exists in the economy. This occurs when the level of aggregate demand in the economy is insufficient to lead to full employment.

- **Budget surplus**

  - This occurs when government spending is lower than government income.

  - By running a surplus, the government is taking money out of the economy, reducing aggregate demand.

  - This is referred to as a 'contractionary' policy.

  - It is often used when an **'inflationary gap'** exists in the economy. This occurs when aggregate demand in the economy is higher than the country can supply – leading to high inflation.

4.2 Monetary policy

Monetary policy (like fiscal policy) can be described as expansionary or contractionary.

An expansionary policy increases the money supply in the economy, helping to increase investment and employment. A contractionary policy decreases the total money supply, helping to reduce demand and easing inflation.

How can the government increase or reduce the money supply?

- **Interest rates**

  - Raising the interest rates will increase the cost of borrowing money for individuals and businesses.

  - This will typically reduce the level of investment by businesses and expenditure by individuals, helping to reduce aggregate demand in the economy.

  - In addition, high rates encourage individuals to save money, further reducing expenditure.

Interest rates

In some countries, such as the UK, interest rates are set by the central bank (i.e. the Bank of England in the UK).

In other countries, rates are directly set by the government.

- **Reserve requirements**

  - Most banks typically operate a fractional reserve system. This means that only a part of their deposits are kept in cash as they assume that not all customers will want their money back at the same time.

  - For instance, if a bank was required to keep 10% of its deposits in cash – for every $1,000 deposited by its customers, it would be able to lend $900 of this to another person or business.

  - Increasing the reserve requirement will reduce the amount of money that banks have available to lend, limiting the money supply. The reduction in the amount of money available to loan will also tend to push interest rates up.

- **Open market operations**

  - By buying and selling its own bonds, the government is able to exert some control over the money supply.

  - For example, by buying back its own bonds, it will release cash back into circulation. When it sells bonds, it receives cash in return, thereby taking it out of circulation.

Quantitative easing

Quantitative easing is a relatively unconventional monetary policy that involves a country's central bank buying financial assets (such as government and corporate bonds) using money that it has generated electronically.

Put more simply, the central bank has essentially printed itself new money that it can spend (although in practice it is unusual for the money to **actually** be printed).

This has the effect of increasing the amount of cash within the economy, hopefully increasing aggregate demand. However, it can cause increased inflation and weaken a country's exchange rate – which both come with their own problems.

It has been used extensively by several countries in the aftermath of the banking crisis in 2008.

4.3 Economics theories

So monetary and fiscal policies provide several 'levers' that the government can use to affect the economy.

But when should it use these levers?

The answer to this question is – it depends! Several economists have proposed different theories about the best ways for governments to look after the economies of their countries. Different governments may follow different theories.

4.3.1 Classical theory

The classical theory suggests that the government **does nothing**.

It was widely believed by classical economists that the economy would naturally move to an equilibrium point with full employment, all by itself.

For instance, in the event of a recession, the price of producing products (wages and raw materials) would fall. This would lead to a reduction in the selling price of the products, which in turn would lead to increased demand for them. Increasing demand for these goods would lead to economic growth, pulling the economy out of recession.

However, this theory was undermined by the Great Depression in the 1920s and 30s when, despite wages falling significantly, the economy did not respond by growing and seemed unable to pull itself out of recession.

This failure of the classical approach led to rival economics theories emerging.

4.3.2 The Keynesian view (demand side)

This was developed by John Maynard Keynes.

Keynes argued that governments needed to manipulate the level of aggregate demand within the economy (i.e. **demand side economics**).

He argued that government intervention was often needed in order to move the economy closer to its ideal equilibrium point (i.e. one where there was full employment).

This was because, if left to itself, the economy could get 'stuck' at unfavourable equilibrium points, as had happened in the Great Depression.

Practically, this means that governments should borrow money and inject it into the economy (run a budget deficit) when economic growth needs to be stimulated.

Governments should increase taxes and run a budget surplus to slow the economy down if it was growing too fast and experiencing significant inflation.

The multiplier

It is difficult to see how a government injection of funds into the economy could lead to prolonged economic growth. If the government borrows $50 million and injects it into the economy, it will at some point have to pay back this money. It will do this by taking $50 million out of the economy through taxation. the net effect on aggregate demand (and therefore national income) would appear to be zero as the initial injection is counterbalanced by leakage in the form of taxation.

This analysis is incomplete as it neglects the fact that the injection of $50 million is spent many times in the economy, boosting national income by more than $50 million.

Example

Imagine the government funds a road construction project. The construction workers then spend their wages in the domestic economy. The shop owners who sold them goods then spend their income and so on. This effect is known as the multiplier.

The multiplier cannot continue infinitely as some of the extra income may be saved or spent on imported goods or paid back to the government in taxes.

4.3.3 The monetarist view (supply side)

Monetarists returned to the classical view that there was only one equilibrium point in an economy: the point where supply equals demand in all markets in the economy.

The only reason that the economy does not find this equilibrium is because it will be hindered by market imperfections.

The role of the government is therefore to remove these imperfections, allowing the economy to naturally find its ideal equilibrium.

Market imperfections tend to include:

- inflation
- government spending and taxation
- price fixing
- minimum wage legislation

- regulation of markets

- abuses of monopoly power.

Monetarist solutions to economic problems are often described as **supply side economics** as they focus on improving the supply of factors of production in the economy (such as making it easier for businesses to access labour, raw materials, etc).

Illustration 5 – Supply-side policies

Between 1979 and 1984, the number of people claiming unemployment benefit in the UK rose from just over 1 million to nearly 2.9 million people. The Conservative Government of the time, following monetarist supply-side policies, adopted the following policies:

- Freed up markets for both factors and goods and services. This involved reducing the power of the trade unions and a reduction in the number of state-owned monopolies.

- Provided government-funded worker retraining schemes.

- Improved information provided by job centres and employment agencies.

- Provided financial support and advice for workers willing to relocate.

- Provided assistance and incentives for firms willing to relocate to areas of high unemployment.

- Lowered state benefits to make it less attractive to depend on state benefits rather than working.

- Reformed taxation with less emphasis on direct taxes (argued to act as a disincentive to work, effort and the supply of enterprise) and more emphasis on indirect taxes.

Test your understanding 11

Which of the following statements is **NOT** consistent with supply side policies?

A   Reduction in unemployment benefit

B   Running a budget surplus

C   Improvements to job centres

D   Reducing the power of unions

Test your understanding 12

Which ONE of the following would cause a fall in the level of aggregate demand in an economy?

A   A decrease in the level of imports

B   A fall in the amount people choose to save

C   A decrease in government expenditure

D   A decrease in the level of income tax

4.4 Achieving policy objectives

We have now identified the key factors that drive a government's approach to managing the economy.

A government will focus on trying to control growth, inflation, unemployment and the balance of payments using a variety of levers. These include both fiscal and monetary policy. Each government may use these levers in different ways, depending on the economics theory they feel works the best.

The final area we need to examine draws on all these areas. How will a government practically manage its economic objectives?

4.4.1 Growth

Policies to promote growth include:

- **Running a budget deficit**
    - This is a classic Keynesian response to a recession.
    - The government pumps money into the economy, triggering increased aggregate demand.

- **Increasing the availability of production factors**
    - This would be a classic monetarist policy and could include, for example, increasing the availability of labour through training schemes.

- **Cutting interest rates**
    - This can be interpreted as either a Keynesian policy (lowering the cost of borrowing to boost aggregate demand) or a monetarist policy (by increasing the money supply).

- **Other policies**
    - These could include:
    - government grants and incentives to boost investment – protectionist measures to reduce imports.

4.4.2 Unemployment

Reducing unemployment is complex. The government approach is likely to depend on the **type** of unemployment that it wants to tackle.

- **Cyclical unemployment**

    - This is also known as demand deficient, persistent or Keynesian unemployment.

    - It is caused by **aggregate demand in the economy being too low to create employment opportunities** for everyone that wants a job.

    - It tends to occur in the 'bust' period of the trade cycle.

    - The Keynesian solution would be to boost aggregate demand (perhaps by running a trade deficit).

    - Monetarists would continue to remove market imperfections, as they feel that this will naturally move the economy further towards full employment.

- **Frictional unemployment**

    - This refers to people who are short-term unemployed as they move between jobs.

    - It is not normally seen as a problem, but can be reduced by increasing the information unemployed people receive about job opportunities (a supply-side policy).

- **Structural or technological unemployment**

    - This occurs when there is a structural change in the economy, leading to a change in the skills required and the location where economic activity takes place.

    - Boosting aggregate demand (a Keynesian policy) will have little impact on this type of unemployment. Monetarist policies are likely to be more effective – such as:

        - government funded retraining schemes

        - tax breaks for redeveloping old industrial sites – business start-up advice and loans.

Illustration 9 – Unemployment

In the 1980s, the UK experienced a huge decline in its traditional heavy industries in the north. At the same time, new high technology industries were established in the south.

Workers in the former heavy industries were at a double disadvantage. Not only were they in the wrong location but they also had the wrong skills required by the new industries.

- **Seasonal unemployment**
    - This occurs naturally in some industries, where demand for goods is highly seasonal, for example in tourism and farming.
    - This can create economic problems in regions that rely heavily on such industries.

- **Real wage unemployment**
    - This is found in industries that are highly unionised.
    - Union negotiations keep wages artificially high using the threat of industrial action, such as strikes. The high wages bill that this creates means that the number of people employed by the industry is reduced.
    - Monetarists would see this as a market imperfection and would look to reduce union powers and abolish minimum wage agreements.

Test your understanding 13

Identify which type of unemployment is being described in the following statements

A   A worker loses their job because of the introduction of new technology

B   After the Wall Street Crash, millions of Americans were unable to find work

C   Jobs in the car industry have been reduced due to a strong union and high wages

D   A management accountant has just been made redundant but is due to start a new job in three weeks' time

E   Bar staff are out of work in November in a Spanish holiday resort

4.4.3 Inflation

As with unemployment, there are a number of different causes of inflation. Government policy will depend on which cause is dominant in the economy.

- **Demand-pull inflation**
    - This occurs when demand for goods and services in the economy is growing faster than the ability of the economy to supply these goods and services. This will lead to price rises.
    - Keynesian policies would focus on reducing aggregate demand through tax rises, cuts in spending and higher interest rates.

- **Cost-push inflation**
    - This is where the underlying cost of the factors of production rise. This makes goods more expensive to make, forcing manufacturers to raise their prices.

- For example, the increase in the price of oil means that transportation and manufacturing costs will rise. This leads to the price of many other goods increasing.

- **Imported inflation**

    - This can occur in countries that have significant levels of imports.

    - If the national currency weakens, the cost of imports will rise, leading to domestic inflation.

    - This can be reduced by policies to strengthen the national currency (which are explored below).

- **Monetary inflation**

    - Increasing the money supply increases the purchasing power of the economy, boosting demand for goods and services. If this expansion occurs faster than expansion in the supply of goods and services, inflation can arise.

    - Monetarists would argue that this should be controlled through increased interest rates, which will reduce the growth in money supply.

- **Expectations effect**

    - Many individuals and businesses will have an expectation that goods and services will increase in price each year due to inflation.

    - In order to protect themselves against these rises, wages and prices will therefore be increased now.

    - This may mean lead to an inflationary spiral, where inflation occurs because there is an expectation that it will occur.

Illustration 10 – Inflation

In 1975 the UK had inflation of nearly 25%. This reflected a number of factors:

- Poor macroeconomic management by government. In seeking to reduce unemployment, the government had injected significant sums into the UK economy. However, due to growing structural problems, the economy was unable to grow and the net result of this increased demand was to trigger an inflationary spiral.

- The effects of the quadrupling of the oil price in 1973/74 were still being felt in the UK economy.

- Strong unions and weak management led to poor control over wage demands.

In summary, the high inflation was a mix of both cost push and demand pull.

Inflation and unemployment combined

Most governments wish both to reduce unemployment and keep inflation low. However, there is fundamental conflict between the two objectives. Research by **Phillips** indicated that there is an inverse relationship between inflation and unemployment, i.e. during periods of low inflation unemployment was high and vice versa. The suggestion here is that, during times of low unemployment, labour can command higher wages as it is in relatively short supply.

Test your understanding 14

What type of inflation is each phrase describing?

A   Workers seek above inflation pay rises

B   Growth in demand for new homes has outstripped supply

C   Retailers have increased their prices in advance of inflation figures to be published next month

D   Copper prices have more than doubled on the world market this year, increasing the cost of electrical cables

Test your understanding 15

- If a deflationary gap exists, what kind of unemployment is most likely to exist in the economy?

- Will running a budget deficit successfully reduce all types of unemployment in an economy?

4.4.4 Balance of payments

If the country has a deficit on its balance of payments, there is a net outflow of funds from the country. This is clearly not supportable in the long-term, as the country will run out of money.

The government can therefore look to reduce the deficit using either expenditure-reducing or expenditure-switching strategies.

- **Expenditure-reducing strategies**

  - These involve the government deliberately shrinking the domestic economy in order to reduce the demand for imports.

  - This reduction could be accomplished by:

    - **contractionary monetary policy**, such as increased interest rates, increasing bank reserve requirements, etc.

    - **running a budget surplus**

- Reducing the size of the economy will also help to reduce inflation, reducing export prices and making the country's exports more competitive.

- However, suppressing demand is likely to lead to increased unemployment.

- **Expenditure-switching strategies**

  - These involve the government trying to encourage consumers to buy domestically produced rather than imported goods.

  - This could be accomplished by:

    - controls on imports, via tariffs or quotas (though this may breach global free trade regulations)

    - increasing exports, by subsidising exporters

    - lowering the exchange rate, making imports more expensive and exports more competitive. This is often referred to as currency **devaluation**.

Test your understanding 16

Which of the following policies for correcting a balance of payments deficit is an expenditure-reducing policy?

A   Cutting the level of public expenditure

B   Devaluation of the currency

C   The imposition of an import tax

D   The use of import quotas

Test your understanding 17

Which of the following might cause a country's exports to decrease?

A   A fall in the exchange rate for that country's currency

B   A reduction in other countries' tariff barriers

C   A decrease in the marginal propensity to import in other countries

D   A rise in that country's imports

Test your understanding 18

Which of the following would not correct a balance of payments deficit?

A   Revaluing the currency upwards

B   Raising domestic interest rates

C   Deflating the economy

D   Imposing import controls

5 Chapter summary

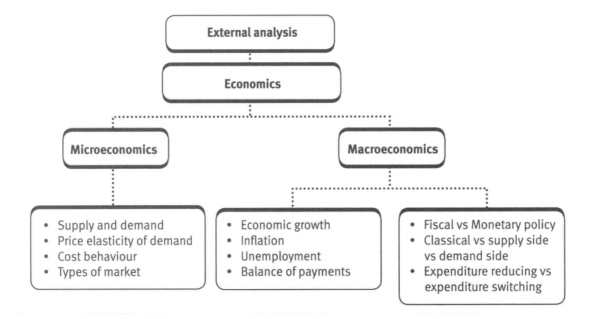

6   Practice questions

Test your understanding 19

Which of the following is most likely to lead to the demand curve for a product shifting to the right (i.e. an increase shift in demand)?

A   Changes in the level of income of customers

B   Falling population

C   Reduction in selling price of the product

D   Increase in selling price of the product

Test your understanding 20

A business currently sells 10,000 units of its product per month. It is planning to reduce the retail price from $1 to $0.90. The price elasticity of demand for the product is currently 1.5. Assuming no other changes, the sales that the business can now expect each month will be:

A   8,500

B   10,500

C   11,000

D   11,500

Test your understanding 21

A product has a price elasticity of demand (PED) of 2.0. Which of the following statements are therefore correct?

A   If the selling price of the product is cut by 10%, demand will fall by 20%

B   If the selling price of the product rises by 10%, demand will fall by 20%

C   If the selling price of the product is cut by 10%, demand will fall by 5%

D   If the selling price of the product rises by 10%, demand will fall by 5%

Test your understanding 22

Which of the following is **not** a factor that affects price elasticity of demand?

A   The availability of substitutes

B   The necessity of the product or service

C   The duration of the price change

D   The change in the number of units demanded

Test your understanding 23

In the long term, as a business grows it tends to become less efficient at controlling costs. What is this effect known as?

A   Equilibrium

B   Diminishing returns

C   Diseconomies of scale

D   Market imperfection

Test your understanding 24

Aggregate demand is made up of **(1)** + investment by firms + government spending + exports – **(2)**

Identify the terms that need to be placed at (1) and (2).

A   **(1)** = capital, **(2)** = imports

B   **(1)** = consumer spending, **(2)** = net borrowing

C   **(1)** = capital, **(2)** = net borrowing

D   **(1)** = consumer spending, **(2)** = imports

Test your understanding 25

Which of the following is a typical consequence of rapid economic growth?

A   Rising unemployment

B   Narrowing gap between rich and poor in society

C   Rising inflation

D   Falling demand for imports

Test your understanding 26

Which of the following is an example of a fiscal policy?

A   Running a budget deficit

B   Raising interest rates

C   Buy back of government bonds

D   Increases to bank reserve requirements

Test your understanding 27

The government of country V is concerned that the economy is growing too quickly. Which of the following policies might they choose to implement in order to slow growth?

A Reduction in bank reserve requirements

B Running a budget deficit

C Selling government bonds

D Lowering interest rates

Test your understanding 28

The government of country H is planning to adopt a supply-side approach to dealing with the country's high unemployment. Which of the following strategies is consistent with a supply-side approach?

A   Do nothing

B   Borrow money from the money markets and increase government spending, creating additional jobs

C   Lower interest rates to make it cheaper for firms to borrow, meaning that they can afford to hire more workers

D   Improve information available to the unemployed to make it easier for them to find work

Test your understanding 29

(a)   The following are policies that governments may use in order to affect their national economies:

A   Taxation levels

B   Interest rates

C   Buying or selling government debt

D   Public borrowing

E   Altering bank reserve requirements

F   Running a budget surplus

G   Quantitative easing

H   Running a budget deficit

Required:

Write down the FOUR options (A–H) which are examples of monetary policies.

(0.5 marks each = 2 marks in total)

(b)   The following are possible effects of government interference in the pricing of goods and services.

A   Excess supply

B   Waste of resources

C   Shortages of supply

D   Misallocation of resources

Required:

Write down which TWO of the four options (A–D) could be caused by the government setting a MAXIMUM price for goods or services which is below the market equilibrium point.

(0.5 marks each = 1 mark in total)

(c)   The following sentences contain gaps which requires the insertion of one of the following words:

A   Expansion

B   Contraction

C   Shortage

D   Surplus

If a product is priced above the equilibrium point in the market, it will lead to the producer having unsold units. This will lead to a reduction in selling price, along with **1** in the level of supply. The fall in selling price will lead to **2** in demand, until eventually equilibrium is reached.

Required:

(i)   Select the word that correctly fills gap 1 above; i.e. select A, B, C or D.

(ii)   Select the word that correctly fills gap 2 above; i.e. select A, B, C or D.

(0.5 marks each = 1 mark in total)

(Total: 4 marks)

Test your understanding answers

Test your understanding 1

The correct answer is D

Correct answer is D since this changes the price of foreign holidays and leads to a movement along the demand curve, not a shift in the curve.

Test your understanding 2

The percentage change in price being suggested is ((£60 − £55) ÷ (£55)) × 100% = 9.09%

The percentage fall in units that this would cause is ((15,000 − 12,000) ÷ 15,000) × 100% = 20%

This leads to a PED of (20% ÷ 9.09%) = **2.20**

This result indicates that the F1200 is price-elastic. The demand for the units is falling at a much faster rate than the price is increasing by. For price-elastic goods such as this, it is typically a bad idea to increase prices as overall revenue and, therefore, profits are likely to fall. The opposite would be true if price elasticity was less than 1.

Test your understanding 3

This is unlikely to significantly affect the demand for medicine. This is because medicine is likely to be highly **inelastic**. Given that the medicines are likely to be seen as a necessity for most individuals, citizens are likely to continue paying for their medication regardless of the cost.

The price of the medicines is currently low and only applies to the wealthier citizens. This means that these payments will only represent a *small proportion of their income*, again suggesting a low elasticity of demand.

Also, given the relatively low prices charged by the government, it is *unlikely that citizens will be able to find cheaper substitutes*. This would indicate that they will continue to buy the medicines at the higher prices.

The increase will presumably be long in duration. This would normally mean that *consumers have more time to find alternatives*, leading to increased elasticity and a fall in demand. However, given the other factors already mentioned, on balance there is likely to be little change in the level of demand.

Test your understanding 4

The correct answer is C

When the price of a good is held above the equilibrium price suppliers will be willing to supply more at this higher price. However, consumers will demand less. The combined effect of this is to create a surplus of the goods.

Test your understanding 5

The correct answer is D

Putting in place a minimum wage is likely to increase the production cost within country F. This will either lead to a contraction of supply, if the cost rises cannot be passed onto customers, or a contraction of demand if businesses raise the prices they charge customers to cover the increased wages bill. Either way, the most likely outcome is a surplus of labour within the country, leading to rising unemployment.

Test your understanding 6

The correct answer is D

Test your understanding 7

The correct answer is C

Lower taxation is not a policy objective. Rather it is a policy instrument that could be used to encourage economic growth.

Test your understanding 8

The correct answer is B

(i) is clearly incorrect. Government spending is also part of the aggregate demand (AD) formula. By changing this, the government could directly affect AD.

In addition, government policy can affect AD. If the government invests in infrastructure (i.e. new roads and railways), this can attract investment in the country, boosting AD.

(ii) is correct as a weakening currency will tend to make imports more expensive, reducing demand for them. Exports will be more competitive, increasing AD.

Test your understanding 9

The correct answer is B

A   **FALSE**

The benefits of economic growth are often very unevenly spread across a population. Those missing out on growth can experience a relative decline in their standard of living.

B   **TRUE**

Rising incomes that accompany economic growth can lead to an increase in imports as consumers choose to spend their income on foreign, rather than domestically produced, goods.

C   **FALSE**

Fixed incomes do not increase in line with inflation, e.g. 10% on $10,000 savings will not increase if a country is experiencing inflation. Those in employment would expect to receive pay rises broadly in line with inflation, ensuring that the spending power of their income is not eroded.

D   **FALSE**

Inflation tends to discourage investment in a national economy in a number of ways. This includes a loss in confidence by both domestic and international investors.

Test your understanding 10

The correct answer is B

A   Less pressure for government to increase taxes. **NO**

During periods of unemployment, government tax receipts will be low but its expenditure (on unemployment and other benefits) will be high. There is therefore increased pressure on government to raise taxes to fund these obligations.

B   Reduced economic output. **YES**

Unemployed people are not economically active and are not adding to the output from the economy. Furthermore, their longer-term ability to contribute may decline as their skills become outdated.

C   Greater inflationary pressure in the economy. **NO**

Lower levels of demand for goods and services are unlikely to put upward pressure on the price of goods and services. Equally, unemployment reduces upward pressure on wages as there is, in effect, an oversupply of labour.

Test your understanding 11

The correct answer is B

- Reduction in unemployment benefit: **yes**

  This acts as an incentive for people to return to work and therefore improves the supply of labour.

- Running a budget surplus: **no**

  Remember, supply side policies refer to attempts to improve the supply of factors in an economy. Stimulating demand through running a budget surplus or deficit is a demand side policy.

- Improvements in job centres: **yes**

  Improving the quality of information available to those seeking work should improve the supply of labour as those out of work are able more easily to identify relevant employment opportunities.

- Reducing the power of the unions: **yes**

  Unions can distort the operation of markets by effectively restricting the supply of labour. Reducing their power removes this market imperfection and is consistent with a monetarist approach.

Test your understanding 12

The correct answer is C

AD = C + I + G + (X – M)

- Reducing government expenditure will decrease aggregate demand.

- Reducing imports, savings and tax will all act to increase aggregate demand.

Test your understanding 13

A   A worker loses their job because of the introduction of new technology – structural.

B   After the Wall Street Crash, millions of Americans were unable to find work – cyclical.

C   Jobs in the car industry have been reduced due to a strong union and high wages – real wage.

D   A management accountant has just been made redundant but is due to start a new job in three weeks time – frictional.

E   Bar staff are out of work in November in a Spanish holiday resort – seasonal.

Test your understanding 14

A   Workers seek above inflation pay rises: cost push.

Above inflation pay rises lead to cost push inflation as wages are part of the factor cost of production.

B   Growth in demand for new homes has outstripped supply: demand-pull.

Where demand is exceeding supply consumers will be prepared to pay higher prices to obtain the goods or services they require. This type of inflation is known as demand-pull.

C   Retailers have increased their prices in advance of inflation figures to be published next month: expectations effect.

This type of inflation is occurring due to the expectations effect.

D   Copper prices have more than doubled on the world market this year, increasing the cost of electrical cables: cost push.

Increase in copper prices represents an increase in the cost of input and would be classified as cost-push inflation.

Test your understanding 15

- When a deflationary gap exists the current equilibrium level of national income is too low to provide employment opportunities for all those seeking work. In other words there is insufficient demand in the economy, i.e. cyclical or demand-deficient unemployment exists.

- Government injection of funds will not have any effect on structural unemployment. Simply stimulating demand under these circumstances will lead to inflation as the additional demand will not be met by an increase in economic output. Alternatively, additional income will simply be spent on imports.

Test your understanding 16

The correct answer is A

The other three are expenditure-switching policies which will make imported goods either more expensive or hard to obtain.

Test your understanding 17

The correct answer is C

A fall in the exchange rate for a country's currency will encourage exports as they will become relatively cheaper to the foreign importer, hence A is incorrect. B is also wrong since reducing tariff barriers will open up export markets giving exporting countries more opportunities. A rise in a country's imports is not clearly related to changes in the same country's exports.

Test your understanding 18

The correct answer is A

Revaluing the currency would worsen the balance of payments deficit by making exports more expensive and imports cheaper.

Test your understanding 19

The correct answer is A

Changes in customer income are most likely to produce an increase shift in demand (i.e. make the demand curve shift to the right). Customers may have more income, leading to an expansion in demand.

Falling population would be likely to shift the demand curve to the left (a decrease shift in demand), as there will be fewer people to buy the products, which is likely to lead to a smaller market for the product to be sold in.

The other two options (increase or decrease in selling price) relate to the normal expansion and contraction in demand as price changes, not a shift in the entire curve itself.

Test your understanding 20

The correct answer is D

Percentage change in price = 10%

PED = 1.5, which means that the quantity demanded will change 1.5 times faster than the price.

Change in quantity demanded is therefore 10% × 1.5 = 15%.

As the price has dropped, demand should have risen by 15%, meaning that sales will rise to (10,000 × 115%) = **11,500 units**.

Test your understanding 21

The correct answer is B

If you're unsure about the answer, get rid of the ones that are obviously incorrect. If the selling price falls, the level of demand is likely to rise. This eliminates A and C.

Remember that PED tells you how fast the quantity demanded changes in relation to changes in selling price. A PED of 2 indicates that the quantity demanded changes twice as fast as the selling price. A 10% change in selling price will therefore cause a 20% shift in demand for the product.

Test your understanding 22

The correct answer is D

The other factors are: the proportion of income spent on the item, habit and the market definition.

Test your understanding 23

The correct answer is C

By definition.

Test your understanding 24

The correct answer is D

By definition.

Test your understanding 25

The correct answer is C

Typically, rapid growth will reduce unemployment and increase demand for imports. However, the benefits of growth are often not distributed evenly throughout society, meaning the gap between rich and poor widens. Increase growth does, on the other hand, lead to more demand, pushing up prices and leading to inflation.

Test your understanding 26

The correct answer is A

Remember that fiscal policies relate to government taxation and spending. Monetary policies (of which the other three options are examples), involves adjusting the amount of cash within the economy.

Test your understanding 27

The correct answer is C

A and D both involve making it easier for consumers and businesses to access credit. Doing so will lead to expansion of the economy.

Running a budget deficit means the government is borrowing cash to pump it into the economy. Again, this would be used to stimulate growth.

Selling government bonds will mean the government is taking money out of the economy, which may help to slow growth.

Test your understanding 28

The correct answer is D

A is the classical approach. B and C are Keynesian, or demand-side, policies designed to manipulate the level of aggregate demand in the economy. D is the only monetarist, or supply-side, policy which aims to help improve the supply of production factors (in this case people) in the economy.

Test your understanding 29

(a) Monetary policies are those that change the amount or availability of currency in circulation and deposited in banks within the economy. This means that the correct options are: **B, C, E and G**. The other options are all to do with the government's taxation and spending policies and are therefore fiscal policies.

(b) If the government sets a maximum price which is below the equilibrium point for the goods or services in question, suppliers will reduce the level of output as the goods will be less profitable than those where no price controls exist and allocate resources to these alternative products. This will lead to shortages in the goods which have a maximum price set on them, as well as mis-allocation of resources to other goods and services. The correct answers are therefore **C and D**.

(c) Pricing above the equilibrium point will usually mean that there is excess supply in the market, due to relatively low levels of demand. Eventually, this will lead to a fall in the selling price and, subsequently, a contraction in supply of the units. The fall in selling price will cause an expansion in demand for the goods. This effect will likely continue until equilibrium is reached. The correct answers are therefore:

   (i)   **B**

   (ii)   **A**

External analysis – social, environmental and technological factors

Chapter learning objectives

Upon completion of this chapter you will be able to:

- explain the medium and long-term effects of social and demographic trends on business outcomes and the economy

- describe the impact of changes in social structure, values, attitudes and tastes on the organisation

- identify and explain the measures that governments may take in response to the medium and long-term impact of demographic change

- explain the effects of technological change on organisation structure and strategy: downsizing, delayering, outsourcing

- describe the impact of information technology and information systems development on business processes

- list ways in which the business can affect or be affected by its physical environment

- describe ways in which businesses can operate more efficiently and effectively to limit damage to the environment

- identify the benefits of economic sustainability to a range of stakeholders.

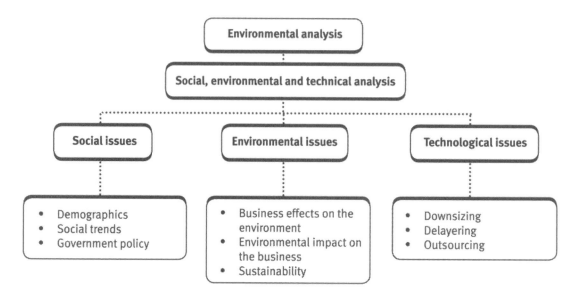

When using PEST analysis, the final factors to be considered are social and technological issues and how these could impact on the organisation.

1 Social and demographic factors

1.1 Demographic trends

 The word **demographics** refers to the composition of the population in any given area – whether a country or an area within a country.

There are a number of important demographic issues that businesses will need to monitor.

These include:

Population size

Population growth (or decline) is the result of a combination of factors, including birth rates, death rates, immigration and emigration.

Many businesses monitor forecasts for population size as a growing population often results in a growing market for their products and services.

Population composition

This often relates to the age of the population, which is usually affected by the relative sizes of the birth and death rates.

In Ireland, around 36% of the population is aged 25 and under, making it an attractive country for businesses needing a large, young workforce.

In the UK, 17% of the population in 2011 was over the age of 65. This is predicted to reach 23% by 2035. Businesses that cater to the needs of retired people will therefore enjoy a growing market.

Population location

In 1950 around 30% of the world's population lived in cities. That figure is expected to rise to 70% by 2050.

Given that space is at more of a premium in cities, businesses that offer space-saving furniture (for example) are likely to see increasing demand for their products.

Wealth

Economic growth in a country often results in higher disposable incomes for its population. This in turn leads to increased demand for goods and services.

The three fastest growing world economies in 2010 were Qatar, Paraguay and Singapore.

Education

An educated workforce is a key driver of economic growth.

Increasing standards of education not only mean that consumers are more discerning, but also allows the expansion of high-tech businesses that need skilled staff.

Health

In many western countries, the population is becoming increasingly overweight. This places greater demands on healthcare providers.

More than 10% of all South Africans are affected by HIV. The country's declining life expectancy (49 years in 2010) is cause for great concern, especially as the population structure has changed, with fewer middle-aged people. This is normally the most economically active and skilled group who support the young and elderly.

Test your understanding 1

A greater percentage of teenagers in the UK are going on to university than ever before with the government putting forward a target figure of 50% by 2010.

Give examples of three firms who will be affected by this and state whether they face an opportunity or a threat.

1.2 Social trends

This examines how society changes over time. There are a number of key ways in which this change occurs, including:

- social structure
- values
- attitudes
- tastes

Organisations need to analyse these social changes and attempt to understand how they will affect their activities.

1.2.1 Social structure

Social structure is often closely related to the concept of social class.

 A social class refers to a group of people who have the same social, economic or educational status.

Changes in social structure can have a significant impact on organisations. In particular, organisations may be able to link the social position of a given group to its buying patterns.

This means that an organisation may be able to improve its marketing by targeting it towards a specific social group. For instance, individuals in a social group with lower disposable income may not be targeted by organisations that make and sell high-priced luxury items.

1.2.2 Values

 Social values are the accepted behaviours and norms that help to bind a social group together.

There are a number of examples of changes in social values that have impacted on a range of organisations and their activities.

These include:

- Increasing concerns about environmental and ethical issues, such as greenhouse gases and animal testing, may spell disaster for firms unwilling to embrace the cultural shift.

- Many women are choosing to pursue careers before having children. This has led to a rise in the average age of a mother on the birth of their first child. These older mothers are often wealthier, leading to increased demand for better quality baby clothing, prams, etc.

- A shift in lifestyle away from a traditional '9 to 5' working day has led to supermarkets opening throughout the night. The Internet and other forms of IT allow people to shop or bank in the middle of the night as a response to this trend.

1.2.3 Attitudes

 Attitudes represent a person or group's like or dislike for something. They are positive or negative views of a person, place, thing or event.

Again, organisations must be able to keep pace with changing attitudes in society. For instance:

- There is an increasing willingness across Europe to seek compensation from organisations for alleged wrongs. This has become known as the 'compensation culture' and can significantly increase costs for organisations.

- Changes in public attitudes to waste have led to opportunities for recycling firms.

- People have become increasingly comfortable with using the Internet and computers. In 2003, 3 million users in the UK had a broadband connection. By 2010, this had risen to 18 million. This has created huge opportunities for online firms and many conventional retailers have set up websites to sell their products.

1.2.4 Tastes

Taste refers to an individual's personal preferences or patterns of choice. On a social level, tastes may be linked to the social group that an individual belongs to.

Most organisations have to take account of changing fashions and tastes in society. Failure to do so can lead to significant reductions in profitability or even the collapse of the organisation.

- Clothing is an excellent case in point, with UK retailer Marks and Spencers suffering significant declines in the early 2000's due to its clothing no longer being seen as fashionable by consumers.

- Other business sectors that see significant changes in fashions over time include cars and furniture.

Social influences

According to **Johnson and Scholes** the social influences that should be monitored include the following.

Population demographics – a term used to describe the composition of the population in any given area, whether a region, a country or an area within a country.

Income distribution – will provide the marketer with some indication of the size of the target markets. Most developed countries, like the UK, have a relatively even distribution spread. However, this is not the case in other nations.

Social mobility – the marketer should be aware of social classes and the population distribution among them. The marketer can use this knowledge to promote products to distinct social classes within the market.

Lifestyle changes – refer to our attitudes and opinions towards things like social values, credit, health and women. Our attitudes have changed in recent years and this information is vital to the marketer.

Consumerism – one of the social trends in recent years has been the rise of consumerism. This trend has increased to such an extent that governments have been pressured to design laws that protect the rights of the consumer.

Levels of education – the level of education has increased dramatically over the last few years. There is now a greater proportion of the population in higher education than ever before.

Test your understanding 2

Which of the following statements is/are correct?

(1) A social trend towards increased materialism will be beneficial to all retailers.

(2) A change in social structure may lead to a change in social attitudes.

A (1) only

B (2) only

C Neither

D Both

1.3 Government policy

For many firms the impact of social and demographic change is primarily through government responses to trends. For example:

Population structure

- Governments of countries with low birth rates often introduce tax advantages and other financial incentives to encourage women to have more children. This is the case in Singapore for example. Another common policy is to encourage immigration. Both Canada and Australia have been promoting this for over a decade.

- Governments in countries with rapidly rising populations often put in place policies to discourage large families, e.g. the 'one child' policy adopted by China.

- The increasing percentage of the population aged over 65 is creating a pensions crisis in many countries. The main concern is that the taxes received from a smaller proportion of workers will be insufficient to meet the pension demands of a growing retired population without huge increases in income tax rates. Typical government responses include raising the retirement age and encouraging private and occupational pension schemes.

Housing

- Increasing demand for new homes in many countries has resulted in governments setting out plans for new housing developments, creating further demand for builders.

Employment

- The percentage of single-parent families in the UK rose from 7% in 1971 to 25% in 2009. The UK government has focused on enabling single parents to return to work through a mixture of childcare vouchers and tax credits. Among others this has created extra demand for childcare services and after-school clubs.

Health

- Concerns over the effects of smoking have resulted in bans on tobacco advertising on television in many countries. Concerns over obesity are giving rise to increasing pressure on governments to legislate in a similar way in the fast food industry.

- In South Africa the government has put in place many initiatives to raise awareness of AIDS and sexual health. The global community is under great pressure to provide cheap drugs to help.

- Some governments have also taken steps to improve the nutritional value of school meals with obvious implications for the suppliers of those meals.

Test your understanding 3

Given increasing health concerns there is pressure for some governments to legislate for more detailed food labelling. Give an example of one firm for whom this will be an opportunity and one for whom this will be a threat.

Test your understanding 4

The average price paid by first-time house buyers in the UK more than doubled between 1998 and 2010. This has led to a shortage of affordable housing resulting in shortages of key staff such as nurses and teachers in many areas. To counter this, there have been national and local government initiatives to ensure that new housing developments include affordable housing.

What implications does this have for a house building firm?

2   Environmental factors

This looks at how an organisation affects or is affected by the world around it – its physical environment. This analysis may be carried out alongside analysis of an organisation's social factors, as discussed in the previous section. This is because companies that fail to look after their environment can often expect a strong negative response from their key stakeholders, such as governments and consumers.

2.1 How can a business affect or be affected by its physical environment?

Before a company can decide on how to look after its environment, it needs to understand the possible impacts a business and its environment may have on each other.

Some suggestions for these include:

Business effects upon the environment	Environmental effects upon the business
• **Pollution**, such as production of rubbish or harmful emissions. • **Wastage of resources**, such as food, water or other raw materials. • **Destruction** of natural habitats. • **Loss of plant and animal species.**	• **Changing climate** may affect a number of businesses – especially those involved in food production. • **Lack of resources** will increase the cost of raw materials – potentially reducing business profits. • **Loss of sales** – if a business has a poor environmental record, customers may no longer wish to trade with it. • **Legislation** – polluting companies may trigger legislation by governments. The additional compliance costs and fines may reduce profits.

Illustration 1 – The impact of the environment upon the business

The number of bees has fallen dramatically over the last few years, with a 34% reduction in numbers in the USA between 2009 and 2010. This has widely been attributed to the use of pesticides by farmers and businesses across the country.

This does not just affect the environment. The fall in the number of bees is having a dramatic effect on commercial crop production in the USA, as they are vital for the pollination of a range of commercial crops, including those used for animal feed.

> The loss of bees worldwide would be directly expected to cost the global economy upwards of $41 bn.
>
> This illustrates that while businesses may have an impact on the environment, the environment can also directly affect the profitability of businesses.

2.2 The ways in which businesses can limit damage to the environment

If a business identifies that it is not acting responsibly towards the environment, there are a number of things it may do to try and limit its impact on the world around it.

These include:

- **Redesign of products to use fewer raw materials** – The technology company Apple, has significantly reduced the amount of harmful materials, such as arsenic, in its product range over the last few years and made its units easier to recycle.

- **Reduction in packaging on products** – Some UK supermarkets have started charging customers for plastic carrier bags in an attempt to reduce the amount of plastic finding its way into landfill sites.

- **Recycling** – A significant number of businesses have started looking for ways to recycle their waste products, such as paper and glass.

- **Improving energy efficiency** – Businesses may have 'energy wardens' – members of staff who are responsible for identifying ways of reducing energy consumption within the business.

- **Careful production planning** – If businesses only produce the number of units required by customers, wastage will be reduced.

 ## 2.3 Sustainability

Nowadays, businesses should look to be environmentally sustainable. Sustainability means that organisations **should use resources in such a way that they do not compromise the needs of future generations**.

For example, a paper manufacturer may consider planting a tree for everyone it fells. This will ensure that future generations will have enough timber to meet their needs.

Taking this approach will benefit a range of stakeholders.

Stakeholder	Benefit
Workers/local community	Reduced waste and pollution will lead to a more pleasant, healthier environment.
Customers	Many customers prefer dealing with businesses that look after the environment as they are seen as being more ethical.
Shareholders	Reduction of waste and increased efficiency can improve business profits. This could lead to higher long term returns for investors.
Public	Reduced pollution can lead to fewer environmental problems, such as acid rain and soil erosion.

The benefits of being more environmentally friendly are evidenced by the large number of businesses adopting this policy.

Test your understanding 5

A is a supermarket company which is considering improving its environmental image. Which of the following would **NOT** help A to limit the damage it is doing to the environment?

A   Charging customers for using plastic carrier bags

B   Improving sales forecasting to reduce wastage of inventory

C   Improving accessibility for less able customers

D   Reducing packaging on fresh food

3   Technological factors

3.1 Introduction

Technological changes can affect a firm in many different ways, such as:

- Organisational structures, e.g. employees working from home but still able to access files and systems at work.

- Product developments, e.g. turntables were effectively replaced by CD players which in turn are being replaced by mp3 players.

- Production changes, e.g. computer-controlled machinery.

- Marketing, e.g. using the internet to sell the product.

3.2 Impact on organisational structure

Technological change has affected organisational structure in a number of key ways:

- Some administrative and managerial roles have been replaced by more effective IT systems.

- Some production roles have been replaced by the use of robots and automated production lines. This has also reduced the need for as many supervisors.

- Improved communications (email, use of secure intranets, wireless networks) mean that employees can work out of the office/at home allowing more flexible work arrangements.

These have resulted in downsizing and delayering in firms.

 Downsizing

Downsizing is a term used for reducing the number of employees in an organisation without necessarily reducing the work or the output.

Downsizing has been a feature of the 1980s and 1990s and many organisations, large and small alike, believe that they have become 'leaner' and 'fitter' as a result.

 Delayering

Often linked to downsizing, delayering is the process of removing layers of management.

This is usually to change the organisation from one with a rigid hierarchical framework with numerous layers of supervisory grades into a 'flatter' organisation with minimal layers of management. Such organisations tend to emphasise team working, with people taking on different roles in different teams.

 Outsourcing

Outsourcing means contracting out aspects of the work of the organisation, previously done in-house, to specialist providers.

In some cases suppliers are given access to the firm's records so they can review production schedules and stock records to ensure that supplies are delivered before they run out.

Outsourcing

Outsourcing is particularly common for IT within an organisation, which may contract another, more skilled, supplier to take over some or all of their IT functions. There are four key types of IT outsourcing:

- **Total** – this is where the third-party supplier provides most or all of the organisation's IT systems and services.

- **Ad-hoc** – occurs when the organisation needs IT support for a short period and hires in external support as needed on a temporary basis.

- **Partial** – this is where some IT functions are outsourced, such as maintenance or support, but others are kept in-house by the organisation.

- **Project management** – similar to ad-hoc, this occurs when the creation and/or implementation of a specific IT system are outsourced to a third part supplier.

Advantages and disadvantages of outsourcing to the organisation

Advantages	Disadvantages
The supplier may have specialist skills and knowledge that the organisation may lack, such as programming.	It may be difficult to bring IT back in-house at a later date, as outsourcing often causes the loss of staff with specialist skills from the organisation.
Outsourcing may operate on a fixed fee contract. This removes any uncertainty about how much the company will pay for its IT in the year.	Outsourcing may lead to the organisation being locked into an unfavourable contract with a poor quality supplier.
Outsourcing may improve business flexibility, allowing the business to vary the level of work the supplier performs, depending on demand.	Outsourcing IT will allow third-party suppliers to gain access to the organisation's information. This may be confidential, leading to a risk of data security breaches.
The supplier may be more efficient at running the IT function for the organisation, leading to cost savings.	By relying on a third-party for its IT, the organisation will have no way to create its own, unique systems. This means that it cannot obtain competitive advantage from its systems.

Illustration 2 – Impact on organisational structure

Wal-Mart, the US store chain, makes its sales data immediately available to its suppliers, through the internet. This sales data allows the suppliers to make their own forecasts of expected future demand for their products through Wal-Mart and plan their production schedules on the basis of these forecasts, rather than waiting for an actual purchase order from Wal-Mart before making any scheduling decisions.

Test your understanding 6

An audit firm has decided to eliminate the role of supervising senior and split the workload between other existing staff. What type of change is being described here?

3.3 Impact of technological change on products

- Technological advances allow many products to become increasingly more sophisticated, e.g. mobile phones are now smaller, can record images and video and be used to access the internet.

- New technology can lead to the emergence of substitutes, e.g. the cinema industry went into decline in the early 1980s as a result of the emergence of the video.

- Some industries have seen their business model completely transformed, e.g. online banking has reduced barriers to entry allowing supermarkets, among others, to move into banking.

- Customer support is often provided by call centres in countries where wage rates are lower. However some firms have reinstated call centres into their home countries after concerns over customer care.

3.4 Impact of technological change on production processes

- The most obvious way that technology has affected production is the use of robots and automated production lines.

- However, IT systems have also been used for more efficient scheduling and monitoring of production, resulting in lower inventory levels, higher quality, elimination of bottlenecks and lower costs.

3.5 Impact of technological change on marketing

As well as the product issues mentioned above, technology has affected all parts of the marketing function.

- Pricing – many retailers monitor competitors' prices to ensure that they are not being undercut. Most 'price watch' schemes are IT-based.

- Promotion – the obvious issue here is the use of websites but promotional methods also include viral and banner advertisements.

- Distribution, e.g. the internet has created a huge opportunity for many firms to sell direct to a wider range of potential customers.

- Market research, e.g. customer databases.

> **Test your understanding 7**
>
> Comment on how technological changes have affected the demand for holiday travel agents.

3.6 Impact of technological change on society as a whole

Society is becoming more dependent upon computer and communications technology. Many would argue that we have left the industrial age behind, and the information age has taken over. Key issues are:

- E-commerce

  (i)   online advertising

  (ii)   online ordering of products

  (iii)   online financial transactions

  (iv)   Electronic data interchange

- Home shopping

- Home banking

- Home learning

- Home entertainment

- Teleworking/telecom muting.

Some industries may disappear, but new ones are emerging. Employment patterns will change.

For example, sales staff and retail jobs could be reduced as home shoppers order directly from centralised warehouses. The new skills needed, will be that of web authoring and new languages such as HTML5 to create attractive and interactive interfaces for the customers.

4 Chapter summary

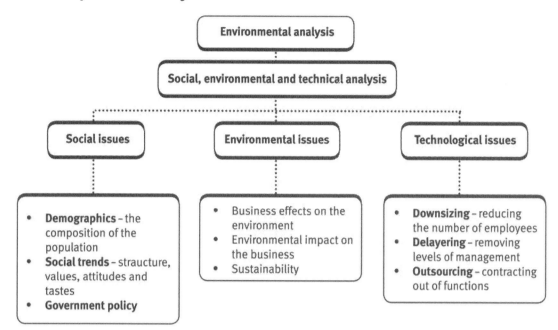

5 Practice questions

Test your understanding 8

'The accepted behaviours and norms that help bind a social group together.'

What is this the definition of?

A   Attitudes

B   Tastes

C   Values

D   Social structure

Test your understanding 9

Downsizing is the process of:

A   Reducing the number of employees

B   Reducing the number of levels of management

C   Contracting out aspects of the organisation's structure

D   Reducing the price charged for products

Test your understanding 10

The average age of a country's population depends on its birth and death rates. Assuming equal rates of change, which of the following would give an overall reduction in the average age of the population?

A   Rising birth rate, rising death rate

B   Rising birth rate, falling death rate

C   Falling birth rate, rising death rate

D   Falling birth rate, falling death rate

Test your understanding 11

X company is a commercial fishing organisation. It owns several large trawlers that it uses to catch large volumes of fish. Once a certain part of the ocean has been trawled, X ensures that no further fish are caught there for at least one year, even though there are still a large number of fish left to be caught. This allows the fish stocks time to replenish.

What is this an example of?

A   Efficiency

B   Recycling

C   Sustainability

D   Effectiveness

Test your understanding 12

Which of the following is likely to be an advantage of an organisation outsourcing some of its less important operations?

A   Increased level of skill within the organisation

B   Increased workload for directors and senior managers

C   Increased time for management to focus on core operations

D   Increased control over the outsourced function

Test your understanding 13

(a) **Required:**

Below are four definitions of terms relating to social trends Match each definition to the appropriate term.

A   The accepted behaviours and norms that help to bind a social group together.

B   Individual personal preferences or patterns of choice.

C   A group of people with the same social, economic or educational status.

D   A person or group's like or dislike for something.

(i)   **Social class. Select ONE of A, B, C or D**

(ii)   **Values. Select ONE of A, B, C or D**

(iii) **Attitudes. Select ONE of A, B, C or D**

(iv) **Tastes. Select ONE of A, B, C or D**

(0.5 marks each, total = 2 marks)

(b) Increased automation has had a number of effects on organisations, including an increase in the level of outsourcing of IT, which can have several benefits for the organisation.

A   The new IT supplier may have skills that the organisation lacks.

B   The organisation will need to hire more members of staff.

C   The organisation's flexibility may increase.

D   There will be reduced risk of data security breaches.

E I   t will be easy for the organisation to bring the IT function back in-house in future, if needed.

F   Outsourcing IT will increase the chances that the organisation will gain competitive advantage over its rivals.

G   Outsourcing may lead to the organisation being locked into an unfavourable contract with a supplier.

Required:

Which TWO of the above are benefits of this approach? Select TWO from (A, B, C, D, E, F, G).

(1 mark each, total = 2 marks)

(Total: 4 marks)

Test your understanding answers

Test your understanding 1

- Firms who rent out properties in university towns and cities – opportunity.

- Providers of stationery and study aids – opportunity.

- Student loan providers – opportunity.

- Any firm which typically takes staff straight after they leave school – threat as there will be fewer suitable candidates available. The number of graduate applicants for jobs may rise, but they may expect higher starting salaries.

Test your understanding 2

The correct answer is B

Increased materialism may not help all retailers – for example, those that sell basic goods may suffer as consumers wish to purchase more luxurious alternatives.

However, changing social structure can cause a shift in social attitudes within a culture.

Test your understanding 3

Opportunity – food labelling specialists (!), sellers of high quality unprocessed foods.

Threats – smaller businesses which cannot afford expensive labelling technology.

Test your understanding 4

The initiatives will be viewed as threats to profitability as the firm will have to rent out or sell properties at below the market rate. It may also have to reduce the prices on other houses in the development because of a perceived fall in their exclusivity.

The trend may, however, present an opportunity. If competitors are unable or unwilling to meet the criteria set out for new developments, then the firm which can will gain approval on more planning applications.

Test your understanding 5

The correct answer is C

While C would be an ethical activity for A to undertake, it would not directly reduce A's impact on the environment.

Test your understanding 6

Given that one level of management is being removed, this could be described as delayering.

(Note: It would also be downsizing if existing supervising seniors are made redundant.)

Test your understanding 7

- Demand for travel agents grew hugely when technology allowed agents to explore availability and book flights from their premises in the 1970.

- More recently the internet has allowed customers to do this from the comfort of their own homes, reducing the demand for agents.

- There has also been an increase in the number on online agents, such as Expedia.co.uk offering to build bespoke holidays.

Test your understanding 8

The correct answer is C

By definition.

Test your understanding 9

The correct answer is A

B is delayering, C is outsourcing and D is simply a price cut.

Test your understanding 10

The correct answer is A

A rising birth rate, means more youngsters within the population, while a rising death rate would indicate fewer older individuals. Combined, this would reduce the average age of the population.

Test your understanding 11

The correct answer is C

Sustainability is the use of resources in such a way that the needs of future generations are not compromised.

Test your understanding 12

The correct answer is C

By outsourcing non-core operations, management time can be freed up for more important activities. This will, however, normally lead to a loss of control over the parts of the organisation that have been outsourced.

Test your understanding 13

(a)   The correct answers are:

   (i)   **C** – this is the definition of social class.

   (ii)   **A** – this is the definition of values.

   (iii) **D** – this is the definition of attitudes.

   (iv)   **B** – this is the definition of tastes.

(b)   The only correct benefits are: **A** and **C**. An IT outsourcing company may have more IT skills than the organisation itself and may also lead to increased flexibility, with the organisation only paying for IT work as and when it is needed.

The other statements are all incorrect, with the exception of G – which is correct, but is a disadvantage of outsourcing.

Competitive factors

Chapter learning objectives

Upon completion of this chapter you will be able to:

- Identify a business's strengths, weaknesses, opportunities and threats (SWOT) in a market and the main sources of competitive advantage

- Identify the main elements within Porter's value chain and explain the meaning of a value network

- Describe the activities of an organisation that affect its competitiveness:
    - purchasing
    - production
    - marketing
    - service

- Explain the factors or forces that influence the level of competitiveness in an industry or sector using Porter's five forces model.

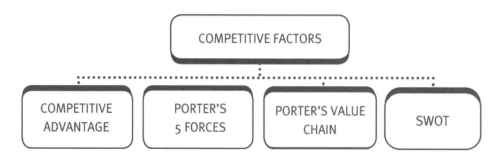

 1 Competitive advantage

Part of a firm's external analysis will involve assessing the degree and sources of competition within the industry. The key issue here is whether the firm has a sustainable competitive advantage.

This will be analysed in three steps:

- the main competitive forces in an industry

- the different ways a firm can achieve a competitive advantage

- how different activities and departments within the firm contribute to its competitiveness.

2 Porter's five forces analysis

2.1 Introduction

As outlined in chapter 6, PEST analysis is particularly good at identifying whether and why certain markets will be expected to grow in the future. However, just because a market is growing, it does not follow that it is possible to make money in it.

Porter's five forces approach looks in detail at the firm's competitive environment by analysing five key areas, or 'forces'.

Together these forces determine the overall profit potential of the industry. Looking at an individual firm, its ability to earn higher profit margins will be determined by whether or not it can manage the five forces more effectively than competitors.

2.2 Porter's five forces model

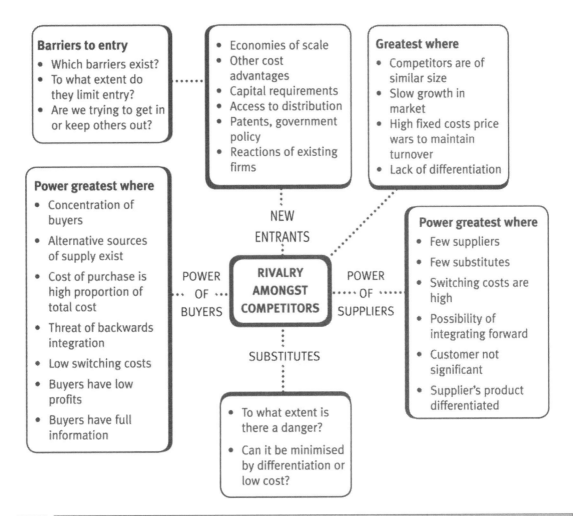

 Porters five forces – additional detail

Competitive rivalry

High competitive rivalry will put pressure on firms to cut prices and/or improve quality to retain customers. The result is reduced margins.

Intensity of existing competition will depend on the following factors:

- Number and relative strength of competitors – where an industry is dominated by a few large companies rivalry is less intense (e.g. petrol industry, CD manufacture).

- Rate of growth – where the market is expanding, competition is low key.

- Where high fixed costs are involved companies will cut prices to marginal cost levels to protect volume, and drive weaker competitors out of the market.

- If buyers can switch easily between suppliers the competition is keen.

- If the exit barrier (i.e. the cost incurred in leaving the market) is high, companies will hang on until forced out, thereby increasing competition and depressing profit.

- An organisation will be highly competitive if its presence in the market is the result of a strategic need.

Threat of entry

New entrants into a market will bring extra capacity and intensify competition. The threat from new entrants will depend upon the strength of the barriers to entry and the likely response of existing competitors to a new entrant. Barriers to entry are factors that make it difficult for a new entrant to gain an initial foothold in a market.

There are six major sources of barriers to entry.

- Economies of scale, where the industry is one where unit costs decline significantly as volume increases, such that a new entrant will be unable to start on a comparable cost basis.

- Product differentiation, where established firms have good brand image and customer loyalty. The costs of overcoming this can be prohibitive.

- Capital requirements, where the industry requires a heavy initial investment (e.g. steel industry, rail transport).

- Switching costs, i.e. one-off costs in moving from one supplier to another (e.g. a garage chain switching car dealership).

- Access to distribution channels may be restricted (e.g. for some major toiletry brands 90% of sales go through 12 buying points), i.e. chemist multiples and major retailers. Therefore it is difficult for a new toiletry product or manufacturer to gain shelf space.

- Cost advantages independent of scale, e.g. patents, special knowledge, favourable access to suppliers, government subsidies.

Threat of substitute products

This threat is across industries (e.g. rail travel versus bus travel versus private car) or within an industry (e.g. long-life milk as a substitute for delivered fresh milk). Porter explains that, 'substitutes limit the potential returns ... by placing a ceiling on the price which firms in the industry can profitably charge'. The better the price-performance alternative offered by substitutes, the more readily customers will switch.

Bargaining power of customers

Powerful customers can force price cuts and/or quality improvements. Either way margins are eroded. Bargaining power is high (as, for instance, Sainsbury and Tesco in relation to their suppliers) when a combination of factors arises.

Such factors could include the following.

- Where a buyer's purchases are a high proportion of the supplier's total business or represent a high proportion of total trade in that market.

- Where a buyer makes a low profit.

- Where the quality of purchases is unimportant or delivery timing is irrelevant, prices will be forced down.

- Where products have been strongly differentiated with good brand image, a retailer would have to stock the complete range to meet customer demands.

Bargaining power of suppliers

The power of suppliers to charge higher prices will be influenced by the following:

- the degree to which switching costs apply and substitutes are available

- the presence of one or two dominant suppliers controlling prices

- the extent to which products offered have a uniqueness of brand, technical performance or design not available elsewhere.

Illustration 1 – Porter's five forces model

Porter's five forces can be applied to the house building industry as follows:

Competitive rivalry – very high

- large number of domestic and international firms

- it is difficult to differentiate your product

- firms typically have high fixed costs.

Threat of entry – high

- For new firms entering the industry the main barriers are as follows:

    - capital requirements are low – construction is labour intensive, most equipment can be hired if necessary

    - some economies of scale – e.g. purchasing bricks – need initial finance to acquire land

    - need good relationships with planning offices to get planning permission

- overall these barriers are low, resulting in a high threat of entry.

Threat of substitutes – high

- Main threat is the availability of second-hand property for rent or purchase.

- This will depend on the country concerned – some countries have housing shortages (e.g. Turkey) whereas others have booming housing property markets.

Power of suppliers – low for materials, higher for land and planning permission

- Material suppliers have low power – numerous suppliers, undifferentiated products.

- Suppliers of prime land sites are in a strong position and can command high prices.

- Local planning office has very high power.

Power of customers – low

- In the housing sector customers have more choice but individually have low buying power.

Summary: key issue is competitive rivalry.

Test your understanding 1

Use **Porter's** five forces to identify the most important competitive force for a burger chain, such as McDonalds.

Test your understanding 2

'Low industry profitability is a barrier to entry.'

Is this statement:

A   True

B   False

3   Generic strategies

This model, developed by Porter, examines the different ways that an organisation can achieve a competitive advantage in its market.

Porter argued that businesses could adopt one of three strategies to gain competitive advantage. Each business can adopt the strategy that best fits their individual circumstances.

Cost leadership

This involves the business making a product of similar quality to its rivals, but at a lower cost. This is normally achieved through internal efficiencies.

Cost leadership will usually allow the organisation to:

- sell its products at a lower price than rivals, increasing its sales; or

- sell its products at the same price as its rivals, but make higher profits.

For example, Casio Electronics Ltd follows a cost leadership approach and has sold over 1 billion pocket calculators. Its calculators are not of inferior quality, but it has organised its operations to minimise its production costs, such as through mass manufacturing its products in countries with low labour costs.

Differentiation

This strategy involves persuading customers that our product is superior to that of our rivals. It can be done by adding additional features to the product or by altering customer perception of the product through advertising or branding. Differentiation will usually allow the business to charge a premium price for its product.

British Airways (BA) is a multinational airline. It has adopted a differentiation approach by offering passengers a higher quality experience than many of its rivals, through offering superior customer service and convenient, more luxurious flights. This has allowed the company to charge a premium for its services.

Focus

This involves aiming at a segment of the market, rather than the market as a whole. A particular group of consumers is identified with the same needs and the business will provide products or services that are tailored to their needs. This tailored approach will typically allow the business to charge a premium for their products.

Saga is an example of a company that has adopted a focus approach. It offers a range of products and services that are tailored for customers over the age of 50.

Conclusion

Porter argued that businesses needed to adopt one of the above three approaches or they would be 'stuck in the middle', which would make it difficult for them to compete successfully.

Test your understanding 3

Company F makes motor vehicles. The cars are similar to those created by F's rivals, but F has managed to achieve significant economies of scale by bulk-buying its material from one main supplier. This has enabled F to see its cars more cheaply than their competitors.

Which of the following strategies has F adopted?

A   Cost leadership

B   Differentiation

C   Focus

D   Stuck in the middle

4   Porter's value chain

4.1 Introduction

Porter developed his value chain to determine whether and how a firm's activities contribute towards its competitive advantage.

4.2 The value chain

The approach involves breaking the firm down into five 'primary' and four 'support' activities, and then looking at each to see if they give a cost advantage or quality advantage.

Primary activities

Activity	Description	Example
Inbound logistics	Receiving, storing and handling raw material inputs.	A just-in-time stock system could give a cost advantage.
Operations	Transformation of the raw materials into finished goods and services.	Using skilled craftsmen could give a quality advantage.
Outbound logistics	Storing, distributing and delivering finished goods to customers.	Outsourcing deliveries could give a cost advantage.
Marketing and sales	Market research + 4Ps.	Sponsorship of a sports celebrity could enhance the image of the product.
Service	All activities that occur after the point of sale, such as installation, training, repair.	Marks & Spencer's friendly approach to returns gives it a perceived quality advantage.

Support (also known as secondary) activities

Activity	Description	Example
Firm infrastructure	How the firm is organised.	Centralised buying could result in cost savings due to bulk discounts.
Technology development	How the firm uses technology.	The latest computer-controlled machinery gives greater flexibility to tailor products to individual customer specifications.
Human resources development	How people contribute to competitive advantage.	Employing expert buyers could enable a supermarket to purchase better wines than competitors.
Procurement	Purchasing, but not just limited to materials.	Buying a building out of town could give a cost advantage over High Street competitors.

Results of analysis

The results of the analysis are often summarised in the following diagram.

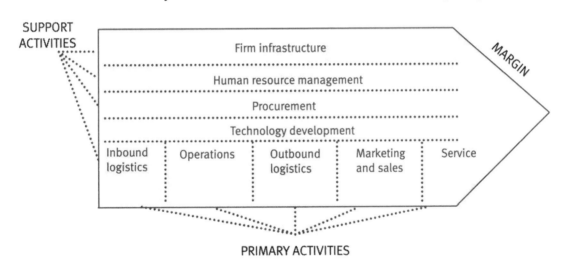

4.3 How different departments contribute to competitive advantage

Porter's value chain can now be used to explain how different departments contribute to competitiveness as follows:

Purchasing

- Cost advantages – sourcing cheaper materials, bulk discounts, centralised buying.

- Quality advantages – sourcing higher quality materials, employing expert buyers.

Production

- Cost advantages – mass production lines, standardisation, employing workers just above the minimum wage, keeping stock levels low.

- Quality advantages – using better quality materials, more quality control procedures, employing highly skilled staff, flexible manufacturing systems, use of technology to ensure better consistency, ongoing training of staff.

Marketing

- Cost advantages – word-of-mouth promotion, sell direct to cut distribution costs.

- Quality advantages – market research can help tailor products to meet customer needs, large promotional budgets, sponsorship, perceived quality pricing, brand development.

Service

- Cost advantages – outsourcing (?), not offering service provision, low paid staff.

- Quality advantages – outsourcing (?), highly skilled staff.

Test your understanding 4

Human Resources (HR) is set up as a service department with a firm. How can this department contribute towards competitive advantage?

Test your understanding 5

TRE Ltd is a company that buys, cleans and then sells vegetables. It has recently introduced a new automated inventory system that allows management to identify older inventory quickly. This will allow the company to reduce its currently high level of wastage.

Which activity within TRE's value chain will the new system improve?

A   Operations

B   Outbound logistics

C   Inbound logistics

D   Procurement

4.4 Value networks

This refers to a set of connections between organisations and individuals interacting with each other to benefit the entire group. It will allow members to share information as well as buy and sell products.

Organisations' value chains don't exist in isolation. There will be links between the inbound logistics of a company and the outbound logistics of its suppliers, for example.

5 Corporate appraisal (SWOT)

SWOT analysis examines the **S**trengths, **W**eaknesses, **O**pportunities and **T**hreats of an organisation.

This is an integral part of strategic analysis. Unlike PEST analysis, which focuses on external environmental issues, SWOT analysis is used to view the internal and external situation that an organisation finds itself in. Strengths and weaknesses examine what an organisation **internally** does well or badly, while opportunities and threats look at positive and negative factors that might impact on the organisation **externally**.

To do this, it draws on PEST analysis, as well as the other models examined in this chapter. Because of this, SWOT analysis is a vital tool that an organisation uses in its long-term strategic planning process.

Resource Based (Internal)

S	W
• The things we are doing well	• The things we are doing badly (need to correct or improve)
• The things we are doing that the competition are not	• The things we are not doing but should be
• Major successes	• Major failures

O	T
• Events or changes in the external environment that can be exploited	• Events or changes in the external environment we need to protect ourselves from or defend ourselves against
• Things likely to go well in the future	• Things likely to go badly in the future

Position Based (External)

The internal and external appraisals of SWOT analysis will be brought together and it is likely that alternative strategies will emerge.

Once identified, management can consider:

- matching strengths to opportunities may highlight new areas for organisational development

or:

- methods of removing weaknesses or dealing with the threats the organisation faces

Test your understanding 6
A company is attempting to analyse its competitive environment. Which of the following models would be most appropriate for it to use?
A SWOT
B PEST
C Five forces
D Value chain

Chapter summary

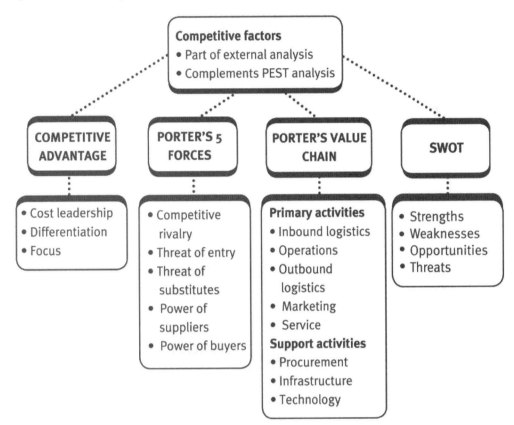

6 Practice questions

Test your understanding 7

JHG sells computers. It has a large number of competitors within this market. It has recently cut its prices and is now selling at a price which is significantly below those if its rivals. JHG believes that it will be difficult for any other company to match its new pricing structure.

Which of Porter's five forces would this strategy NOT help to deal with?

A   Power of suppliers

B   Power of buyers

C   Barriers to entry

D   Competitive rivalry

Test your understanding 8

Which value chain activity relates to how the firm is organised, for example whether purchasing is undertaken centrally?

A   Procurement

B   Infrastructure

C   Operations

D   Inbound logistics

Test your understanding 9

Which of the following is a secondary activity in Porter's value chain?

A   Procurement

B   Service

C   Marketing and sales

D   Outbound logistics

Test your understanding 10

When analysing its strategic position, an organisation may use one of several models, including:

(i)   SWOT

(ii)   Five forces

(iii) PEST

(iv) Value chain

OIU company is undertaking a strategic analysis of its operations. It has discovered government plans to write new legislation that would result in OIU's closure. Which of the strategic models should have identified this issue?

A   (i) and (ii)

B   (ii) and (iii)

C   (i) and (iii)

D   (i) and (iv)

Test your understanding 11

(a)   H plc manufactures and sells a range of motorbikes. It is currently analysing its value chain and is aware that its activities can be classified as either:

A   Primary activities

B   Secondary activities

Required:

Classify the following activities as either A (primary activities) or B (secondary activities):

(i)   **Receiving, storing and handling raw materials.**

(ii)   **Management of personnel and human resources.**

(iii) **Purchasing of materials and other resources.**

(iv) **Advertising to attract potential customers.**

(0.5 marks each, total = 2 marks)

(b) Porter's five forces model helps to identify key market forces that may affect H's business. Four of these forces are:

A Competitive rivalry

B Threat of new entrants

C Threat of substitute products

D Bargaining power of customers

The following sentences contain gaps which specify one of Porter's five forces.

H is concerned that a number of its customers are choosing to purchase cars, rather than motorbikes. This shift in the market indicates that the 1 has increased.

Required:

(i) **Select the force which appropriately fills gap one above; i.e. select A, B, C or D.**

In addition, H and its competitors hold a large number of patents relating to the manufacture and design of motorbikes. This has the effect of reducing the 2 within the market.

Required:

(ii) **Select the force which appropriately fills gap two above; i.e. select A, B, C or D.**

(1 mark each, total = 2 marks)

(Total: 4 marks)

Test your understanding answers

Test your understanding 1

Competitive rivalry – very high

- Many major competitors – e.g. Burger King.

Threat of entry – low

- Significant barriers to entry include economies of scale, capital investment required and strength of incumbents' brand names.

Threat of substitutes – medium

- Many substitutes – e.g. sandwiches, pizzas, etc.

Power of customers – low

- Customers have low switching costs and can easily go elsewhere BUT have very low individual buying power.

Power of suppliers – low

- McDonalds buys from small suppliers all over the world.

Summary: key issue is competitive rivalry.

Test your understanding 2

The correct answer is B – False

While low profitability may make an industry unattractive, it does not make it more difficult for firms to enter should they wish to do so.

Test your understanding 3

The correct answer is A

This would be a classic example of a cost leader.

Test your understanding 4

HR can contribute towards competitive advantage through selection, recruitment, training and appraisal schemes. These can all contribute towards lower staff turnover and greater motivations, which in turn will save costs and improve quality and productivity.

Test your understanding 5

The correct answer is C

Inbound logistics involves receiving, storing and handling of inventory, so a new inventory system would affect this part of the chain.

Test your understanding 6

The correct answer is C

PEST looks at the external environment of the company. The value chain examines the company's activities to see which contribute towards competitive advantage. Porter's five forces is specifically designed to examine the competitive nature of the company's market or industry. SWOT pulls all these models together and examines the overall position of the company.

Test your understanding 7

The correct answer is A

Cutting prices may well help reduce customer bargaining power, as customers will be unable to find a cheaper alternative to JHG's products. Having a low price may help deter new entrants, who will (especially when they are setting up) find it difficult to compete with JHG. In addition, JHG's lower prices will help to attract customers from its rivals, helping to reduce the impact of competitive rivalry on the company.

Test your understanding 8

The correct answer is B

Don't get confused here – procurement is the actual purchasing function itself. Infrastructure looks at how the organisation is organised.

Test your understanding 9

The correct answer is A

The others are all primary activities.

Test your understanding 10

The correct answer is C

The potential new government legislation should be part of the political issues identified in PEST analysis and is a threat within SWOT.

Test your understanding 11

(a) The correct answers are:

  (i) **A** – the activity being described is inbound logistics, which is primary.

  (ii) **B** – the activity being described is human resource management, which is secondary.

  (iii) **B** – the activity being described is procurement, which is secondary.

  (iv) **A** – the activity being described is marketing and sales, which is primary.

(b) The correct answers are:

  (i) **C** – motor cars are not direct competitors to motor bikes and are in a different industry. They are therefore substitute products.

  (ii) **B** – patents held by major motorbike manufacturers will make it difficult for new businesses to enter the market. They act as a barrier to entry.

Professional ethics in accounting and business

Chapter learning objectives

Upon completion of this chapter you will be able to:

- define business ethics and explain the importance of ethics to the organisation and to the individual

- describe and demonstrate the following principles from the IFAC code of ethics, using examples

    - integrity

    - objectivity

    - professional competence

    - confidentiality

    - professional behaviour

- describe organisational values which promote ethical behaviour using examples

    - openness

    - trust

    - honesty

    - respect

    - empowerment

    - accountability

- explain the concept of acting in the public interest

- recognise the purpose of international and organisational codes of ethics and codes of conduct, IFAC, ACCA, etc.

- describe how professional bodies and regulators promote ethical awareness and prevent or punish illegal or unethical behaviour
- identify the factors that distinguish a profession from other types of occupation
- explain the role of the accountant in promoting ethical behaviour
- recognise when and to whom illegal, or unethical conduct by anyone within or connected to the organisation should be reported
- define corporate codes of ethics
- describe the typical contents of a corporate code of ethics
- explain the benefits of a corporate code of ethics to the organisation and its employees
- describe situations where ethical conflicts can arise
- identify the main threats to ethical behaviour
- outline situations at work where ethical dilemmas may be faced
- list the main safeguards against ethical threats and dilemmas.

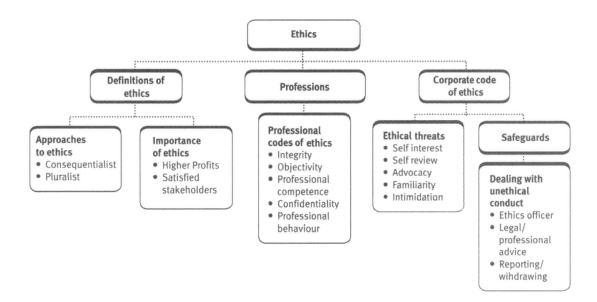

1   Business ethics and their importance

 Ethics is the system of moral principles that examines the concept of right and wrong.

Business ethics is the application of ethical values to business behaviour.

Whether an action is considered to be right or wrong normally depends on a number of different factors, including:

- the consequences – does the end justify the means?

- the motivation behind the action

- guiding principles – e.g. 'treat others as you would be treated'

- key values – such as the importance of human rights.

Illustration 1 – Definition of business ethics

You discover that a colleague at work has been stealing from the company. What do you do? Do you report them to management which might lead to their dismissal and the loss of a friend? Do you keep quiet and risk being punished yourself if your knowledge of the situation later becomes clear? Do you urge the colleague to confess what they've done? Does it depend on the size of the theft, e.g. a $1 pad of paper, or a $1,000 piece of machinery? Does it depend on how friendly you are with the colleague?

You can see that ethical problems require moral judgements that can be extremely difficult and depend on many different factors.

Test your understanding 1

The study of business ethics is purely concerned with legal requirements. Is this statement:

A   True

B   False

Ethical dilemmas

An ethical dilemma involves a situation where a decision-maker has to decide what is the 'right' or 'wrong' thing to do. Examples of ethical dilemmas can be found throughout all aspects of business operations.

Accounting issues:

- Creative accounting to boost or suppress reported profits.

- Directors' pay arrangements – should directors continue to receive large pay packets even if the company is performing poorly?

- Should bribes be paid to facilitate contracts, especially in countries where such payments are commonplace?

- Insider trading, where for example directors may be tempted to buy shares in their company knowing that a favourable announcement about to be made should boost the share price.

Production issues:

- Should the company produce certain products at all, e.g. guns, pornography, tobacco, alcoholic drinks aimed at teenagers?

- Should the company be concerned about the effects on the environment of its production processes?

- Should the company test its products on animals?

Sales and marketing issues:

- Price fixing and anti-competitive behaviour may be overt and illegal or may be more subtle.

- Is it ethical to target advertising at children, e.g. for fast food or for expensive toys at Christmas?

- Should products be advertised by junk mail or spam email?

Personnel (HRM) issues:

- Employees should not be favoured or discriminated against on the basis of gender, race, religion, age, disability, etc.

- The contract of employment must offer a fair balance of power between employee and employer.

- The workplace must be a safe and healthy place to operate in.

1.1 Approaches to ethics

Making ethical decisions is often not an easy process. Individuals may find themselves facing an ethical dilemma and could be unsure of the correct action to take.

There are several possible approaches to making these decisions.

1.1.1 Consequentialist versus pluralist

- **Consequentialist approach**

  This approach states that a decision is right or wrong depending on the consequences or outcomes of that decision. As long as the outcome is right, then the action itself is irrelevant.

  For example, if an individual needs to feed their family, stealing may be seen as morally acceptable if there is no other way of obtaining food.

  This approach can be broken down into two further perspectives:

  Egoism – the action is morally correct as long as the outcome is favourable for the individual making the decision; and

  Utilitarianism – the action is considered to be morally correct if the outcome is favourable for the greatest number of people or 'the greater good'.

  For instance, if an accountant is asked to cover up a major fraud within a company they work for, an egoist approach to ethics may lead to the accountant refusing to do so. This would be because if the fraud is discovered at a later date, the accountant risks serious penalties.

  From a utilitarian point of view, keeping quiet is also likely to be unacceptable as the fraud may well damage the returns to shareholders and could put the livelihoods of employees at risk. As such, reporting the fraud is likely to benefit a greater number of people rather than allowing it to continue.

- **Pluralist approach**

  This approach involves trying to cater to the needs of all stakeholders without seriously compromising the interests of any one group.

  For example, a mining company may wish to open a new mine in order

  to access mineral deposits and earn its shareholders a large profit. However, local residents may be unhappy due to the pollution caused by the mine. A pluralist approach would be to open the mine but ensure that enough money is spent to minimise the damage to the local

  environment, perhaps guaranteeing that the site will be fully restored once mining operations have ceased.

1.1.2 Relativist versus absolutist

- **Relativism**

  This is the view that there is **no universal moral code** with which to judge all actions. This means that whether something can be classed as 'ethical' or not **depends on the circumstances**.

  What if someone stole bread to feed their starving family? Relativists may argue that different people will view this theft differently. Some may feel that stealing is never justified, while others will feel that, given the circumstances, it was a reasonable course of action.

  Relativism's greatest strength is that it accepts that different people and cultures will have different views on what is right and wrong. For organisations that operate internationally, this allows greater flexibility when deciding on what actions to take. This makes them more responsive to local attitudes.

  Unfortunately, relativism is often argued to be an excuse for organisations and individuals to do whatever they like and continue with unethical activities.

- **Absolutism**

  This approach to ethics argues that **certain actions are inherently right or wrong**, regardless of their context or the circumstances that they occur in.

  For example, an absolutist would regard the taking of a human life as entirely unacceptable, regardless of the context; whether it was murder or in self-defence would be irrelevant.

  The main strength of absolutism is that provides a framework of rules that are easy for individuals and companies to follow.

  However, it is often unclear where an absolutist should find this framework of ethical rules – should it be religious in nature? Or simply down to what they feel is universally accepted?

  Absolutism may also lead to problems where absolute rules conflict with one another. For instance, what if you had to steal something to save someone's life?

  Note that absolutism is linked to the idea of **deontological ethics**. This is linked to the work of the German philosopher Immanuel Kant, who suggested that when faced with an ethical dilemma, an individual must look at the action being considered and deciding if it is inherently right or wrong. It ignores the consequences of the decision being made and instead focuses on the individual meeting their moral duties.

Illustration 2 – Approaches to ethics in business

Imagine you are a company that runs a large chain of supermarkets. You have identified an opportunity to expand into country G. This expansion will create large numbers of local jobs and is expected to earn you significant profits.

Local officials in country G have made it clear that, in order to gain the appropriate planning permissions, you will need to pay them money as inducements (bribes). This is common practice for officials in country G, though it is illegal in your home country. What should you do?

The answer depends on your approach to ethics.

Consequentialists would argue that your decision depends on the consequences of paying the bribes.

If you were egoist (looking at your own needs), you would probably pay the bribes as you would still stand to earn a significant profit from the venture.

If you are a utilitarian company, you may also consider paying the bribe as doing so will not only mean that you can earn large profits, but will provide jobs for many locals. Paying the bribe will therefore be for the greater good.

Pluralists would look at ensuring that the needs of none of the stakeholders are seriously compromised by paying the bribe. In this case, while the payment will involve some loss to our shareholders, paying the bribe will still allow us to expand into country G, benefiting everyone.

Relativists would look at the context of the decision to pay the bribe. In this case, bribery is a commonly accepted part of doing business in country G. Therefore, we can be flexible with our approach and may consider paying the bribe.

Absolutists would look at whether paying the bribe was fundamentally incorrect. In this case, bribery is illegal in our home country. An absolutist would therefore be likely to conclude that paying bribes to officials in country G would also be inappropriate, as doing so is always wrong.

Test your understanding 2

Joe is a manager in company A. He has twenty employees who report to him and he has been told that he needs to reduce this number by one.

Joe decides that rather than making a member of staff redundant he will instead reduce each employee's hours by one–twentieth, thereby keeping everyone in a job.

What approach is Joe taking to this decision?

A   Egoist

B   Pluralist

C   Utilitarian

D   Joe is acting unethically

1.2 Why business ethics are important

Businesses are part of society. Society expects its individuals to behave properly, and similarly expects companies to operate to certain standards.

Business ethics is important to both the organisation and the individual.

For the organisation	For the individual
• Good ethics should be seen as a driver of profitability rather than a burden on business.	• Consumer and employee expectations have evolved over recent years.
• An ethical framework is part of good corporate governance and suggests a well-run business.	• Consumers may choose to purchase ethical items (e.g. Fairtrade coffee and bananas), even if they are not the cheapest.
• Investors are reassured about the company's approach to risk management.	• Employees will not blindly accept orders to act in a manner that they personally believe to be unethical.
• Employees will be motivated in the knowledge that they operate in an environment of good ethical corporate behaviour.	

Illustration 3 – Why business ethics are important

The Fairtrade mark is a label on consumer products that guarantees that disadvantaged producers in the developing world are getting a fair deal. For example, the majority of coffee around the world is grown by small farmers who sell their produce through a local co-operative. Fairtrade coffee guarantees to pay a price to producers that covers the cost of sustainable production and also an extra premium that is invested in local development projects.

Consumers in the developed world may be willing to pay a premium price for Fairtrade products, knowing that the products are grown in an ethical and sustainable fashion.

Test your understanding 3

Adhering to ethical practice is always a cost to business. Is this statement:

A True

B False

2 Professional ethics

2.1 What is a profession?

A profession, as opposed to other types of occupation, is characterised by the following factors:

- the mastering of specialised skills during a period of training

- governance by a professional organisation

- compliance with an ethical code

- a process of certification before being allowed to practise.

There are many examples of professions, such as accounting, law, medicine and teaching. A professional accountant (such as an ACCA member), for example, fulfils all four of the above criteria.

In many countries (including the UK) it is also possible for unqualified people to call themselves 'accountants' and set themselves up in business. However, such people are not professional accountants as they do not belong to a professional accountancy body (such as the ACCA) and have no obligation to follow an ethical code.

Test your understanding 4

Which of the following is **NOT** a difference between a professional accountant and an unqualified accountant?

A   A professional accountant has passed exams which prove their level of knowledge

B   A professional accountant has a duty to stay up to date with his or her knowledge

C   A professional accountant is required to comply with relevant legislation

D   A professional accountant must comply with an ethical code

As mentioned above professions are distinguished, in part, by having a code of conduct that all members of that profession are required to follow. This ensures that the profession as a whole does not have its reputation damaged by the questionable actions of some of its individual members.

2.2 Professional codes of ethics

Both the International Federation of Accountants (IFAC) and the ACCA have developed codes of ethics for their members.

The IFAC 'Code of Ethics for Professional Accountants' (issued in June 2005) lays down ethical standards to be applied by practising accountants across the world. IFAC recognise that some jurisdictions may have specific requirements and guidance that differ from its Code, in which case professional accountants should comply with the more stringent rules unless this is prohibited by local laws or regulation.

Note that the IFAC code is now administered by the International Ethics Standards Board for Accountants (IESBA).

IFAC Code of Ethics: Fundermentals Principles

Integrity   Objectivity   Professional competence and due care   Confidentiality   Professional behaviour

The IFAC code

A professional accountant must comply with the Fundamental Principles in the Code at all times. The IFAC Code is based on a conceptual framework approach to problem resolution, rather than a rules-based approach. Professional accountants are required to identify and address threats to complying with the Fundamental Principles, rather than the Code listing a long set of rules that aim to deal with every possible eventuality.

IFAC also takes an interest in ensuring that the accounting profession in general, and auditors in particular, act in the public interest. This means that accountants are expected to act in such a way as to improve the general welfare of the society they operate in, rather than just acting in the best interests of their clients.

The member bodies of IFAC are professional bodies such as the ACCA, so IFAC has no direct ability to punish an accountant who acts contrary to the Code. However IFAC would expect the transgressor's professional body to investigate the matter and punish the accountant if necessary.

The ACCA's 'Code of Ethics and Conduct' is contained in the annual Rulebook issued by the Association. All registered students, affiliates and members of the ACCA are required to comply. The ACCA Code is based on the IFAC Code and takes a similar conceptual framework approach, listing an identical set of Fundamental Principles that must be followed.

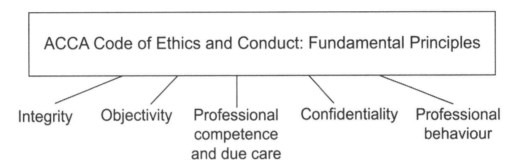

ACCA Code of Ethics and Conduct: Fundamental Principles

Integrity   Objectivity   Professional competence and due care   Confidentiality   Professional behaviour

What do the ACCA and IFAC fundamental principles actually mean?

- **Confidentiality** – Information obtained in a business relationship is not to be disclosed to third parties without specific authority being given to do so, unless there is a legal or professional reason to do so. This information should not be used for the personal advantage of the accountant.

- **Objectivity** – Accountants must ensure that their business or professional judgement is not compromised because of bias or conflict of interest.

- **Integrity** – This implies fair dealing and truthfulness. Accountants should not be associated with any false, misleading or recklessly provided statements.

- **Professional Competence and Due Care** – Accountants are required to have the necessary professional knowledge and skills required to carry out work for clients and must follow all applicable technical and professional standards when carrying out that work.

- **Professional Behaviour** – Accountants must comply with all relevant laws and regulations and must avoid any actions that would bring the profession into disrepute.

 Compliance with the Fundamental Principles

All ACCA members must comply with the Fundamental Principles, whether or not they are in practice. Members must identify threats to compliance with the Principles and apply safeguards to eliminate the threat or to reduce it to an acceptable level such that compliance with the Fundamental Principles is not compromised.

Students, affiliates and members of the ACCA who are in doubt as to their correct course of action in specific ethical dilemmas should contact the ACCA for guidance. Those failing to observe the standards expected of them may be called before the ACCA's Disciplinary Committee and required to explain their conduct.

Illustration 4 – IFAC and ACCA code of ethics

ACCA Disciplinary Committee decision

An ACCA member may be called to appear before the Disciplinary Committee for breach of any of the ethical principles described above, and may be admonished, fined, suspended or excluded from membership.

For example, in January 2004 an ACCA member was convicted in a court of three counts of false accounting. This is contrary to the principles of 'integrity' and 'professional behaviour' so the Disciplinary Committee considered the matter. The member was excluded from ACCA membership and ordered to pay £750 costs.

Test your understanding 5

A works in the accounts department of a large multinational company. If profits for the company are above a certain level, A will receive a large bonus. Because of this, he decides to manipulate some of the expenses, artificially increasing the profits and allowing him to get a bonus.

Which of the fundamental principles has A NOT breached?

A   Confidentiality

B   Professional behaviour

C   Integrity

D   Objectivity

2.3 The role of the accountant in promoting ethical behaviour

At many business meetings, or on many Boards of Directors, it is only the professional accountant who belongs to a profession and therefore has a duty to act in the public interest.

 Public interest refers to the common well-being or general welfare of society. Professional accountants must consider this, as they have a wider duty to act in the best interests of the public at large, as well as to the business and its owners.

The professional accountant therefore has a special role in promoting ethical behaviour throughout the business.

3   Corporate codes of ethics

Most companies (especially if they are large) have approached the concept of business ethics by creating a set of internal policies and instructing employees to follow them. These policies can either be broad generalisations (a corporate ethics statement) or can contain specific rules (a corporate ethics code).

There is no standard list of content – it will vary between different organisations. Typically, however, it may contain guidelines on issues such as honesty, integrity and customer focus.

Many organisations appoint Ethics Officers (also known as Compliance Officers) to monitor the application of the policies and to be available to discuss ethical dilemmas with employees where needed.

The purposes of codes of conduct

Some commentators see the growth in codes of conduct as a cynical attempt by companies to escape legal liability when an employee is caught doing something wrong. The company can try to claim that it is not the company's fault when a rogue employee acts outside the stated rules.

Other commentators argue that codes of conduct are simply a marketing tool that companies can use to highlight to the public how well they behave.

In practice, a code of conduct will only work if management are seen to support it, for example by holding regular seminars at the business to promote ethical practice. The worst situation is where a code of conduct exists, but management openly deride its contents and instruct employees to disobey it.

Illustration 5 – Codes of ethics and codes of conduct

Tesco plc

Tesco states that it is committed to conducting its business in an ethical manner, treating employees, customers, suppliers and shareholders in a fair and honest manner and ensuring that there are constant and open channels of communication.

Tesco has a code of ethics for its employees, including a policy on the receipt of gifts and a grievance procedure to cover employment issues. Employees are able to ring a confidential telephone helpline to raise concerns about any failure to comply with legal obligations, health and safety issues, damage to the environment, etc.

Test your understanding 6

Business code of ethics

Are all the obligations in a company's code of ethics imposed on the employee, or does the company also take on obligations to behave ethically?

4 Ethical threats and dilemmas

4.1 Ethical threats

There are several key threats to ethical behaviour that accountants should attempt to avoid.

These include:

- **Self-interest threat** – this could occur where a financial or other interest influences an accountant's judgement and causes a conflict of interest. For example, by overstating the profits of a company they work for, an accountant may receive higher pay or bonuses.

- **Self-review threat** – this may occur when an accountant is required to re-evaluate their own previous judgement. For instance, if an accountant was asked to review and justify a business decision they made, it would be difficult for them to remain objective.

- **Advocacy** – can be a problem if an accountant is promoting a position or opinion to the point where their subsequent objectivity is compromised. This could occur when acting for a client when in litigation or disputes with third parties.

- **Familiarity threat** – can occur when an accountant becomes sympathetic to the interests of others due to a close personal relationship. This can seriously compromise professional judgement. This could occur if acting for clients over a long period, or when accepting gifts or preferential treatment from clients.

- **Intimidation threat** – occurs when an accountant is deterred from acting objectively by actual or perceived threats. This could be, for example, if an accountant is threatened with dismissal over a disagreement about application of an accounting principle.

4.2 Safeguards against ethical threats – professional bodies

In response to the ethical threats outlined above, the ACCA, along with other professional bodies, have put in place several safeguards to try to reduce or eliminate such threats.

These include:

- Ethics training for all professional accountants – both as part of their initial training and on an ongoing basis

- Creation of corporate governance requirements

- Professional or regulatory monitoring and disciplinary procedures

- Setting of professional standards.

4.3 Safeguards against ethical threats – business

Organisations can also help to reduce the threat of ethical breaches by their employees by, amongst other things, having an effective internal complaints procedure that enables the reporting of unprofessional and unethical behaviour.

They can also create a culture that makes it as easy as possible for employees to follow their professional codes and behave ethically.

There are six values that organisations can apply in order to accomplish this. They can be easily remembered using the acronym HOTTER.

- **H**onesty – employees should be encouraged to be honest at all times – even when this may be seen as detrimental to the organisation itself. For example, a salesperson should never overstate the benefits or features of the product they are selling.

- **O**penness – this means that the organisation should be willing to freely provide information, as needed, to stakeholders. This should make it easier for shareholders, for example, to decide whether to invest in the business or not.

- **T**ransparency – this is similar to openness in many ways and indicates that a company makes it easy for key stakeholders to review its activities. This can be helped by regular audits and the production of detailed reports on business activities.

- **T**rust – organisations need to be trustworthy in their dealings with others and attempt to work in the best interests of as many stakeholders as possible. This could involve, for instance, not overcharging customers.

- **E**mpowerment – this involves giving employees and other stakeholders more ability to make their own decisions. This will improve their self-image and their motivation.

- **R**espect – all employees and stakeholders should be treated with dignity by the organisation regardless of their age, gender, ethnicity, religion or sexuality.

If these principles are part of an organisation's values, it will foster an ethical culture which will make breaches of the IFAC and ACCA codes far less likely.

Test your understanding 7

B is an accountant at AFR Ltd – a small manufacturing company. Last year, B estimated that the launch of a new product, the GJH, would boost AFR's profits. The board of AFR is currently reviewing the performance of the GJH and have asked B to review the launch of the GJH and evaluate whether it was a success.

Which ethical threat is B facing?

A   Self-interest

B   Advocacy

C   Self-review

D   Familiarity

4.4 Dealing with unethical or illegal conduct

If an accountant uncovers unethical or illegal conduct within the organisation they work for, there is a series of steps that they should take to deal with the issue.

(1)   The accountant should first consult with whoever is responsible for governance or ethics within the organisation. This may be a Compliance Office, or the Board of Directors themselves.

(2)   If the problem remains unresolved, the accountant should take legal advice and/or advice from their professional body (e.g. ACCA).

(3)   If the situation still cannot be resolved, the accountant should consider reporting to the relevant authorities (if there is a legal or professional obligation to do so) and withdrawing from the engagement.

Test your understanding 8

K works for a retail company based in country H. She has recently uncovered that her employer is buying in goods from countries with poor labour conditions, even though they have assured their customers that all their goods are ethically sourced. This is not illegal in country H, though there would likely be a significant backlash against the retailer's products if this information were uncovered by the public.

Which of the following statements is correct?

A   As there are no legal implications of the retail company's actions, K should take no action

B   K should immediately report this to her professional body and ask for guidance

C   K should approach the Board of Directors and discuss the issue with them

D   K should report the ethical breach to the public and press as this would be in the public interest

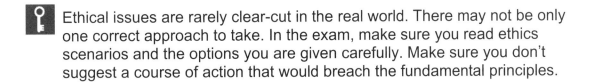

Ethical issues are rarely clear-cut in the real world. There may not be only one correct approach to take. In the exam, make sure you read ethics scenarios and the options you are given carefully. Make sure you don't suggest a course of action that would breach the fundamental principles.

5 Chapter summary

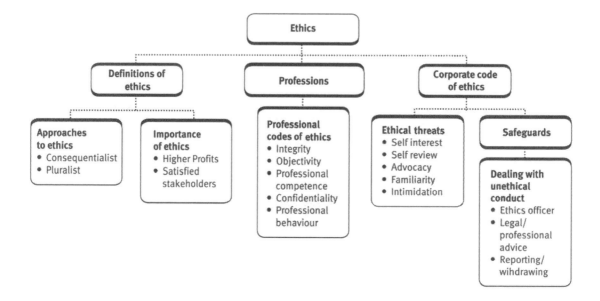

6 Practice questions

Test your understanding 9

AB is a large airline. A recent survey of its passengers indicated that 65% had problems due to other passengers allowing their children to create noise and disturbance on the aircraft. Families make up around 15% of AB's total passengers.

Which of the following courses of action would be regarded as a utilitarian point of view?

A   Do nothing, as families rights should be protected

B   Refuse to allow bookings for families

C   Provide entertainment for children on board to keep them occupied

D   Create a separate section on the planes for families with children

Test your understanding 10

Consider the following two statements:

(i)   Your supervisor at work instructs you to undertake an activity you believe to be illegal. This is an example of an ethical dilemma.

(ii)   Adopting a strong ethical code will tend to improve a company's relationship with investors.

Which of these statements is/are correct?

A   (i) only

B   (ii) only

C   Both

D   Neither

Test your understanding 11

Which of the following will be required before an occupation can be classified as a profession?

A   More than a given number of individuals must be in this occupation

B   The occupation must be governed by a professional organisation

C   Legal or political approval is needed

D   All members must be above a certain age

Test your understanding 12

Harry is an accountant in a large business. The Finance Director has asked him to lie to the other directors about the profitability of the company. Which fundamental ethical principle would Harry be breaching if he agreed to the request?

A   Objectivity

B   Confidentiality

C   Integrity

D   Professional competence

Test your understanding 13

Consider the following statements:

(i)   An auditor should not report unsafe or fraudulent activity within a client organisation, as this would breach the fundamental principle of confidentiality.

(ii)   Acting in the public interest refers to an accountant's duty to consider the general welfare of society in his or her work.

Which of these two statements is/are correct?

A   (i) only

B   (ii) only

C   Both

D   Neither

Test your understanding 14

A professional accountant is working in a South American country that has its own code of ethics for accountants, which is not as strict as that created by IFAC. Which of the following statements is correct?

A   The accountant must comply with the IFAC code, as it is stricter

B   The accountant only needs to comply with the local code

C   The accountant can choose which code to follow

D   The accountant can apply parts of both codes as he or she wishes, as codes of conduct are not mandatory

Test your understanding 15

Ash is an accountant who is currently helping to defend one of his clients, who is currently being prosecuted by the local government for tax evasion. Which ethical threat is Ash exposed to?

A   Self-interest

B   Familiarity

C   Intimidation

D   Advocacy

Test your understanding 16

(a)   The following are all qualities that you may see in a professional at work.

A   Objectivity

B   Honesty

C   Fairness

D   Confidentiality

E   Integrity

F   Professional appearance

G   Professional behaviour

H   Confidence

Required:

Write down which of the FOUR options from A – H contain fundamental principles of ethical behaviour from the IFAC and ACCA codes of ethics.

(0.5 marks each, total = 2 marks)

(b)   The following are examples of ethical threats:

A   Self-interest

B   Self-review

C   Advocacy

D   Familiarity

The following sentences contain gaps which specify the type of ethical threat that is being discussed.

1 tends to occur when an accountant is promoting a position or opinion to the point where their subsequent objectivity is compromised.

Required:

(i)   **Select the ethical threat which appropriately fills gap 1; i.e. select A, B, C or D.**

(1 mark)

If an accountant had to audit the financial results of a company that is owned and run by one of their friends, this would expose them to **2** risk.

Required:

(ii)   **Select the ethical threat which appropriately fills gap 2; i.e. select A, B, C or D.**

(1 mark)

(Total: 4 marks)

Test your understanding answers

Test your understanding 1

The correct answer is B – False

Business ethics is partly concerned with legal requirements, but also with areas that are not covered by the law.

Test your understanding 2

The correct answer is B

The pluralist approach involves trying to find a solution that caters to the needs of all stakeholders – in this case all employees that report to Joe. By reducing the hours slightly for all members of staff, this is the approach Joe is taking.

Test your understanding 3

The correct answer is B – False

The traditional view was always that ethical behaviour was a burden on business. If competitors were behaving unethically, then managers thought they had no choice other than to act unethically themselves. Initiatives such as Fairtrade have proved this traditional view to be false. Adherence to ethical practice can be shown to be a driver of new profit streams rather than as a cost burden.

Test your understanding 4

The correct answer is C

Any accountant, whether professional or otherwise, would be expected to comply with relevant legislation.

Test your understanding 5

The correct answer is A

There is no evidence that A has breached confidentiality in this scenario. However, he has produced an inaccurate profit figure, compromising his integrity. He is also breaching objectivity, as he is allowing self-interest to bring bias into his work. His actions, if discovered, would also bring the profession into disrepute, meaning that he is not displaying professional behaviour.

Test your understanding 6

The obligations in a company's code of ethics flow in both directions, from the company to individual stakeholders, and from stakeholders to the company. For example the company agrees to act ethically towards its employees, but each employee must also act ethically towards the company.

Test your understanding 7

The correct answer is C

B is being asked to re-evaluate his own professional judgement. Should product GJH have underperformed, it will be difficult for B to act impartially as he will want to support the original judgement he made – that the GJH was a good investment.

Test your understanding 8

The correct answer is C

Just because something is legal does not always make it ethical. Accountants must consider both ethics and legality in their work. This means that A is incorrect.

K can consult with her professional body, though this would normally be undertaken **after** discussing it with those responsible for ethics within the retailer itself, as suggested in C.

Finally, K would be breaching the fundamental principle of confidentiality by disclosing the issue to the public. Disclosures can only be made if there is a legal or professional reason to do so – which does not appear to be the case in this scenario.

Test your understanding 9

The correct answer is B

Utilitarians believe that an action is morally correct if it benefits the greatest number of people. The other three options involve either looking after the rights of the smaller group of families that travel (A) or reaching a compromise to try and avoid compromising the needs of any of the stakeholders (C and D).

Test your understanding 10

The correct answer is C

In an ethical dilemma, you have a morally difficult decision to make, involving judgement of what is the right or wrong thing to do in a given situation.

Ethics can improve the relationship between the business and investors, who can be reassured that the company is using their funding fairly.

Test your understanding 11

The correct answer is B

The main requirements are: mastering of skills during a period of training, governance by a professional organisation, compliance with an ethical code and a process of certification for new entrants.

Test your understanding 12

The correct answer is C

Integrity means truthfulness and fair dealing. It states that accountants must not be associated with false or misleading statements.

Test your understanding 13

The correct answer is B

The principle of confidentiality states that an accountant must not disclose information about a client as long as there is no professional or legal reason to do so. In the statement, both examples would give rise to legal reasons to report to the authorities.

Test your understanding 14

The correct answer is A

An accountant must always comply with IFAC codes unless this would be contrary to local regulations.

Test your understanding 15

The correct answer is D

Advocacy occurs when an accountant promotes a position or opinion to the point where their objectivity is lost. This may happen in court cases.

Test your understanding 16

(a) The correct answers are: **A, D, E and G**

(b) The correct answers are:

    (i)   **C** – this is the definition of advocacy.

    (ii)   **D** – this would be a classic example of a familiarity threat.

Governance and social responsibility in business

Chapter learning objectives

Upon completion of this chapter you will be able to:

- explain the concept of separation between ownership and control

- explain the agency concept in relation to corporate governance

- define corporate governance and social responsibility and explain their importance in contemporary organisations

- explain the responsibility of organisations to maintain appropriate standards of corporate governance and corporate social responsibility

- briefly explain the main recommendations of best practice in effective corporate governance: executive and non-executive directors, remuneration committees, audit committees and public oversight

- explain how organisations take account of their social responsibility objectives through analysis of the needs of internal, connected and external stakeholders

- identify the social and environmental responsibilities of business organisations to internal, connected and external stakeholders.

- explain the purposes of committees

- explain the types of committee used by business organisations

- list the advantages and disadvantages of committees

- explain the roles of the Chair and Secretary in a committee.

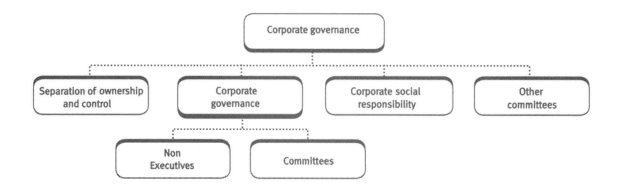

1 Separation of ownership and control

Separation of ownership and control refers to the situation in a company where the people who own the company (the shareholders) are not the same people as those who run the company (the Board of Directors).

This situation tends to occur in larger companies, where there may be many external shareholders who play no role in the day-to-day running of the company.

This separation can bring benefits for both parties.

- Specialist managers can often run the business more efficiently than those who own the company.

- Managers cannot personally contribute all the capital needed to run the business, so they have to bring in external capital from investors who often have no interest in the day-to-day operations of the company.

However, there is a risk that the directors may run the business in their own interests, rather than those of the shareholders and other stakeholders. This is referred to as the '**agency problem**'.

Note that smaller companies often do not have this issue, as in these organisations the directors are also likely to own all of the shares in the company, meaning that there is no separation of ownership and control.

Illustration 1 – The separation of ownership and control

The agency problem in a company

The directors of a large quoted company may hold a board meeting and vote themselves huge salaries, bonus shares if modest profitability targets are achieved, and contractual terms granting each of them huge compensation payments if they are dismissed. These are in the best interests of the directors, but not in the best interests of the shareholders who own the company and in whose interests the directors are meant to be working.

The problem of directors not operating in the company's best interests can be solved by aligning the interests of the directors and the interests of the company. For example, the directors could be paid a small basic salary and bonuses depending on the growth in profits achieved. Directors could be paid partly in shares to make them shareholders so that they have a direct interest in the share price and level of dividends. Adopting such procedures would reduce the agency problem of the directors acting as agents of themselves rather than as agents for the shareholders.

Test your understanding 1

The 'separation of ownership and control' refers to the fact that the owners of a company are always different people to the directors of the company.

Is this statement:

A True

B False

2 Corporate governance

Corporate governance is the set of processes and policies by which a company is directed, administered and controlled. It includes the appropriate role of the Board of Directors and of the auditors of a company.

Definitions of corporate governance

Consider two formal definitions of corporate governance:

- 'Corporate governance is the system by which companies are directed and controlled.'

  The Cadbury Report 'The Financial Aspects of Corporate Governance', 1992

- 'Corporate governance involves a set of relationships between a company's management, its board, its shareholders and other stakeholders. Corporate governance also provides the structure through which the objectives of the company are set, and the means of attaining those objectives and monitoring performance are determined.'

  The OECD 'Principles of Corporate Governance', 2004

The main recommendations of best practice in effective corporate governance tend to include the following areas:

* The membership of the Board of Directors – both executive and non-executive directors (NEDs).

* How directors' remuneration is decided and disclosed.

* The role of both internal and external audit.

* How the public, as a legitimate stakeholder in a large company, has a right to know how the company is being governed.

2.1 Non-executive directors (NEDs)

Whilst company law refers only to 'directors' in general, two types of director have emerged.

Those who are involved in the day-to-day running of the company are known as **executive directors**.

 Non-executive directors (NEDs) are not employees of the company and have no managerial responsibilities, meaning that they do not participate in the day-to-day running of the organisation.

However, NEDs do attend board meetings and therefore have a say in the strategic decision making of the company.

Roles

NEDs have several key roles in the organisation. According to the Higgs report (2003), these include:

* **Strategy** – NEDs should constructively challenge and contribute to the development of strategy.

* **Performance** – NEDs should scrutinise the performance of management in meeting agreed goals and objectives and monitoring senior management.

* **Risk** – NEDs should satisfy themselves that financial information is accurate and that financial controls and systems of risk management are robust and defensible.

* **People** – NEDs are responsible for determining appropriate levels of remuneration for executives and have a prime role in appointing, and where necessary removing, senior management and in succession planning.

Independence

NEDs should be independent as far as possible, in order to ensure that their oversight role can be carried out as effectively and responsibly as possible. This is similar to auditor independence, which is discussed in a later chapter.

NEDs must not:

- have been an employee of the company in the last five years

- have had a material business interest in the company for the last three years

- participate in the company's share options or pension schemes

- have close ties with company directors or senior employees

- serve as a NED for more than nine years with the same company.

If any of these apply to a NED, their independence will be seriously compromised.

Other recommendations

At least half of the board should be independent NEDs (excluding the Chairman of the Board, who is often also a NED). A smaller company should have at least two independent NEDs.

One of the independent NEDs should be appointed to be the 'senior independent director'. They are available to be contacted by shareholders who wish to raise matters outside the normal executive channels of communication.

It is also worth noting that good corporate governance recommends that the role of Chairman (who is responsible for the activities of the Board, such as appointing senior management and strategy development) should be distinct from the Chief Executive Officer (CEO) (who is responsible for the day-to-day running of the company). If one person holds both roles, it will give them too much power and allow them to individually dominate the running of the company.

Executive directors and NEDs would typically be required to stand for reelection by shareholders every three years. NEDs who have been with the company for over nine years must stand for re-election on an annual basis.

 Test your understanding 2

Mrs X retired from the post of Finance Director at AB plc a year ago. The company wishes to retain her experience within the company. Mrs X wishes to continue her involvement with the company as she owns 8% of the share capital of AB.

Because of this, the Managing Director of AB, one of Mrs X's close friends, has offered Mrs X a permanent position on the board as a non-executive director. As a non-executive, she is to be offered a 5% bonus each year if AB outperforms its targets.

Identify the five reasons that Mrs X will not be sufficiently independent in her role as a non-executive director at AB.

2.2 Remuneration committees

A remuneration committee is a committee made up of non-executive directors which is responsible for deciding on the pay and incentives offered to executive directors.

It is an important principle of corporate governance that no director should be involved in setting the level of their own remuneration.

The board of a listed company should therefore establish a remuneration committee of at least three (or two in the case of smaller companies) independent NEDs.

The remuneration committee is responsible for setting the remuneration of all of the executive directors, including pension rights and any compensation payments.

The whole Board of Directors should be responsible for deciding the level of remuneration for NEDs, although the decision may be delegated to a committee of the board.

Advantages and disadvantages of remuneration committees

Advantages of having a remuneration committee:

- It avoids the agency problem of directors deciding their own levels of remuneration.

- It leaves the board free to make strategic decisions about the company's future.

Disadvantages of having a remuneration committee:

- There is a danger of a 'you scratch my back, I'll scratch yours' situation in that the NEDs might recommend high remuneration for the executive directors on the understanding that the executives will recommend high remuneration for the NEDs.

- There will be a cost involved in preparing for and holding committee meetings.

Test your understanding 3

Which of the following can non-executive directors accept as remuneration from the company?

A   A fixed daily rate for their time

B   Shares

C   Pension payments

D   Equity options

2.3 The audit committee

 An **audit committee** consists of independent NEDs who are responsible for monitoring and reviewing the company's internal financial controls and the integrity of the financial statement.

The audit committee acts as an interface between the full board of directors and both the internal and external auditors.

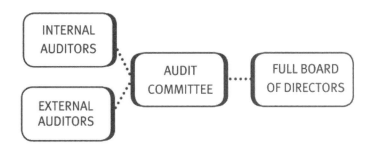

Responsibilities of audit committees

These include the following:

- Reviewing accounting policies and financial statements as a whole to ensure that they are appropriate and balanced.

- Review systems of internal controls and risk management within the organisation. (Note that risk management may be dealt with by a separate committee – the risk committee.)

- Agreement of the work agenda for the internal audit department, as well as reviewing the results of internal audit work.

- Making recommendations to the board, for them to put to the shareholders, relating to the appointment and removal of the external auditors as well as their remuneration and terms of engagement.

- Liaising with the external auditors, in particular relating to the review and monitoring of the external auditor's independence and objectivity as well as the effectiveness of the audit process.

The main advantage of an audit committee is that it allows auditors to report their findings to independent directors. This avoids a number of possible problems, including:

- External auditors do not have to report frauds or errors to the executive directors, who may be responsible for perpetrating them.

- Internal auditors are unlikely to feel comfortable reporting systems weaknesses to the executive directors, who will have designed the systems.

2.4 Nomination committee

A nomination committee is formed in order to ensure that the composition of the board is balanced. It monitors the process for appointment of directors to the board of directors as well as making recommendations for appointments to the board.

Typically, when recommending appointments, the nominations committee needs to consider the overall size of the board, as well as other factors, such as:

* the various skills needed to be present on the board

* the mix of executive and non-executive directors

* the need for continuity in the board

* the need to attract directors from diverse backgrounds to improve the organisation's strategy.

2.5 Public oversight

As mentioned earlier, the public is a legitimate stakeholder in a large company. This means that the public has a 'right to know' how such a company is being governed as well as a right to be involved in the governance process.

The most obvious means of public oversight of corporate governance is via the publication by companies of their Annual Report and financial statements. These will disclose a number of important matters, such as the role and actions of the audit and remuneration committees during the year, as well as the composition of the board.

While companies are required by law to send a copy of this information to every shareholder, most companies will also post a copy on their website or will provide a paper-based copy to any member of the public who requests one.

In addition, most companies are required to submit their annual financial statements to a regulatory body (Companies House in the UK) so that any interested parties can review them.

Some countries and/or industries have set up **public oversight boards**. These organisations monitor whether organisations are complying with relevant rules and regulations and take action against those that fail to meet the required standards.

Illustration 2 – Public oversight of corporate governance

JJB Sports Independent NEDs

Among the independent NEDs at sportswear company JJB Sports is Matthew Pinsent – an Olympic gold medal winning rower. He is well known to the public and has a good reputation, so the public may see him as representing the views of wider society. Pinsent may have little or no experience of big business, but the public would not necessarily see this as a disadvantage in representing them on the board.

2.6 Benefits of corporate governance to the organisation

Corporate governance will increase costs as well as the complexity of the company's decision-making process. So why do companies adopt good corporate governance?

Reasons include:

- **Business success** – improved controls and decision-making will aid corporate success as well as growth in revenues and profits.

- **Investor confidence** – corporate governance will mean that investors are more likely to trust that the company is being well run. This will not only make it easier and cheaper for the company to raise finance, but also has a positive effect on the share price.

- **Minimisation of wastage** – strong corporate governance should help to minimise waste within the organisation, as well as corruption, risks and mismanagement.

- **Listing requirements** – following corporate governance guidelines is required by many stock exchanges (such as the London Stock Exchange) in order to obtain a listing.

3   Corporate social responsibility

Corporate social responsibility (CSR) refers to the idea that a company should be sensitive to the needs and wants of all its stakeholders, rather than just the shareholders.

It refers to an organisation's obligation to maximise its positive impacts upon stakeholders while minimising the negative effects.

Note that CSR is closely linked to **sustainable development**, which suggests that organisations should use resources in such a way that they do not compromise the needs of future generations.

As mentioned above, CSR involves being sensitive to the needs of an organisation's stakeholders. This means that in order to improve its CSR position, an organisation must first understand who its stakeholders are and what they expect.

What is corporate social responsibility?

A formal definition of CSR has been proposed by the World Business Council for Sustainable Development (WBCSD):

'CSR is the continuing commitment by business to behave ethically and contribute to economic development while improving the quality of life of the workforce and their families as well as of the local community and society at large.'

WBCSD meeting in The Netherlands, 1998

The WBCSD see CSR fitting into overall corporate responsibility as follows:

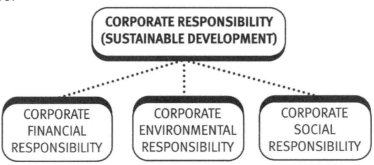

However the distinctions between each category can be blurred. Key issues in the CSR debate include:

- employee rights, e.g. laws to prohibit ageism and other discrimination at work

- environmental protection, e.g. reducing factory emissions of poisons and pollutants

- supplier relations

- community involvement.

Illustration 3 – The meaning of corporate social responsibility

Marks and Spencer

Marks and Spencer promotes itself as a responsible business that takes the challenge of CSR seriously. It aims to listen and respond to the needs of its shareholders and build up good relationships with its employees, suppliers and society at large.

Marks and Spencer approach CSR by following three basic principles:

- products – throughout the three stages of each product's life (production, selling and usage), the aim is to encourage ethically and environmentally responsible behaviour

- people – everyone who works at the company is entitled to a mix of benefits. This approach is also encouraged amongst the company's suppliers, franchisees and other business partners

- places – the company recognises its obligations to the communities in which it trades. Successful retailing requires economically healthy and sustainable communities.

3.1 Stakeholder needs analysis

Stakeholder needs analysis involves an organisation undertaking research to determine:

- Who its key stakeholders are, and;

- What their needs are.

Typical stakeholders (internal, external and connected) and their needs have already been identified in chapter five. However, a typical list is not what should be created here. Each company must sit down with a blank sheet of paper and identify the stakeholders of **their** business.

For example, if a company has $1 m in the bank earning modest interest, then the bank is probably not a key stakeholder. In another company with a $100m debt to the bank and large interest payments, the bank is clearly an extremely important stakeholder.

Once the organisation has identified its stakeholders, it needs to understand what their needs and wants are. There is no better way of accomplishing this than asking them directly. Possible methods include:

- questionnaires

- focus groups

- direct interviews or interviews with representatives.

Illustration 4 – Stakeholder needs analysis

Car manufacturers

As well as being sensitive to the requirements of customers with respect to factors such as price and performance, a car manufacturer should also consider the following:

- public attitudes to pollution

- government policies on road tax and fuel tax

As a result it may choose to develop more environmentally-friendly vehicles as part of its long term strategy even if current demand is for larger cars, say.

Test your understanding 4

Supplier to a supermarket

A supermarket buys its goods on credit and sells them for cash, therefore it has strong cash flows at all times. What are the business needs of a supplier to such a supermarket in its relationship with the supermarket?

To some stakeholders, the company owes obligations arising from the law (e.g. to pay employees their salary each month, or to compensate them if they are made redundant). However, other obligations arise voluntarily due to the company's commitment to CSR (e.g. to discuss their plans with interested pressure groups before a particular plan is adopted).

Illustration 5 – Responsibilities of businesses to stakeholders

888.com

888.com is an internet gambling site that is listed on the London Stock Exchange. It is headquartered in Gibraltar and operates under a licence granted by the Government of Gibraltar. It has responsibilities to the following stakeholders:

- **Shareholders** – since it is listed on the London Stock Exchange it must comply with the rules of that exchange, including adopting the UK Corporate Governance Code.

- **Employees** – to be a good employer to all its members of staff.

- **Customers** – to offer a fair, regulated and secure environment in which to gamble.

- **Government** – to comply with the terms of its licence granted in Gibraltar.

- **The public** – the company chooses to sponsor several sports teams as part of strengthening its brand. The company also tries to address public concerns about the negative aspects of gambling, e.g. by identifying compulsive gamblers on their site and taking appropriate action.

3.2 The importance of CSR

Traditionally adopting a CSR approach to business has been seen as having a number of drawbacks, including:

- Increased cost of sourcing materials from ethical sources (e.g. free-range eggs)

- Having to turn away business from customers considered to be unethical

- The management time that can be taken up by CSR planning and implementation.

However, more recently businesses have been starting to see a number of key benefits to being socially responsible, such as:

- Good CSR can attract customers by enhancing the organisation's reputation

- An ethical approach to business will help to attract and retain good quality employees

- Avoiding pollution will save the money in the long term – many governments are now fining or increasing taxes for more polluting businesses

- Being environmentally friendly can save money – for example being energy efficient will not just benefit the environment, it will also lower the organisation's utilities bill!

Illustration 6 – The importance of CSR to an organisation

BAA plc

BAA owns and operates seven airports in the UK. BAA recognises that they are responsible, both directly and indirectly, for a variety of environmental, social and economic impacts from their operations.

Positive impacts: employing 12,000 people; allowing business people to travel to meetings, thus supporting the global economy; allowing tourists to enrich their cultural experiences; allowing dispersed families to visit each other.

Negative impacts: large consumption of fossil fuels; emission of greenhouse gases; noise affecting people living close to airports.

BAA sees its CSR programme as managing these operational impacts in order to earn the trust of their stakeholders.

For example, local people living near airports are sensitive to the noise of aircraft approaching and taking off. If BAA did nothing about this issue, local people could complain to politicians who could pass laws to curb the number of flights which would damage the company. As part of its CSR programme, BAA will therefore offer to buy the properties of local people concerned about aircraft noise, or will offer to pay for sound-proofing of the properties.

You should consider whether such expenditure is an expense against the company's profits, or an investment in building up a strategic asset of goodwill among the local community.

Test your understanding 5

Which of the following benefits could be realised from a successful CSR programme?

- Improvement in innovation by identifying new market opportunities.

- Improvement in the company's reputation.

- Improvement in relationships with internal and external stakeholders.

- Maintenance of strategic assets such as licences to operate.

Select one from the following four options:

A   (i), (ii) and (iii) only

B   (ii), (iii) and (iv) only

C   (i), (iii) and (iv) only

D   (i), (ii), (iii) and (iv)

4   Committees

So far, we have looked at two committees that are required as part of corporate governance – the audit and remuneration committees. We now need to spend some time looking in detail at how these committees, and indeed committees in general, are run.

4.1 What is a committee?

A committee is a group of people who are appointed to administer, discuss or make reports concerning a subject.

Typically, committees

- tend to be permanent, or at least long-term

- have authority

- follow well-established procedures

- provide a way of making difficult decisions by involving key individuals and departments.

4.2 The purposes of committees

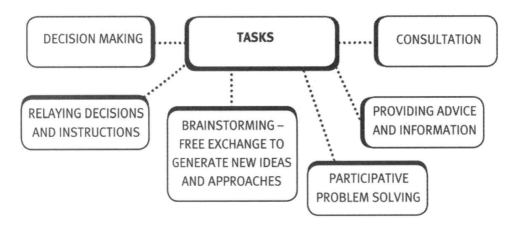

The major purposes of committees include:

- The committee can **brainstorm** new ideas for the organisation.

- They allow a number of people with different skills and knowledge to work together in a **coordinated** manner.

- They can act as a **delaying mechanism**.

- They can help to **make or implement decisions** within the organisation.

- They can **oversee a function or procedure**. For example, public oversight boards are committees formed to minimise the risk of an organisation breaching legislative requirements.

- They can **gather information** about a particular issue.

4.3 Types of committee used by business organisations

There are several specific types of committee that you need to know about for your exam.

- **Executive committee** – this is a committee with administrative powers which meets frequently to manage the affairs of an organisation. The Board of Directors of a company is an example of an executive committee, which is appointed by directors to run the company.

- **Standing committee** – these are formed for a particular purpose on a **permanent basis**.

- **Ad hoc committee** – these are formed to **complete a particular task** and may well be temporary.

- **Sub-committee** – this is simply a **subordinate committee** comprised of members appointed by a parent committee. This could be to look into a particular issue or as a way of helping the parent committee deal with its workload.

Illustration 7 – Examples of business committees

There are many different types of committees within companies, including:

- The Board of Directors – an executive committee formed to oversee the running of the company.

- The Audit Committee – made up of directors who review the company's accounting policies, internal controls and annual financial statements. They also liaise with the company's external auditors.

- The Remuneration Committee – examines the pay and conditions offered to the directors of the company.

- Ethics committees – these oversee the working practices and procedures of an organisation regarding conflicts of interest, confidential information, environmental issues, etc.

Test your understanding 6

H plc has appointed five members of staff to a new committee. This committee's purpose is to investigate a one-off failure in H's production processes that led to the loss of $100,000 worth of products and to make recommendations as to how H can avoid similar problems in the future.

Which type of committee is this?

A   Standing

B   Executive

C   Ad hoc

D   Permanent

4.4 Advantages and disadvantages of committees

Advantages of committees

- Committees bring together individuals with the necessary skills or knowledge for the successful completion of a given task.

- Committees tend to slow the decision-making process down. This means that hasty, poorly-considered decisions are less likely to be made.

- Decisions are likely to be more easily accepted by the organisation as they have been made by a committee with representatives from many departments.

- As mentioned earlier, setting up committees can delay the decision-making process, buying a company time.

- More people are involved in the decision-making process, leading to increased motivation.

- Collective responsibility means that no individual member of the committee is likely to be held responsible for the consequences of the committee's recommendations.

Disadvantages

- Committees tend to be slow at making decisions. This could not only make the organisation miss out on valuable opportunities, but it also increases the costs of the decision-making process.

- Collective responsibility means that no individual is likely to be held accountable for the poor performance of the committee, reducing the motivation of the committee members.

- Members of committees may wish to further the objectives of their own departments. This can lead to conflict within the committee, affecting its effectiveness.

- Committees tend to work based on compromise between the various members. This may mean that they fail to recommend decisive action where needed.

- Committee members normally only attend committees part-time. The rest of the time they will have to continue with their normal work-load. This can mean that members take committee work less seriously and that they are not always able to attend committee meetings, further slowing decision-making down.

- Some 'experienced' committee members may dominate.

4.5 Key roles in the committee

There are likely to be two key roles that are essential for the proper functioning of a committee.

The Chairperson

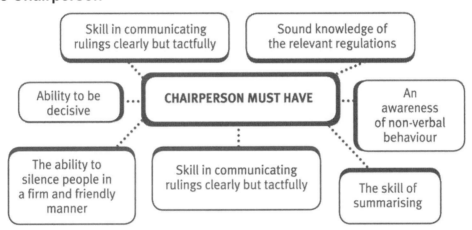

The Chair is a crucial role that involves guiding the proceedings at committee meetings.

The Chair will be responsible for:

- **Keeping the meeting on schedule and agenda** – he or she must ensure all relevant issues are discussed.

- **Maintaining order** – ensuring that only one person at a time speaks.

- **Impartiality** – the Chair must ensure that all parties have a reasonable opportunity to speak and express their views.

- **Summing up** – ascertaining the overall conclusion of the meeting by summing up or putting the issue to a vote and announcing the result.

- **Checking and signing the minutes of the meeting** – this depends on the formality of the meeting itself.

The Secretary

This individual undertakes all the administration relating to the committee and supports the Chair in ensuring the smooth running of the committee.

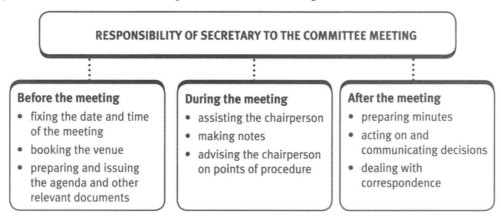

RESPONSIBILITY OF SECRETARY TO THE COMMITTEE MEETING

Before the meeting
- fixing the date and time of the meeting
- booking the venue
- preparing and issuing the agenda and other relevant documents

During the meeting
- assisting the chairperson
- making notes
- advising the chairperson on points of procedure

After the meeting
- preparing minutes
- acting on and communicating decisions
- dealing with correspondence

5 Chapter summary

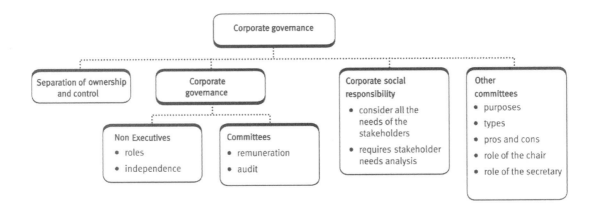

6   Practice questions

Test your understanding 7

Consider the following two statements:

(i)   The separation of ownership and control is only relevant in the context of limited companies.

(ii)   Corporate social responsibility is concerned with a company's obligations to just its external stakeholders.

Which of these statements is/are correct?

A   (i) only

B   (ii) only

C   Both

D   Neither

Test your understanding 8

Which of the following would reduce the agency problem in a large quoted company?

A   Pay the directors a fixed amount of salary each year

B   Pay the directors a bonus of shares based on the reported profits

C   Employ the directors on a rolling five-year contract

D   Offer the directors large compensation payments if they are dismissed

Test your understanding 9

What proportion of the board members of a large UK-listed company should be made up of independent non-executive directors?

A   At least one quarter

B   At least one third

C   At least half

D   At least two thirds

Test your understanding 10

Mrs X has been asked to act as a non-executive director of H plc. Which of the following facts about her would prevent her from taking this role?

(i)   She owns 20% of the share capital of H plc.

(ii) She is to be paid $20,000 per annum as a fee for her new role.

(iii) Up until last month, she was an executive director of H plc.

A   (i) and (ii) only

B   (i) and (iii) only

C   (iii) only

D   (ii) only

Test your understanding 11

What is the primary role of a public oversight board?

A   Oversight of the internal audit function

B   Creation of accounting standards

C   Monitoring corporate compliance with key rules and regulations

D   Writing legislation to target poor corporate behaviour

Test your understanding 12

Which of the following is NOT a major purpose of committees?

A   Gathering of information about a given issue

B   Speeding up the decision-making process

C   Overseeing a function or procedure

D   Co-ordination

Test your understanding 13

Which of the following is an advantage of using a committee rather than an individual to make a decision?

A   Increased accountability for the quality of the decision made

B   Increased speed in decision-making

C   Reduced conflict in the decision-making process

D   Increased acceptance of the decision made by the rest of the organisation

Test your understanding 14

(a) Here are a number of statements relating to non-executive directors:

A   They must not participate in the company's share option schemes.

B   They may participate in the day-to-day running of the organisation.

C   They should not serve on the board of the same company for more than seven years.

D   They may not challenge executive strategies, as the executive directors are directly voted in by the shareholders.

E   They should form just over half of the remuneration committee within the company.

F   They should take a major role in appointing and removing senior management.

G   They should not have had a material business interest in the company for the last three years.

H   They should not have close personal ties to the executive directors.

Required:

Write down which of the FOUR options (A–H) given in the list above are correct with regards to non-executive directors.

(0.5 marks each, total = 2 marks)

(b) The following relate to the disadvantages of operating a system of good corporate social responsibility (CSR):

A   Increased materials costs

B   Reduction in corporate image and reputation

C   Increased scrutiny of corporate activities

D   Having to turn away business

E   Loss of key personnel

F   Management time taken up

G   Reduction in wastage of resources

H   Increased chance of government legislation

Required:

Select FOUR of the above options that are actual disadvantages of CSR to an organisation.

(0.5 marks each, total = 2 marks)

(Total: 4 marks)

Test your understanding answers

Test your understanding 1

The correct answer is B – False

In a small company the directors of the company (perhaps a husband and wife) are often the sole shareholders of the company, so the agency problem does not arise. The problem is potentially most serious in a large quoted company where there is a professional board of directors and many (perhaps thousands or even millions) external shareholders.

Test your understanding 2

1   Mrs A has been an employee of the company within the last five years.

2   She has a significant business interest in AB due to her 8% holding in the shares of the company.

3   She is a close friend of the Managing Director, which will compromise her independence.

4   She is being offered a permanent non-executive position. This is inappropriate.

5   She should not be allowed to participate in any of AB's bonus schemes, share options or pensions schemes.

Test your understanding 3

The correct answer is A

NEDs should be paid fees that reflect the time commitment and the responsibilities of the role, e.g. a fixed daily rate for when they work for the company. Share options should not be granted to NEDs since this would detract from the detached judgement that they should bring, and it would also prevent them from being identified as 'independent' NEDs.

Test your understanding 4

The needs of a supplier to a supermarket are:

- a long-term business relationship so the supplier can plan for the future

- a large value of goods sold on regular orders

- agreed quality standards that both parties can work with

- fair prices

- prompt payments on the agreed dates.

Test your understanding 5

The correct answer is B

Note that these benefits will not be automatically achieved by any expenditure on CSR activities. There must be a well managed coherent programme which is being followed.

Test your understanding 6

The correct answer is C

This committee has been formed for one purpose. Once this has been completed, it will presumably be disbanded. As such is not likely to be a standing committee (also known as a permanent committee). It is not an executive committee as there is no evidence that it has the power to enact its recommended changes – merely to report its findings.

Test your understanding 7

The correct answer is D

The concept of the separation of ownership and control is relevant anywhere that the decision-makers do not bear a major share of the wealth effects of their decisions – such as charities, local and national governments, mutuals, and so on.

Corporate social responsibility is concerned with a company's obligation to all its stakeholders, both internal and external.

Test your understanding 8

The correct answer is B

Paying a bonus in shares would motivate directors to maximise shareholder wealth, helping to align their aims with those of the investors.

Test your understanding 9

The correct answer is C

Test your understanding 10

The correct answer is B

NEDs should not have a material business interest in the company, which a 20% shareholding would represent. In addition, having recently acted as an executive director, it will be difficult for Mrs X to remain objective.

Test your understanding 11

The correct answer is C

By definition.

Test your understanding 12

The correct answer is B

Committees may actually act as a delaying mechanism. Involving groups of people in the decision-making process rarely speeds the process up!

Test your understanding 13

The correct answer is D

Making a decision by committee tends to mean that individuals are able to 'hide' behind the collective responsibility of the group, leading to less accountability. Decisions tend to be slower when made by committee and differences of opinion between committee members may increase conflict. However, having a group make a decision is likely to increase acceptance by the organisation as the committee is likely to be made up of individuals from a range of different parts of the organisation.

Test your understanding 14

(a) The correct answers are: **A, F, G & H**. Note that NEDs are not allowed to run the business on a day-to-day basis (as this is the role of the executive directors). NEDs may not serve on the board for more than **nine** years, they are supposed to challenge any strategies that they feel are not in the best interests of the organisation, and they should make up the entire remuneration committee.

(b) The correct answers are **A, C, D & F**. The others are not likely drawbacks of a CSR approach.

Law and regulation governing accounting

Chapter learning objectives

Upon completion of this chapter you will be able to:

- explain basic legal requirements in relation to retaining and submitting proper records and preparing and auditing financial reports

- explain the broad consequences of failing to comply with the legal requirements for maintaining and filing accounting records

- explain how the international accountancy profession regulates itself through the establishment of reporting standards and their monitoring.

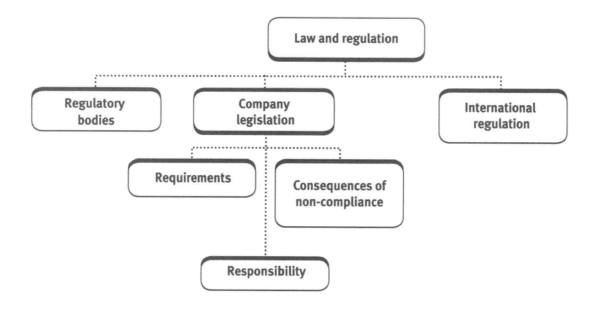

1 Authorities to whom companies are accountable

Many countries have enacted legislation controlling the retention and submission of proper accounting records and financial statements. This legislation predominantly applies to companies, as governments attempt to ensure that they are accountable for their actions.

There are usually several bodies that companies find themselves accountable to.

1.1 Regulatory bodies

In most countries, there is a government department which has been set up to oversee the regulation and accounts of companies. In the UK, this is known as **Companies House**, but it goes by various names in other countries (such as Companies Commission in Malaysia).

Companies are usually required to submit their financial statements to these bodies so that interested parties can inspect them.

In addition to their financial statements, companies may also have to retain and submit certain key documents, such as a Register of Shareholders and a Register of Directors.

Test your understanding 1

Companies are required to submit financial statements to Companies House, or a similar body, so that interested parties can inspect them.

Complete the following table, stating reasons why these parties would want to view the financial statements.

Party	Reason
Audit firm	
Competitor	
Supplier	
Job applicant	
Journalist	
Analyst	

Test your understanding 2

In addition to the financial statements, companies are often required to submit additional information to Companies House (or similar).

Complete the following table, showing why each type of information should be available for public inspection.

Information	Reason why made available
Register of Directors	
Register of Shareholders	
Register of Charges *	

* This shows which assets of the company have a charge over them, meaning that if the company fails to repay a loan the lender (who has 'taken' the charge) can seize the assets and sell them.

1.2 Tax authorities

Companies, as well as individuals, are accountable to the tax authorities in the countries in which they are based. They have to prepare tax returns each year, showing the amount of taxable profits they have earned in the period.

For many countries, businesses will also have to submit returns showing the amount of sales tax (value added tax or VAT) that they owe to the tax authorities.

1.3 Other authorities

Companies and other organisations may be accountable to other regulatory authorities.

For example, in the UK:

- Most businesses in the financial services industry handle client money. The FCA (Financial Conduct Authority) and the PRA (Prudential Regulation Authority) are public bodies that monitor and control the activities of organisations within this industry, to protect clients against failure or poor advice.

- Charities have access to public money, so the Charity Commission is a public body that registers all charities and monitors their activities.

- Utilities, such as gas and electricity providers need to offer a reliable, fair and safe service across the country. OFGEM is a public body in the UK that regulates the activities of these organisations.

Regulated industries normally have to produce some form of accounting information for the regulator.

1.4 Summary

In order to satisfy the relevant authorities, most organisations have to retain their accounting records and information for a minimum period (usually seven years), in case the authorities wish to verify information at a future date.

2 Legislation governing financial statements

For companies legislation covers not only the need to prepare financial statements, but also how they should be prepared – including issues such as frequency and format.

This helps to ensure that interested parties are able to access the financial statements of a company, as well as making sure that they have been prepared in an understandable way.

This legislation varies between countries, but in the UK it is known as the Companies Act 2006 (or CA2006).

2.1 Typical requirements for financial statements

The CA2006 in the UK requires that financial statements are produced that give a **true and fair** view of the position and performance of the company. The term 'true and fair' is not defined in company law, but normally means that the financial statements:

- **follow all appropriate accounting standards**

- **contain information of sufficient quantity to satisfy the reasonable expectations of the users** – indicating that the information must be adequately detailed. For example, it would not be acceptable to list 'current assets' without showing the different categories of current assets.

- **follow generally-accepted practice**

- **should not contain any material misstatement** – the information should be reasonably accurate, and should not contain errors that would be large enough to alter the view of the company's affairs.

Companies are also required to maintain proper accounting records which are sufficient to show and explain the transactions. The content of these records is not defined, but a record of transactions, assets and liabilities would be required as a minimum.

Test your understanding 3

State whether each of the following statements is true or false. If false, explain why.

- If financial statements give a true and fair view it means they are accurate.

- If financial statements give a true and fair view it means there is no fraud.

2.2 Responsibility for financial records

 Under company legislation, directors are responsible for producing financial statements that give a true and fair view.

This is delegated within the company to the Finance Director (FD) or the Chief Financial Officer (CFO). The financial reporting function within the accounting department will assist the FD with this.

If the FD does not have the skills to prepare the financial statements, an external accounting firm may be asked to provide assistance.

Test your understanding 4

Consider the following three statements:

(i)   The FD is required by the Companies Acts to prepare the financial statements.

(ii)   The management accounting section is primarily involved in preparing the financial statements.

(iii)   If a firm of accountants may be hired to help with accounts preparation at the end of the year, then they are responsible for them being true and fair.

Which of these statements is/are correct?

A   (i) only

B   (i) and (ii) only

C   (iii) only

D   None

3   Consequences of compliance failure

Failure to keep proper accounting records or to prepare regular financial statements that give a true and fair view are both criminal offences.

In both cases, the responsibility is that of the directors, who can be fined for failure to comply. Should the company be listed it may have its shares suspended by the stock exchange, meaning that they cannot be traded.

There may be further problems with the tax authorities if records are found to be inaccurate. If the tax authorities launch an investigation and discover that too little tax has been paid, then the company may be guilty of tax evasion, which is illegal.

If the poor accounting records mean that the financial statements do not show a true and fair view, the company's auditors may give a qualified audit report (see later chapter for more detail). This can damage the company's reputation and make it harder and more expensive to raise finance.

Finally, failure to keep adequate accounting records could mean that the company has insufficient information relating to areas such as receivables and payables. It may therefore fail to collect money owed from customers on time, leading to cash flow problems. Failure to pay suppliers on time may lead to lost goodwill as well as the removal of the company's trade credit facilities.

Test your understanding 5

Identify how failure to maintain proper accounting records could lead to corporate failure.

4 International regulation of the accountancy profession

As mentioned above, companies need to follow the requirements of the Companies Act (or equivalent) and the tax authorities of the country in which they operate.

However, the accountancy profession is keen to be 'self-regulating', meaning that the profession would prefer to issue its own regulations and deal with problems itself, rather than relying on legislation.

This has led to companies not only having to follow the requirements of their country's company legislation, but also of various standard-setting bodies which were linked to their country's accountancy profession.

By the 1970's, this meant that there were a wide range of different accounting standards being applied in different countries across the world. It became increasingly difficult for international investors to compare the financial statements of companies in different countries.

To deal with this problem, the International Financial Reporting Standards (IFRS) Foundation (formerly known as the IASCF) was formed to try and harmonise (i.e. make more similar) accounting standards in different countries.

Test your understanding 6

Julia is considering investing in one of two companies.

ABC Limited is a travel company based in the UK. XYZ Limited is an aluminium company based in Jamaica.

List five problems Julia faces in comparing the financial statements of these two companies.

4.1 The role of the IFRS Foundation

The IFRS Foundation is the supervisory body for the IASB (see below) and is responsible for governance issues and ensuring each member body is properly funded.

The principle objectives of the IFRS Foundation are to:

- develop a set of high quality, understandable, enforceable and globally accepted financial reporting standards

- promote the use and rigorous application of these standards

- to take account of the financial reporting needs of emerging economies and small and medium sized entities

- bring about the convergence of national and international financial reporting standards.

The **International Accounting Standards Board (IASB)** is the independent standard setting body of the IFRS Foundation. Its members are responsible for the development and publication of IFRSs and interpretations.

The **IFRS Interpretations Committee (IFRS IC)** reviews widespread accounting issues (in the context of IFRS) on a timely basis and provides authoritative guidance on these issues (IFRICs).

The **IFRS Advisory Council (IFRS AC)** is the formal advisory body to the IASB and the IFRS Foundation. It is comprised of a wide range of members who are affected by the IASB's work. Their objectives include:

- advising the IASB on agenda decisions and priorities in their work

- informing the IASB of the views of the Council with regard to major standard-setting projects and

- giving other advice to the IASB or to the Trustees.

4.2 The role of the IASB

The IASB is an independent standard-setting body which is based in London. It has 14 members from nine countries.

The IASB's aims are to develop a single set of high quality, understandable and enforceable global accounting standards and to co-operate with national accounting standard-setters to achieve convergence in accounting standards around the world.

Standards produced by the IASC, the forerunner to the IASB, are called International Accounting Standards (IASs). Standards produced by the IASB are called International Financial Reporting Standards (IFRSs). Collectively these are international accounting standards.

Nearly 100 countries adopt international standards or amend their national standards to bring them into line with international standards.

A new standard starts life as a Discussion Paper (DP). The IASB assigns a working group to develop a new standard, following input from the SAC, and produces a first draft with some points for discussion. This is then made available for public comment.

The views expressed on the DP are taken into account in producing the next draft, known as an Exposure Draft (ED). Again public comment is invited.

Finally an IFRS is issued. The IFRS may later be amended if necessary.

Test your understanding 7

Over 100 countries have adopted international standards or have amended their national standards to comply with international standards.

Give three reasons why countries would want to do this.

4.3 Regulation within the UK

Accounting standards in the UK are written by the **FRC** (Financial Reporting Council). One of its subsidiary committees – the **ASB** (Accounting Standards Board) controls the creation of UK accounting standards, known as Financial Reporting Standards (FRSs).

Note that the FRSs have replaced most of the earlier UK accounting standards, known as Statements of Standard Accounting Practice (SSAPs), however any SSAPs that have not yet been replaced by an FRS are still in force.

The FRC is then broken down into a number of other committees, including:

- **Auditing Practices Board (APB)** – which establishes standards and guidance for the auditing of companies (which will be examined in more detail in a later chapter).

- **The Professional Oversight Board** – which provides independent oversight and regulation of the accountancy profession within the UK.

- **The Financial Reporting Review Board** – examines the accounts of large organisations and investigates any failure to comply with appropriate accounting practices.

- **The Accounting and Actuarial Disciplinary Board** – which enforces codes of conduct and professional behaviour on accountants within the UK.

5 Chapter summary

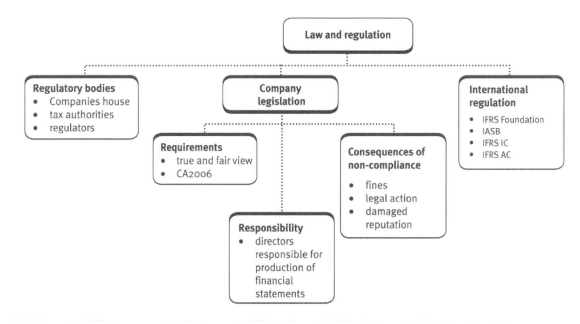

6 Practice questions

Test your understanding 8

The following are typical sanctions that can be imposed on a company.

(1) Qualification of the audit report by the external auditor

(2) Suspension of trading of the company's shares on the stock exchange

(3) Investigation by government officials

(4) Fines by the government registration body

Which two of the above would be imposed on a company for failing to publish its financial statements?

A   (1) and (2)

B   (1) and (3)

C   (2) and (3)

D   (2) and (4)

Test your understanding 9

Which of the following are advantages of having legislation which governs the preparation of financial statements?

A   Guaranteed minimum levels of disclosure of financial matters

B   Companies behave in a more ethical manner

C   Accounts prepared in different countries are more comparable

D   Accounts comply with accounting standards

Test your understanding 10

Which of the following is NOT necessary in order for financial statements to give a true and fair view?

A   They must follow generally accepted practice

B   They must follow all relevant accounting standards

C   They must be free from significant error

D   They must be free from all fraud

Test your understanding 11

SDF plc is a large, multinational company. The Finance Director heads up the department that produces the annual accounts. He is helped by a large external accountancy provider. After the accounts were audited and published, it was discovered that the Finance Director had made a number of errors, meaning that the published accounts were significantly inaccurate.

Whose is responsible for SDF's accounts failing to show a true and fair view?

A The Board of Directors as a whole

B The Finance Director, as he was incompetent

C The accountancy provider as they failed to notice the errors

D The external auditor

Test your understanding 12

Which of the following are produced as part of the process of preparing international accounting standards (IASs)?

A Interpretation

B Exposure draft

C Directive

D Regulation

Test your understanding 13

Which of the following develops and publishes IFRSs and interpretations?

A SAC

B IASB

C I FRS AC

D IFRS IC

Test your understanding answers

Test your understanding 1

Party	Reason
Audit firm	To get background information on client/potential client.
Competitor	To assess market share and profitability of competitor.
Supplier	To consider likelihood of payment before allowing credit.
Job applicant	To gain background information about the company prior to interview, to consider whether company is likely fail.
Journalist	To write an article on the company's results.
Analyst	To make recommendations on purchases to investors/clients.

Test your understanding 2

Information	Reason why made available
Register of Directors	So that people know who the directors are, and what other companies they are directors of. If a director has previously been the director of an insolvent company, then a shareholder may want to reconsider a decision to invest.
Register of Shareholders	So that people can see who the shareholders are and the percentage of shares owned by each. This can help to determine which individuals/other companies will have influence over the company.
Register of Charges	Enables lenders and suppliers to establish which assets are already subject to charge and therefore cannot be sold to pay other creditors if the company fails.

Test your understanding 3

- If financial statements give a true and fair view it means they are accurate.

This is false.

It means that the financial statements are reasonably accurate, not materially misstated, but does not mean that the financial statements are totally accurate.

Some errors in financial statements are inevitable, so they will never be totally accurate. Numbers which are estimates, such as depreciation or allowances for bad debts, are more at risk of error.

- If financial statements give a true and fair view it means there is no fraud.

This is false.

As stated above, true and fair requires that the financial statements are reasonably rather than totally accurate. If a fraud is not material, then it will not cause a material misstatement.

Test your understanding 4

The correct answer is D

The directors are collectively responsible for the preparation of the financial statements, not just the FD. The financial accounting function is involved in the production of the financial statements. The directors are responsible for the preparation of accounts that are true and fair. This cannot be delegated to anyone else.

Test your understanding 5

Poor accounting records could lead to the preparation of financial statements which do not give a true and fair view.

If this is detected by the auditors, they will give a qualified audit opinion.

Banks may refuse to lend money to a company which has a qualified audit opinion.

Shareholders may not wish to invest in a company which has a qualified audit opinion.

Poor accounting records may result in the company failing to 'chase' customers for payment, resulting in cash flow difficulties.

Poor accounting records may result in the company failing to pay suppliers on time and those suppliers refusing future credit.

These factors could lead to cash flow difficulties and ultimately corporate failure.

Test your understanding 6

(1) The companies are in different industries.

(2) The companies are operating in different economic environments.

(3) The companies have prepared their accounts using different national accounting policies.

(4) The companies have probably chosen different accounting policies.

(5) The companies have prepared their accounts in different currencies.

Test your understanding 7

(1) It is easier for multinationals, which encourages investment. A multinational will have subsidiaries in various countries, and if the subsidiaries' financial statements are prepared using international standards, or similar, it will be much simpler for the holding company to prepare the consolidated accounts for the group.

(2) It reassures investors in companies in the country. International standards are perceived as being fair and transparent, so investors will be more likely to trust the financial information given to them.

(3) It is more convenient for the national accounting standard setters, since they don't have to develop their own standards but can instead use international standards.

Test your understanding 8

The correct answer is D

Action can also be taken against the individual directors.

Test your understanding 9

The correct answer is A

Preparation of proper financial statements will not ensure ethical behaviour by an organisation. C requires international accounting standards, not legislation. D is incorrect as legislation and accounting standards are different.

Test your understanding 10

The correct answer is D

True and fair requires that accounts are free from material, or significant error. As long as fraud is immaterial, the accounts could still be considered true and fair.

Test your understanding 11

The correct answer is A

Remember that the Board of Directors is responsible for the financial statements giving a true and fair view. This responsibility cannot be delegated to others.

Test your understanding 12

The correct answer is B

Test your understanding 13

The correct answer is B

Note that IFRSs are the international accounting standards themselves – not a subdivision of the IFRS Foundation.

Accounting and finance functions within business

Chapter learning objectives

Upon completion of this chapter you will be able to:

- identify and describe the main financial accounting functions in business: recording financial information, codifying and processing financial information and preparing financial statements

- explain the various business purposes for which the following financial information is required:

    - the statement of profit or loss

    - the statement of cash flows

    - the statement of financial position

    - sustainability and integrated reports

- explain the contribution of the accounting function to the formulation, implementation and control of the organisation's policies, procedures and performance

- identify and describe the main management accounting and performance management functions in business:

    - recording and analysing costs and revenues

    - providing management accounting information for decision-making

    - planning and preparing budgets and exercising budgetary control

- describe the main purposes of the following types of management accounting reports:

  - cost schedules

  - budgets

  - variance reports

- identify and describe the main finance and treasury functions:

  - calculating and mitigating business tax liabilities

  - evaluating and obtaining finance

  - managing working capital

  - treasury and risk management.

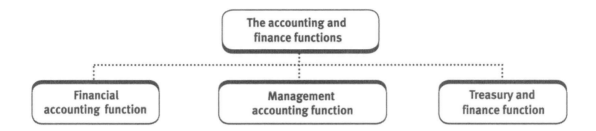

1 The accounting function

1.1 What is accounting?

 Accounting is the systematic recording, reporting and analysis of financial transactions within a business.

In larger organisations, the range of tasks that the accounting function needs to perform is very wide. This often means that the accounts department is split into a number of different functions, each of which deals with a separate set of responsibilities.

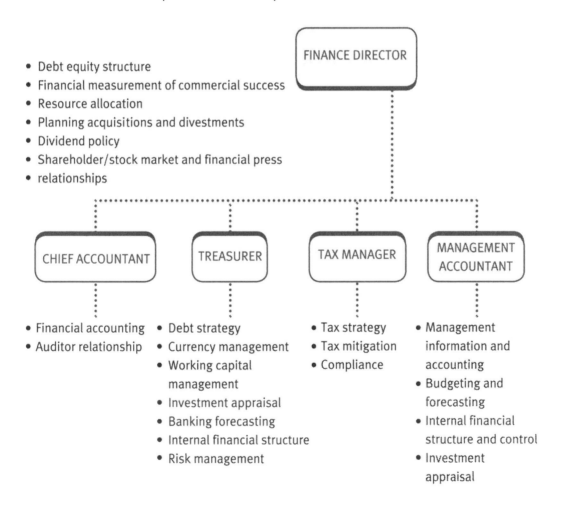

Typical structure of a head office accounting function

For the purposes of this exam, you need to be aware of three key functions within the accounts department:

- the financial accounting function
- the management accounting function and
- the treasury function.

2 The financial accounting function

Financial accounting is concerned with the production of annual financial statements in accordance with the relevant accounting standards and legislation.

Whenever a business transaction takes place (such as a sale, purchase or payment of an expense), there is a need to record the transaction in the organisation's accounting records. The transaction is first entered into the **books of prime entry**.

Books of prime entry

There are five main books of prime entry:

The **purchases day book** is used to record the purchases made by a business, listing the invoices received from suppliers.

The **sales day book** is used to record the sales made by a business, listing the invoices issued to customers.

The **cash book** is used to record the receipts into and payments out of the organisation's bank account.

The **petty cash book** is used to record sundry small payments of cash made by a business, e.g. purchasing tea and biscuits for staff refreshments or reimbursing the travel expenses of job interviewees.

The **journal** is used to keep a proper record of non-routine accounting adjustments made by senior accounts staff.

On a regular basis (often daily or weekly, depending on the volume of transactions), the day books are totalled and these totals are entered into the ledger accounts.

At the end of the accounting year of the business, the balance is calculated on each ledger account and these balances are used to create the financial statements of the organisation for the period.

There are three main financial statements produced by most businesses each year. These are:

- the **statement of profit or loss (SOPL)** (also known as the 'profit and loss account' or the 'income statement') for the year, which details the income as well as the costs incurred in the period. This allows the business to calculate whether it has made a profit (if income exceeds costs) or a loss (if costs exceed income).

- the **statement of financial position (SOFP)** as at the year end, which shows the assets (business resources such as motor vehicles, buildings and cash) and liabilities (money owed to third parties such as banks and suppliers) of the business. This statement also shows the stake that the owners of the business have in the organisation (or their 'capital'). In a company, this is often referred to as 'shareholder's equity'.

- the **statement of cash flows** for the year, which summarises the cash receipts and payments for the year. This helps to show whether the company is solvent (has sufficient cash) and where the cash has been spent in the year.

In summary, the normal sequence of steps in the accounting function is:

| TRANSACTIONS | ··· | DAY BOOKS | ··· | LEDGER ACCOUNTS | ··· | FINANCIAL STATEMENTS |

Test your understanding 1

J has been asked to find four pieces of information about FGH Ltd for his manager from the company's statement of profit or loss (SOPL) and statement of financial position (SOFP). He has been asked to find:

(1) The ratio of current assets to current liabilities

(2) Total shareholders' equity

(3) Gross profit as a percentage of turnover

(4) Total rent paid for the year

Which of the following correctly match the information needed with the financial statement each would be found in?

	1	2	3	4
A	SOFP	SOFP	SOPL	SOPL
B	SOPL	SOPL	SOFP	SOFP
C	SOFP	SOPL	SOFP	SOPL
D	SOPL	SOFP	SOPL	SOFP

2.1 Why do businesses need to prepare financial statements?

The preparation of financial statements is a time-consuming and expensive process. So why do most organisations have an accounting function?

The main reason is to satisfy groups of people who have an interest in the financial performance of the business. These could include:

- **Owners** – interested in how profitable the business is and how well it is being run.

- **Managers** – interested in the company's financial situation so that they can plan effectively for the future.

- **Banks** – may wish to see whether the business can afford the repayments on loans and overdrafts.

- **Employees** – interested in the financial position of the company and the impact this will have on their jobs and wages.

- **Suppliers and customers** – may wish to check the financial stability of the business to ensure it will be able to make payments/supply goods as needed.

- **Government** – may wish to check that the business is obeying relevant laws on reporting and taxation.

Companies must send a copy of their financial statements to each of their shareholders at the end of the year. Large and publicly-quoted companies are also required to appoint external auditors each year to give an independent opinion on whether the financial statements have been drawn up properly and whether they give a true and fair view.

2.2 Integrated reporting

Many organisations adopt an integrated reporting approach which means that their financial statements cover the organisation's financial performance and position (using the three primary financial statements mentioned earlier), but also report on any other relevant information that would be of interest to the users.

Other relevant information might include (but is not limited to):

- major risks the organisation faces and any actions they have taken to deal with these risks

- the organisation's performance regarding ethics and corporate social responsibility (discussed further in chapter 11)

- the organisation's performance with regard to sustainable development (discussed further in chapter 8).

Integrated reporting and 'capital'

Context

With integrated reporting, instead of having environmental and social issues reported in a separate section of the annual report, or a standalone 'sustainability' report, the idea is that one report should capture the strategic and operational actions of management in its holistic approach to business and stakeholder 'wellbeing'.

The management accountant must be able to collaborate with top management in the integration of financial wellbeing with community and stakeholder wellbeing.

Integrated reporting will bring statutory reporting closer to the management accountant and will make management accountants even more important in bridging the gap between stakeholders and the company's reports.

The management accountant will be expected to produce information that:

- is a balance between quantitative and qualitative information

- links past, present and future performance

- considers the regulatory impacts on performance

- provides an analysis of factors that could impact in the future.

There is clearly a need for the profession to accept the challenge for being the mechanism for a new type of transparency and accountability; one that incorporates social and environmental impacts as well as economic ones.

The role of the management accountant in sustainability is as yet not well established. However, it is anticipated that over time, integrated reporting will become the corporate reporting norm. This will offer a productive and rewarding future, not only for the management accountant but for society as a whole.

Six types of 'capital'

The Integrated Reporting Framework recognizes the importance of looking at financial and sustainability performance in an integrated way – one that emphasizes the relationships between what it identifies as the "six capitals":

- **Financial capital**

  This is what we traditionally think of as 'capital' – e.g. shares, bonds or banknotes. It enables the other types of Capital described below to be owned and traded.

- **Manufactured capital**

  This form of capital can be described as comprising of material goods, or fixed assets which contribute to the production process rather than being the output itself – e.g. tools, machines and buildings.

- **Intellectual capital**

  This form of capital can be described as the value of a company or organisation's employee knowledge, business training and any proprietary information that may provide the company with a competitive advantage.

- **Human capital**

  This can be described as consisting of people's health, knowledge, skills and motivation. All these things are needed for productive work.

- **Social and relationship capital**

  This can be described as being concerned with the institutions that help maintain and develop human capital in partnership with others; e.g. Families, communities, businesses, trade unions, schools, and voluntary organisations.

- **Natural capital**

  This can be described as any stock or flow of energy and material within the environment that produces goods and services. It includes

  resources of a renewable and non-renewable materials e.g. land, water, energy and those factors that absorb, neutralise or recycle wastes and processes – e.g. climate regulation, climate change, CO_2 emissions.

The fundamental assumption of the Integrated Reporting Framework is that each of these types of capital – whether internal or external to the business, tangible or intangible – represents a potential source of value that must be managed for the long run in order to deliver sustainable value creation.

 The International Integrated Reporting Council (IIRC)

The IIRC was formed in August 2010 and aims to create a globally accepted framework for a process that results in communication by an organisation about value creation over time.

The IIRC seeks to secure the adoption of an Integrated Reporting Framework (an alternative to the recommendations by the GRI) by report preparers. The Framework sets out several **guiding principles** and **content elements** that have to be considered when preparing an integrated report.

Guiding principles

There are **seven** guiding principles, as follows:

- **Strategic focus and future orientation** – the report should provide an insight into the organisation's strategy and how it relates to the organisation's ability to create value in the short, medium and long term.

- **Connectivity of information** – the report should show a holistic picture of the combination, inter-relatedness and dependencies between the factors that affect the organisation's ability to create value over time.

- **Stakeholder relationships** – the report should provide an insight into the nature and quality of the organisation's relationships with its stakeholders.

- **Materiality** – the report should disclose information about matters that substantively affect the organisation's ability to create value.

- **Conciseness** – the report should be concise and include relevant information only.

- **Reliability and completeness** – the report should include all material matters, both positive and negative, in a balanced way and without material error.

- **Consistency and comparability** – the report should be consistent and comparable over time.

Content elements

There are **eight** content elements:

- **Organisational overview and external environment** – what does the organisation do and what are the circumstances under which it operates?

- **Governance** – how does the organisation's governance structure support its ability to create value in the short, medium and long term?

- **Business model** – what is the organisation's business model?

- **Risks and opportunities** – what are the risks and opportunities that affect the organisation's ability to create value over the short, medium and long term and how is the organisation dealing with them?

- **Strategy and resource allocation** – where does the organisation want to go and how does it intend to get there?

- **Performance** – to what extent has the organisation achieved its strategic objectives for the period?

- **Outlook** – what challenges and uncertainties is the organisation likely to encounter in pursuing its strategy and what are the implications for future performance?

- **Basis of preparation and presentation** – how does the organisation determine what matters to include in the integrated report and are such matters quantified or evaluated?

3 Management accounting

Management accounting is carried out to assist management in discharging their duties to plan, direct and control the operations of the business. It is concerned with the process of measuring, analysing, interpreting and communicating information to management in a form which is easy for them to understand.

Management accountants will use the financial accounting records as a source of data for their work, but they may choose to use any other sources of data (both internal and external) that they feel will be useful for managers.

While there are no legally required formats for management accounts, there are several key management reports that are common to many businesses. Three of the most common are **cost schedules, budgets** and **variance reports**.

3.1 Cost schedules

A **cost schedule** lists the various expenses involved in manufacturing units of a product. This is often shown as a list of the costs incurred when making a unit of each type of product we make. This may be called a **standard cost card**.

Illustration 1 – Standard cost cards

ABC Ltd manufactures toys. One of its products is a wooden train set, which has the following standard costs per unit:

	£
Direct materials (wood and paint)	5.50
Direct labour (time spent cutting and painting)	6.50
Prime cost	12.00
Variable overheads (heat and light)	4.00
Marginal cost	16.00
Fixed overheads (factory rent)	5.00
Total (absorption) cost	21.00

There are several key business decisions that this report can help a business to make:

- **Pricing decisions** – How much should we sell our products for in order to ensure we make a profit?

- **Break-even analysis** – Which products are profitable or loss-making? Is a new product worth producing? Can we sell enough units to cover the costs of making the product?

- **Key factor analysis** – should products be made in-house or should their manufacture be outsourced to somewhere cheaper?

- **Investment appraisal** – should a new machine be bought to replace an old machine? Should we begin a new project, such as launching a new product?

3.2 Budgets

In addition, once the costs per unit have been identified, it should be possible to produce a **budget**. This shows the total planned revenues and costs for our business for the coming period. It is based on the cost schedules mentioned earlier.

Budgets are useful for several reasons. A useful memory aid is the acronym **CRUMPET**.

- **C**o-ordination – the budget provides guidance for managers and ensures they are all working together for the good of the company.

- **R**esponsibility – the budget authorises managers to make expenditure, hire staff and generally follow the plans laid out in the budget.

- **U**tilisation – budgets (especially cash budgets) help managers to get the best out of their business resources in the coming period.

- **M**otivation – the budget can be a useful device for influencing the behaviour of managers and motivating them to perform in line with business objectives.

- **P**lanning – budgets force managers to look ahead. This may help them to identify opportunities for, or threats to, the business and take effective action in advance.

- **E**valuation – budgets are often used as the basis for management appraisal. The manager has performed well if he has met his budgets in the period.

- **T**elling – also called 'communication', budgets ensure that all members of the business understand what is expected from them during the coming period.

One major drawback of budgets is that they are only estimates of what will happen in the coming period. In reality, most businesses will not perfectly achieve the targets set out for them in their budgets.

This means that they will have to prepare a **variance report** at the end of each period.

3.3 Variance reports

A **variance report** compares the budget to the actual results achieved for the budget period and identifies any significant differences, or variances, between the two.

For control purposes, management may need to establish why a particular variance has occurred. Once the reason has been established, a decision can be taken as to what, if any, control measures might be appropriate to:

- prevent adverse variances from occurring again in the future, or

- repeat a favourable variance in the future, or

- bring actual results back on course to achieve the budgeted targets.

3.4 Management accounting and business policy and performance

In addition, the management accounting function has a particularly important role in formulating, implementing and controlling business policy and performance.

For example, a business may have an objective to grow its revenue and profits. It will then need to examine possible ways of achieving this – such as by the launch of new products, or acquisition of a competitor. Finally it will have to assess which of these approaches will achieve its goals and select the best one(s).

The accounting function can clearly contribute to this process. Since the achievement of an organisation's plans is usually measured in monetary terms, accountants are needed to help establish objectives and then evaluate the various possible strategies to identify which are the most financially attractive.

Once a strategy has been selected, such as the launch of a new product, the business must carefully monitor and control it to ensure that it is being implemented properly and performing as desired.

This is usually done by undertaking variance analysis, which was outlined earlier.

3.5 The differences between financial and management accounting

	Management accounting	Financial accounting
Why information is mainly produced	For internal use, e.g. managers and employees	For external use, e.g. shareholders, creditors, banks, government.
Purpose of information	To aid planning, controlling and decision making	To record the financial performance in a period and the financial position at the end of the period.
Legal requirements	None	Limited companies must produce financial accounts.
Formats	Management decide on the information that they require and the most useful way of presenting it	Format and content of financial accounts must follow accounting standards and company law.
Nature of information	Financial and non- financial	Mostly financial.
Time period	Historical and forward-looking	Mainly a historical record.

Test your understanding 2

Consider the following two statements regarding the management accounting function.

(i)   Variance analysis enables a business to identify why the actual financial results were different to those predicted by the budget.

(ii)   Management accounts follow a set, pre-determined format as laid out in relevant accounting standards.

Which of these statements is/are correct?

A   (i) only

B   (ii) only

C   Both

D   Neither

4   The functions of the treasury

Treasury management is the corporate handling of all financial matters, the generation of external and internal funds for business, the management of currencies and cash flows, and the complex strategies, policies and procedures of corporate finance.

The key roles of the treasury and finance functions include:

Working capital management	The treasury section will monitor the organisation's cash balance and working capital to ensure that it never runs out of money.
Cash management	Preparation of cash budgets and arrangement of overdrafts where necessary.
Financing	The treasury section will monitor the organisation's investments and borrowings to ensure the gain as much investment income as possible and incur as little interest expense as possible.
Foreign currency	The treasury section will monitor foreign exchange rates and try to manage the organisation's affairs so that it minimises losses due to changes in foreign exchange rates.
Tax	The treasury section will try to manage the organisation's affairs to legally avoid as much tax as possible.

Foreign currency

Companies may have borrowings in foreign currencies, or may have customers/suppliers who will pay/expect payment in a foreign currency. The treasury department will try to manage affairs to minimise the company's exposure to foreign exchange losses, i.e. minimise losses.

For example, assume a UK company buys goods costing US$1 m from a US company on 1 January 20X1. The goods are due to be paid for on 31 March 20X1. The exchange rate at 1 January is £1:US$1.5, so the goods will cost £666,667 ($1m/1.5). However if the exchange rate changes to, say, £1:US$1.3, then the payment to be made will be £769,231 ($1m/1.3).

The company can manage this risk by entering into a 'forward exchange contract' at 1 January to fix the rate of exchange at which it can buy $1m at 31 March. The rate in the forward exchange contract will depend on what the market thinks will happen to exchange rates. Let us say, for example, that the company can enter into a contract to purchase $1m at the rate of £1:S1.48. The company's cost, in sterling, is then fixed at £675,676 ($1m/1.48).

4.1 Management of working capital

 Working capital is the capital available for conducting the day-to-day operations of an organisation, calculated as the excess of current assets over current liabilities. Thus:

Inventory	X
Trade receivables	X
Cash	X
	───
Total current assets	X
Less: Trade payables	(X)
	───
Working capital balance	X
	───

The treasury and finance function is responsible for deciding on an appropriate level of investment in working capital for the business.

There are advantages in holding either large or small balances of each component of working capital, as shown below.

	Advantage of large balance	Advantage of small balance
Inventory	Customers are happy since they can be immediately provided with good.	Low holding costs. Less risk of obsolescence costs.
Trade receivables	Customers are happy since they like credit.	Less risk of irrecoverable debts. Good for cash flow.
Cash	Creditors are happy since bills can be paid promptly.	More can be invested elsewhere to earn profits.
Trade payables	Preserves your own cash.	Suppliers are happy and may offer discounts.

Management must decide on the appropriate balance to be struck for each component.

Test your understanding 3

Conservative managers will have a policy of holding a large working capital balance, while aggressive management will hold a low working capital balance. Which of the following is a consequence of an aggressive management policy?

A   Increased bad and doubtful debts

B   Increased credit periods attract more customers

C   Increased inventory obsolescence

D   Increased risk of inventory outages

4.2 Evaluating and obtaining finance

The organisation may need additional funding to allow it to grow and invest in new projects. It may therefore need to raise finance from external sources. There are two main types of external finance.

Debt

This involves borrowing cash from a third party and promising to repay them at a later date. Normally, the company will also have to pay interest on the amount borrowed.

There are various sources of debt that an organisation can raise funds from, including bank loans and overdrafts, venture capitalists and through selling bonds or debentures.

The main advantages of raising cash through debt finance are:

- Interest payments are allowable against tax. Note that dividend payments made to shareholders, by contrast, are not an allowable deduction.

- Raising debt finance does not change the ownership of the organisation.

- Debt tends to be cheaper to service than equity, as it is often secured against the assets of the company and takes priority over equity in the event of the business being liquidated.

Equity

This involves selling a stake in the business in order to raise cash. For companies, this involves selling shares to either new or existing shareholders.

Raising equity finance has the following advantages:

- There is no minimum level of dividend that must be paid to shareholders. This means that dividends can be suspended if profits are low and the company cannot afford them. Interest payments on debt finance **must** be paid each year.

- A bank will normally require security on the company's assets before it will offer a loan. Some companies may lack quality assets to offer, making equity more attractive as it does not require security.

Generally

The treasury and finance function will weigh up which source of finance best suits the circumstances of the business.

Test your understanding 4

AHG plc needs to raise £50m to launch a new product. AHG hopes the new product will be a success, but the returns are highly uncertain, with a 30% chance that the launch will be a failure. The product is expected to sell for around 5 years.

AHG is currently trying to decide whether the launch should be financed using a 5 year bank loan, or through raising equity.

Which of the following statements is correct?

A   Equity will be cheaper, as dividends are allowable against tax

B   AHG should choose equity due to the risky nature of the project

C   Equity should be chosen as AHG needs a permanent increase in its finance

D   Debt usually does not require security, meaning it may be easier for AHG to raise

4.3 Determining business tax liabilities

One of the roles of the finance and treasury function is to calculate the business tax liability for the organisation and mitigate, or reduce, that liability as far as possible within the law.

 Tax avoidance is the legal use of the rules of the tax regime to one's own advantage, in order to reduce the amount of tax payable by means that are within the law.

 Tax evasion is the use of illegal means to reduce one's tax liability, for example by deliberately misrepresenting the true state of your affairs to the tax authorities.

The directors of a company have a duty to their shareholders to maximise the post-tax profits that are available for distribution as dividends to the shareholders, thus they have a duty to arrange the company's affairs to avoid taxes as far as possible. However, dishonest reporting to the tax authorities (e.g. declaring less income than actually earned) would be tax evasion and a criminal offence.

While the traditional distinction between tax avoidance and tax evasion is fairly clear, recently authorities have introduced the idea of **tax mitigation** to mean conduct that reduces tax liabilities without frustrating the intentions of Parliament, while **tax avoidance** is used to describe schemes which, while they are legal, are designed to defeat the intentions of Parliament. Thus, once a tax avoidance scheme becomes public knowledge, Parliament will nearly always step in to change the law in order to stop the scheme from working.

Tax avoidance

The traditional view of neutrality towards tax avoidance can be shown by judges' comments in the past, for example Lord Clyde in 1929:

'No man in this country is under the smallest obligation, moral or other, so to arrange his legal relations to his business or to his property as to enable the Inland Revenue to put the largest possible shovel into his stores.'

More recently, even tax avoidance can be regarded with hostility. Some countries such as Australia have a General Anti-Avoidance Rule. Other countries such as the UK have used retrospective legislation to counteract the purpose of some tax avoidance schemes. In general it is safer now to stick with tax mitigation measures.

5   Chapter summary

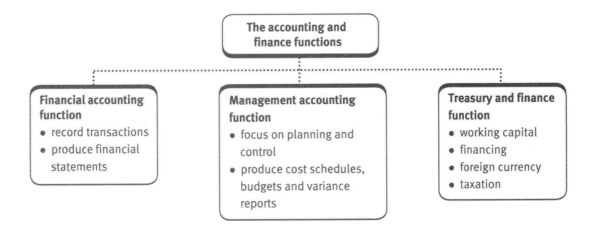

6 Practice questions

Test your understanding 5

Kayla is recording a non-routine business transaction. Which book of prime entry would she most likely record the transaction within?

A   The journal

B   The purchases day book

C   The cash book

D   The general ledger

Test your understanding 6

An analyst wishes to use a company's financial statements to determine whether the business has a significant cash balance or not. He has three main financial statements to choose from:

(1)   Statement of profit or loss (SOPL)

(2)   Statement of financial position (SOFP)

(3)   Statement of cash flows (SCF)

Which of these statements could the analyst use to identify this information?

A   (1) and (3) only

B   (2) and (3) only

C   (2) only

D   (3) only

Test your understanding 7

Which of the following is **not** typically prepared by the management accounting function?

A   Budgets

B   Investment appraisals

C   Business tax calculations

D   Variance reports

Test your understanding 8

The following statements relate to either management or financial accounting.

(1) Format decided by management

(2) Created to aid planning and decision-making

(3) Legally required for companies

(4) Mainly for the use of external stakeholders

Which of these statements relate to management accounting?

A   (1) and (2) only

B   (1) and (3) only

C   (2) and (3) only

D   (3) and (4) only

Test your understanding 9

HGK Ltd is looking to raise additional finance to enable it to open a new store. Which of the following are advantages of HGK raising the finance via debt?

A   Interest payments can usually be delayed if the company is unable to afford them

B   Debt is often considered to be a better source of finance if the return from the project is uncertain

C   Debt finance tends to have a higher annual cost than equity

D   Debt holders are paid before equity holders in the event of the company being liquidated, reducing the cost of finance

Test your understanding 10

Tax ___(1)____ is illegal misrepresentation of one's tax liability, while tax ____(2)____ is simply the legal use of tax legislation to minimise the amount of tax paid by the business.

Which two words correctly fill gaps 1 and 2, respectively?

	Gap (1)	Gap (2)
A	Avoidance	Evasion
B	Evasion	Minimisation
C	Avoidance	Minimisation
D	Evasion	Avoidance

Test your understanding 11

Which of the following responsibilities would normally be dealt with by the treasury function?

A   Break-even analysis

B   Costing of products

C   Production of financial statements

D   Foreign exchange management

Test your understanding answers

Test your understanding 1

The correct answer is A

Test your understanding 2

The correct answer is A

Statement (i) is correct. However, statement (ii) describes a feature of financial accounting, rather than management accounting.

Test your understanding 3

The correct answer is D

Keeping a low level of receivables means that money is collected promptly, decreasing the chance of bad debts. Low receivables would also mean we are offering less credit to customers, which they may find unattractive. Low levels of inventory mean that the company is less exposed to inventory obsolescence, but it does mean the company may run out of inventory if demand is unexpectedly high.

Test your understanding 4

The correct answer is B

A is incorrect, as dividends are not tax allowable – interest is.

B is correct as, in the event of the product being a failure, AHG would not need to make unaffordable repayments to investors if it raises finance from equity.

C is incorrect as AHG only needs the money for 5 years. It could be argued that a 5 year loan would match the term of the project and therefore be more appropriate than equity finance, on which the company will have to pay dividends forever.

D is also incorrect as debt does normally require security from the company. Equity does not.

Test your understanding 5

The correct answer is A

By definition.

Test your understanding 6

The correct answer is B

The cash balance could be determined from the statement of cash flows, which looks at cash movements in the year, or the statement of financial position, which lists the assets at the year end (of which cash is one).

Test your understanding 7

The correct answer is C

This is usually the responsibility of the treasury department.

Test your understanding 8

The correct answer is A

Options 3 and 4 relate to financial accounting.

Test your understanding 9

The correct answer is D

Interest payments cannot normally be delayed (unlike dividends), meaning that they are not good for investing in projects with uncertain returns. Debt finance tends to be cheaper to service than equity because it can be secured against the company's assets and is repaid first in the event of the company being liquidated.

Test your understanding 10

The correct answer is D

By definition.

Test your understanding 11

The correct answer is D

A and B are usually part of the management accounting function, while C is financial accounting.

Financial systems and procedures

Chapter learning objectives

Upon completion of this chapter you will be able to:

- identify an organisation's system requirements in relation to the objectives and policies of the organisation.

- describe the main financial systems used within an organisation:

  - purchases and sales invoicing

  - payroll

  - credit control

  - cash and working capital management

- explain why it is important to adhere to policies and procedures for handling clients' money

- identify weaknesses, potential for error and inefficiencies in accounting systems

- recommend improvements to accounting systems to prevent error and fraud and to improve overall efficiency

- explain why appropriate controls are necessary in relation to business and IT systems and procedures.

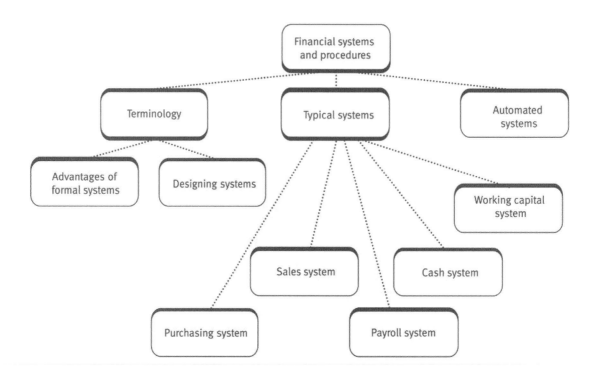

1 Overview of systems

Accounting systems lay down procedures and guidelines that reflect the company's policies. These terms are explained below.

Term	Meaning
System	(i) A group of independent but interrelated elements comprising a unified whole.
	(2) A process for obtaining an objective.
Policy	A guiding principle.
Procedure	(1) A series of acts.
	(2) A set sequence of steps.
Guideline	A recommended approach for conducting a task.

Illustration 1 – Terminology

XYZ Limited has developed a new sales system.

Its policy is to process orders from customers efficiently, and to despatch goods within two days.

The system contains procedures for the ordering, despatching, invoicing, and receipt of payment for goods to ensure the policy is followed.

It also has guidelines on assessing the creditworthiness of new customers.

Test your understanding 7

Give an example of each of these terms within the context of enrolling for an ACCA course: system, policy, procedure and guideline.

1.1 Advantages of formal systems

There are several advantages to having formal, documented systems that staff must follow within the organisation. These include:

- All transactions will be recorded in the same way, and the required information will be recorded in the correct places.

- The 'best' practice, the most efficient way of recording transactions, can be adopted by everyone.

- Staff can refer to the written procedures if they are in doubt as to what to do.

- New staff can be trained more quickly.

- The auditors can follow transactions more easily if they are recorded in the same way.

- Transactions which have not followed the procedure, which could be errors or frauds, may be identified more easily.

 It is particularly important to have formal policies and procedures in place when organisations, such as solicitors or banks, handle money on behalf of their customers. As this money does not belong to the business it is vital to have controls in place to help prevent the loss of client funds – either through fraud, theft or accidental loss. Should such losses occur, it would damage the organisation's reputation, as well as potentially having legal implications.

1.2 Designing financial systems

Each system is made up of a series of procedures. The system designer will need to first consider the objectives of the system, the required outputs, and the likely inputs.

Taking a sales system as an example:

Objectives	To record the value of sales to each customer and the amount outstanding to be collected.
Outputs	An analysis of sales by date and product type. A report showing amounts owing from receivables and how long outstanding.
Inputs	Customers place orders by fax and by telephone.

The designer then needs to consider the most likely sequence of events from input to outputs. For example:

Order received

↓

Goods despatched

↓

Invoice sent to customer

↓

Sale recorded in accounts

↓

Payment received from customer

↓

Outstanding amounts followed up

For each step in the system, a procedure is then designed, using the same format as for the system. The designer should also consider what could go wrong, and incorporate controls into the system to try to prevent such errors.

Let us consider this for the ordering stage of the system:

Objectives	• To receive and process orders quickly and accurately. • To ensure that goods are only despatched where the amount charged will be collectable.
Outputs	• Instruction to despatch department to despatch goods. • Instruction to accounting department to invoice (charge for) goods.
Inputs	• Note of telephone call. • Fax.
What could go wrong	• Details of orders may be lost. • Details of orders may not be passed on to despatch and/or invoicing. • Order may be processed from customer who is unwilling/unable to pay.

A procedure will then be designed to receive, record and process the order, which achieves the above objective and has controls to prevent things going wrong.

Test your understanding 2

Fill in the table, using the example of a student enrolling for an ACCA course.

Objectives	
Outputs	
Inputs	
What could go wrong	

We will now go on to consider several key financial systems that operate within most organisations:

- purchasing and sales

- payroll

- cash

- working capital management

2   The purchasing system

The main stages in the purchasing cycle and the issues to be considered are as follows:

Requisition	• Staff decide what goods/services they wish to purchase and produce a purchase requisition.
	• This is authorised by department supervisor and passed to purchasing/ordering department.
Ordering	• Purchase department places order with suppliers.
	• Obtain several quotations to get the most competitive price.
	• Order may be authorised, especially if for a large amount.
Goods received	• Goods should be inspected to ensure that they are in good condition and the quality is correct.
	• A record should be kept of all goods received.

Invoice received	• Supplier bills company for goods/services.
	• Before recording in the accounts, checks are made to ensure goods were received and that the price is correct (i.e. same as order).
Invoice recorded	• Recorded in company's accounting system, manual or computerised.
Payment made	• A cheque is produced for the amount owing.
	• This will be approved for payment by a senior manager who will first check that the details on the cheque agree with the invoices.

The purchasing cycle

XYZ Limited is a company manufacturing handbags.

Describe what will happen when the company purchases some leather to produce a handbag.

Requisition	• The production department plans what items will be produced and consults with the inventory department to see if sufficient quantities of the required raw materials are available.
	• The inventory clerk realises that there is an insufficient quantity of leather, and so prepares a requisition to order more.
	• (In a computerised system, the inventory system may be linked with the purchasing system and automatically reorders when the inventory quantity falls to a certain level.)
Ordering	• The purchasing clerk checks the price charged by three regular, reliable suppliers, and places an order with the one who charges the best price.
	• A copy of the order is sent to the goods inwards clerk, so that he/she knows to expect these goods, and to the accounting department.
Invoice received	• The invoice is received by the accounting department. The clerk checks that the price charged agrees with the price on the order and that the goods have been received.
	• The invoice is then passed to the requisitioning department for approval, and is coded* according to purchase type.

Invoice recorded	• The invoice is entered into the accounting system (manual or computerised) to the coded account.
Payment made	• At the end of the following month (suppliers normally give a month's credit) payment is made via BACS or CHAPS. This is submitted to the managing director to be signed, together with the invoice to prove it is a valid business expense.

* Information on revenue or expenses is more useful if it can be analysed by type and department. Each specific expense type is given a unique code number, and invoices relating to that expense type are coded with that number. The accounting department then knows what expense heading to allocate it to. In this case, the inventory was purchased by the production department (say, department 03). It is an inventory purchase (e.g. expense type 01) and is to be used to manufacture a particular handbag type (say 06). The invoice would be coded 030106.

Test your understanding 3

Purchasing cycle controls

For each of the stages in the purchasing system provided below, identify what could go wrong and what controls the system designer could implement to try and deal with these problems.

Stage	Administration	What could go wrong	Control measures
Item is required	Requisition order issued in two copies to purchasing dep't and client.		
Purchase order is raised	Purchase order issued in up to four copies to be sent to accounts, orderer, warehouse and purchasing department.		
Goods received	Goods received note is issued in put to four copies, as above.		
Invoice received	One copy raised to accounts department.		
Goods paid or returned	Payment processed or credit note received.		

3 The sales system

The main stages in the sales cycle and the issues to be considered are as follows:

Order received	• Depending on the business, orders may be received by post, by fax, telephone, in person or electronically.
	• A record should be made of incoming orders so that a check can be made that they have all been processed.
Order processed	• A check should be made to ensure that the customer has a valid credit account, or has already paid in cash.
	• A check should be made that the goods are in inventory.
	• An order confirmation may be sent to the customer detailing when the goods will be despatched.
Goods despatched	• The goods are sent to the customer.
	• A document called a goods despatch note is produced, which will be signed by the customer confirming that the goods were received in good condition.
Invoicing	• An invoice is sent to the customer, detailing the amount charged for the goods.
Recorded in the accounts	• The invoice is coded and entered into the accounts.
Payment received	• Payment is received by cheque or credit transfer from customers. Controls should be in place to ensure that the staff are not in a position to misappropriate the payment.
	• The credit controller contacts those customers who are late in paying.

Credit control

It is important that a company only sells goods to those who are able and willing to pay for them. For some businesses, such as a fast food outlet, customers pay in cash or by credit card so the company is assured of payment.

For most businesses, companies buy and sell on credit, meaning that they pay for goods purchased and receive payments themselves for sales some time after the goods/services are delivered. It is vital that a company only gives a credit account after careful consideration of the likelihood of receiving payment.

The credit controller will ask companies who wish to obtain credit to complete an application form and sometimes to give a reference from the bank and an existing supplier. The credit controller then sets a credit limit, which will normally be quite low initially.

The credit controller also monitors which companies are late in paying and 'chases' late payers when necessary.

The sales cycle

XYZ Limited is a company manufacturing handbags.

Describe what will happen when the company receives an order from a department store for some handbags.

Order received	• Order received by post. It will be given a unique number by XYZ Limited so that it can be tracked through the system.
Order processed	• A check is made to ensure that the customer's credit account is still active, and that this order will not put the customer over the credit limit.
	• An order confirmation is sent to the customer detailing the date of despatch.
Goods despatched	• The handbags are sent to the customer, and the goods despatch note signed.
Invoicing	• An invoice is sent for the value of the handbags plus sales tax.
Recorded in the accounts	• The invoice is coded according to handbag type and recorded in the accounts.
Payment received	• The customer pays by credit transfer, and the payment is allocated to the customer account.

Test your understanding 4

Sales system controls

For each of the stages in the sales system provided below, identify what could go wrong and what controls the system designer could implement to try and deal with these problems.

Stage	Administration	What could go wrong	Control measures
Receive order	Two to three copies made of sales order for dispatch and sales department records.		
Dispatch the goods	Goods dispatched note up to five copies for accounts department, driver, customer, sales department and warehouse records.		
Raise an invoice	Sales invoice is copied twice for the customer and accounts department.		
Payment or return of goods	Sales invoice is copied twice for the customer and accounts department.		

4 The payroll system

Variable data:
- Timesheets
- Clock-cards
- Sick leave

Fixed data:
- Pay rates
- Pay rises
- Holidays
- Leavers/new starters

Payroll system

Calculates:
- Gross pay
- Tax
- Net pay

Payroll reports
- for management

Payslips
- for employees

Makes payments
- employees receive net pay
- government receives taxation

The main stages in the payroll system and the issues to be considered are as follows:

Hours worked recorded	• Hourly-paid employees will record details of hours worked. This is usually done using clock cards/timecards/punch cards on which a machine records starting and finishing times of work.
	• Hours worked are usually authorised by a supervisor.
Overtime recorded	• Salaried employees (who are not paid an hourly rate) may receive additional pay for overtime hours. If so, they will submit a timesheet with details of the hours worked.
Pay rates obtained	• Per hour or per month.
	• If it is a manual system, the pay clerk will manually look these up. If it is a computerised system the computer will do so.
	• When pay rates are changed, this must be authorised by a senior manager.

Pay calculated	• Hours × rate, or a set monthly pay. • If calculated manually someone else should check a few of the transactions.
Deductions calculated	• Depending on the country, this could be tax, social security, etc. This will be deducted from the gross pay.
Net pay paid to employee	• Usually via a transfer from company's bank account to employee's bank account. • Occasionally via cash. Supervision is required to prevent theft, and employees should sign to acknowledge receipt of money.

Illustration 2 – The payroll system

XYZ Limited is a company manufacturing handbags.

Describe what will happen when the company prepares the payroll for September 20X6.

Hours worked recorded	• The clock cards from the factory (production) workers are authorised by the factory supervisor and sent to the wages clerk.
Overtime recorded	• Salaried employees who have worked overtime submit a timesheet to their supervisors for approval, and these are then passed to the wages clerk.
Pay rates obtained	• The wages clerk looks up the pay rates.
Pay calculated	• The wages clerk calculates the gross pay. • The accountant selects five employees and checks the calculation.
Deductions calculated	• The wages clerk calculates the deductions. • For the five employees already selected, the accountant checks the calculation of deductions.
Net pay paid to employee	• The wages clerk produces a list showing the net pay to be paid to each employee. • This is approved by a senior manager and details sent to the bank for transfer.

Test your understanding 5

Stage	What could go wrong	Control measures
Variable data	• incorrect levels of work recorded, leading to employees being over/underpaid	
Fixed data	• fraudulent creation of employees that do not exist • failing to record new employees/remove old employees from the payroll • failure to pay at the correct rate • allowing too many/too few holidays for staff	
Calculations	• inaccurate calculations leading to errors in payments to staff or government	
Production of reports and payments	• inaccurate payslips produced • payments made to wrong employees • payments not matching amount calculated	

5 The cash system

- When we refer to the cash system, we are sometimes referring to the banking system, and payments into and from the bank account. This overlaps with our consideration of the sales, purchases and wages systems above. We also need to consider the petty cash system.

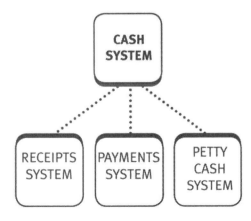

5.1 The receipts system

- Cheques are received from credit customers. These are recorded in the cash book and in the customer's personal account. The cashier then pays the cheques into the company's bank account.

- Controls must be in place to ensure that the cheque cannot be misappropriated before it is paid into the bank. Typical controls would include having two employees open the mail and listing the cheques received, and a supervisor checking that all cheques received were banked.

- Some customers may pay money directly into the company's bank account (often via BACS or CHAPS transfers). The cashier should go through the bank statement carefully, enter details into the cash book, and ensure that details are passed to the sales ledger section to deduct the amount from the customer's balance.

5.2 The payments system

- Companies pay their suppliers, usually monthly and by cheque.

- A cheque requisition is prepared for each payment. This is a form which details the reason why a cheque is required. A cheque will be prepared and the cheque, the cheque requisition and the invoices to be paid will be submitted to a senior manager for approval and to have the cheque signed.

- Cheques for a large amount of money will usually require two signatories.

- If the company pays its suppliers through direct bank transfers (i.e. via BACS), each transfer should be approved by a senior manager before it is set up.

5.3 The petty cash system

- Companies will need to keep a certain amount of cash on hand to pay for small expenses such as postage stamps, biscuits, taxi fares, etc.

- A cheque will be made out to cash, to generate the initial cash for the system.

- As staff claim against the petty cash system, they complete vouchers stating what the payment is for, and attach a receipt to prove the amount.

- At regular intervals a further cheque is made out to cash to replenish the petty cash which has been spent. The supervisor will inspect the receipts and vouchers at that point.

Illustration 3 – The cash system

XYZ Limited is a company manufacturing handbags.

Paul Hewson is the sales manager, and attends a trade exhibition. He wishes to claim the train and taxi fares through the petty cash system.

Describe the process by which he does this.

(1) He fills out a petty cash voucher, detailing the purpose of the claim. He should also record his department and the purpose of the visit so that it can be coded to the correct expense heading.

(2) He staples the receipts to the back.

(3) If the expenditure is over a certain amount, which will vary according to the company, he will need to get authorisation from his supervisor.

(4) The cashier gives him the money.

(5) The cashier records the payment in the petty cash book and codes it as 'sales-travel'.

6 The inventory system

The inventory system is really several systems, which can be summarised as follows:

The production manager will decide on the required inventory purchases bearing in mind the items to be produced and the inventory balance on hand. In some (automated) systems raw materials will be ordered automatically when the balance falls to a certain level.

The goods are received and are stored in the raw materials store.

When goods are required for production, the production manager completes a materials requisition form and gets the goods from the store.

The goods are then made into 'work in progress' (partially complete goods) and eventually finished goods. The length of this process depends on the type of item being produced.

When the goods are sold, a record must be made of the quantity removed from inventory.

At the year end, all inventory will be counted and valued so that the statement of financial position can be produced.

Illustration 4 – The inventory system

XYZ Limited is a company manufacturing handbags.

Describe the inventory system as it relates to the production of a handbag.

(1) The production manager decides what items will be produced and checks the amount of raw materials required and in inventory.

(2) He produces a purchase requisition for the leather, zips, fastenings required.

(3) The goods arrive and are included in the raw material inventory record.

(4) The production department requisitions the raw materials needed.

(5) The handbags are produced, becoming firstly work in progress...

(6) ...and then finished goods.

(7) The finished handbags are added into the finished goods inventory records and then transferred to the warehouse.

(8) The handbags are sold, and deducted from the finished goods records.

7 The purpose of organisational control

Control within an organisation has several purposes:

Purpose	Why this is important
Safeguard company's assets	If assets are stolen or damaged the company will have to spend money to replace then.
Efficiency	Inefficient business practices are a waste of the company's money.
Prevent fraud	Fraud means the loss of valuable resources belonging to the company/shareholders.
Prevent errors	Errors can lead to losses in efficiency (time spent correcting) or a loss of assets (e.g. failing to invoice the correct amount, paying for goods which have not been received).

This ties in with corporate governance, which is covered elsewhere in this workbook. The directors are required to introduce a good system of controls to safeguard the company's assets and protect the shareholders' investments.

Most of our focus will be on financial controls. The company should introduce controls to prevent fraud and error.

The purpose of organisational control

XYZ Limited is a company manufacturing handbags.

Purpose	Example	Why important
Safeguard company's assets	Regular inventory counts and investigation if quantity on hand is not as expected.	Staff could be stealing the handbags to sell privately, so controls need to be in place to protect the inventory.
Efficiency	Should get several quotations before placing a purchase order.	It is a waste of money to spend more than necessary, and it will reduce the profit margins on the bags.
Prevent fraud	Two people should open the post and list the contents.	There could be misappropriation of cheques/cash before they are banked.
Prevent errors	The payroll calculation for a sample of employees should be checked each month.	It is a waste of money to pay them too much in error, and demoralising for the employees to pay them too little in error.

Test your understanding 6

Complete the following table from the perspective of a fast food outlet.

Purpose	Example	Why this is important
Safeguard company's assets		
Efficiency		
Prevent fraud		
Prevent errors		

8 Why controls in systems are important

Controls are important in all systems for the reasons given above.

The specific issues in the systems we have mentioned are as follows:

System	Purpose	Key areas
Purchasing	Safeguard company's assets	• Ensuring that only goods that have been received are paid for. • Ensuring goods are in good condition.
	Efficiency	• Ensuring that the best price is negotiated before buying.
	Prevent fraud	• Preventing purchasing staff accepting payments from suppliers to persuade them to purchase from that supplier.
	Prevent errors	• Ensuring that the correct amount is charged by suppliers. • Ensuring that they all purchases are recorded.

Sales	Safeguard company's assets	• Ensuring goods are only sold to customers who are likely to pay.
	Efficiency	• Ensuring orders are processed promptly so that customers do not go elsewhere.
	Prevent fraud	• Ensuring there is no theft of cash from customers.
	Prevent errors	• Ensuring the correct quantity of goods is despatched and invoiced.
Wages	Safeguard company's assets	• Ensuring that cash wages cannot be stolen.
	Efficiency	• Ensuring that people are only paid for overtime when necessary (approved).
	Prevent fraud	• Ensuring that there are no 'ghost' employees, people being paid but who do not work for the company. • Ensuring employees do not claim pay for hours they have not worked.
Cash	Safeguard company's assets	• Ensuring cash is kept safe from theft.
	Efficiency	• Ensuring cash is banked promptly, so as to gain interest.
	Prevent fraud	• Ensuring employees do not claim for expenses not incurred.
	Prevent errors	• Ensuring the entries in the cash book are correct.
Inventory	Safeguard company's assets	• Ensuring inventory is kept free from damage.
	Efficiency	• Ensuring inventory is only produced when it can be sold quickly.
	Prevent fraud	• Ensuring inventory cannot be stolen by employees.
	Prevent errors	• Ensuring costs of finished goods are calculated properly.

Illustration 5 – Why controls in systems are important

XYZ Limited is a company manufacturing handbags.

Complete this table, stating two controls which could be in operation to achieve each of the objectives listed for the inventory system.

Safeguard company's assets.	Ensuring inventory is kept free from damage.	• Store room kept tidy and clean. • Handbags put into plastic bags and boxes as soon as finished.
Efficiency	Ensuring inventory is only produced when it can be sold quickly.	• Forecasts of sales of each handbag style made by sales department. • Raw materials and production only scheduled when there is demand for bags.
Prevent fraud	Ensuring inventory cannot be stolen by employees.	• Warehouse to be kept locked and all inventory movements recorded. • Regular inventory counts and investigations of discrepancies.
Prevent errors	Ensuring costs of finished goods are calculated properly.	• Checks of calculations by another person. • Comparison against previous periods and estimates.

Test your understanding 7

Ben recently began trade as a mechanic. His business has been a great success and, due to the volume of work, he has decided to hire a part-time bookkeeper. Ben wishes to have as little as possible to do with the finances of his business.

At the end of each day he tells the bookkeeper which jobs have been undertaken that day and which customers they relate to. The bookkeeper then records the transactions, matches the work described to the price list and raises invoices as appropriate. She processes any receipts from customers as they arrive.

In addition, the bookkeeper processes all purchases invoices that come into the business and makes payments as needed. Ben has no further involvement in the accounting system.

Identify the major weaknesses in Ben's accounting system. What improvements could he make to deal with them?

9 Automated systems

Automated (computerised) systems are nowadays used by most organisations with the exception of very small firms.

Large companies will have accounting software especially written for their needs ('bespoke systems') whereas smaller companies will purchase a standardised accounting package that has been written to suit any company ('off-the-shelf package').

Automated systems show the following features:

Uniform processing of transactions	Every transaction will be performed in exactly the same way.
Lack of segregation of functions	One person in the company, the IT manager has a lot of power as he/she can access all the data within the company.
Potential for data to be corrupted easily	An inexpert operator could accidentally corrupt data. Computer files can become corrupted on their own. Alternatively, users may input data incorrectly.
Potential for increased management supervision	Management can monitor the activities of subordinates easily. Exception reports can be used to highlight unusual transactions.

The records maintained under manual and automated systems are similar, but the use of an automated system allows the data to be analysed more easily in a variety of ways. For example, it would be very time-consuming to produce a report showing how long customers have owed money under a manual system, but very quick using an automated system.

Illustration 8 – Automated systems

XYZ Limited is a company manufacturing handbags.

Describe five specific advantages to XYZ Limited of automating its financial systems.

(1) It can easily prepare an analysis of which products have sold at what quantities, and use this to determine its marketing strategy and production plans.

(2) It can easily prepare an aged inventory analysis, so as to identify slow-moving designs.

(3) It can use an aged receivables analysis to focus collection work on slow-paying customers.

(4) It can use passwords to protect confidential information.

(5) It can prepare an exception report detailing potential 'ghost' employees and then investigate. For example, an employee who has not taken holiday in the last 12 months or been sick may not actually exist.

Test your understanding 8

ABC Limited is an ACCA tuition provider.

Give three examples of information that would be useful to the business and easily obtained using a computerised system.

10 A comparison of manual and automated systems

- Manual and automated systems both have their advantages and disadvantages. Some of these are listed below:

Manual systems	
Advantages	**Disadvantages**
Low capital cost	Slower at performing calculations
No computer experience required	More likely to make calculation errors
Easy to correct errors (e.g. whitening fluid)	Analysis of information is more time-consuming
Ledgers are portable	Less easy to audit
Can review transactions for logical sense while entering/performing calculations	

Advantages	**Disadvantages**
Quicker	Capital cost
Can perform more complex calculations	Training cost, especially for older staff
Fewer errors	Less easy to correct errors
More security (passwords)	Systems can crash
Easier to sort and analyse data	

Advantages and disadvantages of automating financial systems

Advantages	
Quicker	The computer can process transactions, e.g. add up enrolment revenue, more quickly than a person with a calculator.
Fewer errors	The computer will not make mistakes in adding up.
More security (passwords)	Only authorised personnel will be able to access data, e.g. enrolment data, payroll data.
Easier to sort and analyse data	Can produce an analysis of, for example, enrolment timing to make decisions on future strategy.

Disadvantages	
Capital cost	The setup costs will depend on the system, but the company would need as a minimum several terminals (for enrolment and other financial records) plus printers and software.
Training cost, especially for older staff	Staff would need to be trained in how to operate the system.
Less easy to correct errors	If errors are made, especially when the automated system is first introduced, it could be very complex to correct them.
Systems could crash	If the company does not back up regularly it could lose data.

Chapter summary

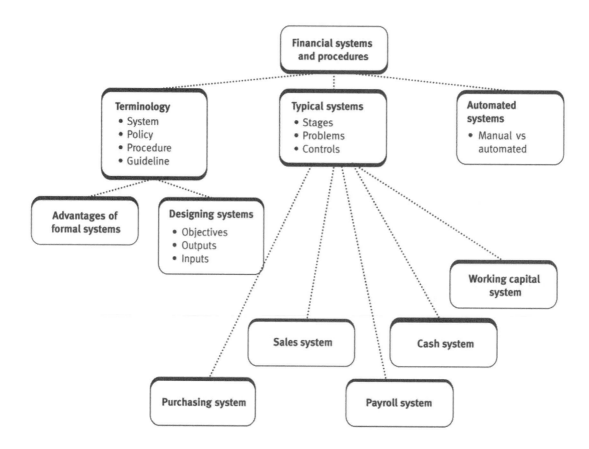

11 Practice questions

Test your understanding 9

You are given the following extract: 'The clerk multiplies the hours worked by the hourly rate to determine the gross pay....'

What does this extract describe?

A   A system

B   A policy

C   A procedure

D   A guideline

Test your understanding 10

A is trying to design a system for the processing of orders from customers.

Which of the following is not likely to be an objective of this system?

A   To ensure that orders are processed promptly

B   To ensure that goods are only dispatched to customers who are likely to pay

C   To ensure that all orders are recorded

D   To ensure that customers sign to accept the goods

Test your understanding 11

Which of the following is not a stage in a standard purchases system?

A   Receipt of goods

B   Receipt of cash

C   Placing of order

D   Matching of invoices with orders and goods received notes

Test your understanding 12

Which of the following would be earliest in the sales cycle for a company selling goods on credit to wholesalers?

A   Receipt of payment

B   Dispatch of goods

C   Receipt of order

D   Dispatch of invoice

Test your understanding 13

Consider the following stages in the inventory control system:

(i)   Transfer to warehouse

(ii)   Requisition of raw materials

(iii)   Year end inventory check (stock-take)

(iv)   Purchase of raw materials

What order will these stages usually be performed in?

A   (i), (iv), (ii), (iii)

B   (ii), (iii), (i), (iv)

C   (ii), (iv), (iii), (i)

D   (ii), (iv), (i), (iii)

Test your understanding 14

Which of these controls relates to the purchasing system?

A   Agreeing invoices to goods received notes

B   Checking creditworthiness

C   Authorising timesheets

D   Keeping the finished goods warehouse locked

Test your understanding 15

Which of these controls relates to the sales system?

A   Matching of cash payments to invoices received

B   Calculating overtime payments

C   Authorisation of requisition forms

D   Matching of cash received to invoices sent

Test your understanding 16

Which of the following is not a feature of an automated system?

A   Uniform processing of transactions

B   Lack of segregation of functions

C   Reduced chance of data corruption

D   Potential for increased management supervision

Test your understanding 17

The primary purposes of control within an organisation are to safeguard company assets, improve efficiency and prevent fraud and errors.

Is this statement:

A   True

B   False

Test your understanding 18

Consider the following system features:

(i)   Low capital costs

(ii)   Less potential for errors

(iii)   Improved security

(iv)   Transactions can easily be reviewed for logical sense

Which of these are features of an automated system?

A   (i) and (iv) only

B   (ii) and (iii) only

C   (i) and (iii) only

D   (ii) and (iv) only

Test your understanding answers

Test your understanding 1

System	The process by which a student selects which paper he/she wants to take, enrols for the course at a tuition provider and pays.
Policy	The tuition provider has a policy that only students who have been briefed about ACCA can enrol.
Procedure	The student details are entered onto the computer and a student registration card is produced.
Guideline	Students are recommended to sit no more than three papers if in full-time employment.

Test your understanding 2

Objectives	To record accurately and efficiently which students are doing which paper and how much they have paid.
Outputs	• A class register. • An analysis of sales revenue by paper and class.
Inputs	• Personal enrolments ('walk in'). • Mailed enrolment forms. • Faxed enrolment forms. • Emailed/online enrolment.
What could go wrong	• The wrong amount could be charged. • Students could be enrolled for a class which is full. • Enrolling staff could misappropriate the payments made. • Faxes, mailed enrolments, etc. could be lost and not processed.

Test your understanding 3

Stage	Administration	What could go wrong	Control measures
Item is required	Requisition order issued in two copies to purchasing and client.	• Incorrect item requisitioned • Item ordered that is not needed	• Requisition order to be signed off by purchasing manager.
Purchase order is raised	Purchase order issued in up to four copies to be sent to accounts, individual who placed the order warehouse and purchasing department.	• Copies not sent to all necessary recipients	• Purchase order to be matched to requisition order once created. • All recipients to sign to indicate they have received a copy of the purchase order.
Goods received	Goods received note is issued in up to four copies, as above.	• Goods received note not sent to all necessary recipients • Goods received note not allocated to supplier account. • Incorrect or defective goods received.	• GRN to be processed as soon as received and matched to purchase order. Unmatched purchase orders to be investigated. • Check condition of the goods received • Regular purchase ledger reconciliations

Invoice received	One copy raised to accounts department.	• Invoice not processed, or entered inaccurately	• Invoice amount to be matched to original purchase order. • Regular purchase ledger reconciliations. • Record promptly.
Goods paid or returned	Payment processed or credit note received.	• Incorrect payment made (in error or fraudulently) • Payment or return not allocated to supplier account	• Match payment amount to original invoice. • Regular purchase ledger reconciliations. • Ensure that payment is correctly authorised.

Test your understanding 4

Stage	Administration	What could go wrong	Control measures
Receive order	Sales order two to three copies – for dispatch and sales department records.	• Failure to process invoice • Order not copied to all departments	• Checks on all orders received • Relevant departments sign upon receipt of order • Authorisation required for sale to new customers

Dispatch the goods	Goods dispatched note up to five copies for accounts dep't, driver, customer, sales dep't and warehouse records.	• Goods not dispatched to customer • GDN not created for all relevant recipients • Incorrect goods sent to customer	• GDN agreed to original order and checked against goods to be sent to customer • All orders received reviewed after a number of days to ensure sent to customer
Raise an invoice	Sales invoice is copied twice for the customer and accounts dep't.	Invoice not raised Incorrect invoice raised Invoice not allocated to a customer account	• All orders to be reviewed periodically and matched to invoices • Regular sales ledger reconciliations to be undertaken • Invoice matched to GDN
Payment or return of goods	Payment processed or credit note (if applicable) copied twice to customer and accounts dep't.	Payment or receipt not allocated to a customer account • Customer fails to pay	• Regular sales ledger reconciliations to be undertaken • Segregation of duties • Monitor and chase overdue accounts

Test your understanding 5

Stage	What could go wrong	Control measures
Variable data	• incorrect levels of work recorded, leading to employees being over/underpaid	• all overtime and work information to be verified and authorised by management
Fixed data	• fraudulent creation of employees that do not exist • failing to record new employees/remove old employees from the payroll • failure to pay at the correct rate • allowing too many/too few holidays for staff	• segregation of duties within the payroll department • changes to fixed employee data to be authorised by senior management • staff data regularly reviewed and updated • verification of employee identity
Calculations	• inaccurate calculations leading to errors in payments to staff or government	• random checks on all payroll calculations • use of automated payroll systems
Production of reports and payments	• inaccurate payslips produced • payments made to wrong employees • payments not matching amount calculated	• match sample of payslips to calculations made • automated payroll system • reconciliation of payments made to payroll calculations • authorisation of wage payment

Test your understanding 6

Purpose	Example	Why this is important
Safeguard company's assets	Supervision and security cameras to ensure servers can't keep cash from customers rather than recording sale in cash register.	Cash is very susceptible to theft, since a thief can spend it immediately. Controls should therefore be in place to minimise the chances of loss of assets in this way.
Efficiency	Company should monitor demand at different times of the day, and ensure that the correct amount of food is cooked.	If too much food is cooked it may need to be thrown away if not sold in time. If too little food is cooked, customers will have to wait and will become impatient.
Prevent fraud	The cash register should be set so that when the server selects the item the customer requires from a menu the price will be selected automatically.	In a fast-moving, noisy environment the servers could charge the wrong price in error.
Prevent errors	Two people present when cashing up.	High risk environment as transactions are generally all made in cash.

Test your understanding 7

Major weaknesses

- The bookkeeper receives information verbally from Ben regarding the day's transactions. There is a very real risk that she may record the information incorrectly, leading to inaccurate invoices being sent to customers. This could also lead to inaccurate financial statements ultimately being produced.

- There is potential for fraud within Ben's systems. Should the bookkeeper be dishonest, she could easily steal receipts from customers as they arrive, or raise false purchase invoices which would be paid to her. With no checks or controls within the system, this should be of serious concern to Ben.

- There is no checking of the accounting system at any stage. This means that there is a high chance of fraud and errors throughout the system.

Possible improvements

- Ben should keep a written record of the jobs he has undertaken each day for the bookkeeper. In addition, he should then check the sales invoices to ensure this has been recorded correctly.

- Ben should consider segregating duties. For example, the raising of sales invoices should be kept separate from the processing of receipts. Ben could either perform one of these tasks for himself, or hire someone to do it for him.

- Ultimately, Ben may have to be more involved with the maintenance of his financial records than he might like to be.

Test your understanding 8

(1) Number of students in each class.

(2) The timing of enrolments, i.e. how many students enrolled early to take advantage of 'early bird' discounts.

(3) The correlation between attendance at class and exam mark.

Test your understanding 9

The correct answer is C

This is a single procedure – not a system, which would involve a number of different stages.

Test your understanding 10

The correct answer is D

While getting customers to sign for receipt of the goods is likely to be a procedure that A builds into the system, it is unlikely to be an **objective** of the system.

Test your understanding 11

The correct answer is B

The purchases system will involve making payments to suppliers, not receiving money from them.

Test your understanding 12

The correct answer is C

The correct order is likely to be C, B, D then A.

Test your understanding 13

The correct answer is D

By definition.

Test your understanding 14

The correct answer is A

B relates to the sales system, C would help with the payroll system, while D would be a control as part of the inventory system.

Test your understanding 15

The correct answer is D

A and C are controls of the purchasing system, while B relates to the payroll system.

Test your understanding 16

The correct answer is C

It is possible for inexpert users to accidentally corrupt data on an automated system.

Test your understanding 17

The correct answer is A – True

By definition.

Test your understanding 18

The correct answer is B

Manual systems tend to be cheaper to set up and make it easy for transactions to be reviewed for logical sense as they are being manually input.

The relationship between accounting and other business functions

Chapter learning objectives

Upon completion of this chapter you will be able to:

- explain the relationship between accounting and other key functions within the business such as procurement, production and marketing

- explain financial considerations in production and production planning

- identify the financial issues associated with marketing

- identify the financial costs and benefits of effective service provision.

1 Introduction

In the last chapter, we looked at the various financial systems that operate within most organisations. We will now go on to examine how these systems interact with the organisation's accounting function.

2 Purchasing (procurement)

The purchasing/buying function is responsible for placing and following up orders. It co-ordinates with the accounting department as follows:

Establishing credit terms	The accounting department will work with the buying department to liaise with suppliers to obtain a credit account and to negotiate credit terms which are acceptable.
Prices	The accounting department can advise the buying department on the maximum price that should be paid to maintain margins.
Payment	Payments may be approved by the buying department but are made by the accounting department.
Data capture, e.g. orders	Order details will be input by the buying department and details passed to accounting department.
Inventory	The purchasing department will consult with the inventory section of the accounting department to determine the quantity of items already in stock and therefore the quantity required.
Budgeting	The accounting department will consult with the buying department on likely costs in preparing budgets.

Illustration 1 – Purchasing

XYZ Limited is a company manufacturing handbags.

Describe how the buying department liaises with the accounting department when buying some leather to make handbags from DEF Limited, a new supplier.

Establishing credit terms	The buying department will advise the accounting department that the preferred supplier is DEF. The accounting department contacts the credit controller at DEF and provides the information required to set up a credit account.
Prices	The accounting department obtains the cost estimate for the handbag being produced. It discusses with the buying department how much can be paid for the leather in order to maintain margins.
Payment	The payment for the leather is approved by the buying department and then made by the accounting department.
Data capture, e.g. orders	Order details for the leather will be input by the buying department and details passed to the accounting department to check that the price on the invoice is correct.
Inventory	Before placing the order, the buying department will consult with the inventory section to determine how much suitable leather is already in stock.

Test your understanding 1

Complete the following table, showing how the purchase and accounting departments would liaise in the case of a company with a chain of fast-food outlets.

Establishing credit terms	
Prices	
Payment	
Data capture, e.g. orders	
Inventory	
Budgeting	

3 Production

The production department plans and oversees the production of goods. It liaises with the accounting department as follows:

Cost measurement, allocation, absorption	The production department measures quantities of materials and time used; the management accountant gives a monetary value to them. Costs are then allocated and absorbed to calculate production costs based on advice given by the production department.
Budgeting	The production department will decide how many items of what type are to be produced. The cost of producing these will be determined by the accounting and production departments together, and incorporated into the overall budget.
Cost v quality	The production and accounting departments will discuss the features that can be included in products and the raw materials that should be used. They should agree which better quality materials and features justify the extra cost, and discuss how to maximise quality and profit.
Inventory	The production department will liaise with the inventory section to ensure that there are sufficient raw materials in inventory for the production that is planned.

Illustration 2 – Production

XYZ Limited is a company manufacturing handbags.

The company has commissioned a designer to design a new style of handbag and discussions are taking place about the materials to be used and the quantity to be produced.

Describe how the accounting and production departments would liaise over this.

Cost measurement, allocation, absorption	The production department would estimate the quantity of raw materials required and (in conjunction with the purchase department) estimate their cost. Together with the accounting department overheads will be allocated to determine the full cost of the handbag.
Budgeting	The production department, accounting department and marketing department will discuss how many bags are likely to be sold at what price and determine how many should be produced. A budget can then be produced.
Cost v quality	The production, accounting (and marketing) departments will discuss the various grades of leather and the material that could be used, their costs, and the extra price that could be charged for better quality material. They will decide on the best combination of cost/quality/profit.
Inventory	The production department will discuss with the inventory section of the accounting department the materials required. Some existing materials may be usable for the new product or entirely new materials may need to be purchased.

4   Marketing

We have already examined the marketing function in more detail in chapter 2.

The marketing department co-ordinates with the accounting department as follows:

Budgeting	The accounting department will discuss the likely sales volume of each product with the marketing department, in order to produce the sales budget.
Advertising	The accounting department will help the marketing department in setting a budget, and in monitoring whether it is cost effective. For example, they could help in measuring new business generated as a result of different advertising campaigns.

Pricing	The accounting department will have input into the price that is charged. Often products are priced at cost plus a percentage. Even if the marketing department determines the price based on market forces they need to consult with the accounting department to ensure that costs are covered.
Market share	The accounting department can provide the marketing department with information on sales volumes for each product, to help the marketing department in determining market share.

In many companies there can be a great deal of antagonism between marketing and accounting, especially over pricing and cost control.

5 Service provision

Companies very often provide services to customers, at the same time as a sale or afterwards, e.g. a computer retailer may charge an extra fee to help customers set up their system, or a car dealer may provide car servicing.

5.1 The nature of services

Services are said to have four main features.

- **Intangibility** – services are activities undertaken by the organization on behalf of its customers and therefore cannot be packaged for the customer to take away with them. They often have few, if any, physical aspects. For example, a taxi driver provides a service, carrying customers from one location to another. The customers do not have a permanent, tangible product they can keep.

- **Inseparability** – services are often created by the organisation at the same time as they are consumed by the customer. For instance, a taxi driver will create the service they offer as they are carrying a passenger to their desired location. The service cannot therefore be easily distinguished from the person or organisation providing the service.

- **Perishability** – services cannot be stored for later. For example, a taxi driver cannot take a customer to the same location at the same point in time twice. Once the journey is over, the service has been consumed.

- **Variability** – each service is unique and cannot usually be repeated in exactly the same way, making offering a standardised service to customers very difficult.

5.2 The relationship between service provision and accounting

There are several issues about which the service departments may need the input of the accounting department.

Charge-out rates	This is the hourly rate which the company charges clients. It should be higher than salary, as it should include a share of overheads, e.g. training and any profit the company wishes to make. However if the charge-out rate is too high customers will not use the service. Many accounting firms base charge-out rates for their staff on roughly three times that person's salary.
Estimating costs	Problems arise in determining the amount of overhead to be included in the charge-out rate. Also, if the service takes longer to provide than expected, the company may not be able to pass on the extra cost.
Problems measuring benefits	Market conditions may mean that the charge-out rate contains a very low profit element. The company may question whether it is worth carrying out these services. The problem is that the benefits are intangible and not easy no measure, but nevertheless real. A company with effective service provision has happier customers, and happy customers are more likely to buy from the company in future, therefore leading to lower selling costs. But it is very difficult to measure these benefits.

Illustration 3 – Service provision

GHI Limited is a retailer of computers.

GHI offers a service to customers whereby they will go to the customer's house and set up their new system.

What factors should be taken into account in determining the fee to be charged for this service?

- wages cost of the employee

- employer's social security cost

- transport costs

- other indirect employee costs, such as training

- how long the job will take

- GHI's required return on the service

- cost savings due to providing service, e.g. fewer calls to GHI's 'problem hotline'

- fee charged by competitors for the same service

- price charged for the computer (if computer price is low, charge more for this service and vice versa).

Test your understanding 2

JKL Limited is a car dealer, dealing in new and second-hand cars.

JKL also has a service department which services cars for customers and others. The fee charged to customers will include parts used and an hourly rate for the time spent by service personnel.

List the factors that should be taken into account by JKL in determining the hourly rate to be charged for such services.

Test your understanding 3

JKL Limited is a car dealer, dealing in new and second-hand cars.

JKL also has a service department which services cars for customers and others. The fee charged to customers will include parts used and an hourly rate for the time spent by service personnel.

List the benefits to JKL of providing such a service.

Chapter summary

6 Practice questions

Test your understanding 4

Which of the following is an example of co-ordination between the purchasing and accounting departments?

A   Establishing credit terms

B   Determining sales prices

C   Allocating costs

D   Calculating pay rises

Test your understanding 5

Which of the following is not an example of co-ordination between the marketing and accounting department?

A   Review cost/benefit of advertising

B   Pricing

C   Assessing market share

D   Assessing creditworthiness

Test your understanding 6

Which of the following is a likely advantage of providing a good service?

A   Greater customer satisfaction

B   Higher payroll costs

C   Higher inventory turnover

D   Economies of scale

Test your understanding 7

'Most services provided by an organisation will be created at the same time as they are consumed.'

Which feature of services is being described?

A   Intangibility

B   Inseparability

C   Perishability

D   Variability

Test your understanding answers

Test your understanding 1

Establishing credit terms	The accounting department will work with the buying department to liaise with suppliers to obtain a credit account and to negotiate credit terms which are acceptable. Since the fast-food company will be buying large quantities of just a few items, it should be able to negotiate good terms.
Prices	The accounting department can advise the buying department on the maximum price that should be paid to maintain margins. Achieving low cost is vital in this type of business where prices are low.
Payment	The purchasing department approves the invoices, and the accounting department pays them.
Data capture, e.g. orders	Order details will be input by the buying department and details passed to the accounting department so that the price can be checked when the invoice comes in.
Inventory	The purchasing department will consult with the inventory section of the accounting department to determine the quantity of items already in inventory and therefore the quantity required. They will also discuss likely usage of raw materials in the near future.
Budgeting	The accounting department will consult with the buying department on likely costs in preparing budgets, as the buying department will have more focus on trends in raw materials costs.

Test your understanding 2

- Wages cost of the employee.
- Employer's social security cost.
- Other indirect employee costs, such as training.
- JKL's required return on the service.
- Fee charged by competitors for the same service.
- The depreciation charge on service equipment used (a share of this overhead should be included in the charge-out rate).
- Other service department overheads, e.g. service receptionists, waiting area.

Test your understanding 3

- JKL can offer customers a one-stop solution for all their motoring needs.

- Customers would think it strange/inconvenient if there were no service department.

- JKL can enhance overall customer satisfaction by providing good service.

- Customers may buy a new car when they see new models on display.

- If JKL does not offer service functions, customers will go elsewhere for servicing and may buy cars elsewhere.

Test your understanding 4

The correct answer is A

B relates to marketing, C relates to production and D relates to personnel.

Test your understanding 5

The correct answer is D

This would be an example of co-ordination between the sales and accounting departments.

Test your understanding 6

The correct answer is A

Note that provision of services would be unlikely to affect the sale of physical units, so inventory turnover would be unaffected.

Test your understanding 7

The correct answer is B

By definition.

Audit and financial control

Chapter learning objectives

Upon completion of this chapter you will be able to:

- identify and describe the main audit and assurance roles in business
  - internal
  - external audit
- explain the main functions on the internal auditor and the external auditor and how they differ
- explain basic legal requirements in relation to preparing and auditing financial statements
- explain internal control and internal check
- explain the importance of internal financial controls in an organisation
- describe the responsibilities of management for internal financial control
- describe the features of effective internal financial control procedures in an organisation, including authorisation
- identify and describe the types of information technology and information systems used by the business for internal control
- identify and describe features for protecting the security of IT systems and software within business
- describe general and application controls in business.

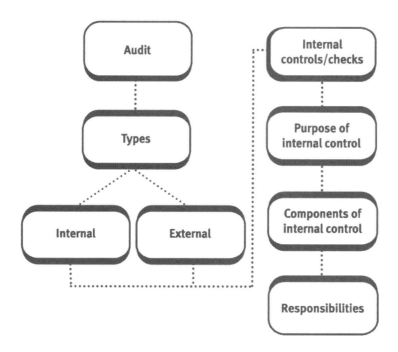

1 The meaning of internal control and internal check

 Internal control is the process designed and effected by management to provide reasonable assurance about the achievement of the entity's objectives with regard to:

- reliability of financial reporting

- effectiveness and efficiency of operations, and

- compliance with applicable laws and regulations.

Definition based on the Auditing Practices Board

'Glossary of Terms'.

Example of internal control

For example, an accounts department might have a policy to check the additions and multiplications on a purchase invoice received, before it is approved for payment. This control would help to ensure that the correct amounts are paid to the organisation's suppliers, and would therefore improve the reliability of the amounts reported as purchases.

 Internal check is an element of internal control, concerned with ensuring that no single task is executed from start to finish by only one person. Each individual's work is subject to an independent check by another person in the course of that other person's duties.

KAPLAN PUBLISHING

Internal check – more detail

The purpose of internal checking is to reduce the likelihood of errors and fraud. Errors should be reduced since an employee will take more care over their work if they know it is going to be looked at by someone else, and any errors which are made should be spotted by the second person so that corrections can be made. Similarly an employee will be dissuaded from defrauding the company if they know that their work will be checked and that it is likely that their fraud will be discovered.

Clearly it is possible that two or more employees could collude together to defraud their company, so it is risky to rely on a single internal control at any stage of operations. However a comprehensive suite of controls should reduce the risk of material error or fraud to an acceptably low level.

Illustration 1 – The meaning of internal control and internal check

Consider a company that sells bottled drinks to supermarkets and other retailers. The company maintains its inventories in a central warehouse. Internal controls would be established by management to ensure the security of the inventories (so that they are not stolen by employees or third parties) and to ensure the accuracy of the accounting figures for inventories included in the financial statements.

Typical controls could be:

- physical controls – keeping the front door locked when not in use, and banning visitors from entering the warehouse storage area

- regular inventory counts – the inventories held could be counted every six months to check the accuracy of the continuous inventory records.

An internal check on inventory quantities could be implemented at each inventory count by ensuring that no individual counts the items that they are responsible for maintaining. In this way it would not be possible for an employee to steal items of inventory, and then to pretend at the regular count that the stolen items were still there in the warehouse. Such a theft would require collusion between employees if it is going to remain undetected.

Test your understanding 1

'A company's internal controls can be so well designed that they eliminate the risk of failing to achieve the company's objectives.'

Is this statement:

A   True

B   False

2 The purpose of internal control

The purpose of internal control is implied by the definition given earlier, to help management achieve the entity's objectives, especially in terms of ensuring:

- the orderly and efficient conduct of the business

- the safeguarding of assets

- the prevention and detection of fraud and error

- the accuracy and completeness of the accounting records, and

- the timely preparation of reliable financial information.

Why do companies need internal controls?

Internal controls are there to prevent risks occurring or to minimise the impact of risks (i.e. to help prevent things going wrong). Even when controls are in place documents may still get lost or portable assets may go missing. The level and extent of internal controls required depend on what the risks are if such controls fail. It is particularly important that stringent controls exist where there are associated legal requirements.

 Internal controls – more detail

Documents are batched and pre-numbered so staff can check that there are none missing. If any sales invoices go missing debts may not be collected and income may be understated; cash flow would therefore also be affected resulting in payment difficulties.

If purchase invoices go missing the company would be overstating profits and if money owing to those payables was spent elsewhere, cash flow problems could result later.

But what if the amounts involved are small? Does one invoice really matter? Experience shows that if one invoice has gone missing it is highly likely that several more are also missing, and the larger the organisation gets, the bigger the numbers get, and the tighter the controls have to be to prevent significant errors.

Authorisation controls are another type of internal control and are particularly important. For example, suppose that a clerk routinely authorises false purchase invoices raised by a friend outside the company. The company pays the invoices and the friend and the clerk share the proceeds. This is a very common type of fraud.

Controls to prevent this require payments to be authorised only with reference to purchase invoices that are attached to goods received notes, or authorisations for the receipt of services by managers completely unconnected with the accounting function.

3 The components of internal control

- the control environment
- the entity's risk assessment process
- the information system relevant to financial reporting
- control activities
- monitoring of controls.

The term 'internal control' can refer to any of these five components.

 The **control environment** is the overall attitude of management regarding internal controls and their importance. It encompasses management's philosophy, e.g. a commitment to integrity and ethical values, a formal organisation structure and proper training of staff.

 The control environment – more detail

The control environment sets the tone of the organisation in terms of the control consciousness of its employees. It is the foundation for effective internal control, providing discipline and structure. For example, if senior management openly engage in unethical behaviour, and urge fellow employees to ignore internal rules, then the whole tone of the organisation will be damaged and internal control will be weak.

 The **risk assessment process** is an entity's process for identifying and responding to business risks.

 Business risk – more detail

Business risk is the possibility that an event or transaction could occur that will adversely affect the organisation's ability to achieve its objectives and execute its strategies. It is conventionally split between internal and external factors, as below.

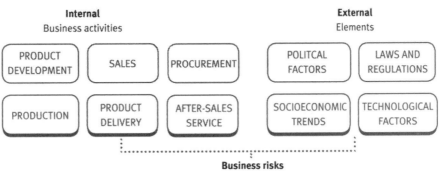

Once risks have been identified, management must investigate their significance, the likelihood of their occurrence, and how they should be managed.

The **information system** relevant to financial reporting objectives consists of the procedures and records established to process the transactions that the entity carries out, and to maintain accountability for the related assets, liabilities and equity balances. Many information systems make extensive use of information technology (IT).

The information system – more detail

The information system must be able to:

- identify and record all valid transactions

- describe the transactions in sufficient detail to permit proper classification for financial reporting

- measure the transactions to permit the recording of their proper monetary value in the financial statements

- determine the correct accounting period in which transactions should be recognised

- present properly the transactions and related disclosures in the financial statements.

 Control activities are the policies and procedures that help ensure that management directives are carried out, for example that necessary actions are taken to address risks that threaten the achievement of the entity's objectives. Control activities, whether within IT or manual systems, have various objectives and are applied at various organisational and functional levels.

Different books identify different categories of control activities. One possibility is:

- **A**uthorisation

- **C**omparison

- **C**omputer controls

- **A**rithmetical controls

- **M**aintaining a trial balance and control accounts

- **A**ccounting reconciliations

- **P**hysical controls

- **S**egregation of duties

(Use the mnemonic **ACCA MAPS** to remember these categories.)

Control activities – more detail

Control activities can take several forms.

Authorisation involves members of staff having to obtain approval from managers or other key members of staff for various transactions, especially those that are considered significant/material to the organisation. These could include expense claim forms, purchases or cash transfers – amongst others.

Comparison involves looking at analysis and reports in order to identify management or control issues from past performance. For example, a comparison of actual and budgeted figures might highlight business risks if implementation of the budget is slipping, or bookkeeping problems if the variance is due to errors in the recorded figures.

Computer controls tend to be of two separate types – general and application controls. These will be examined in more detail later. Both are designed to ensure that computer systems operate as intended.

Arithmetical controls check for minor errors or frauds that would not have otherwise been detected. Figures can be recalculated to check that they are correct.

Maintaining a trial balance and control accounts will often enable the organisation to easily see if errors or frauds have occurred by way of a simple review.

Accounts reconciliation, such as receivables and payables ledger reconciliations and bank reconciliations are useful tools in identifying errors and frauds and can be performed on a regular basis (using the control accounts mentioned above).

Physical controls are often overlooked, but they are just as important as administrative or accounting procedures. For example, there is no point in having an efficient inventory tracking system if there is inadequate security to prevent staff or third parties from simply stealing high value items.

Segregation of duties splits any given transaction into three elements: authorisation, recording and maintaining custody of assets. This is a potentially effective means of preventing fraud because it will require collusion between at least two members of staff. For example, ordering goods for personal use will be impossible because one member of staff must place the order and another will receive (have custody of) the goods. It would require both staff members to work together to defraud the system.

Management in an organisation are responsible for weighing up the costs and benefits of possible controls and establishing an appropriate internal control system. Below are listed a number of possible controls – try to decide which of the 'ACCA MAP' categories each control belongs to.

- Approval and control of **documents and transactions of importance** – in a purchases system, for example, there should be pre-set authority limits. An order up to the value of $1,000 could be approved by a department head, up to $5,000 by any one director, and beyond this by the board as a whole.

- Controls over **computerised applications** and the IT environment.

- Checking the **arithmetical accuracy** of the records – such controls include checking the casts on a purchase invoice (i.e. whether the invoice has been added up correctly), and recalculating the sales tax on sales invoices.

- Maintaining and reviewing **control accounts** and **trial balances** – control accounts include sales and purchase ledger control accounts, bank reconciliations and non-current asset registers.

- Comparing the results of **cash, security** and **inventory counts** with the accounting records.

- Comparing **internal data** with **external sources** of information – this might include supplier statement reconciliations.

- Comparing and analysing the financial results with budgeted amounts.

- Producing and reviewing **exception reports**, e.g. lists of purchasing transactions above certain limits or payments made without a purchase order.

- **Limiting direct physical access** to assets and records – an important general principle with respect to assets and records is that of **segregation of duties**. In particular there should be a division of responsibilities for:

  - **authorising** or initiating the transaction

  - the physical **custody** and control of assets involved

  - **recording** the transaction.

No one person should be in a position both to misappropriate an asset and to conceal the act by falsifying the records. For example, in a sales system the duties of receiving money from receivables and writing up the sales ledger should be separated. If not, money could be misappropriated and the records falsified to cover this.

Monitoring of controls is a process to assess the quality of internal control performance over time. It involves assessing the design and operation of controls on a timely basis and taking necessary corrective actions.

Management must decide whether existing control procedures are adequate. This could change over time. For example, a system might become overwhelmed if the entity grows too rapidly.

The operation of controls must also be checked. Compliance failures may arise because of lack of staff motivation or through poor training and supervision.

 Controls – more detail

In practice, the choice of controls may reflect a comparison of the cost of operating individual controls against the benefits expected to be derived from them.

Many of the internal controls which would be relevant to larger enterprises are not practical, appropriate or necessary in small enterprises. Managements of small enterprises have less need to depend on formal internal controls for the reliability of the records and other information, because of their personal contact with, or involvement in, the operation of the enterprise itself.

In many larger companies, internal audit will contribute to the monitoring of control activities, however the extent of internal audit's involvement is up to management to decide.

3.1 Alternative analysis of internal controls

There are three key types of control that can be considered.

Preventive controls

These are controls that prevent errors or frauds occurring. For example, authorisation controls should prevent fraudulent or invalid transactions taking place. Other preventive controls include segregation of duties, recruiting and training the right staff and having an effective control culture.

Detective controls

These are controls that detect if any problems have occurred. They are designed to pick up errors that have not been prevented. These could be exception reports that reveal that controls have been bypassed (for example, large amounts paid without being authorised). Other examples could include reconciliations, supervision and internal checks.

Corrective controls

These are controls that address any problems that have occurred. So when problems are identified, the controls ensure that they are properly rectified. Examples of corrective controls include follow-up procedures and management action.

Clearly the most powerful type of control is **preventative**. It is more effective to have a control that stops problems occurring rather than detecting or correcting them once they have occurred. There is always a possibility that it is too late to sort out the problem.

> **Test your understanding 2**
>
> For each of the following five components of internal control, give one specific example of an internal control that you might find in a well controlled company:
>
> * Control environment
>
> * Risk assessment process
>
> * Information system
>
> * Control activities
>
> * Monitoring of controls

4 Information technology and internal control

4.1 The use of IT in internal controls

For many businesses, IT can be a valuable tool when setting internal controls in two main areas.

Financial controls – this involves IT being used as a check for the financial data in the organisation. This could include ensuring the security of financial data, such as through the use of passwords and authorisation, but it could also allow organisations to make sure that financial procedures are followed.

For example, many businesses have IT based sales ledger facilities. The system could be set to prevent staff making sales to customers who have already reached their credit limit.

Operational controls – this is where IT is used as a control on the day-to-day activities of the business.

For example, a manufacturing business may have automated systems that check each unit and reject any that are defective.

4.2 The protection of IT systems and software within business

While IT has a role to play in the creation and implementation of internal controls, controls must also be put in place to ensure that an organisation's IT systems are operating correctly and are meeting their objectives.

These controls fall into two main categories.

4.2.1 General controls

These review the reliability of the data generated by the IT systems and check that they are operating correctly.

General controls include:

- **Physical controls** – these involve controls to avoid unauthorised access to computer equipment, such as security personnel, door locks and card entry systems. They will also include safeguards against possible environmental damage to the computer equipment, such as surge protectors in case of lightning strikes or other power surges.

- **Hardware and software configuration** – these controls are designed to ensure that any new IT is tested and installed correctly into the system to minimise the risk of errors or damage to the systems.

- **Logical access** – these controls are designed to prevent unauthorised access to the organisation's information systems. These could include password systems.

- **Disaster recovery** – these will ensure that the organisation will be able to continue operating despite adverse conditions. For example, off-site backup may be kept of all systems.

- **Output controls** – these ensure that the outputs from the system are both complete and secure. This could include controls over who outputs (such as reports or lists) are distributed to within the organisation.

- **Technical support** – it is important that all the users of the organisation's IT systems are competent. Training policies and technical support for workers can be a valuable control.

4.2.2 Application controls

These controls are fully automated and tend to be designed to ensure that the data input into the system is complete and accurate.

These controls will vary from system to system, but are often designed to ensure:

- **completeness** – has all necessary data been input?

- **authorisation** – is the person inputting the data authorised to do so?

- **identification** – can the person inputting the information be uniquely identified?

- **validity** – is the information being input by the user valid?

- **forensic checks** – is the information being input by the user mathematically accurate?

Illustration 3 – Application controls in practice

Imagine an employee in a bank entering a new customer's details onto an IT system. They will have to input data about (amongst other things) the customer's name, address, age, earnings and existing cash balances. Application controls are designed to ensure that this data is input accurately.

The system will most likely require the employee to log in using a unique password and ID. This ensures that they are **authorised** to enter new customer information and also enables the bank to **identify** the employee if there is a problem in the future (i.e. the new customer is found to be entered fraudulently).

The system may automatically refuse to process the application if one piece of information is missing, such as the age. This ensures **completeness**.

The system may also sense-check the information being input to ensure that it is **valid**. For instance, if the customer's post code or telephone number is not in the correct format, the system may refuse to accept the information and will not accept the new customer details.

5 Management responsibility

It is the directors (and senior management's) responsibility to establish proper internal control arrangements within their company. This responsibility may derive from statutory requirements or from general corporate governance arrangements.

Legal responsibilities of directors

Company law varies from country to country, but typically the directors of a company are required by law to keep proper accounting records, to safeguard the assets of the company, and hence to take reasonable steps to prevent and detect fraud and other irregularities. Such requirements imply the necessity for proper internal control.

This requirement is set out more clearly in the UK Corporate Governance Code. Principle C2 of the Code states that:

'The board is responsible for determining the nature and extent of the significant risks it is willing to take in achieving its strategic objectives. The board should maintain sound risk management and internal control systems.'

Provision C2.1 of the Code goes on to explain that the board should, at least annually, conduct a review of the effectiveness of the system of internal controls and should report to shareholders that they have done so. This review must cover all material controls, including financial, operational and compliance controls.

Management responsibility – further detail

The Turnbull Report (not nameable in your exam) was issued in 1999 to give guidance to directors on how to comply with these sections of the UK Corporate Governance Code. This Report again emphasises that:

> 'The board of directors is responsible for the company's system of internal control.'

Furthermore it is the role of management to implement board policies on risk and control, and all employees have some responsibility for internal control as part of their accountability for achieving objectives.

Management should report regularly to the board on the risks faced and the effectiveness of the system of internal control in managing those risks.

In its annual assessment of internal control, the board should consider:

- The changes in the nature and extent of significant risks since the last annual assessment.

- The scope of management's ongoing monitoring of risks, including the reports management have made to the board and any relevant work by internal audit.

- The incidence of any significant control failings or weaknesses that have been identified during the year.

Internal financial control is part of overall internal control. Although the auditors, for example, will be particularly interested in testing and reporting on the financial controls, the board is responsible for all the controls in the company: financial, operational and compliance controls.

6 The meaning of internal auditing and external auditing

In studying auditing, it is necessary to distinguish between internal auditing and external auditing.

 Internal auditing is an independent activity, established by management to examine and evaluate the organisation's risk management processes and systems of control, and to make recommendations for the achievement of company objectives.

 External auditing is the independent examination of the evidence from which the financial statements are derived, in order to give the reader of those statements confidence as to the truth and fairness of the state of affairs which they disclose.

Alternative definitions of internal and external audit

Alternative definitions are as follows:

Internal auditing is an appraisal activity established within an entity as a service to the entity. Its functions include, amongst other things, examining, evaluating and monitoring the adequacy and effectiveness of internal control.

Auditing Practices Board 'Glossary of Terms'

Internal auditing is an independent, objective assurance and consulting activity designed to add value and improve an organisation's operations. It helps an organisation accomplish its objectives by bringing a systematic, disciplined approach to evaluate and improve the effectiveness of risk management, control and governance processes.

The Institute of Internal Auditors 'Official Definition'

The objective of an (external) audit of financial statements is to enable the auditor to express an opinion whether the financial statements are prepared, in all material respects, in accordance with an applicable financial reporting framework.

Auditing Practices Board 'Glossary of Terms'

An external audit is a periodic examination of the books of account and records of an entity carried out by an independent third party (the auditor) to ensure that they have been properly maintained, are accurate and comply with established concepts, principles, accounting standards, legal requirements and give a true and fair view of the financial state of the entity.

CIMA 'Official Terminology'

You should recognise the following key points from these definitions:

- internal auditing is established by the management of a company to help them manage the company, by reporting to management on the company's risks and systems of control

- external auditing is required by law in large companies and public companies. Independent auditors inspect the accounting records and systems, in order to report to the shareholders on whether the published financial statements give a true and fair view.

The differences between the two sorts of auditing will be discussed further in the next sections overleaf.

The differences in roles can be summarised in tabular form.

Differences between internal and external audit

	Internal auditing	External auditing
Role	To advise management on whether the organisation has sound systems of internal controls to protect the organisation against loss.	To provide an opinion to the shareholders on whether the financial statements give a true and fair view.
Legal basis	Generally not a legal requirement. However the UK Corporate Governance Code recommends that if a listed company does not have an internal audit department, it should annually assess the need for one.	Legal requirement for large companies, public companies and many public bodies.
Scope of work	Determined by management. Covers all areas of the organisation, operational as well as financial.	Determined by the auditor in order to carry out his statutory duty to report. Financial focus.
Approach	Increasingly risk-based. Assess risks. Evaluate systems of controls. Test operations of systems. Make recommendations for improvements.	Increasingly risk-based. Test underlying transactions that form the basis of the financial statements.
Responsibility	To advise and make recommendations on internal control and corporate governance.	To form an opinion on whether the financial statements give a true and fair view.

 Differences between internal and external audit – further detail

External audit

Someone independent from outside the company being audited is brought in to examine the annual published financial statements.

They will issue a report that:

- explains the audit process
- gives opinions as to the **truth and fairness** of the accounts, and whether they have been **properly prepared.**

The process is highly regulated so that those likely to place reliance on published accounts are protected from poor or inconsistent auditing.

- Many organisations (typically large companies) are legally required to have an external audit.

- Only certain people are legally allowed to be external auditors.

- The external audit process is regulated by law, and by audit standards to ensure consistent quality.

Internal audit

Management may wish to have other things checked. For example:

- effectiveness of accounting systems

- effectiveness of internal control systems

- value for money audit, looking at the economy, efficiency and effectiveness of operations

- whether internal policies are being upheld

- anything else!

In the past, there was no legal requirement for this – it was up to management to decide. However, it is increasingly expected, and in the future may become a requirement, for some companies (especially if listed on a stock exchange).

A company may use internal employees to do these tasks, or may hire outside specialists (e.g. a firm of accountants) to provide the services required.

Key differences

Independence

External auditors must be, and be seen to be, independent of their clients, so that their opinions can be trusted.

Internal audit opinions would also be of more benefit if they were totally independent. However, internal auditors are appointed by the directors and report to the directors (and could be employees) so it is far harder to maintain independence. One way of reducing this problem is to require internal auditors to report to an audit committee.

Legal

External audits are legally required for many companies. Internal audit is recommended, and almost expected, for many companies – but there is no legal requirement in most countries (e.g. the UK) at present.

Appointment and reporting

External auditors are usually appointed by the shareholders, and also report to the shareholders. Internal auditors are appointed by directors and report to directors.

Process/work

External audits are controlled by the law, but mostly by audit standards. Guidance for internal audit is limited to fundamental principles and a small quantity of standards, so there is greater flexibility in how the work is done.

Test your understanding 3

'The internal audit is simply a necessary cost that must be incurred by a company and offers few tangible benefits for the organisation.'

Is this statement:

A   True

B   False

Test your understanding 4

Why might a bank insist on an external audit of a company's accounts before lending money to the company?

The purposes of internal audit

Company directors have a legal requirement to produce true and fair annual financial statements. To help ensure this is done, companies are required to have their published financial statements audited by an external team of experts (external auditors).

Directors also need assurance on other financial matters. This assurance is primarily for their own internal use, although in recent years pressure has grown for increasingly more of such work to be made publicly available.

This additional work is carried out by internal auditors, who may be company employees or outside experts from a firm of accountants.

Internal audit

Internal audit is part of the organisational control of a business; it is one of the methods used by management to ensure the efficient and orderly running of the business as a whole, and is part of the overall control environment.

Internal auditors' work has expanded in recent years, and the role of internal audit often now includes:

- helping to set corporate objectives

- helping to design and monitor performance measures for these objectives.

Corporate governance

A properly functioning internal audit department is part of good corporate governance, as recognised by all national and international corporate governance codes.

Internal audit enables management to perform proper risk assessments (another central theme of corporate governance codes) by means of properly understanding the strengths and weaknesses of all parts of the control systems in the business.

The function of internal audit in the context of corporate risk management

Internal audit has a particular interest in evaluating the company's risk management structures. Internal audit can:

- manage the basic data used by management to identify risks

- identify techniques for prioritising and managing risks

- report on the effectiveness of risk management solutions (e.g. internal controls).

The structure and operation of an internal audit function

The UK Corporate Governance Code on corporate governance states that companies without an internal audit function should **annually review the need for one**.

Where there is an internal audit function, the board should **annually review its scope of work**, authority and resources.

Ideally, the internal audit function should be staffed with **qualified, experienced staff**, whose work is closely monitored by an audit committee.

Scope of internal audit

- Internal audit staff are typically expected to carry out a variety of tasks:

- reviewing internal controls and financial reports

- reviewing risk management systems

- carrying out special assignments (e.g. fraud investigations)

- conducting operational reviews (e.g. into efficiency of parts of the business).

Limitations of internal audit

- Internal auditors have an unavoidable independence problem. They are employed by the management of the company and yet are expected to give an objective opinion on matters for which management are responsible.

- Internal audit will only succeed if it is properly staffed and resourced.

- If internal auditors identify fraud, they may be unwilling to disclose it for fear of the repercussions (which could involve the collapse of the company and the loss of their jobs).

These limitations can be reduced if an **audit committee**:

- sets the work agenda for internal audit

- receives internal audit reports

- is able to ensure the internal audit is properly resourced

- has a 'voice' at main board level.

The purposes of external audit

External audit

The purpose of external audit, as set out in the Auditing Practices Board (APB) definition, is for the external auditor to report his opinion on whether the financial statements give a true and fair view in accordance with an identified financial reporting framework (e.g. UK accounting standards and company law). An unqualified opinion (i.e. a reported opinion that the financial statements do give a true and fair view) makes the financial statements more reliable in the eyes of the readers of the statements.

An external audit may also have secondary objectives:

- The fact that employees of the company know that their work may be inspected by external auditors may encourage them to document their work properly and dissuade them from fraud.

- The fact that the external auditors will inspect the company's accounting system means that they may be able to suggest improvements to the system which could tighten the controls.

Advantages of an external audit

- Disputes between management may be more easily settled. For instance, a partnership which has complicated profit-sharing arrangements may require an independent examination of those accounts to ensure as far as possible an accurate assessment and division of those profits.

- Major changes in ownership may be facilitated if past accounts contain an unqualified audit report, for instance, where two sole traders merge their business to form a new partnership.

- Applications to third parties for finance may be enhanced by audited accounts. However, do remember that a bank, for instance, is likely to be far more concerned about the future of the business and available security than the past historical cost accounts, audited or otherwise.

- The audit is likely to involve an in-depth examination of the business and so may enable the auditor to give more constructive advice to management on improving the efficiency of the business.

Disadvantages of an external audit

- The audit fee! Clearly the services of an auditor must be paid for. It is for this reason that few partnerships and even fewer sole traders are likely to have their accounts audited. The accountant's role as the preparer of financial statements, as a tax adviser and general financial adviser, becomes much more important to such concerns.

- The audit involves the client's staff and management in giving time to providing information to the auditor. Professional auditors should therefore plan their audit carefully to minimise the disruption which their work will cause.

Test your understanding 5

'Internal audit may be carried out by employees of the company being audited, or may be carried out by external accountants who are paid for delivering this service.'

Is this statement:

A   True

B   False

Test your understanding 6

In a large company, to whom do internal auditors normally report their conclusions?

A   Executive directors

B   Board of directors

C   Shareholders

D   Non-executive directors

7 Internal control and audit

We have now examined the internal controls within an organisation as well as the role of the internal and external auditor. It is worth noting that these two topics are closely related and an organisation's internal controls will be of great interest to both types of auditor.

7.1 Why internal control interests the external auditor

The principal reason why internal control interests the external auditor is that reliance on internal controls will reduce the amount of substantive testing of transactions and resultant balances in the ledger accounts required.

Substantive tests are tests for accuracy and they are used to establish facts.

At an early stage in their work the auditors will have to decide the extent to which they believe they can place reliance on the internal controls of the enterprise. As the audit proceeds, that decision will be kept under review and, depending on the results of their examination, they may decide to place more or less reliance on these controls.

Internal control and the external auditor – further detail

The operation of internal controls should ensure the completeness and accuracy of the accounting records. If the auditors are satisfied that the internal control system is functioning properly, there is therefore a reduced risk of error in the accounting records.

It is very important to the auditor to establish what internal control system exists and then to test that system to find out whether it is working properly.

Another reason that the auditor needs to consider the adequacy of the accounting system is that the auditor typically has a statutory responsibility to form an opinion as to whether proper accounting records have been kept. This implies the operation of a sound system of internal control.

By recording the accounting system and checking its operation by tests of control, the auditor can reduce the amount of detailed substantive procedures. The total amount of work is reduced as a result and a more efficient audit achieved.

7.2 Why internal control interests the internal auditor

A key objective of the internal auditor is to review the organisation's system of internal control and to provide assurance that the corporate governance requirements are being met. Therefore internal controls are fundamental to the work of the internal auditor. Like external auditors, internal auditors have to make decisions on the extent of reliance on controls to manage risks and therefore the level of testing to be carried out.

Internal control and the internal auditor – further detail

An objective and adequately resourced internal audit function should be in a position to provide the Board with much of the assurance it requires regarding **the effectiveness** of the **system of internal control**.

Therefore, both the internal and external auditors have a common interest in confirming the system of internal control.

To provide assurance, internal audit needs to check:

- that the controls in place are adequate to guard against the risks identified

- that the controls are operating effectively.

This requires a decision on whether the right controls are in place for the type and level of risk identified. The auditor will be interested not just in whether there are sufficient controls but in examples of over-control and inefficiencies. Traditionally, internal audit staff were seen as 'business prevention', because they were seen as adding in additional 'unnecessary' controls. However, increasingly, internal auditors need to be adding value and therefore will review the cost effectiveness as well as the adequacy of controls.

Test your understanding 7

Would an external auditor prefer to carry out an audit using exclusively substantive testing, or would he prefer to be able to rely on the internal controls of the business having carried out tests on those controls?

8 Ensuring the effectiveness of internal financial procedures

Effectiveness is a measure of the extent to which organisational objectives are being achieved. Management's objectives for internal financial procedures will be as described earlier, namely as ensuring:

- the orderly and efficient conduct of the business

- the safeguarding of assets

- the prevention and detection of fraud and error

- the accuracy and completeness of the accounting records and

- the timely preparation of reliable financial information.

The best way for management to set about achieving these objectives will be to establish a strong set of internal financial controls within the organisation, i.e. to implement all five components of internal control in the financial reporting function.

Internal auditors can be used to recommend improvements in internal financial control. As an incidental by-product of their work, external auditors may also recommend improvements in control.

Internal controls ad business objectives

By implementing a high quality corporate governance regime and a strong internal control system, management can be confident that financial objectives will be met as far as practicable.

Corporate Governance

The board	Employees	Internal audit	External audit
• balance of executive and non-executive directors (NEDs) • supplied with information to enable it to carry out its duties • overall responsibility for the internal control system	• proper training • awareness of the need for ethical behaviour	• operational internal audit assignments will investigate standards of internal control	• will report weaknesses in internal control discovered during the course of their audit work

Internal control

Good control environment	Regular risk assessment process	Good information system and communication of information	Appropriate control activities	Monitoring of controls

Test your understanding 8

'The reporting of internal control weaknesses to management is the primary objective of external audit.'

Is this statement:

A   True

B   False

Chapter summary

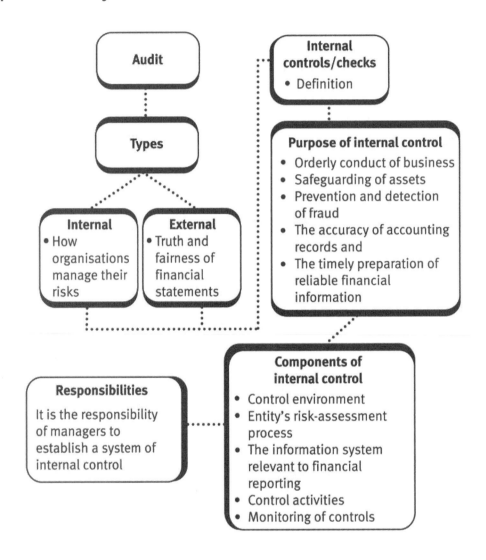

9 Practice questions

Test your understanding 9

An internal audit function is usually legally required in:

A   All large organisations

B   Large companies only

C   All companies

D   None of the above

Test your understanding 10

External auditor reports are addressed to which of the following groups:

A   The executive directors

B   The audit committee

C   The shareholders

D   The board of directors

Test your understanding 11

The primary purpose of an internal audit is to:

A   Ensure that the financial statements are true and fair

B   Prepare management accounts

C   Review risk management processes and internal controls

D   Suggest operational strategies to the directors

Test your understanding 12

All of an organisation's internal controls would be of interest to the external auditor.

Is this statement:

A   True

B   False

Test your understanding 13

Which of the following groups is responsible for the creation and operation of satisfactory operating controls within an organisation?

A   The board of directors

B   The audit committee

C   The internal auditors

D   The external auditors

Test your understanding 14

Which of the following is **not** one of the components of internal control?

A   The entity's risk assessment

B   The documentation of control procedures

C   The monitoring of controls

D   The control environment

Test your understanding 15

Which category of controls would proper segregation of duties be classified as part of?

A   Preventative

B   Detective

C   Corrective

D   Reactive

Test your understanding 16

Contrasting the actual performance of a business with the budgeted performance for the period is an example of which control activity?

A   Arithmetical controls

B   Accounting reconciliations

C   Comparison

D   Physical controls

Test your understanding 17

Here are four short references to control activities.

A   Staff have to gain approval from management for various transactions.

B   This control activity can be sub-divided into general and application controls.

C   Security staff are hired to reduce the risk of inventory theft by customers.

D   The bank balance is periodically agreed to the balance shown on the financial statements.

Required:

(a)   **Identify the description above which is associated with each of the following control activities, by selecting A, B, C, D or None.**

    (i)   **Computer controls**

    (ii)   **Authorisation**

    (iii)   **Segregation of duties**

    (iv)   **Accounting reconciliations**

    (v)   **Physical control**

(b)   Below are a number of statements relating to internal and external audit.

    A   The scope of work is determined by management

    B   Work performed involves testing the underlying transactions within the organisation.

    C   Legally required for large or public companies and many public bodies.

    D   Responsible for making recommendations on internal control and corporate governance.

    E   Produces an opinion on whether financial statements are 'true and fair'

    F   The UK Corporate Governance Code recommends that, if not already undertaken, the need for one should be assessed annually.

Required:

Write down which three of the above statements relate to external audit by selecting THREE of the letters from (A–F).

(0.5 marks each, total = 4 marks)

Test your understanding answers

Test your understanding 1

The correct answer is B – False

There will always be a residual risk of not achieving the company's objectives, however well the internal controls are designed. Internal controls will always have inherent limitations, such as the possibility that they will be circumvented by employees colluding together, or the possibility that they fail due to human error. It is for this reason that one must talk of internal controls providing **reasonable assurance** about achieving the organisation's financial reporting objectives, not absolute assurance.

Test your understanding 2

Control environment – communication of ethical values to personnel through policy statements and codes of conduct.

Risk assessment process – management monitors changes in the operating environment to plan for the future.

Information system – quarterly management accounts are presented to the board of directors for their consideration.

Control activities – an annual inventory count is held to confirm the quantities of inventories physically held.

Monitoring of controls – internal audit conduct a regular review of sales personnel's compliance with the company's terms of sales contracts.

Of course, your examples may be very different, but you should have identified one control for each of the five components.

Test your understanding 3

The correct answer is B – False

The benefits of internal audit should exceed the costs. The IIA definition stresses that internal audit is a value-adding activity by helping an organisation to manage its risks and achieve its objectives. If an organisation believes that the costs of internal audit would exceed the benefits, then it shouldn't operate that internal audit function. This is a choice to be made by the directors of a company; there is no requirement to operate an internal audit department.

Test your understanding 4

Before a bank lends money to a company, it wants to be reasonably certain that it will get its money back, plus interest. The bank will look at the company's recent financial statements to ensure that the company is financially healthy. However the bank will want to be sure that the financial statements can be relied upon to give a true and fair view. Thus the bank will typically insist that the accounts are subject to an external audit.

Test your understanding 5

The correct answer is A – True

Internal auditors can either be employees of the company being audited, or may be external experts brought in. Compare this with external auditors who have to be external to the company; employees of the company are not allowed to carry out an external audit of that company.

Test your understanding 6

The correct answer is D

Internal audit reports to the management of the company. In a smaller company, internal audit is likely to report directly to the board of directors of the company being audited. In a larger company where there is an audit committee, internal audit is likely to report to the audit committee, which will be made up of non-executive directors.

Test your understanding 7

The appropriate audit strategy must be tailored to the characteristics of the organisation being audited. In the audit of a small business, the most appropriate audit approach will usually be exclusively substantive testing, i.e. direct testing of the balances appearing in the financial statements. In the audit of a large business, this would not be efficient. The external auditor would then prefer to test the internal controls in the accounting system and, provided that the controls are proved to be working properly, he can then rely on those controls and carry out a reduced amount of substantive testing, and still be in a position where he has gathered sufficient audit evidence to form an opinion on whether the financial statements give a true and fair view.

Test your understanding 8

The correct answer is B – False

The primary objective of external audit is to report to the shareholders on whether the financial statements give a true and fair view. However external auditors will examine the internal financial controls as part of their audit work, and if they discover weaknesses in those controls, they will communicate those weaknesses to management (normally to the audit committee if one exists) together with their recommendations as to how those weaknesses can be addressed.

Test your understanding 9

The correct answer is D

In most countries, internal audit is not legally required. The UK Corporate Governance Code requires listed companies that do not have an internal audit function to review the need for one annually, but there is no requirement to have an internal audit department.

Test your understanding 10

The correct answer is C

The external audit report is addressed to the shareholders of the company being audited.

Test your understanding 11

The correct answer is C

Note that A is the primary purpose of an external audit. Management accounts preparation would normally be undertaken by management accountants.

Test your understanding 12

The correct answer is B – False

The external auditor is only interested in those controls that affect whether the financial statements are true and fair. Some controls may be on areas that are immaterial (such as controls over petty cash balances) or over areas that have no audit relevance (such as controls over scheduling in factories). These would not be of interest to the external auditor.

Test your understanding 13

The correct answer is A

The board of directors has ultimate responsibility for ensuring the satisfactory nature of internal controls.

Test your understanding 14

The correct answer is B

The five components are: the control environment, the risk assessment process, the information system, control activities and the monitoring of controls.

Test your understanding 15

The correct answer is A

Preventative controls are designed to prevent risks from occurring. Segregation of duties ensures that one individual cannot process an entire transaction on their own, reducing errors and meaning fraud is only possible with collusion. Note that 'reactive' is not a category of control.

Test your understanding 16

The correct answer is C

Comparing actual to budget is an example of comparison control from the ACCA MAP mnemonic.

Test your understanding 17

(a)   The correct answers are:

    (i)   **B**

    (ii)   **A**

    (iii) **None**

    (iv) **D**

    (v)   **C**

(b)   The correct answers are **B, C & E**. The other statements all relate to internal audit.

Fraud, fraudulent behaviour, and their prevention in business

Chapter learning objectives

Upon completion of this chapter you will be able to:

- explain the circumstances under which fraud is likely to arise

- identify different types of fraud in the organisation

- explain the implications of fraud for the organisation

- explain the role and duties of individual managers in the fraud detection and prevention process

- define the term money laundering

- give examples of recognised offences under typical money laundering regulation

- identify methods for detecting and preventing money laundering

- explain how suspicions of money laundering should be reported to the appropriate authorities

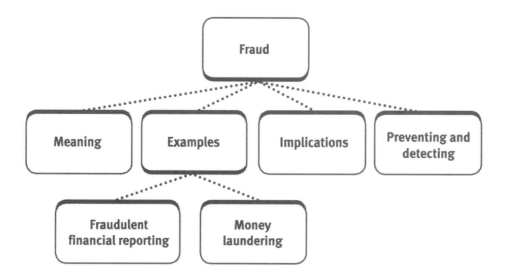

1 The meaning of fraud

Fraud is an intentional act involving the use of deception to obtain an unjust or illegal advantage – essentially 'theft by deception'. Fraud is a criminal offence, punishable by a fine or imprisonment.

- **Error** refers to unintentional mistakes. Error is an inevitable part of human nature, so systems of internal checks are essential in order to prevent or detect any possible errors.

- **Irregularity** is something contrary to a particular rule or standard.

- **Misstatement** is something stated wrongly. Misstatement can arise due to fraud, irregularity or error.

The difference between fraud, error, irregularity and misstatement

Fraud should be contrasted with **error**. While fraud is an intentional act, error is unintentional. For example, if a purchase ledger clerk deliberately enters a false invoice from a friend into the purchase ledger, hoping that it will be paid so that the clerk and the friend can split the proceeds, this is a fraud. However if the clerk accidentally enters an invoice twice into the ledger, this is an error.

An **irregularity** would occur if a petty cash system designed to limit individual vouchers to less than $50, but allowed a single voucher of $70 to be processed.

An example of **misstatement** may be when a balance sheet shows a building at cost $1 m, whereas the actual cost was $1.3m. This misstatement could have been either a purposeful fraud, or an accidental error.

As far as the financial statements are concerned, fraud comprises both the use of deception to obtain an unjust or illegal financial advantage and intentional misrepresentations affecting the financial statements. It is ultimately up to the courts to decide in each instance whether fraud has occurred, for example:

- deliberate falsification of documents/records

- deliberate ignoring of errors requiring correction

- deliberate suppression of relevant information.

Who may carry out fraud?

Note that fraud may be carried out by management, employees or third parties. For example:

- Managers may deliberately select inappropriate accounting policies.

- Employees may steal the proceeds of cash sales and omit to enter the sale into the accounting records.

- Third parties may send bogus invoices to the company, hoping that they will be paid in error.

Test your understanding 1

A rogue trader has sent your company a bogus invoice for advertising in a non-existent publication. The rogue spoke to a purchase ledger clerk at your company and convinced her that the company had placed several previous advertisements in the publication in the past, so that this repeat advertisement was genuine. The clerk was innocently fooled into passing the invoice for payment.

(a) Has the rogue committed a fraud?

(b) Has the clerk committed a fraud?

(c) Will the rogue be paid?

2 The prerequisites of fraud

There are three prerequisites that are required for fraud to occur:

- **dishonesty** – relates to a lack of integrity or honesty. An honest employee will be unlikely to commit a fraud.

- **opportunity** – the individual must have the opportunity or opening for a fraud to be committed. These opportunities will often be created due to weak internal controls.

- **motivation** – the individual must feel that the rewards that can be earned by the fraud will outweigh the potential costs if they are caught.

All three are usually required – for example an honest employee is unlikely to commit fraud even if given the opportunity and motive.

Factors that might indicate an increased risk of fraud and error include (amongst others):

- **management domination by one person, or a small group of people** – dominant individuals often find it easy to circumvent controls and procedures.

- **unnecessarily complex corporate structure** – this makes it harder to trace transactions, meaning it is easier for employees to hide fraud.

- **poor staff morale** – if staff dislike the company they work for, it may give them additional motivation to perpetrate frauds.

- **personnel who do not take leave/holidays** – this may indicate that staff members are unwilling to pass their duties over to other members of staff in case they identify fraudulent activities.

- **lavish lifestyles of employees** – if an employee is clearly living beyond their means, it may indicate they are committing fraud in order to fund it.

- **inadequate segregation of duties** – if tasks are not shared between employees, the risk of fraud rises.

- **lack of monitoring of control systems** – for controls to be effective, they need to be monitored on a regular basis.

- **unusual transactions** – in cash, or direct to numbered bank accounts.

- **payments for services disproportionate to effort** may also be an indication of fraudulent activity.

If management has established a strong system of internal control (remember the five components of internal control studied in an earlier chapter), then the potential for fraud is greatly reduced.

The role of internal audit in preventing and detecting fraud

It is up to the directors to decide what internal audit should do, but normally, where there is an effective internal audit department, the internal auditors will be given the responsibility to test the internal control system and to recommend improvements. The better the control system, the less likely it is that fraud will be attempted, or will succeed if it is attempted.

The directors may also ask the internal auditors to carry out a specific investigation into situations where fraud has been discovered, to learn lessons for the future and ensure that such a fraud cannot be repeated.

The role of the audit committee in preventing and detecting fraud

The precise role of the audit committee will vary from company to company, but the UK Corporate Governance Code recommends that the audit committee should keep under review the company's internal control and risk management systems. They should implement improvements where weaknesses are found, in order to reduce the probability of fraud being carried out.

The audit committee should also ensure that there are arrangements in place whereby employees of the company can, in confidence, raise concerns about possible improprieties that they are concerned about ('whistle-blowing' arrangements). Employees may wish to report their suspicions about the behaviour of fellow employees through this channel of communication to those in authority.

3 Examples of fraud in a business organisation

'Forewarned is forearmed', so the saying goes. By studying examples of fraud seen previously in businesses, you should be better able to assess the risk that such frauds may occur in your business, enabling you to respond properly to the threat.

Frauds can be carried out by managers, employees or by third parties of the organisation in question.

Example frauds by management

- financial statement fraud, e.g. 'window dressing' and 'cooking the books'
- misappropriation of assets
- false insurance claims
- using the company's assets for personal use.

Example frauds by employees

- sales ledger fraud – 'teeming and lading', stealing cash sales and cheques received
- purchase ledger fraud
- skimming schemes
- payroll fraud.

Example frauds by third parties

- false billing fraud
- bank account fraud
- advance fee fraud
- Ponzi schemes.

Example frauds – more detail

The frauds listed above are briefly described below.

Misappropriation of assets

Although all employees of a company may steal assets to a minor degree (e.g. taking pads of paper or other stationery home with them), management are able to conceal more major thefts by amending the accounting records. For example:

- They may steal physical assets (e.g. inventory or non-current assets)
  and adjust the accounts to show that these items were written off.

- They may sell intellectual property (e.g. plans of a new product) to a competitor for cash.

Such frauds are usually hard to detect, because the accounting records look to be in order.

False insurance claims

A manager may steal a high value asset (e.g. a notebook computer) and claim that it was stolen from him while on company business. The company then lodges an insurance claim to remedy its loss. The insurance company is defrauded.

Using the company's assets for personal use

Some instances are minor (e.g. sending personal emails from company computers), but management are in a position to take matters further (e.g. using the company's assets as collateral for a personal loan in favour of the manager).

Sales ledger frauds

There are several possibilities:

- Stealing receipts from debtors (e.g. cheques received in the post) and then writing off the sales ledger balance as a bad debt.

- Pocketing the proceeds of cash sales and never entering them in the accounting records.

- 'Teeming and lading' frauds in which the receipts from one debtor are pocketed by the fraudster, with this sales ledger balance being cleared by a subsequent receipt from another debtor. (See the illustration below for an example.)

Purchase ledger frauds

A dummy purchase invoice can be entered into the purchase ledger records, with the cash being paid to a bank account set up for the purpose by the fraudulent purchase ledger clerk. Alternatively a purchase ledger clerk can collude with a third party to inflate the amount of an invoice, with the surplus amount being shared between the protagonists.

Skimming schemes

In a skimming scheme the fraudster diverts small amounts from a large number of transactions, believing that no one will bother to investigate the small differences individually, although in aggregate they can total to a worthwhile sum.

Payroll fraud

A typical example is to add a bogus employee to the payroll and to pay their monthly 'salary' into a bank account set up for the purpose by the fraudster.

False billing fraud

This has been described earlier. Typically a fraudster will send a bogus invoice to a company, claiming that it is in respect of the company's inclusion in a non-existent trade directory, or similar.

Bank account fraud

Some companies print their bank account details on their invoices, inviting debtors to pay money directly into the account. Alternatively they may pay their bills by cheques that show both the bank account numbers and what the required signature looks like. Unfortunately this gives fraudsters the information they need, for example to set up standing orders and direct debits out of the account and into a bank account under their control. This situation is avoided by designating the account 'deposit only' so that no one can set up a standing order, etc. on the account.

Advance fee fraud

This is a confidence trick where a company is invited to pay a modest fee up front in the promise of being paid a large amount in the future. The typical form is an email from Nigeria claiming that they want to transfer a large sum of money out of the country but need some money immediately to pay the necessary fees to get the money released. Of course, if any fees are paid, the promised large sum never materialises. Such emails have become so common that they are known as '419 frauds' after the section of the Nigerian criminal code that they violate. Indeed many companies now routinely filter out all emails from Nigeria in their anti-spam settings, which has upset legitimate Nigerian businesses.

Since the Nigerian email has become so notorious, new variations on the theme have been developed, such as being told that you have won a large sum in a lottery or have been left money in a will, but you must pay an administrative fee before the money can be released. An astonishingly large number of people in the west still seem to fall foul of these bogus offers, and the offers will continue to be sent while people are still taken in by them.

Ponzi (pyramid) schemes

A Ponzi scheme is a fraudulent investment offer that involves paying abnormally high returns to early investors out of the new money paid in by subsequent investors, rather than from any genuine underlying business. Charles Ponzi emigrated to America in 1903 and set up his savings scheme in Boston offering 50% interest in 45 days, or 'double your money' in 90 days. About 40,000 people sent him a total of $15m for the scheme. When it inevitably collapsed, only about $5m was returned to the investors. The lesson to learn is that if a scheme looks 'too good to be true' then it probably is. You should only invest in schemes where you understand the underlying business rationale of the investment. Modern Ponzi schemes use financial jargon to confuse potential investors, claiming to earn their huge profits by 'hedge futures trading' or 'global currency arbitrage' or similar. Often there is no underlying business at all, and the scheme will always collapse in the end, usually with the initial promoters vanishing with all the assets of the scheme.

A more recent example of a Ponzi scheme was that perpetrated by Bernie Madoff, which is thought to be the largest financial fraud in the history of the US, with losses amounting to around $65bn.

Illustration 1 – Teeming and lading

'Teeming and lading' is a 'juggling' fraud normally on the sales ledger whereby the receipts of later debtors are allocated to pay off earlier debtors. For example Company X might invoice customers for $100 per day who, for the sake of simplicity, all pay their bills after one week. On day 8 the company will receive $100 from the sales of day 1. The accounts clerk steals this money. On day 9 the company receives $100 from the sales of day 2, but the clerk pretends that this money is in respect of the sales of day 1, and so on each day. In practice, as the fraudster grows in confidence, he often steals larger and larger sums, which increase the amount of earlier invoices that he is settling through later receipts.

As long as the organisation regularly issues invoices for similar amounts and the fraudster takes no holidays to allow someone else to see what is happening, such a fraud can continue for some time. Each debtor balance is settled in due course, so no one realises anything is wrong. Usually, one day the fraudster fails to turn up for work, and is never seen again while he keeps the proceeds of the fraud.

Methods to discourage teeming and lading frauds include:

- rotating duties within the accounts department

- insisting that everyone takes their annual holidays

- sending regular statements to debtors

- internal audit could carry out a circularisation of debtors, asking them to confirm the balances that they are recorded as owing to the company

- employing honest employees in the first place, e.g. checking references given by job applicants when they apply to work at the company.

Test your understanding 2

Teeming and lading frauds cannot be carried out within the purchase ledger system.

Is this statement:

A   True

B   False

4   Fraudulent financial reporting

Fraudulent financial reporting involves intentional misstatements (including omissions of amounts or disclosures) in financial statements in order to deceive financial statement users.

Examples of fraudulent financial reporting include:

- recording fictitious entries in the accounting records, particularly those
  close to the accounting year end (see 'window dressing' below)

- inappropriately adjusting assumptions or judgements used to estimate account balances

- omitting, advancing or delaying recognition in the financial statements of transactions that have occurred during the year

- concealing facts that could affect the amounts recorded in the financial statements

- altering records related to significant and unusual transactions.

In daily language, such schemes can be referred to as **'cooking the books'**. Other descriptions are **'creative accounting'** and **'earnings management'**. All these schemes may or may not comply with the letter of standard accounting rules, but they are usually contrary to the spirit of these rules. Ultimately it is up to the courts to decide whether a particular scheme is fraudulent, but hopefully the external auditors will have persuaded the directors of a company against a fraudulent scheme long before it gets to court.

Examples of creative accounting include:

- window dressing

- delaying or accelerating a company's expenses

- inaccurate revaluation of company assets

- manipulation of revenue recognition

- off-balance sheet accounting.

Creative accounting – more detail

Window dressing

Window dressing involves misrepresentation of information, such as the entering into of transactions before the year end that are often reversed out after the year end, the substance of which was primarily to improve the appearance of the company's financial statements.

For example, a company might have promised its shareholders that it would achieve $10m sales during the year. In December it becomes clear

that sales of only $9.5m are going to be achieved. One possibility would be to enter a sale for $0.5m in the December accounts, and then to issue a credit note to the customer for $0.5m in January. The customer doesn't mind, and the shareholders are happy because $10m of sales were recorded for the year. However the entering of the $0.5m sale in the records was arguably fraudulent. A more subtle approach would be to get in touch with a regular customer in December, and offer them a special discount if they will bring forward $0.5m of their intended January purchases to December. Again, everybody is happy, and the question of whether a fraud has occurred is less clear-cut.

Delaying or accelerating a company's expenses

Showing an expense as an asset on the balance sheet rather than writing it off immediately against profits is a quick way to improve your reported profits, as practised spectacularly by WorldCom before its collapse. This is contrary to acceptable accounting practices.

Accelerating a company's expenses may appear a strange objective. However if a new bonus scheme is being introduced that will pay you a bonus if next year's profits are high, you might be tempted to charge as many expenses as you can to this year, thus improving next year's reported profit figure.

Manipulation of revenue recognition

If a company is engaged on a long-term contract, they are supposed to recognise the revenues from the contract on a reasonable basis as the contract is fulfilled. It would be fraudulent to recognise all the revenue in the first year of the contract and none in subsequent years.

A similar problem arises when sales are recorded as soon as goods are ordered by customers, rather than when they are shipped to the customer. This practice has been tried by several Internet retail sites, but again is contrary to acceptable accounting practice.

Off-balance sheet accounting

A balance sheet is supposed to include all the assets and liabilities of the organisation. Off-balance sheet accounting is the deliberate exclusion of certain assets and liabilities from the published balance sheet, meaning that shareholders are misled about the organisation's financial obligations.

One example is a short-term lease. If you lease a building for, say, two years then under current accounting practices you do not have to show the asset or the related obligation to pay the rental amounts on the balance sheet. You have the use of the asset and you have a contractual obligation to pay the rentals, but neither the asset nor the liability are shown on your balance sheet.

Test your understanding 3

Suggest four reasons why the management of a company might want to cook the books.

5 Money laundering

Money laundering is the exchange of 'dirty' money and assets that have been criminally obtained for 'clean' money and assets that have no clear link to criminal activity.

While the term 'money' is used, in reality this can refer to **any** criminally obtained property including cash, securities and tangible assets.

Typical money laundering legislation recognises three main offences relating to money laundering:

- **Laundering** – this may involve acquiring, using or possessing criminal property, handling or being involved with criminal activity, investing the proceeds of criminal activity or transferring criminal property. In the UK, it carries a maximum 14 year prison sentence along with fines.

- **Failure to report** – failing to disclose proof or suspicion of money laundering can carry a maximum 5 year prison term, along with fines.

- **Tipping off** – disclosure of information which may prejudice a money-laundering investigation carries a maximum 2 year prison term.

Money laundering itself normally follows three distinct phases:

- **Placement** – this refers to the placing of illegally obtained cash or assets into a legitimate business (i.e. the purchase of shares in a company with stolen money).

- **Layering** – this relates to the transfer of money between businesses or locations in order to conceal their original source (i.e. wiring money between banks to make its original source harder to trace).

- **Integration** – after layering, the money now appears to have come from a legitimate source.

For example, an individual might buy shares in a business using stolen cash (placement).These shares can then be sold shortly after and the money transferred back into another bank account owned by the launderer (layering). The cash now appears to have come from a legitimate source: i.e. the sale of shares in a company (integration).

In many countries, relevant companies are required by law to put in place controls and procedures to identify money laundering transactions. These relevant companies are usually those who deal with large volumes of cash or high value item, such as banks and bureaux de change.

The controls and procedures required by law will often include, amongst others:

- Identification of large or unusual transactions.

- Scrutinising of unusual patterns of transactions.

- Taking steps to ensure all customers can be identified.

- Creation of the role of **Money Laundering Reporting Officer** (MLRO), an employee who will be responsible for oversight of the organisation's money laundering activities and who employees can report any suspected money laundering activities to.

- Undertaking appropriate **customer due diligence** – this involves the organisation acting to ensure that its customers are who they claim to be. For individuals this would involve checking their personal identification, such as their passport and/or driving licence. The government requires this due diligence to be undertaken, as a minimum:

  - when establishing a new business relationship (i.e. the first time a customer is dealt with)

  - when dealing with an occasional transaction of €15,000 or more (transactions that are not carried out within a normal, ongoing business relationship – this includes identifying 'linked' transactions where individual transactions of €15,000 or more have been broken down into smaller transactions to avoid detection)

  - when money laundering or the financing of terrorism is suspected

- when the organisation has doubts about the accuracy of the identification information it has previously obtained from the customer

- when a customer's circumstances change.

It is also important that a business has a defined reporting process for any suspected money laundering. This will normally involve:

- employees reporting suspicious activity to the MLRO,

- the MLRO investigating further; and

- if there are grounds for reasonable suspicion, the MLRO should report to the relevant authorities (in the UK this would be the Serious Organised Crime Agency (SOCA)).

Illustration 3 – Money laundering in the UK

In the UK, criminals were using high value €500 notes to launder money through some bureaux de change. 'Dirty' sterling cash obtained through criminal activities was being exchanged for large numbers of 'clean' €500 notes.

Police were alerted by one bank when a single bureau de change asked them for €4m in €500 notes. This represented more €500 notes than were sold to holiday-makers throughout the whole of the UK post office network of 12,500 branches in a year.

The bank's money laundering controls were triggered by the large and unusual size of the transaction and they alerted the authorities. The bureau de change was raided by police and closed down.

As a control over future money laundering activities using high value notes, the €500 note has been withdrawn from sale in the UK.

Test your understanding 4

A bank employee becomes suspicious of a customer who has made several large deposits of cash into their account. He is concerned they may be laundering money. Who should he report his suspicions to?

A   The customer

B   The police

C   Immediate line manager

D   Money Laundering Reporting Officer

6   The possible implications of fraud to the company

There is a spectrum of implications of fraud, from the immaterial to the critical. Including

- Loss of shareholder confidence

- Loss of assets

- Financial difficulties

- Collapse of the company

- Fines by tax and other authorities.

What happens after a fraud has been uncovered?

When a material sum of money has been lost, companies will often look around for someone external to blame, regardless of the fact that it is management who have failed in their responsibility to prevent fraud from occurring. In particular the external auditors are known to carry insurance against being sued, so they are often a first target to be sued for negligence by a company that has lost money through fraud. If the external auditors had given an audit opinion that the accounts showed a true and fair view for the period while a material fraud was occurring, then there may possibly be a legal case for negligence that the company could bring against the auditors.

If an employee has been caught red-handed while attempting a fraud, many companies seem to believe that instant dismissal is the best policy, hoping that the problem will then disappear. In practice the fraudulent employee is likely to get a new job and to defraud his new employer. Thus it is best for society if a defrauded company risks some adverse publicity by reporting the fraudulent employee to the police so that the employee can be punished by law, rather than repeating their fraudulent behaviour again and again in the belief that they will never be punished.

Once a fraud has been identified, internal audit should be sent to the department to investigate the circumstances and to make recommendations to improve the controls in the area to deter future fraud. Internal audit should report their findings to the audit committee who can monitor whether the recommendations are swiftly implemented by management.

7   Measures to prevent and detect fraud

The principal strategy of any organisation to prevent and detect fraud is to establish an effective internal control system. You should recall from an earlier chapter that internal control comprises five components:

- the control environment

- the risk assessment process

- the information system

- control activities, and

- monitoring of controls.

The first step of any fraud prevention system is therefore to ensure that each of the five components above is set up and working properly, for example as in the table below.

Component	Example in practice
Control environment	A formal organisation structure assigns authority and responsibility throughout the company.
Risk assessment process (identifying how procedures can be circumvented with an intention to commit fraud).	The company employs IT experts who can advise on incorporating new technologies into the production process.
Information system	Monthly management accounts are submitted to senior management so that they can monitor the company's performance on a timely basis.
Control activities	Segregation of duties is enforced in the accounts department.
Monitoring of controls	Internal audit are charged with reviewing the effectiveness of internal controls throughout the business.

Effective internal controls help ensure that the company is not unnecessarily exposed to avoidable risks.

Effective financial controls, including the maintenance of proper accounting records, are an important element of internal control. But the internal control system must go beyond financial controls to cover the control environment and culture of control established by management.

All internal controls play a role in helping to manage the risks that are significant to the achievement of a company's objectives. Since a company's objectives and the environment within which it operates are constantly evolving, the risks it faces are continually changing. An effective system of internal control therefore requires a regular evaluation of the risks to which the company is exposed. Since profits can be viewed in economic terms as the reward for successful risk taking, the objective of internal controls must be to manage risk properly rather than to eliminate it.

Test your understanding 5

Internal controls over payroll

Consider the internal controls that you would expect to find in a well run payroll department in a manufacturing company. The first column of the table below identifies certain of the key tasks that the department is responsible for. The second column identifies some of the risks that must be countered by control procedures. Fill in the control procedures that you might see, in the third column of the table below.

Payroll department task	Risk/objectives	Procedures
Salary information collected from clock cards, timesheets, etc.	• Staff punch clock cards for friends. • Timesheets claim false hours. • Overtime is claimed that was never worked.	
Adjustments made for: • **starters** • **leavers** • **pay rises** • **overtime**	• Start/leaving dates wrong. • Staff who leave continue to get paid. • Payroll details changed to redirect money. • Fake pay rises put through. • New employees do not exist.	
Gross wages calculated	• Inaccurate calculations.	
Taxes (and other items) deducted	• Calculations could be wrong. • Failure to update system for tax changes.	
Pay list produced for bank	• Incomplete set of pay slip. • Pay list incorrect.	
Employees and tax authorities paid	• Wrong amounts paid to tax authorities. • Taxes paid late. • Employees paid late. • Where staff are paid in cash, the cash is stolen.	

8 The duties of management in preventing and detecting fraud

The duties of 'management' can be split between:

- **the duties of the board of directors** – to maintain a sound system of internal control

- **the duties of the audit committee** – to monitor and review internal control and risk

- **the duties of employees generally (including senior employees below board level)** – will include fraud prevention and detection.

The responsibilities of directors – more detail

The board of directors is required by the UK Corporate Governance Code to maintain a sound system of internal control. At least annually, the board should conduct a review of the effectiveness of the internal control system and should report to shareholders that they have done so. A sound internal control system is the first line of defence in the prevention and detection of fraud.

Generally, the directors are responsible for taking all reasonable steps necessary to prevent and detect fraud.

The audit committee is required by the UK Corporate Governance Code to monitor and review the company's internal control and risk management systems. This should ensure the continuing effectiveness of the controls in preventing and detecting fraud.

The specific duties of employees are set out in their contract of employment and in what they are told to do by their supervisors, but there will always be an implied duty to act honestly and to report suspected or actual frauds encountered to supervisors. Fraud prevention and detection is the responsibility of every employee in a company, not just the board of directors.

Test your understanding 6

Fraud prevention in a small company

A small company may have informal working arrangements and few specific control policies and procedures. How can the directors still ensure that fraudulent behaviour is prevented and detected?

Bribery and corruption

Introduction

Bribery is now recognized to be one of the world's greatest challenges.

For example, KPMG surveyed FTSE 100 companies in August 2009 and found that two thirds said it was not possible to do business in some countries without being involved in bribery, yet only 35 per cent had stopped doing business there.

The ethical position

Accountants need to very careful when deciding whether to accept gifts, hospitality and inducements, especially if 'excessive', as these may be perceived to be bribes. From an ethical point of view, bribery can be viewed as a threat to objectivity and also compromises the fundamental principles of integrity and professional behaviour.

The legal position

Many countries have strict laws relating to bribery and corruption.

For example, firms are allowed to provide hospitality. This could take the form of providing tickets to sporting events, taking clients to dinner or

offering gifts to clients as a reflection of good relations. However where hospitality may be a cover for bribing someone, the authorities would look at such things as the level of hospitality offered, the way in which it was provided and the level of influence the person receiving it had on the business decision in question.

The UK Bribery Act (2010), for example, creates the following offences:

(1) Bribing a person to induce or reward them to perform a relevant function improperly (active bribery).

(2) Requesting, accepting or receiving a bribe as a reward for performing a relevant function improperly (passive bribery).

(3) Using a bribe to influence a foreign official to gain a business advantage.

(4) Failing to prevent bribery on behalf of a commercial organisation.

The UK Act is unusual in that a business can be guilty of an offence if an employee or associate commits an offence even if the management are not aware of, or condoned, the unlawful behaviour. If prosecuted under the act, then the company can invoke in its defence only that it 'had in place adequate procedures designed to prevent persons associated [with the company] from undertaking such conduct'.

This emphasises the importance of having a robust system of internal controls, a strong anti-bribery culture and an effective internal audit department to help prevent and detect bribery and corruption.

Chapter summary

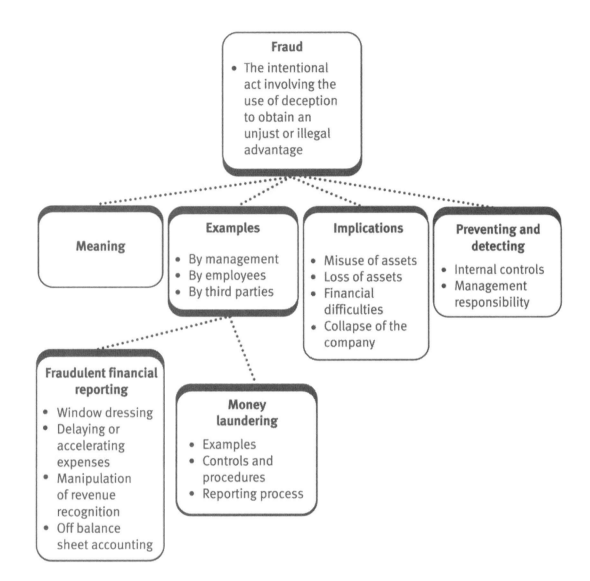

9 Practice questions

Test your understanding 7

Which of the following is not a necessary requirement of a fraud?

A   A deliberate act

B   Collusion between two or more people

C   Deception

D   Aiming to gain as a result of the fraud

Test your understanding 8

Which of the following suggests an increased risk of fraud and error in the recording of an organisation's transactions?

A   Simple corporate structure

B   Employees who take regular holidays

C   High staff morale

D   Employee bonus based on sales achieved

Test your understanding 9

Which of the following types of fraud is not carried out by a third party to the organisation?

A   Advance fee

B   Ponzi scheme

C   False billing

D   Window dressing

Test your understanding 10

Why would auditors be interested in examining large credit notes issued at the start of the financial year?

A   They may suggest non-current assets are being stolen

B   They may suggest window-dressing of sales

C   They may suggest cash is being stolen

D   They may suggest purchases are being misstated

Test your understanding 11

Who is primarily responsible for the prevention and detection of fraud in an organisation?

A   The non-executive directors

B   The entire board of directors

C   The internal auditors

D   The external auditors

Test your understanding 12

An internal control, which is required by law, can be excluded from implementation in a company if the expected costs of operating the control exceed the expected benefits of the control.

Is this statement:

A   True

B   False

Test your understanding 13

Which of the following controls would discourage a teeming and lading fraud from occurring in the payments received department?

A   Two people should be present at the opening of mail

B   Records are made when mail containing monies is opened

C   Regular rotation of duties in the department

D   Control account reconciliations should be performed each month

Test your understanding 14

Which of the following would not be an offence under typical money laundering legislation?

A   Possessing stolen property

B   Investing the proceeds of the sale of stolen goods

C   Theft of cash and other assets

D   Transferring stolen property

Test your understanding 15

'Layering' refers to the transfer of money between businesses or locations in order to conceal their original source.

Is this statement:

A   True

B   False

Test your understanding answers

Test your understanding 1

(a) Yes. He is deliberately deceiving the company, hoping to be paid an amount of money.

(b) No. She has no dishonest intent, but has made a mistake in believing the rogue.

(c) It depends on the other controls in force. If the company has no other controls over payments apart from the clerk's authorisation, then the rogue will be paid. Hopefully there are other controls (e.g. supervisory controls) that will prevent any payment being made in such an instance.

Test your understanding 2

The correct answer is B – False

Although teeming and lading frauds normally occur in the sales system, they may also be carried out in the purchases system. It is a matter of pocketing money now and juggling the records to make it appear that everything is normal.

For example, if an organisation receives an invoice for $100 daily, and pays these invoices after seven days, then a fraudulent clerk can pocket the payment on day 8 (i.e. pay the cheque/bank transfer into an account that he controls) which should have been used to pay the purchase from day 1. He then uses the payment on day 9 to pay the creditor from day 1, and so on. Once again, the creditors will be happy that they are being paid, so nothing looks amiss. It is only when the clerk fails to turn up for work, and the creditors dispute the balance that they owe, that the fraud is discovered.

Test your understanding 3

(1) Management bonuses might depend on achieving a stated profit level.

(2) Management may wish to boost the share price to please shareholders, by reporting high profits.

(3) Management may fear that their company will face a takeover threat and they will lose their jobs unless high profits are reported.

(4) There may be conditions attached to loans that have been taken out (e.g. minimum acceptable accounting ratios) and the company is in danger of breaching these conditions.

Test your understanding 4

The correct answer is D

He should report his suspicions to his bank's MLRO, who will investigate further and decide how to proceed.

Test your understanding 5

Payroll department task	Risk/objectives	Procedures
Salary information collected from clock cards, timesheets, etc.	• Staff punch clock cards for friends. • Timesheets claim false hours. • Overtime is claimed that was never worked.	• All timesheets signed off as correct by line managers. • Clock card machine in open view. • Clocking in/out supervised. • Clock cards kept somewhere secure when not in use. • Clock cards sequenced, and sequence checked each day. • Clock cards checked to personnel records, to ensure no fake employees. • All overtime authorised in advance, and reviewed when claimed.

Adjustments made for: • **starters** • **leavers** • **pay rises** • **overtime**	• Start/leaving dates wrong. • Staff who leave continue to get paid. • Payroll details changed to redirect money. • Fake pay rises put through. • New employees do not exist.	• Take up references, and check qualifications, of new staff. • New staff sign personnel form, with photo. • Random headcounts. • Leaver's form, signed by leaver and manager. • Personnel records kept secure. • All pay data on computer password protected. • Regular check of pay data to personnel files.
Gross wages calculated	• Inaccurate calculations.	• Random check of calculations by manager. • Use computerised payroll package. • Use outside payroll bureau.
Taxes (and other items) deducted	• Calculations could be wrong. • Failure to update system for tax changes.	• Random checks of calculations by manager. • Any amendments to tax data authorised by manager. • Regular check of tax rates to law.

Pay list produced for bank	• Incomplete set of pay slip. • Pay list incorrect.	• Payslips numbered, and checked back to calculations and personnel files. • Pay list reviewed by managers to ensure figures look reasonable. • Pay list authorised before sending to bank.
Employees and tax authorities paid	• Wrong amounts paid to tax authorities. • Taxes paid late. • Employees paid late. • Where staff are paid in cash, the cash is stolen.	• Use payroll control account, and follow up on differences. • Have set system of payment to ensure deadlines not missed. • Avoid paying in cash. • Where cash wages exist, use sealed envelopes. • Employee counts wages, and signs for them. • Only actual employee can receive and sign for wages. • Uncollected wages kept in safe until collection.

Test your understanding 6

If there are few control activities, then the other components of internal control become more important. In particular, the directors of a small company should promote a strong control environment, recruiting employees of the highest calibre in the first place and keeping them happy with decent pay and conditions. A commitment to ethical values, integrity and competence should be communicated throughout the company.

A small company is unlikely to have an internal audit department, but members of the accounts department may have a roving brief to recommend improvements in control.

While the external audit of a small company's accounts is not mandatory in most jurisdictions, a company may choose voluntarily to have an external audit. This would both help to prevent fraud (since employees know that their work may be inspected by auditors at a later date) and should have a reasonable chance of detecting any material fraud that has occurred.

Test your understanding 7

The correct answer is B

Collusion is not necessary for fraud. One person can carry out a fraud alone – for example the petty cashier can steal money for themselves and draw up a bogus petty cash invoice for the stolen cash.

Test your understanding 8

The correct answer is D

If employees are paid bonuses based on the level of sales they achieve, they may be tempted to invent non-existent sales in order to receive bonuses. The others would all indicate a reduced risk of fraud.

Test your understanding 9

The correct answer is D

Window dressing involves management entering into transactions before the year end which are then reversed out after the year end. As such, it is unlikely that this could be perpetrated by third parties.

Test your understanding 10

The correct answer is B

Credit notes issued at the starts of one accounting period may indicate that sales in the previous period have been overstated.

Test your understanding 11

The correct answer is B

The responsibility rests with the directors as a whole (executive and non-executive).

Test your understanding 12

The correct answer is B – False

If a control is required by law, it must be implemented regardless of the cost.

Test your understanding 13

The correct answer is C

Rotation of duties would prevent a teeming and lading fraud continuing for long, so should discourage it from happening in the first place. The remaining options would not ensure that the receipts are being allocated against the correct balances and would therefore not discourage this fraud.

Test your understanding 14

The correct answer is C

While this is usually illegal, it would not fall under the heading of money laundering itself.

Test your understanding 15

The correct answer is A – True

By definition. Make sure you can define placement, layering and integration.

Leadership, management and supervision

Chapter learning objectives

Upon completion of this chapter you will be able to:

- define leadership, management and supervision and explain the distinction between these terms

- explain the nature of management:

    - scientific/classical theories of management – Fayol, Taylor

    - the human relations school – Mayo

    - the functions of a manager – Mintzberg, Drucker

- explain the areas of managerial authority and responsibility

- explain the situational, functional and contingency approaches to leadership, with reference to the theories of Adair, Fiedler, Bennis, Kotter and Heifetz

- describe leadership styles and contexts using the models of Ashridge and Blake and Mouton.

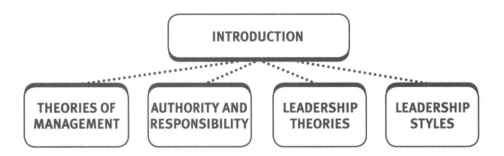

1 What do leadership, management and supervision mean?

1.1 Leadership

 Leadership is an interpersonal influence directed toward the achievement of a goal or goals.

Leadership is therefore a conscious activity and is concerned with setting goals and then inspiring people to achieve them.

1.2 Management

 Management is the effective use and co-ordination of business resources in order to achieve key objectives with maximum efficiency.

Managers have an overall aim of ensuring that everything that needs to be done within an organisation is done on time and to an appropriate standard. They are usually given authority in the organisation, which will enable them to ensure that staff follow their instructions. We will examine this in more detail shortly.

Note that a manager is not necessarily a leader. A manager will only be a leader if he or she is able to influence people to achieve the goals of the organisation without relying on the use of formal authority.

---

e.g **Illustration 1 – Differences between managers and leaders**

The manager administers; the leader innovates.

The manager relies on control; the leader inspires trust.

The manager has his eye on the bottom line; the leader looks to the future.

1.3 Supervision

 A supervisor is a person given responsibility for planning and controlling the work of a group of employees. They are responsible for ensuring that specified tasks are performed correctly and efficiently by the group.

Supervisors are therefore the lowest level of management and act as an interface between management and the workforce.

Supervisors work on the front line of the organisation. This means that they have several key functions:

- As well as supervision, they will also undertake technical or operational work, alongside the group they oversee.

- Supervisors will typically be expected to provide advice and support to their teams in order to help solve problems.

- They will usually monitor work by means of detailed, daily information. Supervisors will often then have to periodically summarise this information and pass it to more senior management for review.

Test your understanding 1

Jason is a supervisor within the purchasing department of a large company. His team are responsible for raising purchase orders for raw materials used in the production of the company's products. The department has been set a limit as to how much raw material they are allowed to purchase each week.

Which of the following will **not** be one of Jason's normal functions as a supervisor?

A   Raising purchase orders for raw materials

B   Reporting the total value of purchase orders raised to management on a weekly basis

C   Dealing with queries from his team

D   Changing the size of the purchasing limits

---

2   Managerial authority and responsibility

2.1 Authority

As we outlined earlier, managers have the authority to ensure staff follow their instructions. This raises the question – what do we mean by 'authority'?

Authority refers to the relationship between the participants within an organisation.

There are several definitions, but among the best are:

 Authority is the right to give orders and the power to exact obedience. **Fayol**

Authority is the right to do something, or ask someone else to do something, and expect it to be done.

2.2 Responsibility

Responsibility is the liability of a person to be called to account for his or her actions.

It expresses the obligation a person has to fulfil a given task. A person is said to be responsible for a piece of work when he or she is required to ensure that the work is done.

Note that responsibility cannot be delegated to others.

If a manager is responsible for a given task, he may choose to delegate it to a member of his team. If they fail to perform the task in a satisfactory manner, the manager is still responsible (are accountable) for this failure. This is because it was the manager's choice to delegate the task as well as the manager's failure to ensure it was accomplished in a satisfactory way.

Test your understanding 2

Which of the following statements regarding authority and responsibility is correct?

A   Authority cannot be delegated to subordinates

B   Authority is the obligation a person has to fulfil a task they have been set

C   Responsibility is the right to do something because of your position within an organisation

D   Responsibility cannot be delegated to subordinates

2.3 Power

Try not to get confused between authority and power. Authority is the **right** to do something, while power is the **ability** to do something.

For example, a manager may have the authority, or the right, to ask one of his team to undertake a certain task. However, the team member could simply refuse. Power is what enables the manager to ensure that the team member will comply with his request.

French and Raven identified five types, or sources, of power.

- **Reward power** – this occurs when one person is able to reward another person for carrying out their orders or meeting other requirements. For example, some managers may be able to offer pay rises to their subordinates.

- **Coercive power** – this is based on one person having the ability to punish another person for failing to carry out their orders satisfactorily. This could include the threat of pay cuts or demotion.

- **Expert power** – this occurs when one person is regarded by others as having special expertise or knowledge that others do not.

- **Referent power** – is based on the personal qualities of the individual and often occurs when one person identifies with, or wishes to imitate another.

- **Legitimate power** – this is power derived from being in a position of authority within the organisation. For instance, other employees may follow the instructions of the senior managers simply because of their position at the top of the organisation's hierarchy.

Other possible sources of power may include:

- **Resource power** – this is power based on control over key resources. For example, a union may have power over an organisation as it can control whether the organisation's employees go on strike. The union therefore controls a key resource – staff.

- **Negative power** – the ability to use disruptive behaviour and attitudes to prevent things from happening. Again, a union could have this power over an organisation as it can implement strike action, disrupting the organisation's ability to operate.

Test your understanding 3

If a manager justifies an instruction to a subordinate by saying 'because I am a qualified accountant' the manager is relying on which of the following bases of power?

A   Referent

B   Reward

C   Legitimate

D   Expert

Note that it is possible to be a manager who has authority over a group of workers, but has no power to make them act in a certain way. This may lead to a serious lack of control by the manager.

Alternatively, it is possible to have no formal authority from the organisation, but still have power over people. Even junior staff members with specialised IT skills, for example, may fall into this category as they have 'expert' power.

2.4 The link between authority and responsibility

All managers should have both responsibility and authority appropriate to their role. If these are not in balance, it can cause serious problems.

- **Responsibility without authority** – this may occur when a manager is held responsible for, say, time-keeping, but does not have the authority to discipline subordinates who are regularly late. The manager is likely to become frustrated and demotivated as they lack the power and authority needed to meet the targets they have been made responsible for.

- **Authority without responsibility** – a personnel department may have the authority to employ new members of staff, but are not held responsible for the quality of the employees that they have selected. Managers who are not made accountable for their decisions and actions may act irresponsibly, as they do not expect to suffer any negative consequences.

Test your understanding 4

John has just joined a small accounts department. The financial controller is taken ill. John has been told that he needs to prepare the management accounts and requires information regarding salaries. The payroll department are not happy about giving John the information required. What is the underlying cause of the problem?

A   Authority without responsibility

B   Responsibility without authority

3   Theories of management

Successfully managing employees can therefore become complex. To try and make it easier, several theorists have identified different ways of viewing the nature and role of managers.

3.1 Classical theories of management

The classical school of management theories were developed during the Industrial Revolution of the mid-to-late 1800s and early 1900s. They are largely concerned with improving efficiency and productivity.

3.1.1 Fayol – The five functions of management

Fayol suggested that management of all organisations could be split into five broad areas:

- Planning
- Organising
- Commanding
- Co-ordinating
- Controlling

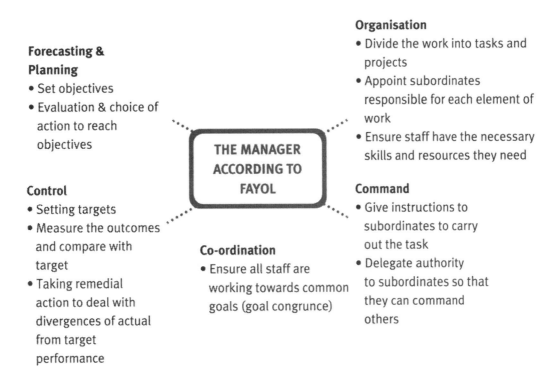

Forecasting & Planning
- Set objectives
- Evaluation & choice of action to reach objectives

Control
- Setting targets
- Measure the outcomes and compare with target
- Taking remedial action to deal with divergences of actual from target performance

THE MANAGER ACCORDING TO FAYOL

Co-ordination
- Ensure all staff are working towards common goals (goal congrunce)

Organisation
- Divide the work into tasks and projects
- Appoint subordinates responsible for each element of work
- Ensure staff have the necessary skills and resources they need

Command
- Give instructions to subordinates to carry out the task
- Delegate authority to subordinates so that they can command others

While this is, nowadays, seen as a relatively old-fashioned model, it is still considered to be the foundation for much of later management theory.

3.1.2 Taylor – Scientific Management

Taylor believed that by analysing work in a scientific manner, it was possible to find **the one best way** to perform a task.

He felt that by organising work in the most efficient way, the organisation's productivity would be increased, allowing them to reward employees with additional remuneration, which Taylor stated was their **only** motivation.

To accomplish this, Taylor's scientific management consisted of four key principles:

- Tasks should be analysed in detail to determine the most efficient methods to use – i.e. they should be planned to maximise efficiency.

- Staff members should be scientifically managed. Only the most suitable people should be chosen, trained and developed for each job.

- Managers should make all key decisions and provide detailed instructions to workers to ensure that work was carried out in the most efficient way possible.

- Work was to be divided between managers and workers, with close co-operation between both groups to maximise efficiency.

Illustration 2 – Taylor's studies

Taylor suggested that if workers were moving 12.5 tonnes of iron ore per day, and they could be incentivised (by money) to try and move 47.5 tonnes per day, left to their own devices they would probably become exhausted and fail to reach their goal.

However, by first conducting experiments to determine the amount of resting that was necessary, the worker's manager could determine the optimal time of lifting and resting so that workers could lift 47.5 tonnes per day without tiring.

Interestingly, only 1 in 8 iron ore workers were capable of doing this. They were not extraordinary people, but their physical capabilities were suited to moving iron ore. This led Taylor to conclude that workers should be selected according to how well they are suited to a job.

3.1.3 Criticisms of the classical models

While there are areas where these classical models are still relevant, most modern theorists would argue that a more progressive approach is needed where:

- it is recognised that there is not always a 'best' way of doing a particular job

- managers realise that employees can have valuable insights into a job and can make important suggestions for improvements, and

- many workers are motivated by factors other than financial rewards.

Illustration 3 – Theories of management

The classical approach is still being utilised today since this is the principle applied in most call centres: targets are set for the number of calls to be taken in a predetermined time period and reward is based on the achievement of the target.

Test your understanding 5

Which of the following statements best describes the classical approach to management?

A   Different employees will be motivated by different things

B   Communication should be encouraged

C   One best approach exists

D   An employee is considered an input to the organisational system

3.2 The human relations school

This model was developed by **Elton Mayo**, during his five-year study at the Hawthorne Works of the Western Electric Company in Chicago.

Mayo argued that:

* employee behaviour depends primarily on group relations and management-worker communication, rather than working practices or physical conditions (e.g. lighting and noise)

* wage levels were not the dominant motivating factor for most workers

* ultimately, worker attitudes, group relationships and leadership style were the key factors that determined productivity.

This approach recognised the role of interpersonal relations in determining workplace behaviour and it demonstrated that factors other than pay can motivate workers.

3.3 Modern writers

Several of the more modern writers on management focussed on the various functions of a manager.

3.3.1 Drucker – Five basic operations

Drucker argued that all managers perform five basic functions.

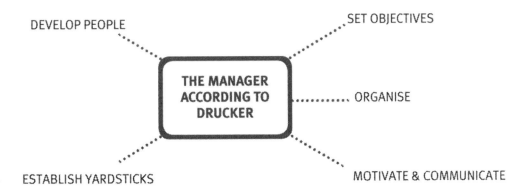

DEVELOP PEOPLE | SET OBJECTIVES

THE MANAGER ACCORDING TO DRUCKER .... ORGANISE

ESTABLISH YARDSTICKS | MOTIVATE & COMMUNICATE

> **Drucker – five basic operations**
>
> * **Set objectives** – determining what they should be and what the goals in each area should be. Managers decide what has to be done to reach these objectives and make them effective by communicating them to the people who are going to perform them.
>
> * **Organise** – analysing the activities, decisions and relations needed. Managers classify the work, divide it into manageable activities and further divide the activities into manageable jobs. They group the units and jobs, and select people for the management of the units and for the jobs to be done.

- **Motivate and communicate** – making a team out of the people that are responsible for various jobs.

- **Establish yardsticks** – by making measurements available, which are focused on the performance of the whole organisation and which, at the same time, focus on the work of the individual and help them to do it. Managers analyse, appraise and interpret performance.

- **Develop people**, including themselves.

3.3.2 Mintzberg – The ten skills of the manager

Mintzberg identified ten skills that managers need if they are to maximise their effectiveness. The skills are grouped into three main categories – interpersonal, informational and decisional.

Interpersonal		
Figurehead	Symbolic role, manager obliged to carry out social, inspirational, legal and ceremonial duties.	E.g. receiving visitors and making presentations.
Leader	Manager's relationship with subordinates, especially in allocating tasks, hiring, training and motivating staff.	E.g. seeking to build teamwork and foster employee commitment
Liaison	The development of a network of contacts outside the chain of command through which information and favours can be traded for mutual benefits.	E.g. lunches with suppliers or customers.
Informational		
Monitor	The manager collects and sorts out information which is used to build up a general understanding of the organisation and its environment as a basis for decision making.	E.g. reading reports and interrogating subordinates.
Disseminator	To be a disseminator means to spread the information widely.	E.g. passing privileged information to subordinates.
Spokesperson	Managers transmit information to various external groups by acting in a PR capacity, lobbying for the organisation, informing the public about the organisation's performance, plans and policies.	E.g. a sales presentation to prospective customers.

Decisional		
Entrepreneur	Managers should be looking continually for problems and opportunities when situations requiring improvement are discovered.	E.g. launching a new idea or introducing procedures such as a cost reduction programme.
Disturbance handler	A manager has to respond to pressures over which the department has no control.	E.g. strikes.
Resource allocator	Choosing from among competing demands for money, equipment, personnel and management time.	E.g. approving expenditure on a project.
Negotiator	Managers must take charge when their organisation engages in negotiations with others. In these negotiations, the manager acts as a figurehead, spokesperson and resource allocator.	E.g. drawing up contracts with suppliers.

Test your understanding 6

According to Mintzberg, managers need to be able to collect and sort information to enable effective decisions to be made.

Which of Mintzberg's ten skills is this a description of?

A   Leader

B   Monitor

C   Resource allocator

D   Liaison

4   Leadership

As mentioned earlier, a leader is someone who exerts influence over other people. Being a leader can be an important part of being a manager so, again, there are a number of theories that a leader can learn in order to make them more successful.

There are three main groups of leadership theories: trait theories, style theories and contingency theories.

4.1 Trait theories

These argue that good leaders have certain natural attributes or qualities that allow them to lead (such as a cheerful personality, or fairness). Leaders are therefore born, not made.

Trait theories have been largely discredited.

4.2 Style theories

These argue that certain leadership approaches or 'styles' can be learnt and used by a manager, depending on the situation.

There are two main style theories that you need to be aware of.

4.2.1 Blake and Mouton – The managerial grid

Robert Blake and James Mouton carried out research into managerial behaviour and observed two basic dimensions of leadership: concern for production (or task performance) and concern for people.

Based on the results of staff questionnaires, managers can then be plotted onto Blake and Mouton's grid.

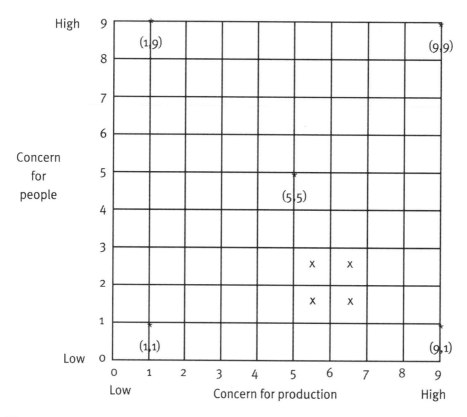

The key points on the grid are as follows:

1.1 Management impoverished – this manager only makes minimum effort in either area and will make the smallest possible effort required to get the job done.

1.9 'Country Club' management – this manager is thoughtful and attentive to the needs of the people, which leads to a comfortable, friendly organisation atmosphere but very little work is actually achieved.

9.1 Task management – this manager is only concerned with production and arranges work in such a way that people interference is minimised.

5.5 'Middle of the road management' – this is a manager who is ambivalent in style towards the task and people, but achieves only moderately good results on both dimensions.

9.9 Team management – this manager integrates the two areas to foster working together and high production to produce true team leadership.

Blake and Mouton's grid can be used to assess the current behavioural style of a manager and then plan appropriate training and development to enable them to move towards 9.9.

Test your understanding 7
Using the scores shown on the above grid (in the text), make suggestions as to how this particular manager could improve his/her managerial style.

Benefits	Drawbacks
• The grid shows areas where management faults can be identified and can then provide the basis for training and for management development. • As an appraisal and management development tool to inform managers that attention to both task and people is possible and desirable. • Managers can determine how they are viewed by their subordinates.	• The grid assumes that leadership style can be categorised into the two dimensions and that results can be plotted on the grid. • The position of team management is accepted as the best form of leadership. This may not be practical or indeed advisable. In many industries, concern for the task may be more important than concern for people, and vice versa and will always depend on the individual situation.

4.2.2 Ashridge Management College

The research at Ashridge Management College distinguished four main management styles.

- **Tells (autocratic)** – the manager makes all the decisions and issues instructions which are to be obeyed without question.

- **Sells (persuasive)** – the manager still makes all the decisions, but believes that team members must be motivated to accept them in order to carry them out properly.

- **Consults (participative)** – the manager confers with the team and takes their views into account, although still retains the final say.

- **Joins (democratic)** – the leader and the team members make the decision together on the basis of consensus.

Ashridge discovered that most people preferred operating under the 'consults' style, though the most important thing was consistency – staff disliked it when managers changed between different styles.

Note that different styles may well be needed in different situations.

- 'Tells' may be best in a crisis, or when quick decisions need to be made. The 'consults' and 'joins' approaches may be best under normal conditions, but they can take longer to reach a decision.

- Note that 'tells' or 'sells' may be best for demotivated or unskilled workers, who may lack the skills or willingness to participate in the decision-making process.

Test your understanding 8

For each of the statements made by managers listed below, choose an Ashridge leadership style that best describes the statement.

Statement	Style
'Produce this report immediately because HR have an urgent need for the information.'	
'Let's agree on what should be included in this report.'	
'Produce this report immediately or else.'	
'Tell me what you think we should include in the report and I'll decide about it later.'	

4.3 Contingency theories

These suggest that there is no correct style, or approach. Instead, successful leadership involves adapting to the particular circumstances in which the leader finds themselves.

4.3.1 Adair – Action-centred leadership

Adair suggested that any leader has to strive to balance three inter-related goals in order to be effective. These three goals relate to the needs of the group, the individual and the task.

Test your understanding 9

The table below includes needs that managers have to action. Suggest whether they are likely to be associated with individual, task or group needs.

Need	Task/group/individual
Decision making	
Peace keeping	
Training	

4.3.2 Fiedler – contingency theory

Fiedler studied the relationship between the style of leadership and the effectiveness of the work group. First, he identified two distinct styles of leadership.

- **Psychologically distant managers (PDMs)**

  - seek to keep their distance from subordinates by formalising roles and relationships within the team

  - are withdrawn and reserved in their interpersonal relationships

  - prefer formal communication and consultation methods rather than seeking informal opinions

  - are primarily task-oriented

- **Psychologically close managers (PCMs)**

  - do not seek to formalise roles and relationships

  - prefer informal contacts to regular staff meetings

  - are primarily person-oriented rather than task-oriented

So which of the two styles is the most effective? Fiedler argued that this depended on the circumstances the manager found themselves in. He identified three key variables within the leadership situation:

- the relationship between the leader and the group (trust, respect, etc.)

- the extent to which the task is defined and structured

- the power of the leader in relation to the group.

Fiedler suggested that the situation is most favourable for the manager when they have a strong relationship with the group they are managing, group tasks are well defined and the power of the leader to reward and punish the team is high.

Fiedler's research indicated that a PDM approach works best when the situation is either very favourable or very unfavourable to the leader.

A PCM approach works best when the situation is only moderately favourable for the leader.

Long-term and short-term conflicts

Fiedler's suggestion is actually quite logical.

In the event that circumstances are favourable for the leader (well defined task, strong relationship with the group, high power) there is no need to try and spend time building a close relationship with the team, as the relationship is already strong. A task-oriented approach is therefore likely to be the most productive.

In the event of strongly unfavourable circumstances (poorly defined task, poor working relationship, low power), the leader needs a task-oriented approach again. This is because a poorly-defined task is more complex and time-consuming. There is simply insufficient time available to build positive relations with the team **and** accomplish the task at hand.

Anywhere in the middle of these two extremes, there will be time to build more favourable relations with the team, which may lead to improved productivity. Therefore a PCM approach is likely to be the best.

Test your understanding 10

Carrie is currently leading a team that is currently trying to launch a new IT system for F plc. Unfortunately, F has been very vague about the requirements of the new system, which is causing Carrie's team significant difficulties.

Carrie doesn't really get on well with her team, who seem to dislike her management style. Carrie has felt very frustrated in recent weeks, as she feels that several members of her team need disciplining because of their poor behaviour, but Carrie does not have the authority to do this.

According to Fiedler, which leadership style should Carrie adopt? Justify your answer.

Test your understanding 11

The accounts manager holds a departmental meeting every Monday at 10.00 am. How would **Fiedler** define this manager?

A   Psychologically distant

B   Psychologically close

4.3.3 Bennis – Transformational leadership

Bennis argued that there were two types of leaders:

* **Transactional leaders** – these leaders see the relationship with their followers in terms of a trade: they give followers the rewards they want in exchange for service, loyalty and compliance.

- **Transformational leaders** – see their role as inspiring and motivating others to work at levels beyond mere compliance. Only transformational leadership is said to be able to change team/organisational cultures and move them in a new direction.

Bennis – generic skills

Bennis also suggested that there was no 'right way' to lead. However, he set out some generic skills that strong leaders should display:

- **the management of attention** – leaders must create a compelling cause or vision that will inspire and focus the attentions of those that they are leading

- **the management of meaning** – leaders must be able to communicate this cause or vision effectively to their group

- **the management of trust** – a good leader must be consistent and honest in all their interactions with their group; and

- **the management of self** – leaders should always be aware of their own strengths and weaknesses.

4.3.4 Kotter – Managing change

Kotter set out the following change approaches to deal with resistance:

Participation and involvement	This approach aims to involve employees, usually by allowing some input into decision making.	Employees are more likely to support changes made and give positive commitment as they 'own' the change.
Education and communication	This approach aims to keep employees informed, usually through presentations about the reasons for the required change.	This approach relies on the hopeful belief that communication about the benefits of change to employees will result in their acceptance of the need to exercise the changes necessary.
Facilitation and support	For example training or counselling.	Employees may need help to overcome their fears and anxieties about change.
Manipulation and co-optation	The information that is disseminated is selective and distorted to only emphasise the benefits of the change.	Involves covert attempts to sidestep potential resistance.
Negotiation and agreement	This approach enables several parties with opposing interests to bargain.	This bargaining leads to a situation of compromise and agreement.

Test your understanding 12

Training in the use of a new information system is a means of overcoming resistance to change by:

A   Facilitation and support

B   Education and communication

C   Participation and involvement

D   Negotiation and agreement

4.3.5 Heifetz – Leadership to motivate

Heifetz argues that the main role of managers is to help people to face reality and mobilise them to make changes where necessary. A true leader doesn't necessarily have all the answers – instead they encourage people to tackle tough challenges themselves.

In addition, Heifetz suggested that anyone within an organisation may have provide some degree of leadership in certain circumstances. This means that leaders may sometimes simply emerge, rather than being formally appointed by the organisation. This is referred to as 'dispersed leadership'.

4.3.6 Contingency theories – conclusion

Contingency theories are often seen as the most practical, as they encourage leaders to understand their current circumstances and adapt their approach accordingly. However, in practice, most managers find it difficult to vary their leadership approach on a regular basis – instead simply finding a style that they are comfortable with and sticking with it.

Test your understanding 13

Leaders need to consider task needs, group needs and individual needs if they wish to be effective.

Which writer's theory on leadership does this statement correspond to?

A   Heifetz

B   Fiedler

C   Bennis

D   Adair

5   Chapter summary

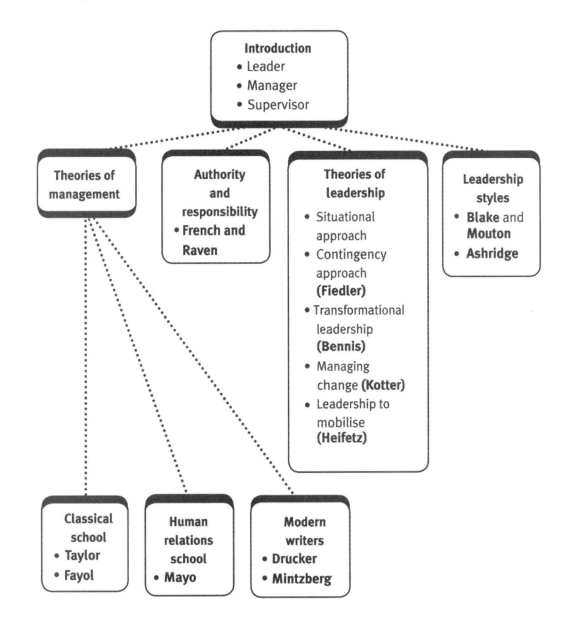

6 Practice questions

Test your understanding 14

Which of the following is **not** one of the elements of management as identified by Fayol?

A   Control

B   Co-ordination

C   Commitment

D   Command

Test your understanding 15

Bennis argued that effective leaders needed to display certain generic skills. Which of the following is one of these skills?

A   The management of self

B   The management of finance

C   The management of objectives

D   The management of authority

Test your understanding 16

C manages a small team of workers. He has recently asked his team for suggestions as to how they can improve their efficiency. The team members have made several suggestions, but C does not feel they are practical and has decided to adopt a different approach.

According to the Ashridge Management College, what management style is C demonstrating?

A   Joins

B   Tells

C   Consults

D   Sells

Test your understanding 17

In a recent staff survey, manager F has been identified as highly focused on meeting production needs, but having little real concern for the wellbeing of the employees who report to her.

According to Blake and Mouton, which key point on the managerial grid is F being placed at by the staff survey?

A   Impoverished

B   Team management

C   Country club

D   Task management

Test your understanding 18

There are a number of different models that can be used to improve an individual's management skills.

(a)   The following are basic operations that managers may have to perform.

A   Entrepreneur

B   Set objectives

C   Forecasting and planning

D   Establish yardsticks

E   Co-ordination

F   Develop people

G   Figurehead

H   Control

Required:

Write down which three options given (A – H) are the basic management operations identified by Drucker?

(0.5 marks each, total = 1.5 marks)

(b) The following are four short references to the function of management:

A   The manager's approach should depend on whether their situation is favourable or unfavourable.

B   Leaders must consider task, individual and group needs in order to be successful.

C   There is one best way to perform a task and staff are only motivated by financial rewards.

D   Anyone within an organisation can act as a leader in certain circumstances.

Required:

Identify the description above which is associated with each of the following theorists, by selecting A, B, C, D or None.

(i)   **Heifetz**

(ii) **Fiedler**

(iii) **Adair**

(iv) **Bennis**

(v)   **Taylor**

(0.5 marks each, total = 2.5 marks)

(Total: 4 marks)

Test your understanding answers

Test your understanding 1

The correct answer is D

A supervisor is supposed to help control staff and apply the policies and strategies set by more senior management. As such, a supervisor would not normally be responsible for changing the objectives they have been set by senior management.

Test your understanding 2

The correct answer is D

A is incorrect. Authority can be delegated, as a manager can give a more junior member of staff the right to give orders in a certain area or for a certain length of time.

The definitions for B and C have been reversed.

D is correct, as responsibility can never be delegated.

Test your understanding 3

The correct answer is D

Test your understanding 4

The correct answer is B

John has been given the responsibility for completing a task but without the authority.

Test your understanding 5

The correct answer is C

The classical approach is to assume that the same approach to management will work for all employees and in all situations.

Test your understanding 6

The correct answer is B

By definition.

Test your understanding 7

The manager illustrated in the above grid is showing good concern for production (although this can be strengthened further) but is weak in terms of concern for employees. Further investigation would then be carried out to determine why this is the case and in what ways such a lack of concern is exhibited. Then rectifying action can be taken.

For example:

- Attend a training course on people skills and motivation.

- Involve staff in more decisions.

- Treat staff as valuable assets; adopt an open door policy.

Test your understanding 8

Statement	Style
'Produce this report immediately because HR have an urgent need for the information.'	Sells
'Let's agree on what should be included in this report.'	Joins
'Produce this report immediately or else.'	Tells
'Tell me what you think we should include in the report and I'll decide about it later.'	Consults

Test your understanding 9

Need	Task/group/individual
Decision making	Task
Peace keeping	Group
Training	Individual

Test your understanding 10

Carrie's situation is clearly unfavourable for her:

- she has little power over her team, as evidenced by her inability to discipline them

- the lack of information from F plc means that the task her group is trying to undertake is unstructured

- she has a poor working relationship with her team.

According to Fiedler, Carrie should therefore adopt a psychologically distant approach to her management of the team and become task-oriented.

Test your understanding 11

The correct answer is A – psychologically distant manager.

Test your understanding 12

The correct answer is A

Be careful not to get this approach confused with 'education and communication'.

Test your understanding 13

The correct answer is D

Test your understanding 14

The correct answer is C

The five elements are planning, control, organisation, command and co-ordination.

Test your understanding 15

The correct answer is A

Leaders must be able to identify their own strengths and weaknesses – or management of self. The others are management of attention, meaning and trust.

Test your understanding 16

The correct answer is C

C is asking employees for their opinions, but still retains the final say about what changes are made. This is consistent with a participative (consults) style.

Test your understanding 17

The correct answer is D

F is focused on meeting production, but not on employee welfare. This plots her at 9,1 on the managerial grid – a task manager. Impoverished indicates no concern for production or employees, country club indicates little concern for production but high concern for employees and team management indicates a high degree of concern for both people and production.

Test your understanding 18

(a) The correct options are: B, D and F. A and G were suggested by Mintzberg, while C, E and H were those proposed by Fayol.

(b) The correct answers are:

(i) D

(ii) A

(iii) B

(iv) None – Bennis suggested that leaders were transformational or transactional

(v) C

Recruitment and selection of employees

Chapter learning objectives

Upon completion of this chapter you will be able to:

- explain the importance of effective recruitment and selection to the organisation

- describe the recruitment and selection process and explain the stages in this process

- describe the roles of those involved in the recruitment and selection processes

- describe the methods through which organisations seek to meet their recruitment needs

- explain the advantages and disadvantages of different recruitment and selection methods

- explain the purposes of a diversity policy within the human resources plan

- explain the purpose and benefits of an equal opportunities policy within human resource planning

- explain the practical steps that an organisation may take to ensure the effectiveness of its diversity and equal opportunities policy.

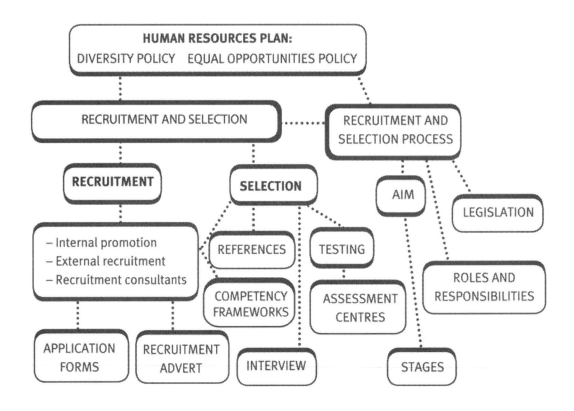

1   Recruitment and selection

1.1 Recruitment and selection

Recruitment and selection are part of the same process. However, they are slightly different to each other.

 Recruitment involves attracting a range of suitable candidates for a given role within the organisation.

It is the process of contacting the labour market (both inside and outside the organisation), communicating opportunities and information and generating interest.

 Selection processes are aimed at choosing the most suitable candidate for the specified position.

The aim of selection is to identify, from those coming forward, the individuals most likely to fulfil the requirements of the organisation.

 The overall aim of the recruitment and selection process is to obtain the quantity and quality of employees required to fulfil the objectives of the organisation.

1.2 The importance of recruitment and selection

Employees are critical to the success of most organisations. It is therefore vital to ensure that the correct staff are selected, who have the appropriate skills and fit well into the social structure of the organisation.

If an unsuitable person is hired for a role, they are likely to be discontent, will be unlikely to give of their best and will be more likely to leave, either voluntarily or involuntarily.

The consequences of poor recruitment and selection can therefore include:

- high staff turnover

- the high cost of advertising for vacancies

- management time involved in selection and training

- the expense of dismissal

- the negative effects of high staff turnover on general morale and motivation within the organisation

- reduced business opportunities

- reduced quality of the organisation's products or services, leading to customer dissatisfaction.

Illustration 1 – Recruitment and selection in a downturn

In periods of economic recession, recruitment and selection would appear to be less important, as large numbers of people will be looking for employment, meaning a field of candidates should be easy to attract.

However, even in times of high unemployment, organisations must ensure they only hire the correct people with the skills and abilities that they need. This can become more difficult when there are larger numbers of applicants.

Test your understanding 1

The economic situation in a country (or specific area of a country) may have a marked effect on the ability of an organisation to attract suitable candidates.

Is this statement:

A   True

B   False

2 The recruitment and selection process

Successfully finding the right candidate for a given role tends to require nine different stages, split between recruitment and selection.

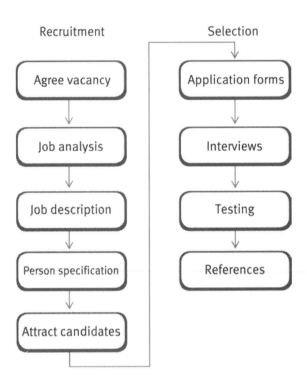

We will now look at each of these stages in more detail.

2.1 Agree the vacancy to be filled

When an employee leaves an organisation, the vacancy they leave presents an opportunity to the business to either reassess the requirements of the job, or to consider restructuring. The organisation could consider:

- analysing the role in more detail – what is its purpose? Has it changed? This could lead to:

  - not replacing the employee – could the vacant role be handled by existing staff through retraining, promotion or adjustment of workloads?

  - replacing the employee with a part-time worker – alternatives to full-time employment include home working, job-sharing or flexitime contracts.

2.2 Job analysis

The process of job analysis starts with a detailed study and description of the tasks that make up the job.

These include:

2.3 Job description

Once management fully understand the role that they wish to fill, they can prepare a job description.

 A job description is a broad statement of the purpose, scope duties and responsibilities of the job.

A typical job description will tend to include:

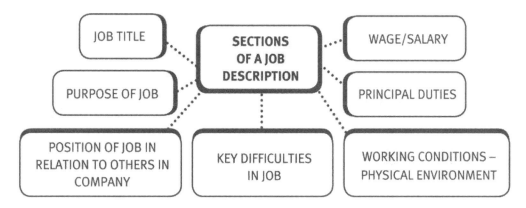

Job descriptions have several main purposes, including:

- They form the basis for advertising the role to prospective candidates

- They can be used to help select the right candidate for the role (see below)

- They are often used as a basis for writing the contract of employment for the role

- They can be used as a way of setting targets for employees, once hired.

2.4 Person specification

Once management have a job description, they can attempt to define the key attributes and qualities that the jobholder should ideally have. Prospective candidates can then be compared to this specification as part of the selection process.

Alec Rodgers devised a seven-point plan which suggests the content of a person specification. You can remember this using the acronym SCIPDAG.

- **S**pecial aptitudes – what skills and abilities should the candidate have? (i.e. manual dexterity, skill with words and numbers).

- **C**ircumstances – does the job have any special demands (such as the requirement to work unsociable hours).

- **I**nterests – is the person active or social in their personal life? This may aid their success in the job.

- **P**hysical makeup – what is the appropriate personal appearance and level of health required by the job?

- **D**isposition – what sort of nature should the ideal candidate have? Do they need to be social, or calm in a crisis and good under pressure?

- **A**ttainments – does the ideal candidate need any specific qualifications or achievements for the role?

- **G**eneral intelligence – should the ideal candidate be average or above average to be successful in the role?

An example of a person specification for an accountant could include:

Requirement	Essential or desirable?
Qualifications	
Professional qualification	Essential
Degree level	Desirable
Experience	
Experience of working in a similar role	Essential
Experience of dealing with clients	Desirable
Skills and competencies	
Excellent communication skills	Essential
Ability to present complex information	Essential
Excellent numerical skills	Essential
Team player	Desirable
Ability to work flexibly	Desirable
Personal attributes	
Self-motivated	Essential
Able to use own initiative	Essential
Attention to detail	Essential
Prepared to learn new skills	Desirable
Other	
Ability to use Microsoft Word and Sage	Essential
Willing to participate in client meetings	Essential

KAPLAN PUBLISHING

2.5 Attracting candidates

This stage involves persuading relevant candidates to apply for the role the organisation wishes to fill.

The first thing to consider when attracting a candidate, is whether to recruit externally or use an existing member of staff to fill the role. This could be done via:

- promotion of existing staff

- secondment (temporary transfer to another department or office) of existing staff which may, or may not, become permanent

- closing the job down by sharing out duties and responsibilities among existing staff

- rotating jobs among staff, so that the vacant job is covered by different staff periodically.

The advantages of internal and external recruitment include:

Internal	External
• Motivating for employees	• Obtain specialist skills
• Part of career development plan	• Inject 'new blood' into company
• 'Know' the staff already	BUT
• Candidate understands work	• May create dissatisfaction in existing employees
• Save time and money	• May cost more (higher wages and recruitment costs)
• No induction necessary	

If the business decides to recruit externally, it must consider two key issues – where to find suitable candidates and how to advertise the job in such a way that it attracts relevant candidates.

2.5.1 Potential sources

It is important to know where suitable candidates are likely to be found, in order to make contact with them. Sources could include:

- employment service job centres and agencies

- private recruitment consultants

- career advisory offices

- universities, colleges and schools

- the general public

If the business decides to use private recruitment consultants to source candidates, it would need to carefully consider:

- whether the organisation has sufficient internal expertise to find and attract relevant candidates, or whether it would benefit from the help of an experienced external consultant

- the cost of using consultants, compared with the cost of advertising and attracting candidates itself

- the level of expertise required of potential employees and therefore the appropriate knowledge required of the consultants

- whether there is sufficient time to select a consultant and teach them about the vacancy and the type of person that is required.

 Test your understanding 2

BOM plc is a multinational company that operates several nuclear power stations across three countries. It is currently considering the recruitment of a new safety inspector for one of its plants.

The role is extremely complex and demanding, requiring highly specialised knowledge and skills. BOM's existing inspector will be leaving in one month due to ill health and BOM is legally required to have an inspector in each plant it operates at all times. BOM's senior management have indicated that money is no object when hiring a replacement.

Outline the reasons why BOM should not attempt to hire a new safety inspector using an external recruitment consultant.

2.5.2 Advertising

The objective of recruitment advertising is to attract the interest of suitable candidates in the vacancy that the organisation wishes to fill.

The advertisement itself should:

- be concise, but comprehensive enough to be an accurate description of the job, its requirements and rewards

- be attractive to as many people as possible

- be positive and honest about the organisation, to avoid dissatisfaction

- when the candidate actually comes into contact with the organisation

- include information on how to apply for the role, including any deadlines.

There is no 'correct' advertising medium for a business to use. The medium chosen will typically depend on several factors, including:

- **the type of organisation** – a corner shop will clearly advertise for new staff members in very different places to a large multinational company!

- **the type of job being advertised** – more senior positions may be advertised nationally, while junior positions may only warrant local advertising

- **the readership and circulation of the medium** – how many people it will reach

- **the cost of the advertising** – national newspapers will usually cost more than local newspapers or radio advertisements

- **the frequency and duration of the advertisements** – the longer the planned advertising will last, the more the organisation will need to consider the cost of medium chosen.

Issues to take account of could include:

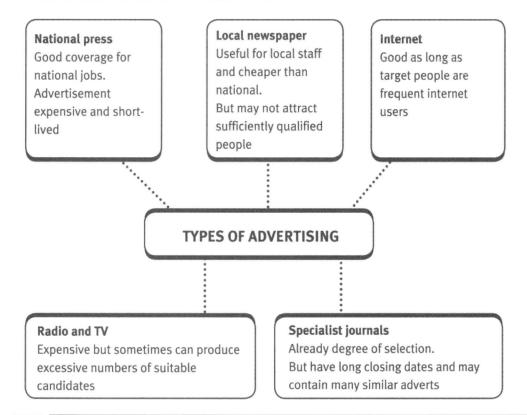

National press
Good coverage for national jobs.
Advertisement expensive and short-lived

Local newspaper
Useful for local staff and cheaper than national.
But may not attract sufficiently qualified people

Internet
Good as long as target people are frequent internet users

TYPES OF ADVERTISING

Radio and TV
Expensive but sometimes can produce excessive numbers of suitable candidates

Specialist journals
Already degree of selection.
But have long closing dates and may contain many similar adverts

Test your understanding 3

If you were looking for a job in an accounting department what information would you expect to find in the advertisement?

If the advertising has been successful, the organisation could now have a large number of potential candidates who have expressed an interest in the vacancy. The organisation therefore has to look at how to identify and select the best candidate(s).

2.6 Application forms

The first, and often easiest, way of filtering out less suitable applicants is through the use of application forms. These will provide the organisation with relevant information about the candidates. This will allow the organisation to:

- eliminate unsatisfactory applicants

- save interview time

- form initial personnel records for successful candidates

2.7 Selection interviews

Once the least appropriate candidates have been rejected using their application forms, the remaining applicants can be interviewed.

The purpose of an interview is to:

- find the best person for the job

- ensure that the candidate understands what the job involves and what the career prospects are

- make the candidate feel that they have been treated fairly in the selection process.

There are various types of interview that an organisation may use, including:

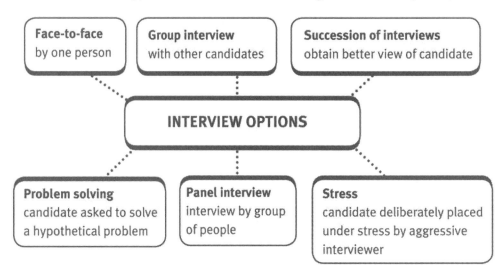

Interviews have several key advantages and disadvantages as a way of selecting candidates.

Advantages of the interview technique	Disadvantages of the interview technique
• places candidate at ease • highly interactive, allowing flexible question and answers • opportunities to use non-verbal communication • opportunities to assess appearance, interpersonal and communication skills • opportunities to evaluate rapport between the candidate and the potential colleagues/bosses.	• too brief to 'get to know' candidates • interview is an artificial situation • halo effect from initial impression • qualitative factors such as motivation, honesty or integrity are difficult to assess • prejudice – stereotyping groups of people • lack of interviewer preparation, skill, training and practice • subjectivity and bias.

Test your understanding 4

A has been asked to attend a job interview. He has been told that he will be interviewed by the Finance Director first, followed by the Human Resources Director.

What type of interview is A going to experience?

A   Group

B   Panel

C   Stress

D   Succession

2.8 Selection testing

Testing can be undertaken either before or after the interview has taken place.

The two basic types of test are:

- **Proficiency and attainment** – these are used to examine the applicant's competences, skills and abilities in areas that will be required in the job they have applied for.

- **Psychometric** – these are more general and test psychological factors, such as aptitude, intelligence and personality.

There are a range of specific tests that you need to be aware of, including:

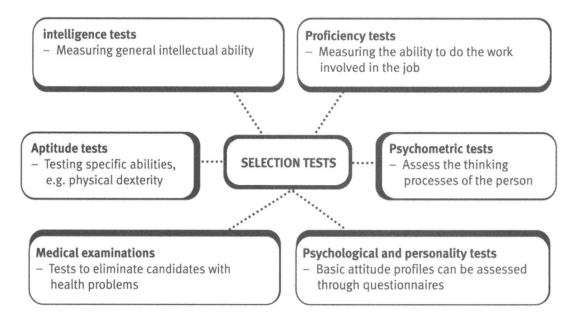

2.8.1 Assessment centres (group assessments)

Assessment centres involve candidates being observed and evaluated by trained assessors as they are given a selection of pre-programmed exercises or trials.

These exercises may include:

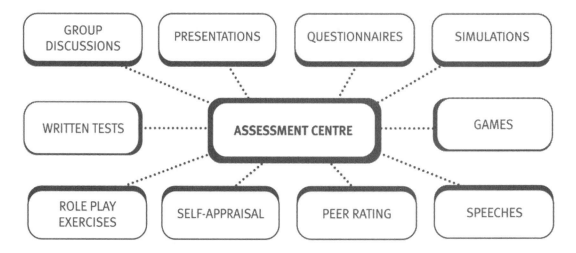

Assessors will be looking for evidence that candidates have certain abilities that are important in the job they have applied for. These criteria will change from job to job, but may include leadership or communication skills, for example.

Assessment centre

The assessment centre is really a combination of many forms of selection. Groups of around six to ten candidates are brought together for one to three days of intensive assessment. As well as being multi-method, other characteristics of assessment centres are that they use several assessors and they assess several dimensions of performance required in the higher-level positions.

The advantages of assessment centres include:

- a high degree of acceptability and user confidence

- avoidance of a single-assessor bias

- reliability in predicting potential success (if the system is well conducted)

- the development of skills in the assessors, which may be useful in their own managerial responsibilities

- benefits to the assessed individuals, including experience of managerial/supervisory situations, opportunity for self-assessment and job-relevant feedback and opportunities to discuss career prospects openly with senior management.

2.8.2 Limitations of testing

Testing – whether in groups or as individuals – has several drawbacks, including:

- There is often no direct relationship between ability in the test and ability in the job itself.

- They are subject to coaching and practice efforts.

- Interpretation of test results is often complex and requires training and experience.

- Many tests can be highly subjective (especially personality tests).

- It may be difficult to exclude bias from the tests.

Test your understanding 5

Why are assessment centres part of a competency-based selection process used by many major employers when recruiting staff for their graduate training scheme?

2.9 References

The purpose of references is to confirm facts about the candidate and increase the degree of confidence felt about information they provided during the selection process.

References should contain two types of information:

- Straightforward, factual information, confirming the nature of the applicant's previous job, period of employment, pay and circumstances of leaving.

- Opinions about the applicant's personality and other attributes, though these are open to bias and should therefore be treated with caution.

Many organisations ask for a minimum of two references – including references from past employers as well as personal references (which are likely to be more biased in favour of the candidate).

References, while useful, have to be viewed with caution. Allowances must be made for:

- prejudice (favourable or unfavourable)

- charity (withholding detrimental remarks)

- fear of being actionable for libel (although references are privileged, as long as they are factually correct and devoid of malice).

3 Responsibility for recruitment and selection

3.1 Who is involved in recruitment and selection?

- **Senior management** tend to be responsible for identifying the overall needs of the organisation and they are usually involved in recruiting people (from within or outside the organisation) for senior positions.

- **A Human Resources (HR) department** may be present in larger organisations. They may take overall responsibility for the recruitment and selection process.

- **Line managers** are likely to be the prospective managers for more junior candidates. In smaller businesses they may, therefore, have sole responsibility for selection.

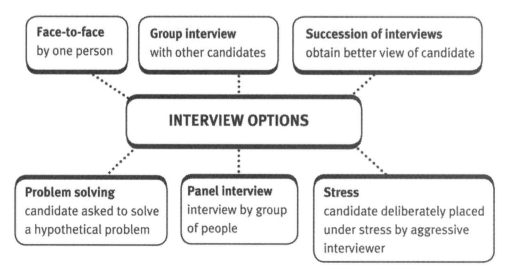

Test your understanding 6

An organisation is undertaking a programme of recruitment, and the human resources department has decided that it may be appropriate to use recruitment consultants.

Describe any five tasks that recruitment consultants would undertake on behalf of the organisation.

4 Equal opportunities

Equal opportunities refers to the belief that there should be an equal chance for all workers to apply and be selected for jobs, to be trained and promoted in employment and to have employment terminated fairly.

The two main principles of equal opportunities are:

- Employers should only discriminate according to ability, experience and potential.

- All employment decisions should be based solely on a person's ability to do the job in question, with no consideration being taken of a person's gender, age, religion, racial origin, sexuality, disability or marital status (amongst others).

4.1 Reasons for adopting an equal opportunities policy

These include:

- It is morally wrong to treat parts of the population as inferior or inadequate.

- Organisations do not benefit from excluding any potential source of talent.

- Many countries now have legislation to prevent discrimination, meaning many organisations have a legal responsibility to adopt equal opportunities.

- The organisation will be able to improve its image as a good employer, helping to attract and retain staff and build customer loyalty.

Test your understanding 7

It is very noticeable in some organisations that there is opposition by employers to recruit older staff. What arguments might they put forward for adopting such a policy?

Test your understanding 8

What practices might an organisation with anti-discrimination policies apply to the recruitment and selection process?

4.2 Types of discrimination

There are three types of discrimination that an equal opportunities policy will attempt to prevent:

- **Direct discrimination** – this occurs when an employer treats an employee less favourably than another, due to their gender, race, etc. For example, if a driving job was only open to male applicants, this would be direct discrimination.

  This may be allowed by law in certain, tightly defined, circumstances.

- **Indirect discrimination** – this occurs when a working condition or rule disadvantages one group of people more than another. For instance, a requirement for male employees to be clean-shaven would put some religious groups at a disadvantage.

  Indirect discrimination is often illegal, unless it is necessary for the working of the business and there is no way round it.

- **Victimisation** – this means an employer treating an employee less favourably because they have made, or tried to make, a complaint about discrimination.

You may have heard of the term **positive discrimination**. This refers to the practise of giving preference to protected groups, such as ethnic minorities, older workers or women. This is also not permitted under most legislation.

> ### Test your understanding 9
>
> Which of the following is **not** an example of indirect discrimination?
>
> A   Asking in interviews whether the candidate was planning to have a family in the near future
>
> B   Advertising for job vacancies exclusively in magazines predominantly read by men
>
> C   Specifying in a job advertisement that only people under the age of thirty should apply for the vacancy
>
> D   Giving less favourable terms to part-time workers, who are predominantly women

4.3 The legal position

Employment legislation varies significantly from country to country, but typically prevents discrimination in various areas, including:

- selection of candidates to interview or employ
- provision of promotion, training or other benefits (including pay)
- working conditions
- dismissal, or other disadvantages.

In the UK, this legislation outlaws discrimination based on:

- Age

- Disability

- Gender reassignment

- Marriage and civil partnership

- Pregnancy and maternity

- Race

- Religion or belief

- Sex (gender)

- Sexual orientation

4.4 Equal opportunities policies

Many organisations not only follow relevant legislation, but actively establish their own, internal equal opportunities policy.

In order for this to be successful, the organisation needs to:

- involve members of minority groups and senior management in the creation of the policies

- communicate the policy to all members of staff

- create action plans as to how the organisation will implement the policies

- monitor whether the policies are being applied within the company. For instance, the company could monitor the number of women leaving and joining the business or the number of complaints received about discrimination

- the organisation may want to consider the creation of the role of Equal Opportunities Manager, to help oversee this area of business activities.

 ## 5 Diversity

Diversity and equal opportunities are related ideas, though they are distinct from each other. Diversity involves valuing all individuals for their differences and variety.

As well as the organisation embracing people from different genders, races and sexual orientations, as in equal opportunities, diversity goes further and extends to appreciating the differences in employee's attitudes, working habits, personalities and experiences.

The main differences between diversity and equal opportunities are:

Diversity	Equal opportunities
• voluntary	• government initiated
• productivity driven	• legally driven
• qualitative	• quantitative
• opportunity-focused	• problem-focused
• inclusive	• targeted
• proactive.	• reactive.

5.1 The benefits of a diverse workforce

One of the goals of diversity is having a workforce that is 'representative' of the composition of the organisation's operational environment (the external community).

Benefits should include:

- increased competitive advantage

- maximisation of the organisation's HR potential

- increased creativity and innovation

- a broader range of skills present within the organisation

- better customer relations and service to diverse customers

- ability to recruit the best talent from the entire labour pool

- improved working relations in an atmosphere of inclusion.

5.2 Monitoring

Once an organisation is committed to diversity in its workforce, it will need to proactively monitor and manage the needs of its workforce. This will become more complex the more diverse the organisation's employees become, as individuals and groups have different needs and wants that the employer will need to take account of. Managing their needs will therefore involve:

- tolerance of individual differences

- effective communication and motivation of diverse workers

- managing workers with increasingly diverse family structures and responsibilities

- managing the adjustments to be made by an increasingly aged workforce

- managing increasingly diverse career aspirations/patterns and ways of organising working life (including flexible working)

- confronting issues of literacy, numeracy and differences in qualifications in an international work force.

Illustration 2 – Diversity assessments

Diversity assessments are formal reviews of the structure of the workforce, to check whether or not there is an appropriate mixture of people from different backgrounds.

For example, a diversity assessment might find that there are very few women or very few men from a particular racial or religious background in senior management positions. Measures for correcting this imbalance can then be considered – for example by asking why the imbalance has arisen and then taking steps to deal with the problem.

It is a structured process to gather information about the experience of current employees and, if desired, former employees using:

- focus groups of current employees

- personal interviews with senior managers

- telephone interviews of employees who have left the organisation.

A diversity assessment provides information about what helps and hinders:

- the creation of an inclusive work environment where all employees can flourish

- career advancement

- teamwork

- high morale, commitment and productivity

- retention of diverse employees

- recruitment and hiring of diverse individuals.

6 Chapter summary

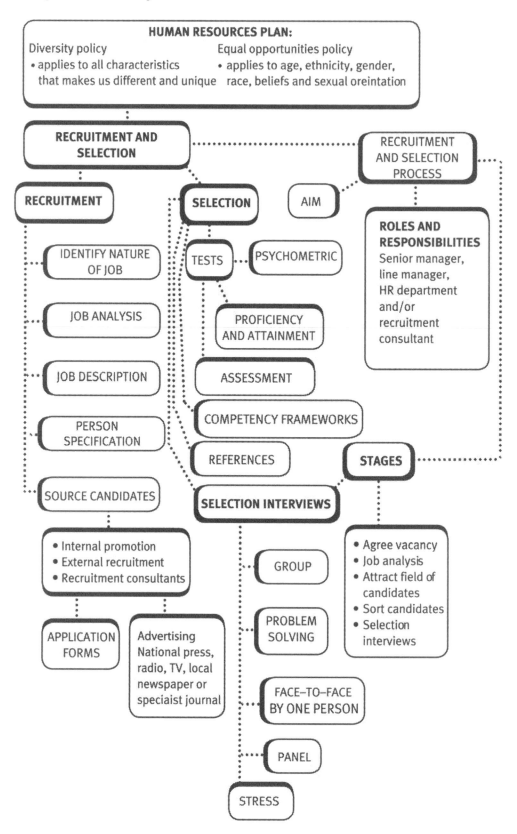

HUMAN RESOURCES PLAN:

Diversity policy
• applies to all characteristics that makes us different and unique

Equal opportunities policy
• applies to age, ethnicity, gender, race, beliefs and sexual oreintation

RECRUITMENT AND SELECTION

RECRUITMENT AND SELECTION PROCESS

RECRUITMENT

SELECTION

AIM

IDENTIFY NATURE OF JOB

TESTS

PSYCHOMETRIC

ROLES AND RESPONSIBILITIES
Senior manager, line manager, HR department and/or recruitment consultant

JOB ANALYSIS

PROFICIENCY AND ATTAINMENT

JOB DESCRIPTION

ASSESSMENT

PERSON SPECIFICATION

COMPETENCY FRAMEWORKS

REFERENCES

STAGES

SOURCE CANDIDATES

SELECTION INTERVIEWS

• Internal promotion
• External recruitment
• Recruitment consultants

GROUP

• Agree vacancy
• Job analysis
• Attract field of candidates
• Sort candidates
• Selection interviews

APPLICATION FORMS

Advertising National press, radio, TV, local newspaper or speciaist journal

PROBLEM SOLVING

FACE–TO–FACE BY ONE PERSON

PANEL

STRESS

7 Practice questions

Test your understanding 10

C Ltd is a company that makes chemicals for sale across the world. It needs to hire a new member of staff for a role in its chemical engineering centre. This role is highly specialised and complex, with the employee required to have a large number of skills and competences.

C is considering using a popular recruitment consultant to help it locate a suitable candidate. Which of the following statements is correct regarding this choice?

A   It will always be cheaper for C to use a consultant rather than attempting to find appropriate candidates themselves

B   The recruitment consultants may lack the skills and knowledge required to locate an appropriate candidate

C   It is likely that the recruitment consultants will find suitable candidates more quickly than C itself

D   Recruitment consultants are typically only used to find unskilled or semi-skilled workers

Test your understanding 11

Which of the following is **not** part of Rodger's seven point plan for the content of a person specification?

A   Physical makeup

B   Attainments

C   Circumstances

D   Age

Test your understanding 12

GBN plc manufactures farming equipment and is looking to hire a large number of unskilled workers for a new factory that it is about to open in a city in the south of country U. Which of the following is likely to be the most appropriate location for GBN to advertise for these jobs?

A   GBN's own website

B   National television

C   Local newspapers or radio

D   Farming trade publications and journals

Test your understanding 13

Psychometric tests check a candidate's competences, skills and abilities relating to the job they have applied for. This can be useful as a way of ensuring that only appropriate candidates are selected for each role.

Is this statement

A True

B False

Test your understanding 14

Which of the following is **not** a reason for adopting an equal opportunities policy within an organisation?

A   Legal requirement

B   Improved organisational reputation

C   Reduction in labour costs

D   Ethically correct

Test your understanding 15

A has placed an advert in her local paper for an employee to work in her shop. The advert states that A is looking for 'a female shop assistant, who must be under the age of twenty-five and should be married.'

(i)   Direct discrimination

(ii)   Indirect discrimination

(iii) Victimisation

Which of the three types of discrimination stated above has A included in her advertisement?

A   (i) only

B   (ii) only

C   (i) and (ii)

D   (i), (ii) and (iii)

Test your understanding answers

Test your understanding 1

The correct answer is A – True

Economic uncertainty may cause people to remain in their present job and discourage them from moving elsewhere, particularly if finance from building societies and banks is difficult to obtain. Married people with children may be less disposed to move and movement will mainly be among younger persons. Growth industries may therefore find it difficult to obtain people with the required experience.

Test your understanding 2

External consultants would probably be inappropriate for several reasons.

Firstly, the role of the new employee is extremely complex. An external consultant is unlikely to have the specialist knowledge needed to understand which candidates they need to attract.

Secondly, the replacement must be found urgently. BOM may not have time to find, select and explain the position to an external consultant. It may be faster to keep the recruitment process in-house.

Note that while an external consultant may be more expensive, BOM has stated that money is no object, meaning that this is unlikely to be a consideration in their decision.

Test your understanding 3

You would expect it to include information about:

- the organisation: its main business and location, at least
- the job: title, main duties and responsibilities, and special features
- conditions: special factors affecting the job
- qualifications and experience (required, and preferred); other attributes, aptitudes and/or knowledge required
- rewards: salary, benefits, opportunities for training, career development, and so on
- application process: how to apply, to whom, and by what date.

Test your understanding 4

The correct answer is D

Test your understanding 5

The graduate training schemes that some major employers offer are intended as a fast track to senior management and assessment centres are designed to evaluate whether the candidate possesses the core competencies that are needed to be successful at a senior level in the business. The idea is that the job description and person specification as traditionally written do not illustrate the actual skills (mental competencies) required in the job. Also, if there is mass recruitment, or recruitment of people without previous work experience (e.g. graduates, police cadets, nurses) there is little to go on. Exercises might include technical tests (of dexterity or problem identification), aptitude tests (of mechanical ability, spatial awareness, computer literacy), psychometric tests (intelligence, verbal/mathematical reasoning, personality) in-tray exercises, group discussions, presentations, etc. They are intended to allow selectors to gain an insight into personal qualities, such as management skills, leadership skills and team membership suitability.

Test your understanding 6

Choose any five of the following tasks undertaken by recruitment consultants:

- understand the practices, procedures and relevance of job descriptions, person specifications and selection criteria, help in their construction and advise on their uses

- advise on the appropriateness of recruitment criteria and develop measures by which applicant might be assessed

- design the vacancy advertisements, ensuring that the advertisement is properly constructed and contains the correct information so as to attract interest from appropriate candidates

- assist with or undertake the screening of applications following the advertisements, ensuring that the procedure for application has been followed

- assist with or undertake the screening of applicants, ensuring that unsuitable applicants are removed and suitable applicants noted

- assist management by listing potential candidates and supporting the list with brief personal illustrations, notes and, if required, recommendations

- ensure that advice is given on the conduct and procedures of the interview, the structure of the interviewing panel and ensure that all candidates provide satisfactory information

- advise on the appropriateness or otherwise of the means of testing applicants, or undertake other screening such as psychometric tests as required by management

- select the team to undertake the interviews, ensuring that the team consists of individuals with appropriate skills and who have an interest in and knowledge of, the vacancy

- alternatively, the consultants themselves might conduct the interview and selection process, but only upon the direct instruction of the management within definite prescribed guidelines.

Test your understanding 7

They may use the following excuses:

- the organisation has a 'young' culture or image

- the older worker is less skilled or has less experience with new technology or IT-based work

- older workers are prone to sickness more than younger employees

- age-based pay systems mean paying more for older staff (even though most organisations operate performance-based pay systems)

- the organisation has a young customer base that older staff would not relate to

- the payback period on training will be too short.

Test your understanding 8

An organisation with anti-discrimination policies might apply some of the following practices:

- recruitment – job advertisements should not discriminate on the grounds of sex, e.g. it would be appropriate to advertise a vacancy for a 'sales person' rather than for a 'salesman'

- selection – interviewers at selection interviews should avoid questions such as: 'Do you intend to get married and have children soon' (sex discrimination), or 'Are you able to work on religious holidays' (discrimination on the grounds of religious belief)

- selection, training and promotion – applying policies based strictly on the ability, experience and potential of employees

- pay – applying an equal pay policy.

Test your understanding 9

The correct answer is C

C is an example of direct discrimination. The others may disadvantage a particular group of people (such as women in A, B and D).

Test your understanding 10

The correct answer is B

Given the highly skilled and technical nature of the role, the consultants may struggle to understand what type of candidate is needed. This may also tend to mean that it will be more expensive and slower for C use a consultant instead of attempting to locate candidates itself. Note that consultants can be used to locate all types of employees, so D is incorrect.

Test your understanding 11

The correct answer is D

The 7 are – special aptitudes, circumstances, interests, physical makeup, disposition, attainments and general intelligence. Age is not a factor (and could have diversity/equal opportunity issues if included).

Test your understanding 12

The correct answer is C

GBN's own website and trade journals are unlikely to attract unskilled individuals, as they will have little or no need for farm equipment. National television is likely to unnecessarily expensive, especially as GBN is attempting to recruit workers for a single factory in the south of the country. Local newspaper and radio advertising in the area where the new factory is to be located would be the most sensible option.

Test your understanding 13

The correct answer is B – False

The description given is that of proficiency testing. Psychometric tests look at psychological factors, such as aptitude, intelligence and personality.

Test your understanding 14

The correct answer is C

Equal opportunities does not mean that workers can be paid less. There should therefore be no reduction in the wages bill because of this.

Test your understanding 15

The correct answer is A

Direct discrimination occurs when an employer treats one group less favourably than another. In this case, A has discriminated against men, the over-25s and unmarried women directly in her advertisement.

Individual, group and team behaviour

Chapter learning objectives

Upon completion of this chapter you will be able to:

- describe the main characteristics of individual and group behaviour

- outline the contributions of individuals and teams to organisational success

- identify individual and team approaches to work

- explain the differences between a group and a team

- define the purposes of a team

- explain the role of the manager in building the team and developing individuals within the team.

    - Belbin's team roles theory

    - Tuckman's theory of team development

- list the characteristics of effective and ineffective teams

- describe tools and techniques that can be used to build the team and improve team effectiveness.

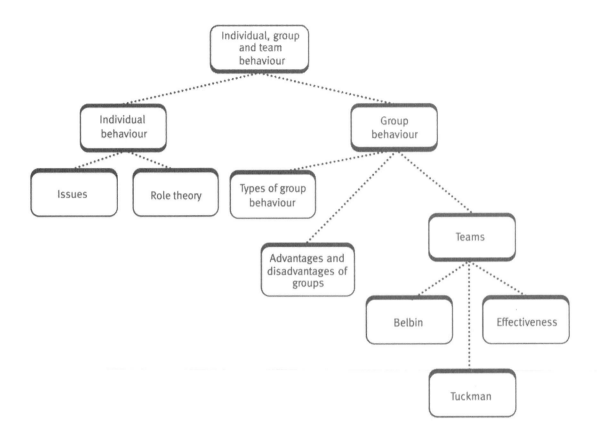

1 Individuals

1.1 Characteristics of individual behaviour

Although individual behaviour patterns vary significantly, the underlying issues relating to behaviour are the same for all people.

Typical issues that affect individual behaviour and performance at work include:

- **Motivation level** – this relates to people's desire to perform tasks and put effort into their job. It can be affected by many factors, including reward levels, recognition, social interactions at work and working conditions.

- **Perception** – individuals select, organise and interpret the stimuli they receive. Messages from managers are always subject to distortion, with the subordinate selecting parts of the message and interpreting it in light of their own experiences, wants and needs.

- **Attitudes** – these are persistent feelings and behavioural tendencies directed towards specific people, groups, ideas or objects.

- **Personality** – this is the combination of emotional, attitudinal and behavioural responses of an individual.

When looking after staff, managers need to be aware of the differences in these four areas between individual members of staff.

Test your understanding 1

A manager has recently emailed two individuals in his team, asking for them to submit reports to him. One worker did so, while the other failed to. The second worker, when asked, stated that she thought that the wording of the email meant that it did not apply to her.

Which characteristic of individual behaviour is the manager having difficulties with?

A   Motivation

B   Perception

C   Attitude

D   Personality

1.2 Role theory

This model suggests that the behaviour of individuals depends on other people's expectations of them and how they are supposed to behave in a given situation.

A role is the pattern of behaviour expected by someone who occupies a particular position.

There are several key terms relating to role theory that you should be aware of:

- **Role behaviour** – certain types of behaviour can be associated with a particular role in an organisation. For instance, a member of staff who expects to be promoted shortly may begin acting as if they have already been put in charge.

- **Role set** – this describes the people who respond to an individual in a particular role. For example, a clerk and junior barristers would form part of a senior barrister's role set.

- **Role signs** – these are visible indications of a role. Styles of dress and uniforms are typical examples of role signs. For example, in the military, different uniforms and styles of address indicate status and position in the hierarchy.

Role theory also identifies several problems that these expected patterns of behaviour may cause.

- **Role ambiguity** – this arises when an individual is unsure of what role they are to play, or others are unclear of that person's role and so hold back co-operation. This can arise, for example, when a new member joins an established group.

- **Role conflict** – this occurs when individuals find a clash between different roles they have adopted. If an accountant uncovers a fraud perpetrated by one of their friends, their roles as a professional and a friend may conflict with each other.

- **Role incompatibility** – this occurs when individuals experience expectations from outside groups about their role that are different to their own role expectations.

Test your understanding 2

T works as the finance director for a small company. She has recently been asked by the Human Resource department to take charge of hiring a new member of staff for her team. She wishes to hire the best candidate that she has interviewed, but knows that this will cost more than she has been allowed in her departmental budget by the Board of Directors.

What is T experiencing?

A   Role ambiguity

B   Role incompatibility

C   Role conflict

D   Role behaviour

2 Groups

A group is any collection of individuals who perceive themselves to be a group.

They have the following characteristics:

- **A sense of identity** – the group has defined boundaries and it is clear who is within the group and who is not.

- **Loyalty to the group** – group members accept one another and have certain standard behaviours that the follow. This binds the group together and excludes others.

- **Purpose and leadership** – a group has a purpose and individuals are chosen to join the group in order to help the group achieve its goals.

There tend to be two main types of group:

- **Informal groups** – these are groups that individuals voluntarily join to meet their social or security needs. Individual members are dependent on each other and influence each other's behaviour, for example, employees who sit together and chat at lunchtime.

- **Formal groups** – these are groups that are created to carry out specific tasks, communicate and solve problems. Membership is normally determined by the organisation – for example, a project team put together to deliver a new payroll system.

Test your understanding 3

Would a number of people waiting for a bus be described as:

A   A formal group

B   An informal group

C   Neither of the above

2.1 Group behaviour

When dealing with other individuals within a group, people can adopt different types of behaviour.

- **Assertive** – this is direct, honest and professional communication. It often involves insisting on your rights without violating the rights of others.

- **Aggressive** – this violates another person's rights and can often lead to conflict.

- **Passive behaviour** – is giving into another person in the belief that their rights are more important than yours.

Illustration 1 – Different types of behaviour

A subordinate has given his manager a report that the manager requested. Upon review, the manager discovers that it is full of errors and it needs to be passed back to the subordinate so he can correct the mistakes.

An **assertive** manager might say: 'I would like you to re-work this report because there are several mistakes in it.'

An **aggressive** manager might say: 'I don't know how you dared to give me a report that has this many mistakes in it.'

A **passive** manager might say: 'The mistakes in the report were probably my fault for not explaining it to you properly.'

Test your understanding 4

A colleague telephones you when you are working on some invoices that you particularly want to finish. He says he wants to talk about next weeks safety meeting. You prefer to discuss it later. Give both an assertive response and an aggressive response.

3 The contribution of individuals and teams to organisational success

Groups usually have several key benefits over individuals. These include:

- a **mixture of skills and abilities** in the group, often improving the number of creative ideas and appreciation of different points of view. This can also aid problem solving.

- **synergy** – the pooling of ideas and energy within a group may mean greater efficiency than if the workers were acting as individuals. This is sometimes known as the **2 + 2 = 5** principle.

- **increased flexibility**, as the team can easily be configured in different ways, with different people taking over different tasks.

- **better control**, with opportunities for individual performance to be reviewed and controlled by other group members.

- **increased motivation**, if worker's social needs are being met within their group.

- **improved communication** between workers.

- **healthy competition within the organisation** – by splitting employees into groups, some rivalry can be created which may help boost organisational performance. For instance, a sales department may be split into groups. The group with the highest sales will be rewarded, motivating all the groups to work harder.

However, placing employees in groups is not always more efficient. There are a number of problems inherent in group work. These include:

- group **decision-making can be slow** as discussion is needed to come to any agreement.

- groups **tend to produce decisions that are compromises**, rather than decisions that are most beneficial to the business.

- **group pressure to conform** where members of a close-knit team agree to decisions that they know are wrong because other members of the group support them and they wish to fit in.

- groups have a **lack of individual responsibility** meaning that the responsibility for any decisions made is shared between all members. This means that groups may take riskier decisions than individuals.

- groups risk having **too much social interaction**; meetings may become social events, with little practical work being undertaken.

- groups may cause increased **competition and conflict**, which may be destructive.

Managers will therefore need to monitor groups carefully to ensure that corrective action is taken if these problems are noted.

4   Teams

A team is more than a group. A team can be described as any group of people who must significantly relate with each other in order to accomplish shared objectives.

Teams usually:

- share a common goal

- enjoy working together

- are committed to achieving certain goals

- are made up of diverse individuals

- are loyal to their team and its project

- have a sense of team spirit.

A team is therefore a formal group. It will have its own culture, leader and will be geared towards achieving a particular objective.

Test your understanding 5

Would an orchestra be considered a team?

A   Yes

B   No

4.1 Belbin's team roles theory

Belbin suggested that, in order for a team to operate effectively, it needed a balance of nine different roles.

Leader (Co-ordinator)	Pulls group together to work towards a shared goal
Shaper	Promotes activity, dominant, extrovert
Plant	Thoughtful and thought provoking, ideas person
Monitor-evaluator	Criticises others ideas, brings the team down to earth
Resource-investigator	Extrovert, networker, looks for alternative solutions
Implementer (company worker)	Administrator, organiser. Turns ideas into practical solutions
Team worker	Concerned with relationships within the group
Completer-finisher	The progress chaser
Specialist (expert)	Provides knowledge and/or skills required by the project

Note that Belbin was not arguing that every team has to have a minimum of nine members. Individuals within the team could take on more than one role each. As long as all the roles are filled, the team will be more likely to be effective.

Belbin's team roles

- Leader (Co-ordinator) – a balanced and disciplined person, good at working with others.

- Shaper – a dominant, extrovert personality, task driven to the point of passion, a force for action.

- Plant – often introverted, but intellectually bright and imaginative who acts as a source of ideas and innovation.

- Monitor-evaluator – not creative but analytical, often tactless, examines ideas and spots flaws.

- Resource-investigator – popular social member of the team, a useful source of contacts but not ideas. Good at communicating both with other members of the group and externally.

- Implementer (company worker) – the administrator and organiser, a trustworthy person.

- Team-worker – concerned with the maintenance of the team. Usually perceptive and diplomatic.

- Completer-finisher – enjoys the detail, pushes the team to meet targets.

- Specialist (expert) – joins the team when specialist advice is required on matters outside the competence of the team.

Test your understanding 6

Neville is in charge of a group of 12 people involved in complex work. This is of an ongoing nature. The group has been working together amicably and successfully for a considerable time. Its members value Neville's leadership and the back-up given by Olivia. She elaborates on Neville's instructions and deals on his behalf with group members queries, especially when he is absent on the group's business.

Much of the success of the group has been due to Peter, who is creative at problem solving, and Rosalinde who has an encyclopaedic knowledge of sources of supply and information. Quentin is an expert on charting and records, and Sheila is invaluable at sorting out disagreements and keeping everyone cheerful. The remaining members of the group also have roles, which are acceptable to themselves and to the others.

Required:

Which of Belbin's role classifications do the following group members most closely comply with?

Neville

Olivia

Peter

Rosalind

Quentin

Sheila

4.2 Tuckman's stages of group development

Tuckman argued that all teams progress through four main stages of development.

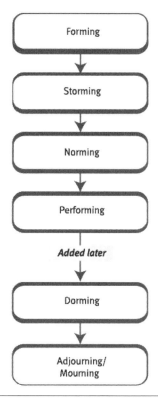

Forming	The team initially comes together.
Storming	The conflict stage where roles and processes are challenged.
Norming	Co-operation begins and roles are agreed.
Performing	The team begins to be productive.
Dorming	Complacency starts within the team.
Adjourning (mourning)	The team completes its objectives and disbands.

Tuckman's group stages in more detail

Tuckman helps identify what needs to be done to weld the team together. The stages are:

- **Forming** – At this initial stage, the group is no more than a collection of individuals who are seeking to define the purpose of the group and how it will operate.

- **Storming** – most groups go through this conflict stage. In this stage norms of attitude, behaviour, etc., are challenged and rejected. Members compete for chosen roles within the group. If successful, this stage will have forged a stronger team with greater knowledge of each other and their objectives.

- **Norming** – This stage establishes the norms under which the group will operate. Members experiment and test group reaction as the norms become established. Typically, the norming stage will establish how the group will take decisions, behaviour patterns, level of trust and openness, individual's roles, etc.

- **Performing** – Once this final stage has been reached, the group is capable of operating to full potential, since the difficulties of adjustment, leadership contests, etc should have been resolved.

All groups do not automatically follow these four stages in this sequence. Not all groups pass through all the stages – some get stuck in the middle and remain inefficient and ineffective. Managers will want to identify such teams and look at ways of dealing with this.

Subsequently two more stages have been added to Tuckman's original four.

- **Dorming** – If a team remains for a long time in the performing phase, there is a danger that it will be operating on automatic pilot. 'Groupthink' occurs to the extent that the group may be unaware of changing circumstances. Instead, maintaining the team becomes one of its prime objectives.

- **Adjourning (mourning)** – The team has fulfilled its objectives and is due to be closed down. This is likely to upset team members who are used to working in the team and can lead to anxiety and insecurity among the team members.

Test your understanding 7

Following on from TYU above, suppose the following has occurred:

- Recently, Olivia resigned for family reasons.

- Because the workload has been increasing, Neville recruited four new people to the group.

- Neville now finds that various members of the group complain to him about what they are expected to do and about other people's failings.

- Peter and Rosalinde have been unusually helpful to Neville, but have had several serious arguments between themselves and with others.

Required:

Relating your answer to Tuckman, analyse the situation before and after the changes.

4.3 Team effectiveness

Peters and Waterman define the five key aspects of successful teams as:

- The team should be relatively **small** – inevitably each member will want to represent the interests of their section/department, meaning that larger teams will be slower and harder to manage.

- The team should have **a limited duration**, existing only to achieve a particular task.

- Membership should be **voluntary** – a team member who does not want to be part of the group is unlikely to be a fully participating member.

- **Communication should be informal and unstructured** – there should be little documentation and no status barriers.

- The team should be **action-oriented**, meaning that the team should create a plan for action and decide what needs doing to accomplish their goals.

Test your understanding 8

Consider the following types of group behaviour:

(i)   Avoidance of conflict

(ii)   Small number of members

(iii)   Lack of communication

(iv)   Strong pressure for group members to conform

(v)   Clear objectives

(vi)   Dominant individual members

Which of these would not be characteristics of an ineffective group?

A   (i), (ii), (iv) and (v)

B   (ii) and (v)

C   (i), (ii), (v) and (vi)

D   (i) and (iv)

4.4 Building the team and improving effectiveness

Teams are not always able to achieve their goals without some outside intervention or support from management. As such, managers may attempt to create 'team-building' exercises for workers.

Team building exercises are tasks designed to develop group members and their ability to work together.

Team building exercises tend to be based around developing the team in several areas, including:

*   **improved communication**, such as through the use of problem solving exercises which force all team members to discuss a problem the group is facing.

*   **building trust** between team members, which will help the individual members work as a group.

*   **social interaction** between the individuals in the team can help to reduce conflict and increase the cohesion of the group.

In addition to formal team-building exercises, managers can attempt to reinforce the individual identity of the team, strengthening team members' sense of belonging and improving the efficiency of the group. This can be accomplished in a number of ways, including giving the team its own name, its own office/space or its own uniforms.

4.5 Measuring team effectiveness

There are many possible ways of measuring team effectiveness, including:

- the degree to which the team achieved its stated objectives and the quality of its output.

- team member satisfaction – this could be measured, amongst other things, by using labour turnover or absenteeism rates.

- efficiency – the resources used to achieve team objectives.

Management could measure these through the use of questionnaires for team members, interviews, or direct observation of the team.

Team rewards could then be designed to not only motivate the individuals within the group, but also encourage co-operation and responsibility sharing between the team as a whole.

Test your understanding 9

Which of the following would be expected to be characteristics of an effective team?

(i)   High labour turnover

(ii)   Low absenteeism

(iii)   High productivity

A   (i) only

B   (i) and (ii) only

C   (ii) and (iii) only

D   (iii) only

5 Chapter summary

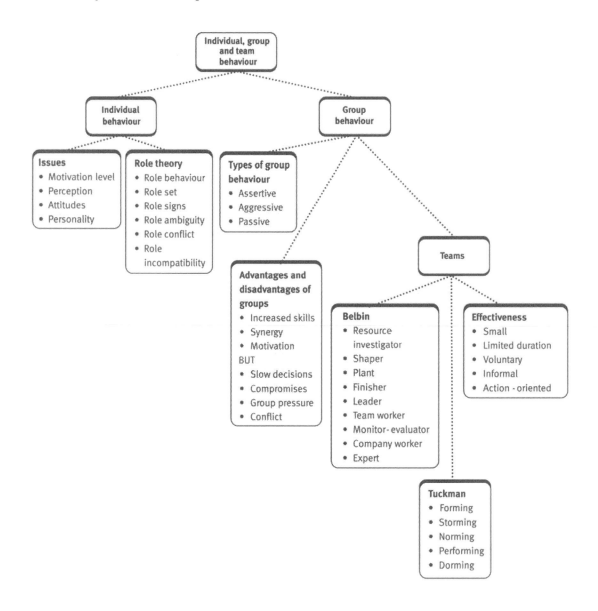

6 Practice questions

Test your understanding 10

Y has recently started a new job in a store. She has been asked to wear a uniform that identifies her as a junior member of staff and which is quite different from those worn by store managers.

According to role theory, what is Y's uniform an example of?

A Role behaviour

B Role set

C Role conflict

D Role signs

Test your understanding 11

Assertive behaviour violates another individual's rights and often leads to conflict.

Is this statement:

A True

B False

Test your understanding 12

Consider the following statements regarding group effectiveness:

(i)   Group decision making may be slower than individual decision making.

(ii)   Competition may exist in groups, which is always destructive.

(iii)   Groups tend to produce decisions that are compromises and may be less effective than those made by individuals.

(iv)   Individuals decisions are subject to more controls than those made by groups.

Which of these statements is/are correct?

A   (i) and (ii) only

B   (i), (ii) and (iv) only

C   (i) and (iii) only

D   (i), (iii) and (iv) only

Test your understanding 13

Which of the following types of behaviour is more likely to defuse conflict when dealing with other people?

A   Assertive

B   Aggressive

C   Passive

Test your understanding 14

There are a number of models that look at the formation and development of teams, including Belbin and Tuckman's models.

Required:

(a)   **Consider the following individuals within a team. For each one, identify which of Belbin's team roles are being described.**

    A   Develops new ideas to help the team achieve their objectives.

    B   Constantly checks up on team progress and tries to ensure that all tasks are completed on schedule.

    C   An extrovert individual who is strongly action-oriented.

    D   Identifies the flaws and inaccuracies in other team members' work.

    (i)   **Shaper. Select ONE from A, B, C or D**

    (ii)   **Monitor-evaluator. Select ONE from A, B, C or D**

    (iii)   **Plant. Select ONE from A, B, C or D**

    (iv)   **Finisher. Select ONE from A, B, C or D**

               (0.5 marks each, total = 2 marks)

(b) A team has been brought together within company G in order to design a new product. The Product Development manager has visited the team on two separate occasions to check on their progress. He is aware that team development passes through several stages, including:

A   Storming

B   Performing

C   Norming

D   Dorming

The following sentences contain gaps which specify the appropriate stage of team development that the group has reached.

On his first visit, the Product Development manager noted that the team had little or no conflict and was busy trying to decide how the group should organise its workload. The manager therefore concluded that the team was at the 1 stage.

Required:

(i)   **Select the correct stage of team development which appropriately fills gap 1 above; i.e. select A, B, C or D.**

On his second visit, the Product Development manager felt that the team had reached the 2 stage, as they felt they had accomplished all major tasks they had been set and the team was meeting for largely social reasons.

Required:

(ii)   **Select the correct stage of team development which appropriately fills gap 2 above; i.e. select A, B, C or D.**

Test your understanding answers

Test your understanding 1

The correct answer is B

The two individuals have interpreted the email in different ways – indicating that they have different perceptions of what the email meant.

Test your understanding 2

The correct answer is B

T has two functions – to set and control the budgets for her department and to hire an appropriate new member of staff. Given the high cost of hiring a skilled new employee, these two roles are currently incompatible.

Test your understanding 3

The correct answer is C

Consider group attributes

- There would be no sense of identity as there are no acknowledged boundaries of the group.

- The loyalty only comes from the norms that might be expected – orderly queue (not always adhered to).

- While they share common individual aims (to catch a bus), there is no collective objective (e.g. I will still get on the bus even if there is no room for others).

- The people are unlikely to choose a leader.

In conclusion, they would be considered as a random crowd rather than a group. If they know each other or have to wait a long time, then they could develop into an informal group.

Test your understanding 4

An assertive response might be "Fine. I'm happy to talk about the safety meeting, but right now I'd like to finish these invoices. How about ringing me back later this afternoon?"

An aggressive response might be "Fine. You can't expect me to think about a safety meeting. I'm in the middle of doing some invoices. You'll have to ring me back later?"

Test your understanding 5

The correct answer is A – Yes

An orchestra is a team made up of talented individuals. The conductor attempts to blend them together to make an excellent team performance.

Test your understanding 6

Neville – Leader

Olivia – Shaper

Peter – Plant-evaluator and innovator

Rosalinde – resource-investigator

Quentin – Company worker

Sheila – Team worker

Test your understanding 7

Before the changes – the team could be described as at the performing stage of team development.

After the changes – the recruitment of four new people to the group has taken the team back to the forming and storming stages.

Test your understanding 8

The correct answer is B

The following are typical examples of behaviour characteristics of ineffective groups:

- tense atmosphere

- no clear objectives

- members not listening to each other

- dominating characters

- group pressure – individuals feeling they need to agree with decisions even when they believe them to be wrong

- conflict is avoided – Tuckman suggests conflict is required and needs to be managed in order to develop team norms.

Test your understanding 9

The correct answer is C

High labour turnover could indicate problems inside the group, with individuals not wishing to remain members for long.

Low absenteeism and high productivity would both indicate a well-balanced, effective team.

Test your understanding 10

The correct answer is D

A role sign is a visible indication of an individual's role within the organisation. A uniform is a classic example of this.

Role sets are a description of the people who respond to an individual in a particular role, while role behaviour is the behaviour associated with a particular role in an organisation.

Test your understanding 11

The correct answer is B – False

Assertive behaviour is direct, honest and professional communication. The definition given is that of aggressive behaviour.

Test your understanding 12

The correct answer is C

Because of the number of potentially differing opinions, group decisions tend to be slower and often end up simply being compromises. While competition may exist in groups, this may be beneficial and is not always destructive. Note that groups enable more effective control over decisions, as the group members can oversee each other's work.

Test your understanding 13

The correct answer is A

Aggressive behaviour is more likely to lead to conflict, while passive behaviour ignores the conflict.

Test your understanding 14

(a) The correct answers are (by definition):

    (i)   C

    (ii) D

    (iii) A

    (iv) B

(b) The correct stages are:

    (i)   **C** – this is the norming stage, where the group is trying to agree on individual roles and how decisions are made.

    (ii) **D** – the team appears to have outlived its usefulness and productivity has fallen. This would make the team appear to be at the dorming stage.

Motivating individuals and groups

Chapter learning objectives

Upon completion of this chapter you will be able to:

- define motivation and explain its importance to the organisation, teams and individuals

- explain content and process theories of motivation: Maslow, Herzberg, McGregor and Vroom

- explain and identify types of intrinsic and extrinsic reward

- explain how reward systems can be designed and implemented to motivate teams and individuals.

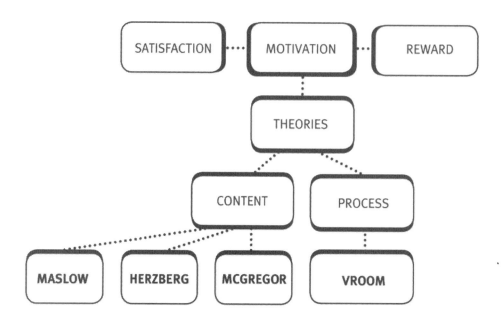

1 What is motivation?

In an organisation, motivation refers to the willingness of individuals to perform certain tasks or actions. It is the incentive or reason for them behaving in a particular way.

In practice, motivation is taken as meaning how hard an employee is willing to work in their job. It goes beyond employees merely following rules and orders and looks at how **dedicated** they are.

Having motivated staff members has a range of benefits – from the perspectives of both the organisation and the individuals or teams themselves. These include:

Organisation perspective	Individual perspective	Team perspective
Harder working employees	Greater job satisfaction	Increased co-operation
Fewer mistakes and errors	Improved health, due to less stress	More commitment to team needs
Less waste of time and resources	Improved career prospects	Better ideas generation and evaluation
More suggestions and ideas generated	Finding the job more interesting and enjoyable	
Increased job satisfaction and therefore lower staff turnover		

More customer satisfaction due to better service from staff		

As there are so many advantages to having motivated workers, motivation is a key issue for most managers.

Unfortunately, motivation is difficult to measure directly, meaning that managers have to look at other factors that may indicate the level of motivation within the organisation, often including staff turnover or productivity levels.

However, remember that these factors could also be caused by issues other than employee motivation. For instance, low productivity could be caused by poor working practices within the organisation, rather than unhappy staff.

The difference between motivation and satisfaction

It is important to distinguish between motivation and **satisfaction**. Motivation looks at how hard someone is willing to work, while satisfaction looks at whether they are **content with their existing job and not looking for another**.

While the two are linked, they are different. In the short term, it is possible to have one without the other, but in the long term you normally need both to retain an employee.

Consider someone working for an aggressive manager who constantly shouts at them. They may be motivated to avoid further abuse from their manager, but are probably looking for another job! The poor working conditions will eventually reduce their motivation as well.

Test your understanding 1

For each of the characteristics listed below, indicate whether they are due to satisfaction or motivation:

A   low staff turnover

B   fewer mistakes

C   higher productivity

2 Motivation theories

Motivation theories fall into two groups.

Content theories	Process theories
• Ask the question '**what**' are the things that motivate people? They are also referred to as '**need theories**' and assume that human beings have a set of needs or desired outcomes which can be satisfied through work.	• Ask the question '**how**' are people motivated. They attempt to explain how individuals start, sustain and direct behaviour and assume that individuals are able to select their own goals and means of achieving those goals through a process of calculation.
• Content theories assume that everyone responds to motivating factors in the same way and that **there is one best way to motivate everybody**.	• Process theories change the emphasis from needs to the **goals** and **processes** by which workers are motivated.

2.1 Content theories

2.1.1 Maslow's hierarchy of needs

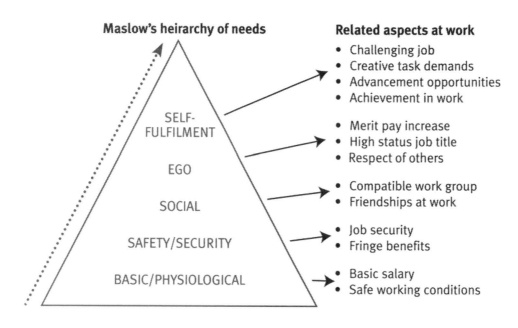

The hierarchy of needs – more detail

Maslow's theory may be summarised by saying that everyone wants certain things throughout life, and these can be placed in five ascending categories, namely:

- **Basic or physiological needs** – the things needed to stay alive, such as food, shelter and clothing. Such needs can be satisfied by money.

- **Safety or security needs** – people want protection against unemployment, the consequences of sickness and retirement as well as being safeguarded against unfair treatment. These needs can be satisfied by the rules of employment, i.e. pension scheme, sick fund, employment legislation, etc.

- **Social needs** – the vast majority of people want to be part of a group and it is only through group activities that this need can be satisfied. Thus the way that work is organised, enabling people to feel part of a group, is fundamental to satisfaction of this need.

- **Ego needs** – these needs may be expressed as wanting the esteem and respect of other people and thinking well of oneself. While status and promotion can offer short-term satisfaction, building up the job itself and giving people a greater say in how their work is organised gives satisfaction of a more permanent nature. An example might be being asked to lead groups on a course.

- **Self-fulfilment needs** – this is quite simply the need to achieve something worthwhile in life. It is a need that is satisfied only by continuing success, for example opening and running a new office.

Test your understanding 2

Which level of Maslow's hierarchy do the following factors relate to?

A   New job title

B   Large pay rises

C   Sick pay

D   Christmas parties

E   Challenging work

F   Enough cash to live on

Test your understanding 3

Violet is the managing director (MD) of a successful design company and runs the board of directors. She has a generous pay package and pension arrangements. In a recent newspaper interview, she described her job as 'constantly challenging and always changing'. Which level of Maslow's hierarchy of needs is Violet likely to have reached?

A   Ego

B   Social

C   Security

D   Self-fulfilment

Criticisms of Maslow's hierarchy

- Individuals have different needs and may not necessarily reach them in the same order as each other.

- Individuals may seek to satisfy several needs at the same time.

- Not all needs are, or can be, satisfied through work.

Test your understanding 4

Why might a graduate starting a new job who had already satisfied the basic needs on Maslow's hierarchy then seek to satisfy needs in a different order?

2.1.2 Herzberg's two-factor theory

Herzberg's model examined two sets of factors that can be used to help get the best out of workers.

Hygiene factors

These are issues that must be addressed to avoid workers becoming dissatisfied with their jobs. They include:

- policies and procedures for staff treatment

- appropriate level of pay and conditions for the job

- suitable levels of supervision

- team working and interpersonal relationships at work

- pleasant physical working environment.

The absence of these will reduce satisfaction levels and lead to employees looking for work elsewhere. However, **their presence will not result in positive motivation**.

Motivators

These are issues that will motivate workers and stimulate improved performance. According to Herzberg, they included:

- a sense of achievement

- recognition of good work by management

- increasing levels of responsibility

- career progression and status increases

- enjoying the job itself.

You will notice that the main motivators are to do with the value and satisfaction gained from the job itself and are **largely non-financial in nature**. Herzberg argued that the potential boost to employee motivation caused by increases to pay were in fact extremely limited.

Instead, Herzberg suggested three types of **job design** that could be an effective tool for motivating employees.

Job design

- **Job enrichment (vertical job enlargement)**

  This is a deliberate, planned process to improve the responsibility, challenge and creativity of a job.

  It involves giving an employee a greater level of responsibility and autonomy within their job – often involving problem solving or delegation. For instance, an accountant who is currently responsible for producing quarterly management accounts could have their role enriched so that they also have to submit and explain them to senior management. The accountant could also be made responsible for dealing with any unexpected variances that have arisen.

- **Job enlargement (horizontal job enlargement)**

  This is an attempt to widen the employee's job by giving them a larger workload. It does not involve higher level work – simply more of the existing work that the employee already undertakes.

  While some employees may see larger roles as higher-status, Herzberg argued that there was relatively little motivational benefit.

- **Job rotation**

  This is the planned rotation of staff between jobs to alleviate monotony and provide a fresh, challenging job.

  The documented example quotes a warehouse gang of four workers, where the worst job was tying the necks of sacks at the base of the hopper after filling. Job rotation would ensure that equal time was spent by each individual on each job.

  While this would reduce boredom for workers, Herzberg argued that it would often simply improve satisfaction, rather than providing motivation.

Test your understanding 5

Which of the following factors can be both a hygiene factor and a motivator for employees?

Multiple choices

A   Pay

B   The quality of management

C   Working conditions

D   The level of responsibility the individual is given

Test your understanding 6

Modern trends in job design have been aimed at the quality of working life for the worker and labour flexibility. Which of Herzberg's three definitions would these be attributed to?

A   Job rotation

B   Job enrichment

C   Job enlargement

Problems with Hertzberg's job designs

Note that Herzberg's job designs do have problems.

- **Job enrichment** – giving an employee higher-level work will eventually lead to an increase in the level of hygiene factors they require to be satisfied. If an employee feels that they are doing the work of a manager, for example, they will eventually expect to be paid as such. Failure to do this will lead to dissatisfaction.

- **Job enlargement** – has limited usefulness for motivation. If an employee is already doing a tedious or repetitive job, merely giving them more of this to do is unlikely to motivate them. In addition, the employee will have to do more work – again leading them to eventually expect higher pay and conditions to compensate them.

- **Job rotation** – while interesting for the employee, changing roles can also be stressful, requiring the employee to learn new skills. In addition, in more complex roles, the organisation will have to have ongoing training for the workers that are being rotated. This will be time-consuming and expensive.

2.1.3 McGregor's Theory X and Y

McGregor suggested that managers make assumptions about their staff – both how they think and behave. These assumptions, which McGregor called **Theory X** or **Theory Y**, then dictate the manager's approach to supervising their group.

Theory X assumptions:

Employees are assumed to:

- dislike work

- have to be coerced, threatened or forced to get them to work adequately

- dislike taking responsibility, preferring to be directed and told what to do.

Managers therefore adopt an **authoritarian, repressive style with tight controls**. Effectively the workforce is a problem that needs to be overcome by management.

Theory Y assumptions:

Employees are assumed to:

- enjoy work, with physical and mental effort being as natural as play or rest

- be able to be motivated to take responsibility

- are able to exercise self-control and self-direction in order to achieve their goals.

Managers who make these assumptions about their workers are more **participative or democratic in their approac**h. Employees are viewed as assets to be encouraged and empowered.

Application

In reality, few managers tend to see their employees as precisely Theory X or Theory Y. Normally, managers will see their staff somewhere between these two extremes.

The model is designed to make managers aware of the assumptions about their staff that they are making in their management approach, as well as the need to match their management style to the nature of their staff. A Theory X workforce should not be managed using a democratic approach, while the manager of a Theory Y workforce will not get the best of their staff with an autocratic management style.

Test your understanding 7

According to Douglas McGregor

A   Theory X people dislike work, need direction and avoid responsibility

B   Theory Y people dislike work, need direction and avoid responsibility

C   People trying to satisfy ego needs dislike work, need direction and avoid responsibility

D   Hygiene factors determine whether people like work, need direction or take responsibility

2.2 Process theories

2.2.1 Vroom's expectancy theory

Vroom believed that people will only be motivated to do tasks if they are confident that the tasks will help them to reach their goals.

Vroom's theory can be stated as a formula:

Force	**= valence × expectancy**
where	
Force	= the strength of a person's motivation
valence	= the strength of an individual's preference for an outcome
expectancy	= the probability of success

Vroom's expectancy theory

Imagine you have been offered the chance to star on a prize show where you will be asked 50 questions in order to win a cash prize. Would you want to appear on the show or not? In other words, would you be motivated to attempt to win the cash?

According to Vroom's model, it would depend on two things:

- **Valence** – this looks at your preference for the outcome. If the prize is only a small amount of money, you may be tempted not to bother. A large prize may increase your motivation to try and win.

- **Expectancy** – this looks at your perception of your probability of success. If the questions are all on a topic that you have little knowledge of, you will be much less likely to appear on the show. If the questions are on a topic you are familiar with, you will perceive your chances of winning as higher, making you more motivated to appear on the show.

Test your understanding 8

Sonya lacks confidence. Her boss wants to motivate her by showing her that she has regularly exceeded targets in the past. Which aspect of the Vroom model is being focused on here?

A   Valence

B   Expectancy

3   Rewards and incentives

A reward is something given, to an individual or group, in recognition of their services, efforts or achievements.

The rewards that an organisation offers to its employees can either be **intrinsic** or **extrinsic**.

- **Intrinsic rewards** – these arise from the performance of the job itself. Intrinsic rewards include the feeling of satisfaction that comes from doing a job well, being allowed to make higher level decisions or being interested in your job.

- **Extrinsic rewards** – these are separate from (or external to) the job itself and are dependent on the decisions of others (i.e. the workers have no control over these rewards). Pay, working conditions and benefits are all examples of extrinsic rewards.

Note that extrinsic rewards are closely linked to Herzberg's hygiene factors, while intrinsic factors tie in to Herzberg's motivators.

Test your understanding 9

Which one of the following is an intrinsic reward?

A   Company car

B   Extra holiday entitlement

C   On the job training of new recruits

D   Bonus payment

3.1 Reward systems

The offering of positive rewards to employees is a key motivational issue for most organisations. However, rewards systems should be carefully designed in order to ensure that they:

- are fair and consistent for all employees, even for those workers with different job sizes or required levels of skill

- are sufficient to attract and retain staff

- maintain and improve levels of employee performance

- reward progression and promotion

- comply with legislation and regulation (i.e. minimum wage laws)

- control salary costs.

Employees can be rewarded in a number of ways, including through ongoing development and training (which will boost their future career prospects). This links back to Maslow's hierarchy of needs, as continuous development will help to meet self-fulfilment and ego needs.

However, most employees will be particularly interested in their remuneration. One way that businesses tie the performance of their employees to their pay is through the use of incentive schemes.

There are three main types of incentive scheme:

- **Performance related pay (PRP)**

  - **Piecework** – reward related to the pace of work or amount of effort. The faster the employee works, the higher the output and the greater the reward.

  - **Management by objectives (MBO)** – key results are identified for which rewards will be paid on top of salary.

  - **Points system** – this is an extension to MBO reward systems, where a range of rewards is available based on a point system derived from the scale of improvement made, such as the amount of cost reduction achieved.

  - **Commission** – paid on the performance of an individual and typically paid to salaried staff in sales functions, where the commission earned is a proportion of total sales made.

- **Bonus schemes** – usually a one off as opposed to PRP schemes which are usually a continual management policy. Bonuses may also be awarded to teams or groups that have met or beaten certain targets. Group bonuses can help the team to pull together and work as a cohesive unit, but may lead to conflict if some members of the team are seen to be doing less work than others.

- **Profit sharing** – usually available to a wide group of employees (often company wide) where payments are made in the light of the overall profitability of the company. Share issues may be part of the scheme.

Incentives need to encourage effort or action towards the delivery of organisational objectives, so there may be potential conflict when contrasting long and short term objectives. (e.g. sales staff offering discounts to customers to win extra orders this year to get a bonus, at the expense of next year's sales)

- **Long-term incentive schemes** will be those that are designed to continually motivate and deliver organisational objectives.

- **Short-term incentive schemes** will be those that motivate in the short-term but do not deliver on-going motivation and are often achieved at the detriment of longer term objectives.

Test your understanding 10

Consider the following statements regarding reward and incentive schemes.

(i) Incentive schemes should have a balance of long-term and short-term measures to ensure staff consider the immediate and future needs of the organisation.

(ii) A 'points system' refers to the payment of bonuses to employees when the organisation achieves a profit above a pre-determined level.

Which of these statements is/are correct?

A (i) only

B (ii) only

C Both

D Neither

4 Chapter summary

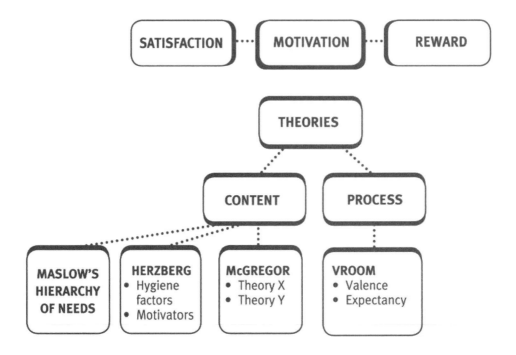

5 Practice questions

Test your understanding 11

Highly satisfied employees always show increased levels of productivity in an organisation, compare to dissatisfied employees.

Is this statement true or false?

A   True

B   False

Test your understanding 12

B is a caretaker at a school where his wife is a teacher. They have three young children and have just moved into a new house – which they cannot afford on B's wife's salary alone. Which of Maslow's hierarchy of needs is likely to be motivating B?

A   Basic

B   Safety

C   Social

D   Ego

Test your understanding 13

Parallels can be drawn between Maslow's hierarchy of needs and Herzberg's two-factor theory. For example, Maslow's 'ego' need can be linked to the motivating factor of recognition.

Which hygiene factor from the following would best match with Maslow's social needs?

A   Sports facilities

B   Pay

C   Pension

D   Working conditions

Test your understanding 14

Which of the following is NOT an issue that needs taking account of when setting the basic salary level for employees?

A   Rewards offered by similar or rival organisations

B   Legislation and regulation

C   Motivation of employees

D   Control of total salary costs for the organisation

Test your understanding 15

(a)   Consider the following rewards offered to employees.

    A   Salary

    B   Career progression

    C   Holiday entitlement

    D   Sick pay allowances

    E   Enjoyment of the job

    F   Level of satisfaction

    G   Higher level decision-making

    H   Maternity entitlement

Required:

Write down which of the four options (A – H) are extrinsic rewards.

(0.5 marks each, total = 2 marks)

(b) There are a number of different theories surrounding the motivation of employees. The following are examples of specific terms from these models.

A   Theory X

B   Theory Y

C   Valence

D   Expectancy

The following sentences contain gaps which specify the appropriate term from the above list.

If a manager acts in an autocratic manner and fails to include staff when making decisions, this may be a sign that he is a **1** manager.

Required:

(i) **Select the correct term which appropriately fills gap 1 above; i.e. select A, B, C or D**

(1 mark)

In order to motivate employees, a manager increase the bonus they can earn each year, from 10% of their salary to 20% of their salary. This increases the 2 of the reward, increasing motivation.

Required:

(ii) **Select the correct term which appropriately fills gap 2 above; i.e. select A, B, C or D**

(1 mark)

(Total: 4 marks)

Test your understanding answers

Test your understanding 1

A   Satisfaction

B   Motivation

C   Motivation

Explanation: a satisfied worker will be more content with their job and will trust their employer. Motivation is required for the employee to work harder and take more care over their work.

Test your understanding 2

A   Ego

B   Ego

C   Safety

D   Social

E   Self-fulfilment

F   Basic

Test your understanding 3

The correct answer is D

Violet appears to be at the self-fulfillment stage. She has certainly achieved security (through her attractive pay and pension scheme), her social needs are likely to be met due to being part of the board of directors, and her ego needs are likely to be met by her role as MD. The fact that she describes her job as challenging and interesting would tend to also indicate she has reached self-fulfillment in her role.

Test your understanding 4

A graduate starting a new job, who has already satisfied their basic needs on Maslow's hierarchy may seek to meet their social needs before worrying about job security and the long term security of pension arrangements.

Test your understanding 5

The correct answer is A

Herzberg argued that the quality of management and working conditions are hygiene factors, and the level of responsibility is a motivator. He also argued that pay is a hygiene factor, particularly basic pay. However, pay can also be used as an incentive/motivator, for example by offering the prospect of a cash bonus for achieving a performance target.

Test your understanding 6

The correct answer is A

Labour flexibility would include functional flexibility (multi-skilling) which would allow employees to move around the organisation depending on demand required in each department, this could be linked to job rotation.

Test your understanding 7

The correct answer is A

McGregor suggested the ideas of Theory X and Y so the answer has to be A or B.

Test your understanding 8

The correct answer is B

The perceived profitability of success is being modified, not the value of the reward.

Test your understanding 9

The correct answer is C

This would be considered as increased responsibility therefore an intrinsic value.

Test your understanding 10

The correct answer is A

Points systems refer to a situation where a range of rewards is available based on the scale of the improvement made in the period.

Test your understanding 11

The correct answer is B

Remember that satisfaction looks at whether the worker is content with their existing job and not looking for another. It does not necessarily mean that they are working harder within their role.

Test your understanding 12

The correct answer is A

As it stands, B has taken his job to allow him to pay for a house for him and his family. He is unlikely to be motivated by anything other than basic needs (for the moment).

Test your understanding 13

The correct answer is A

The social needs of workers could, at least in part, be met by the provision of sports facilities.

Test your understanding 14

The correct answer is C

Most motivational models argue that basic salary is unlikely to act as a motivator.

Test your understanding 15

(a) Extrinsic rewards are those that are separate from the job itself and which are dependent on the decisions of others. This matches options **A, C, D** and **H**.

(b) The correct answers are:

   (i) **A** – by definition.

   (ii) **C** – the valence refers to strength of the employees' preference for the outcome. By increasing the amount of the bonus, the manager is increasing employee desire to attain it, which means that they will be more motivated.

Learning and training at work

Chapter learning objectives

Upon completion of this chapter you will be able to:

- explain the importance of learning and development in the workplace

- describe the learning process: Honey and Mumford, Kolb

- describe the role of the human resources department and individual managers in the learning process

- describe the training and development process: identifying needs, setting objectives, programme design, delivery and validation

- explain the terms 'training', 'development' and 'education' and the characteristics of each

- list the benefits of effective training and development in the workplace.

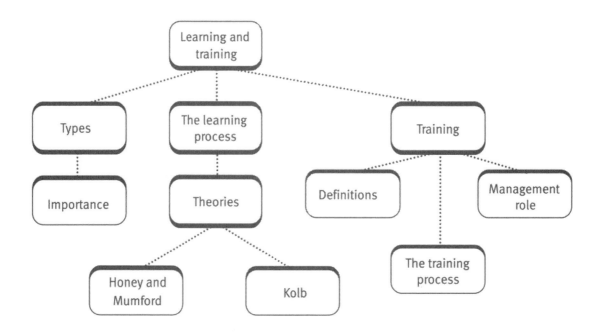

1   Learning

 Learning can be defined as 'the process of acquiring knowledge through experience, which leads to changes in behaviour'. It includes acquiring new skills, knowledge or attitudes, or a combination of all three.

Types of learning

There are three types of learning:

- **Formal** – this is undertaken deliberately and occurs when individuals 'learn' and 'study'. It is often classroom-based and highly structured.

- **Informal** – this is also usually deliberate, but is not highly structured. Examples include self-directed learning, networking, coaching and mentoring.

- **Incidental** – this is a by-product of another activity. For example, attending a formal classroom course may also help a student to learn how to keep their attention focused for a long period.

The pace of learning changes with familiarity, an effect known as the 'learning curve'. The shape of this curve depends on the type of work or task and the individual.

A fictitious curve for learning from a study guide may look something like this:

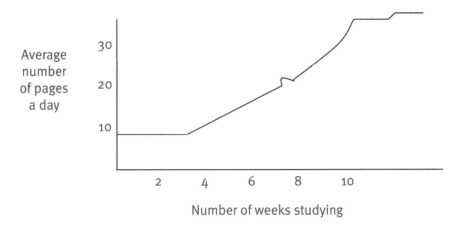

Average
number
of pages
a day

Number of weeks studying

 The rate of learning

Experience has shown that learning does not take place at a steady rate.

Initially progress will be slow, with sudden improvements followed by further progress for a period of time.

There will be a final levelling off when, without enormous effort, little further progress will be achieved.

1.1 The importance of learning in the workplace

Some employers (often smaller businesses) see investment in learning in the workplace as a drain on their resources – using up valuable time and money.

However, work-based learning has a number of key advantages:

- It can lead to increased competence, understanding, self-esteem and morale – leading to improved productivity.

- It may improve the level of creativity and innovation of workers in the organisation, giving an advantage over competitors.

- People who enjoy learning are more likely to be flexible in times of constant change.

- If workers are not given learning opportunities, there is a risk that they will feel undervalued and will lose motivation.

 Many management writers have stated that if you want to develop an organisation, then you must develop its people first and they will develop the organisation.

1.2 The learning organisation

The 'learning organisation' describes any organisation that facilitates the learning of all members and continuously transforms itself.

Typically they:

- generate and transfer knowledge throughout the organisation

- learn from others and from past experience

- tolerate risk and failure as learning opportunities

- have a systematic, ongoing, collective and scientific approach to problem-solving.

This may give them a significant advantage over competitors, especially in fast-changing markets.

2   The learning process

It is important to understand how people learn new things, as this will allow an organisation to create suitable training programmes for its employees. Two theories that help with this are those proposed by **Kolb** and **Honey & Mumford**.

2.1 Kolb: experiential learning cycle

Kolb suggested that learning is a series of steps based on everyday experience. He argued that classroom learning is false and that actual learning comes from actually undertaking tasks and learning from them.

Kolb identified four learning stages that must be addressed:

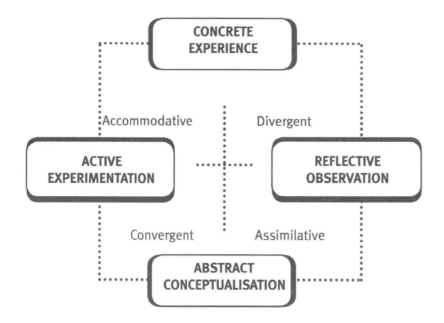

According to Kolb, successful learning is a cycle that progresses through all four stages. For instance, if you want to learn how to use a new computer system:

- **Concrete experience** – you may decide to start using the new computer system, without any training or guidance.

- **Reflective observation** – having failed to accomplish everything you wanted, you spend some time identifying the problems you had and which tasks you were unable to perform successfully on the new system.

- **Abstract conceptualisation** – having identified the problem areas, you go to the instruction manual and look up how to undertake these tasks.

- **Active experimentation** – once you have read the instructions relating to the areas you were uncertain about, you then go back to the computer system and try them again to see if you are now able to perform all the tasks you needed to accomplish.

Kolb argues this is an ongoing loop, as using the system again may well trigger new problems or issues (new concrete experiences) which trigger the cycle again.

Note that it doesn't matter where you start on the cycle. You could start at the abstract conceptualisation stage and begin by reading the instruction manual before using the system. Alternatively, you could watch someone else using the system first – beginning at the reflective observation stage.

Kolb also identifies four different learning styles adopted by individual learners (as shown on the diagram above), based on where they start on the learning cycle.

Each style is a combination of two elements from the cycle.

- **Divergent** – feeling and watching – these people prefer to watch rather than do, reflecting on what they are seeing from various angles before trying it for themselves.

- **Assimilative** – watching and thinking – these individuals take a concise, logical approach. They prefer good, clear explanations rather than undertaking practical examples. They then need time to think through what they have seen.

- **Convergent** – thinking and doing – prefer to apply ideas and enjoy testing ideas out in practice to see if they really work.

- **Accommodative** – doing and feeling – strong preference for concrete experiences and active experimentation (hands-on approach).

2.2 Honey and Mumford: learning styles

Honey and Mumford built on Kolb's earlier work and came up with four alternative classifications of learning styles. They argued people learn more effectively if they are aware of their learning style preferences.

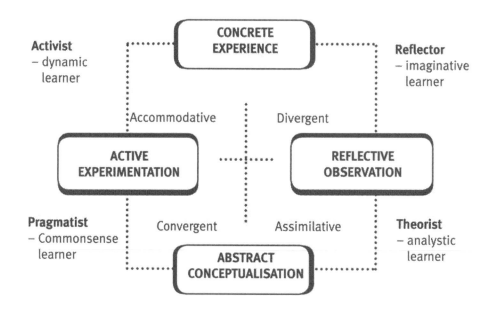

	Activists – involve themselves fully without bias to new experiences. They are open-minded, enthusiastic, constantly searching for new challenges but are bored with implementation and long-term consolidation. They enjoy learning through games, competitive teamwork tasks and role-plays.
	**Reflectors** – prefer to step back to ponder and observe others before taking action. They are in general cautious, may be perceived as indecisive and tend to adopt a low profile. The reflector prefers learning activities that are observational (like carrying out an investigation).
	**Theorists** – adapt and integrate information in a step-by-step logical way. They prefer to maximise certainty and feel uncomfortable with subjective judgements, lateral thinking and anything flippant. The theorist prefers activities that explore the interrelationship between ideas and principles.
	**Pragmatists** – are keen to try out ideas, theories and techniques to see if they work in practice. They are essentially practical, down-to-earth people, like making practical decisions, act quickly on ideas that attract them and tend to be impatient with open-ended discussions. The pragmatist prefers learning activities that are as close as possible to direct work experience.

Learning styles – more detail

Individual preferences mean that:

- Dynamic learners – activists – are primarily interested in self-discovery; they ask 'What if?' questions. In terms of learning they need a variety of new and challenging activities where they can have a lot of the limelight – business games, competitive tasks, role-playing exercises. This learner wants to touch everything. Problem solving, small group discussions or games, peer feedback, and self-directed work assignments all help this learner, who likes to see everything and determine their own criteria for the relevance of the materials. Imaginative learners – reflectors – are primarily interested in personal meaning. They question, Why? To instruct imaginative learners, teachers need to motivate and provide expert interpretation. Their preferred method of teaching is simulation or discussion. They need time to think over, assimilate and prepare for activities, or review what has happened and reach decisions without pressures and tight deadlines. Lectures are helpful to this learner. They look for an instructor who is both a taskmaster and a guide.

- Analytic learners – theorists – are primarily interested in facts as they lead to conceptual understanding. They question, What? Teachers need to give them the facts that deepen understanding. These learners need opportunities to question, probe and explore methodically the assumptions and logic, and the interrelationships between ideas and events, using case studies, theoretical readings and reflective thinking exercises.

- Common sense learners – pragmatists – are primarily interested in how things work. To instruct this type of learner teachers need to act as coach. Students need to practise techniques with coaching/feedback from a credible expert, and they must see a link between the subject matter and a problem or opportunity on the job. Group work and peer feedback often leads to success.

Illustration 1 – Honey and Mumford

It is generally agreed that a combination of different types of learners will make an effective team in an organisation. In discussing an issue, the most likely question the Reflector will pursue is **why** it is important; the Theorist, in contrast, will be interested in **what** it is all about; the Pragmatist will be concerned with **how** it can be applied in the real world; and the Activist will be keen to know **what** would happen if they were to apply it here and now.

Test your understanding 1

Mandeep works for a sales department. The processes for raising a sales invoice have recently changed. He has asked to watch another member of staff, who has been trained in the new process, raise a sales invoice before he attempts to do it himself.

According to Kolb, where is Mandeep starting on the learning cycle?

A   Concrete experience

B   Active experimentation

C   Reflective observation

D   Abstract conceptualisation

2.3 Implications of the learning models

Most individuals exhibit a clear preference for one style of learning and may struggle to switch between them. People with such a clear style preference will therefore tend to learn more effectively if learning is geared to their personal preferences.

People who have a clear learning style preference, for whatever reason, will tend to learn more effectively if learning is geared to their preference. For instance – according to **Kolb**:

- people who prefer the 'assimilating' learning style will not be comfortable being thrown in at the deep end without notes and instructions

- people who prefer to use an 'accommodating' learning style are likely to become frustrated if they are forced to read lots of instructions and rules, and are unable to get hands-on experience as soon as possible.

A feature of **Honey and Mumford's** model is that it provides suggestions about the best ways for individuals to learn. The most effective learning methods are different for each learning style.

- **Activists** – have a practical approach to training, are flexible and optimistic. They prefer practical problems, enjoy participation and challenge, are easily bored and have a dislike of theory. They must have hands-on training.

- **Theorists** – require their learning to be programmed and structured; designed to allow time for analysis; and provided by people who share the same preference for ideas and analysis.

- **Reflectors** – need an observational approach to training. They need to work at their own pace – slow, cautious and non-participative – where conclusions are carefully thought out. They do not find learning easy especially if rushed.

- **Pragmatists** – need to see a direct value and link between training and real problems and aim to do things better. They enjoy learning new techniques and tasks and are good at finding improved ways of doing things.

Test your understanding 2

(a)   What style of learner will:

Learn best from:	Be less likely to learn from:
• activities where they can observe other people first • being given time to think things over • the opportunity to discuss ideas with others • having time to prepare?	• situations where they are 'thrown in' without adequate time to plan or think • role play in front of others • activities where they are told what to do • having to make shortcuts for the sake of expediency?

(b)   Draw up a similar chart for one other style.

3   What are training, development and education?

- **Education** is defined as 'the activities which aim at developing the knowledge skills, moral values and understanding required in all aspects of life rather than a knowledge skill related to only a limited field of activity'.

  Education is usually intended to mean basic instruction in knowledge and skills designed to help people make the most of life in general. It is therefore personal and broadly based.

  The quality of education can therefore only be completely assessed when the learner moves on to future jobs or tasks.

- **Training** is 'the planned and systematic modification of behaviour through learning events, programmes and instruction which enable individuals to achieve the level of knowledge, skills and competence to carry out their work effectively'.

  Training therefore usually implies a planned process to modify attitudes, skills or behaviour that will help the individual to improve their performance in their job. It is therefore job-oriented rather than personal.

  Training can be evaluated upon the learner's return to work.

- **Development** is 'the growth or realisation of a person's ability and potential through conscious or unconscious learning and educational experiences'.

  Development therefore takes a broader view of the acquisition of skills and knowledge than training, concerned more with changes in attitude,

  behaviour and potential than with immediate skills. It relates more to helping the growth of the individual for future roles.

  It is often argued that development is therefore more general, more future-oriented and more individually-oriented than training.

4 The training and development process

4.1 The benefits of training and development

Organisations should view training and development of staff as an investment. The benefits for the learner and the organisation include:

For the individual:

- improved skills and (dependent on the type of training) qualifications
- increased confidence and job satisfaction.

For the organisation:

- increased motivation of employees, leading to higher productivity
- increased competence and confidence, meaning higher quality and fewer mistakes
- low staff turnover, saving the organisation time and money
- skilled workforce, leading to more innovation and a better customer experience.

Due to the obvious importance of training and development, a systematic approach should be taken in order to maximise its effectiveness. To help with this, organisations may find it helpful to view training and development as a step-by-step process.

4.2 Step 1: Identification of training needs

How does a company know that it needs to train its workers? There are a number of possible methods. These include:

- Formal training needs analysis (TNA)

  This involves identification of the skills, knowledge and experience needed for a particular job and comparing this to the skills, knowledge and experience of the current job-holder. If the job-holder is lacking any of these required skills, this is referred to as a learning gap, which can be filled using training.

  TNA may also be triggered by external changes to the organisation, such as new government legislation.

- **Performance appraisal**

  Most line managers appraise their staff or carry out a performance review at least annually. During this, the manager can review past performance, discuss the employee's aspirations and use this to identify possible training and development opportunities in the future.

- **Observation**

  There may be signs that staff require additional training, such as poor productivity or high numbers of mistakes. There is evidence that inadequate training leads to workers failing to meet production targets, leading to frustration. This means that, in addition, managers should monitor labour turnover, absenteeism rates or the level of grievances within the organisation.

  While these problems may be caused by a range of factors, poor training and development could be the reason behind them.

- **Organisational strategy**

  Training and development must be linked to the overall business strategy. There should be senior support for the training programme and it must be seen to support the needs of the organisation itself. Training merely for the sake of training is likely to be a waste of time and money.

Test your understanding 3

Consider the following statement:

'Formal training needs analysis (TNA) is always triggered by changes that are external to the organisation, such as changes in legislation.'

Is this statement:

A   True

B   False

4.3 Stage 2: Setting objectives for training

This stage examines what the proposed training programme is supposed to accomplish. What impact do we want it to have on our staff?

Objectives need to be clearly stated, measurable and specific, outlining the effect that training should have on the performance and abilities of the employee being trained.

Illustration 2 – Training objectives

When an organisation considers sending a junior member of its accounts department on a professional accountancy course, they will have several learning objectives, including:

- The employee will be able to achieve a pass mark in all of his accountancy exams.

- The employee will be able to produce an error-free analysis of the organisation's management accounts each month without supervision.

A car manufacturing company may wish to train its employees in how to assemble the various engine components efficiently. Its key learning objective may therefore be:

- All trained employees will be able to assemble four engines per hour and make no more than one mistake per day.

4.4 Stage 3: Programme design and delivery

Training and development of individuals can include:

- formal training courses – both in-house and external
- mentoring
- coaching
- computer-based learning
- self-managed learning.

Groups may have slightly different training and development methods, including:

- lectures
- discussions
- case studies and role play
- business games.

The organisation must decide whether to implement the training externally (by using a college, university or other training organisation) or in-house. If in-house is chosen, infrastructure and staffing must be carefully considered.

4.5 Stage 4: Evaluation and validation of the training programme

Once complete, evaluation of the training programme aims to assess whether it was successful and whether the training achieved its objectives. It will also enable the organisation to ensure that it is using the right tools for training.

It has been suggested that there are five levels at which evaluation can take place.

Levels of evaluation	Achieved by:
1. Reactions – of the trainees to the training, their feelings about how enjoyable and useful it has been, etc.	• End-of-course questionnaires – obtain immediate feedback on the perceived value of the training but may not be the best way of evaluating the effectiveness of the programme.
2. Learning – what new skills and knowledge have been acquired or what changes in attitude have taken place as a result of the training.	• Attainment tests – limited to the immediate knowledge and skills improvement and may not indicate whether the learning will be transferred to the workplace or job. • Interviews – appraisal or performance reviews provide an opportunity to discuss the individual's progress during and after a training and development programme.
3. Job behaviour – at this level evaluation tries to measure the extent to which trainees have applied their training on the job.	• Observation – the end results of the learning and development can be assessed by observation of improvements in job performance levels. • Career development – the speed of promotion of an individual may be used as an indication of the effectiveness of the training and development and also the level of support given to the development plan by the organisation.
4. Organisation – training may be assessed in terms of the ways in which changes in job behaviour affect the functioning of the organisation.	• At the departmental level the effective training and development of staff can mean the achievement of targets, goals and objectives measured in terms of output, productivity, quality, etc.
5. Ultimate value – this is a measure of the training in terms of how the organisation as a whole has benefited.	• Measured in terms of greater profitability, survival or growth.

Whatever evaluation method is used it should be done before, during and after the event.

- Before the event will clarify the existing skills, knowledge and attitudes to help the trainer plan the event and provide a yardstick by which to measure them.

- During the event will identify the rate of learning, allowing the trainer to pace the learning to suit the trainee and offer remedial help where needed.

- After the event can be immediately after the training or over a long time. It should link back to the objectives of the training (discussed in an earlier stage) and check that they have been accomplished.

Test your understanding 4

Consider the following statements:

(i) Decisions about training are only ever made after a formal training needs analysis.

(ii) Training should be delegated to external providers if the organisation lacks the skills or infrastructure in-house.

Which of these statements is/are correct?

A (i) only

B (ii) only

C Both

D Neither

---

5 The role of management in the learning process

There are a number of people or groups who share responsibility for training and development of employees.

The human resources (HR) department

The HR department has overall, high-level responsibility for training and development. This will often mean that they will need to:

- create frameworks for job appraisals and the analysis of learning gaps

- identify when and if training is needed within the organisation

- design career pathways for employees (such as the creation of different employee grades along with the responsibilities that go along with each grade)

- informing employees about learning, training development opportunities that are available to them.

Line managers

While the HR department takes a high-level view of learning, line managers are likely to have responsibilities for helping to apply HR department resources to their own group or department. This may involve:

- identification of learning and training needs of the group or department they are responsible for

- monitoring the abilities and knowledge levels of individual workers within their team

- organising specific training programmes

- offering informal training, such as coaching and mentoring to employees as needed.

Don't forget that, ultimately, the learners themselves have a responsibility to seek out learning and development opportunities and then take full advantage of them.

6   Chapter summary

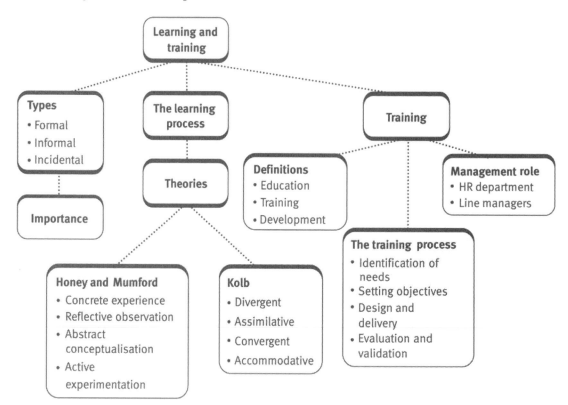

7 Practice questions

Test your understanding 5

J is an employee at Y company. He has recently been sent on a course by his company to help him learn about basic accountancy principles. This is an example of:

A   Education

B   Re-skilling

C   Training

D   Development

Test your understanding 6

Development is the 'planned and systematic modification of behaviour through learning events, programmes and instruction, which enables individuals to achieve the level of knowledge, skills and competence to carry out their work effectively.'

Is this statement:

A   True

B   False

Test your understanding 7

H has been given a new role at her workplace. To prepare, she makes sure that she has read all the relevant documentation and technical summaries relating to her new role.

According to Kolb, what stage of learning is H beginning at?

A   Active experimentation

B   Abstract conceptualisation

C   Reflective observation

D   Concrete experience

Test your understanding 8

A theorist learns best from:

(i)   Activities where they can observe other people first

(ii) Being given time to think things over

(iii) Having time to prepare

(iv) Structured learning

Which of these statements are correct when considering the learning style of a theorist?

A   (i) and (ii) only

B   All four statements

C   (i), (ii) and (iii) only

D   (iv) only

Test your understanding 9

Honey and Mumford argued that there were four possible styles of learning that might apply to individuals.

Required:

(a) **For each example given below, identify which of Honey and Mumford's learning styles is most appropriate.**

    A   E prefers to learn by investigation, with plenty of time being provided to think about the results that he has obtained.

    B   D likes to learn about definite facts and figures. She dislikes having to do any practical work.

    C   T likes to learn through teamwork and role-playing. He tends to get bored easily with longer, theoretical exercises.

    D   V prefers to learn by trying out what she has learned and seeing if it works in practice.

    (i)   **Reflector. Select ONE of A, B, C or D**

    (ii)   **Activist. Select ONE of A, B, C or D**

    (iii) **Pragmatist. Select ONE of A, B, C or D**

    (iv)   **Theorist. Select ONE of A, B, C or D**

          (0.5 marks each, total = 2 marks)

(b)   Training is often seen as beneficial to organisations.

    A   Toleration of risk and failure

    B   Lower cost base

    C   Reduced profit margins

    D   Efficient generation and transfer of knowledge

    E   Low levels of staff needed

    F   Inability to compete with rivals

    G   Little or no training of employees

    Required:

    Which TWO of the above are typical features of a 'learning organisation'? Select TWO from (A, B, C, D, E, F, G).

    (2 marks)

    (Total: 4 marks)

Test your understanding answers

Test your understanding 1

The correct answer is C

Mandeep is watching others first and reflecting on the experience before undertaking it himself.

Test your understanding 2

(a)   Reflector

(b)   Other learning styles (only one of the following was required).

Activists are likely to learn from:	**Activists** are less likely to learn from:
• new experiences and activities • exercises where they become involved • role play, business games and short-term tasks • excitement and drama • being 'thrown in at the deep end'.	• lectures, explanations, reading and observing • theoretical sessions • activities involving analysing data • activities where they are told precisely what to do • repeat activities (such as practising a skill).
Theorists learn best from:	**Theorists** are less likely to learn from:
• structured learning • slower paced learning that allows time for analysis • being surrounded by other people who learn in the same way.	• shallow unclear situations • unstructured situations, especially with no clear point • being asked to make a decision without a policy • situations with emotional overtones • being rushed into any exercise without its relevance being explained.

Pragmatists learn best from:	Pragmatists are less likely to learn from:
• exercises where the link to the job is explained or obvious • practical relevant activities • situations where implementation is important (as well as learning) • drawing up action plans to use back at work • the opportunity to learn from a coach or copy a role model.	• activities with no clear relevance to their job • no clear practical aspects or guidelines on how to do things • situations where people seem to lack a goal • situations where there is no relevant reward to the exercise • situations where the trainer is perceived to be 'out of touch' with their world.

Test your understanding 3

The correct answer is B – False

Formal TNA is often undertaken as part of identification of training needs within an organisation. This does not have to be triggered by external environmental changes.

Test your understanding 4

The correct answer is B

Statement (i) is incorrect, as training decisions can be made after appraisals, interviews, or as part of an ongoing organisational strategy (amongst others).

Test your understanding 5

The correct answer is C

This is an example of training. J is learning a new skill relating to a particular area or activity. Development is learning for growth of the individual and is not related specifically to a present or future job. Education is personal and broadly based.

Test your understanding 6

The correct answer is B – False

The definition given is that of training.

Test your understanding 7

The correct answer is B

H is attempting to understand her new role in theory before she begins. This is an example of abstract conceptualisation.

Test your understanding 8

The correct answer is D

The first three relate to reflectors.

Test your understanding 9

(a)　The correct answers (by definition) are:

　　(i)　**A**

　　(ii)　**C**

　　(iii)　**D**

　　(iv)　**B**

(b)　Learning organisations are those that facilitate the learning of all members and continuously transform themselves. This has nothing specifically to do with costs and profit margins, though it will normally give an organisation the edge over its rivals. The correct answers are therefore **A** and **D**.

Review and appraisal of individual performance

Chapter learning objectives

Upon completion of this chapter you will be able to:

- explain the importance of performance assessment

- explain how organisations assess the performance of human resources

- define performance appraisal and describe its purposes

- describe the performance appraisal process

- explain the benefits of effective appraisal

- identify the barriers to effective appraisal and how these may be overcome

- explain how the effectiveness of performance appraisal may be evaluated.

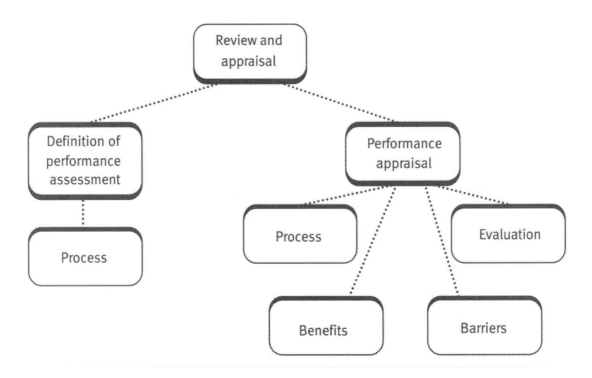

1 Performance assessment

1.1 What is performance assessment?

 Performance assessment is 'the regular and systematic review of performance and the assessment of potential with the aim of producing action programmes to develop both work and individuals'.

It aims to improve the efficiency of the organisation by ensuring that the individual employees are performing to the best of their abilities and by developing their potential for improvement.

Typically, assessing employee performance involves measuring both quantitative measures (i.e. how many units the worker has produced, or how much chargeable time they have billed) and qualitative measures (i.e. their attitude, how they have interacted with other members of staff).

It is crucial that valid criteria are used when assessing employee performance. This is made more complex because most jobs have many dimensions, meaning that the assessment must look at a number of different criteria in order to accurately reflect the employee's performance.

Assessment criteria may include the following:

- **Volume of work produced**
  - within time period
  - evidence of work planning
  - personal time management
  - effectiveness of work under pressure

- **Knowledge of work**
  - gained through experience
  - gained through training courses
  - gained prior to employment
- **Quality of work**
  - level of analytical ability
  - level of technical knowledge
  - accuracy
  - judgement exercised
  - cost effectiveness
- **Management skills**
  - communication skills
  - motivation skills
  - training and development skills
  - delegation skills
- **Personal skills**
  - decision-making capabilities
  - flexibility
  - adaptability
  - assertiveness
  - team involvement
  - motivation

1.2 The process of performance assessment

Organisations follow four main steps when assessing performance of employees:

- **Set targets** – at the start of the period, the manager and employee should agree on which goals and targets the employee is going to work towards. These usually include:
  - areas that the employee needs to improve (perhaps where the employee is currently making mistakes)
  - targets that link in to the overall business goals (such as increasing activity by five percent)
  - development and training targets that will benefit the employee (and the company) and therefore increase motivation.

It is important that employees understand and agree to these targets. If they do not 'buy into' them, they will not put any effort in to accomplishing the goals set – especially if they do not feel that the targets are achievable. This can lead to demotivation.

- **Monitor** – during the period, the manager should monitor employee performance and provide regular feedback. Managers can offer rewards for good performance and support and help where it looks as though the employee is failing to meet their targets.

- **Review** – at the end of the period, the manager and employee will usually have a formal appraisal where they discuss the employee's performance and investigate how successful the employee has been at meeting the pre-agreed targets.

- **Action plan** – the manager and employee then agree on new targets that will be set for the coming period.

Illustration 1 – Performance assessment in context

While many people view the performance assessment process as beginning after six or 12 months of employment and view it as a review of how the employee has performed for the previous period, a successful performance management process begins during the hiring process. It continues as an ongoing cycle from recruitment, through selection, induction/orientation, and goal setting and on to performance appraisal and evaluation. This process occurs in three stages with the following components:

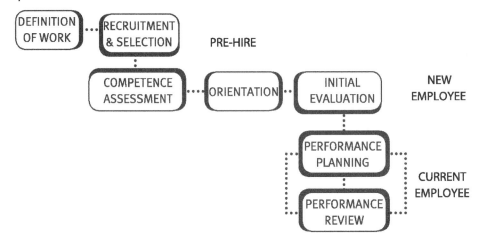

There are a few types of staff appraisal processes in use:

- Review and comparison – consists of the individual being assessed and analysed in terms of objectives, tasks, workflows and results achieved. These are then compared with previously agreed statements of required results and performance levels.

> - Management by objectives – managers agree certain objectives with their subordinates and then review the results achieved. It is based on the idea that if subordinates know their objectives they are more likely to reach them.
>
> - The task-centred method – relates to what the subordinate is doing and how they do it. It avoids the more formal approach to staff appraisal and adopts a continual assessment approach.

Test your understanding 1

Feedback should typically only be provided to employees at the end of each period, when their performance over the entire period can be discussed.

Is this statement:

A   True

B   False

2   Performance appraisal

Appraisal is normally a formal process by which the progress, performance, results and sometimes personality of an employee are reviewed and assessed by his or her immediate superior.

2.1 Purposes of appraisals

From the individual employee's point of view, these will include:

- providing a basis for remuneration for the coming period

- ensuring that work of particular merit is recognised

- providing a forum for the employee to voice concerns about work areas that the employee is unhappy with

- establishment of what is expected of the individual in the coming period and how the employee will be assessed by the business

- identification of training and development needs

- determination of the future employment of the individual, such as whether they remain in the same job, get transferred, promoted, etc.

To the employer, the objectives include:

- monitoring of human resource selection processes against results – has the organisation been hiring the right people?

- identification of the best candidates for promotion, early retirement, etc.

- identification of problems or difficulties with the job that had not been previously realised

- helping to formulate the training plan by identifying weaknesses or skills gaps in employees

- helping to formulate a human resources plan – for example, are key staff members over-worked? Do new employees therefore need hiring to provide additional help?

- improvement of communication between managers and subordinates.

Illustration 2 – Appraisal

Karl works for a call centre and is set targets for the number of calls he takes in the year, the number of customers who say they were satisfied with his performance and the number of complaints he receives in the year.

At the end of the year, the appraisal will allow both Karl and his manager to compare his actual performance against these targets. Any areas where he deviates from the targets (in either a positive or negative way) can be discussed and are likely to form the basis of Karl's annual bonus and pay rise for next year.

Any areas that Karl is struggling with, or would like to gain additional skills and knowledge in, can be used to identify training and development opportunities for the coming year.

Finally, the appraisal can then be used to agree what Karl's targets will be for next year.

Test your understanding 2

Which of the following is an objective of the appraisal process to an employer?

A   It enables them to identify underperforming employees for punishment

B   It helps the business to recruit the best possible employees

C   It helps to identify employees' skills gaps

D   It reinforces management authority over employees

2.2 The performance appraisal process

```
┌─────────────┐       ┌─────────────────┐      ┌──────────────┐
│ JOB ANALYSIS │······ │  CORPORATE PLAN  │      │ PERFORMANCE  │
│             │       │                 │      │  STANDARDS   │
└─────────────┘       └─────────────────┘      └──────────────┘

┌─────────────┐       ┌─────────────────────┐  ┌──────────────┐
│    JOB      │       │  IDENTIFICATION OF   │  │    PERSON    │
│ REQUIREMENTS │··     │ CRITERIA FOR ASSESSMENT │·│ SPECIFICATIONS│
└─────────────┘       └─────────────────────┘  └──────────────┘

┌─────────────┐       ┌─────────────────────┐
│ JOB-HOLDER'S │··     │ APPRAISAL REPORT/FORM │
│ PERFORMANCE  │       │                     │
└─────────────┘       └─────────────────────┘

                      ┌─────────────────────┐
                      │     APPRAISAL        │
                      │    (INTERVIEW)       │
                      └─────────────────────┘
    FEEDBACK
┌─────────────┐       ┌─────────────────────┐
│  FOLLOW UP   │       │  AGREED CONCLUSION   │
│ MONITORING   │       │  AND ACTION PLAN     │
└─────────────┘       └─────────────────────┘
```

This diagram can be explained by looking at its four main stages.

- **Identify the criteria for assessment**

    This involves examining the corporate plan of the business and deciding what targets should be set for the employee in order to help the business meet its objectives. It is usually based upon job analysis, job requirements, performance standards and person specifications.

- **Production of an appraisal report**

    The manager will then prepare an appraisal report, detailing the appraisee's performance in the agreed criteria. Sometimes the appraisee will also write a report and the two will be compared.

    In some organisations, staff are expected to perform self-appraisal, with managers reviewing the output at the end of the process. While it saves the manager time, employees may find it difficult to be truly honest with themselves about their strengths and weaknesses.

- **Appraisal interview**

    The manager will usually interview the appraisee, allowing an exchange of views about the appraisal reports, along with discussion and agreement on action points, training and targets for the coming period.

    The effectiveness of this interview will depend on the skill of the superior conducting the interview. **Maier** identified three types of approach to appraisal interviews:

Tell and sell – the appraiser adopts the strategy of a salesperson, trying to persuade and convince the subordinate that the appraisal is fair and that they can and must change in certain ways. It is a one-way communication system.

Tell and listen – the appraiser listens to the job-holder's perception of their job and their problems, expectations and aims and does not dominate the interview. As it is important to listen to the subordinate and be prepared to change an evaluation in the light of new evidence, this method is likely to more effective.

Joint problem solving – this represents a shift in emphasis from the first two methods. The appraiser uses many social skills to encourage the interviewee to do a self-assessment, admit their own problems and suggest solutions, with the appraiser acting as a coach and counsellor.

- **Follow up/conclusion and action plan**

  This involves giving out the results of the appraisal, monitoring the progress of the action plan, carrying out agreed actions on training and development and giving regular feedback.

Test your understanding 3

L is currently being appraised by her manager, C. C has told L that her performance has been poor during the year and explained why. L disagreed and explained the reason that she has been unable to meet her targets. C therefore amended her appraisal score to 'satisfactory'.

Which type of appraisal interview is L having?

A   Democratic

B   Tell and listen

C   Joint problem solving

D   Tell and sell

Illustration 3 – Criteria to assess staff performance

A key issue that has to do with the criteria of effectiveness is the question of whether they should focus on the activities (tasks) of the job-holder or the results (objectives) achieved. For example, a salesperson might be assessed in terms of activities, i.e. number of cold calls or speed of dealing with complaints or in terms of results, i.e. total sales volume or number of new customers. Measures of results do not reflect how those outcomes were achieved.

There are advantages and disadvantages of using either results or activities as criteria. Appraisal based on results has the advantage of encouraging and rewarding the outcomes desired by the organisation. However, it has the disadvantage that it might encourage people to break rules or go against company policy to achieve what is desired. It may lead to frustration if the failure to achieve results is due to factors beyond the control of the individual. Assessment in terms of results does not generate information about how the person is doing the job and hence has limited value in suggesting ways of improving performance.

A major advantage of appraising in terms of activities is that it helps generate information that can help in the training and development of poor performers. However, it may only encourage people to concentrate on their activities at the expense of results achieved. This can lead to excessive bureaucratic emphasis on the means and procedures employed rather than on the accomplishments and results.

2.3 Benefits of effective appraisal

Staff appraisal can have benefits for both the employer (the organisation) and the employee:

Benefits for the employer	Benefits for the employee
• It provides a formal system for assessing the performance and potential of employees, with a view to identifying candidates for promotion. • It provides a system for identifying ways of improving the competence of employees, in order to raise the general level of efficiency and effectiveness of the work force. • It is a valuable system for human resource planning, and ensuring that employees are ready for promotion, to fill management job vacancies that arise. • If it is well managed, communications can be improved between managers and staff and so improve working relationships.	• The employee gets feedback about performance at work, and an assessment of competence. • A formal appraisal system offers the employee an opportunity to discuss future prospects and ambitions. • An appraisal interview may be used as a basis for considering pay and rewards. • Appraisal can be used to identify and agree measures for further training and development, to improve the employee's competence.

2.4 Barriers to effective staff appraisal

If not handled carefully, appraisals can cause demotivation for employees. Various studies have indicated that criticism of employees can have a negative effect on their goal achievement and self-confidence.

Lockett suggested that there are six main barriers to effective appraisals.

Appraisal as confrontation	• Differing views regarding performance.
	• Feedback is subjective – the manager is biased, allowing personality differences to get in the way of actual performance.
	• Feedback is badly delivered.
	• Assessment is based on yesterday's performance not on the whole year.
	• Disagreement over prospects and solutions.
Appraisal as judgement	• Appraisal is seen as a one-sided process – the manager is judge, jury and counsel for the prosecution.
	• Appraisal is imposed.
Appraisal as chat	• Lack of will from either party.
	• An unproductive conversation.
	• No outcomes set.
Appraisal as bureaucracy	• A traditional ceremony.
	• No purpose or worth, simply a 'box-ticking' exercise.
Appraisal as an annual event	• A traditional ceremony.
	• No real focus on goals for the coming year, simply a way of 'finishing off' the current period.
Appraisal as unfinished business	• Frustration at limited appraisal time.
	• No belief that issues will be followed up.

Test your understanding 4

Appraisals are always good for motivation.

Is this statement:

A   True

B   False

2.5 Overcoming the barriers to effective appraisals

One of the main barriers to effective appraisal is the view of employees that the annual appraisal is not important and that nothing is done after the appraisal interview is finished.

To deal with this, consider the following practical ideas:

- make sure there is a system of follow-up and feedback relating to the appraisal

- agreements between the employee and manager relating to further training and development should be made part of the official record of the appraisal interview

- the agreed action plan should be reported to senior management and/or the HR department

- the manager should ensure that any training and development agreed on is arranged and this should be discussed at the next appraisal meeting.

More generally, best practice for appraisals is given by the 4 Fs:

- **Firm** – managers should be willing to discuss negative as well as favourable aspects of performance.

- **Factual** – subjective aspects of performance should be avoided.

- **Fair** – all employees should be treated the same.

- **Frequent** – appraisals should be held on a regular basis rather than just when a problem arises.

Test your understanding 5

As part of a regular appraisal, a manager has stated that one of his employees is 'strongly disliked' by all her co-workers.

Which aspect of appraisal best practice is the manager failing to display?

A   Firmness

B   Fairness

C   Frequency of appraisal

D   Factual discussion

2.6 Evaluating the effectiveness of performance appraisal

Evaluating the appraisal process can involve the following:

- calculating the costs and benefits of the appraisal process

- monitoring performance results to see if there have been improvements

- checking the uptake of training and development opportunities

- asking appraisers and appraisees for their opinions on the process

- review of other indicators, such as staff turnover – a figure that is too high or too low could indicate a problem in the organisation.

More generally, **Lockett** argued that the appraisal process should be monitored to ensure its:

- **Relevance** – does the system have a useful purpose and is it relevant to the needs of both the organisation and the individual? Do the appraisal criteria link to the needs of both parties?

- **Fairness** – is there reasonable objectivity and standardisation of criteria throughout the organisation?

- **Serious intent** – is the management committed to the system or has it simply been thrust on them by the HR department? Do the appraisers have training in interviewing and assessment techniques? Is there a demonstrable link between performance and reward?

- **Co-operation** – is the appraisal a participative, problem-solving activity, with the appraisee being given time and encouragement to prepare for it? Is a jointly agreed conclusion arrived at by the end of the appraisal?

- **Efficiency** – is it costly and difficult to administer and does it seem too time-consuming compared with the value of its outcome?

Test your understanding 6

A firm has an employee turnover of 2% per annum. This indicates that their review and appraisal process must be excellent.

Is this statement:

A   True

B   False

2.7 Staff turnover

The causes of staff leaving fall into three categories:

- **Discharge** – as a result of an employee's unsuitability, disciplinary action or redundancy.

- **Unavoidable** – because of marriage, moving house, illness or death.

- **Avoidable** – due to pay, working conditions, relationships with work colleagues.

From records, the staff turnover can be calculated by dividing either the total separations (those leaving the organisation) or the total replacements by the average number in the workforce, and expressing the result as a percentage. Examination of this figure may highlight vital information, e.g. poor selection techniques or poor working conditions.

The process of staff appraisal and assessment should highlight any causes of dissatisfaction, find solutions and remedy them before the employee loses motivation, looks for another job and resigns.

3 Chapter summary

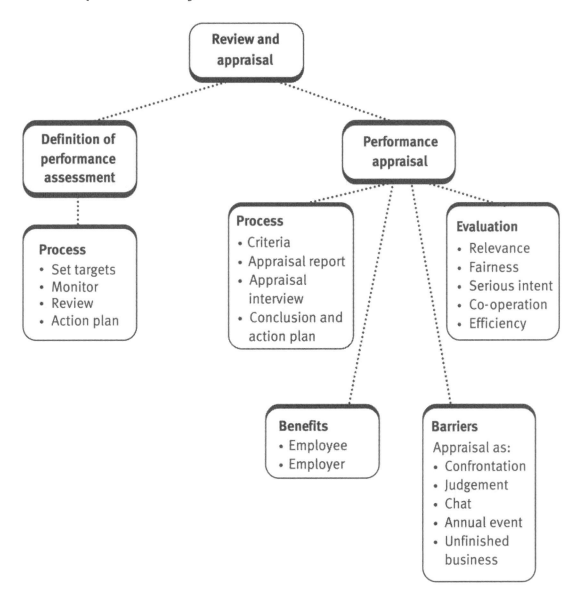

4 Practice questions

Test your understanding 7

An 'avoidable' reason for staff leaving could be:

A   Illness

B   Employee gross misconduct

C   Poor working conditions

D   Redundancy

Test your understanding 8

Consider the following stages in the performance appraisal process:

(i)   Action plan and monitoring

(ii)   Production of an appraisal report

(iii)   Identification of assessment criteria from the corporate plan

(iv)   Appraisal interviews

Identify which of the following options places these stages in the correct order.

A   (ii), (i), (iii), (iv)

B   (ii), (iii), (iv), (i)

C   (iii), (iv), (ii), (i)

D   (iii), (ii), (iv), (i)

Test your understanding 9

J has recently undergone an appraisal interview, where he was told that his attitude at work was excellent and that he was pleasant to work with. What type of employee performance measurement is J's appraisal focused on?

A   Qualitative

B   Quantitative

Test your understanding 10

GHF is a large company which is currently undertaking an appraisal of the performance of its employees. Many employees have complained that the outcome of their appraisal had no link to the pay rise or rewards that they received.

According to Lockett, what aspect of a successful appraisal process appears to be missing in GHF?

A   Relevance

B   Serious intent

C   Co-operation

D   Efficiency

Test your understanding answers

Test your understanding 1

The correct answer is B – False

While feedback will be provided at the end of the period, is should also be provided regularly throughout the period to help employees improve their performance.

Test your understanding 2

The correct answer is C

The appraisal process is certainly not designed to find employees that need to be punished and only applies to existing employees, meaning that it will not help the organisation with its recruitment. It is also designed to improve communication between managers and employees, not reinforce the differences between them.

Test your understanding 3

The correct answer is B

This is an example of the 'tell and listen' approach. C has informed L of his concerns, but then listens to her reply and is willing to change his initial conclusions because of this.

Test your understanding 4

The correct answer is B

While appraisals are often good for motivation, if they are done poorly they can actually demotivate workers.

Good for motivation	Bad for motivation
• Feedback on performance is regarded as essential in motivation because it gives people a chance to evaluate their achievement and make future calculations about the amount of effort required to achieve objectives and rewards • Agreement of challenging but attainable targets for performance motivates people by clarifying goals and by the value of incentives offered • A positive approach to appraisals allows people to solve their work problems and apply creative thinking.	• People do not react well to criticism, especially at work • If people have a favourable self-image, they may be impervious to criticism but if these people are not criticised but are given an 'easy' appraisal they will continue as they are – confirmed in their behaviour and sense of self-worth – even doing a bad job • Where people have a poor self-image, they may be discouraged by low level criticism.

Test your understanding 5

The correct answer is D

The manager is making a subjective statement, which should be avoided. Appraisals should be kept factual.

Test your understanding 6

The correct answer is B – False

This statistic reveals that the labour force would turn over once in 50 years. It is to be congratulated for having a stable and secure workforce but it could be in trouble if there is no young blood to bridge the generation gap and cover any retirements. It may also indicate that there is too little pressure on staff to perform and that they have grown 'comfortable' in their jobs.

Test your understanding 7

The correct answer is C

Avoidable reasons are those that can be avoided by the organisation. This would include working conditions and pay. The other options given are either 'discharge' or 'unavoidable' reasons.

Test your understanding 8

The correct answer is D

By definition.

Test your understanding 9

The correct answer is A

Qualitative measures look at less tangible aspects of the employee's performance, which may be difficult to measure – such as attitude and how well they work with others.

Quantitative measures are those that examine more easily measured aspects of the employee's performance, such as the number of units they produced in the period.

Test your understanding 10

The correct answer is B

There is no indication that the appraisals are being taken seriously by GHF, as they are not basing employee rewards on the appraisal outcomes. Note that the targets that GHF sets as part of the appraisal process may well be linked to their corporate objectives and would therefore still be relevant.

Personal effectiveness at work

Chapter learning objectives

Upon completion of this chapter you will be able to:

- explain the importance of effective time management

- describe the barriers to effective time management and how they may be overcome

- describe the role of information technology in improving personal effectiveness

- identify the main ways in which people and teams can be ineffective at work

- explain how individual or team ineffectiveness can affect organisational performance

- describe the features of a competence framework

- explain how a competence framework underpins professional development needs

- explain how personal and continuous professional development can increase personal effectiveness at work

- explain the purpose and benefits of coaching, mentoring and counselling in promoting employee effectiveness

- describe how a personal development plan should be formulated, implemented, monitored and reviewed by the individual

- identify situations where conflict at work can arise

- describe how conflict can affect personal and organisational performance

- explain how conflict can be avoided

- identify ways in which conflict can be resolved or referred.

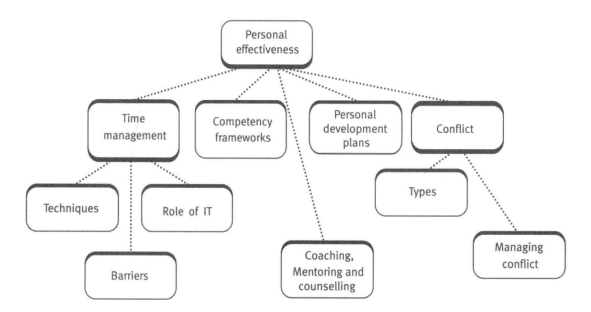

The accountancy profession is often demanding – requiring individuals to perform a large volume of technical work both accurately and before key deadlines, such as the month or year end. This section of the syllabus is designed to ensure that you have the skills necessary to work effectively in this challenging environment.

1 Time management

1.1 What is time management?

Time management is the process of planning and controlling the amount of time that is spent on specific activities, usually with the aim of increasing overall efficiency or productivity.

Time management has several key purposes. These include:

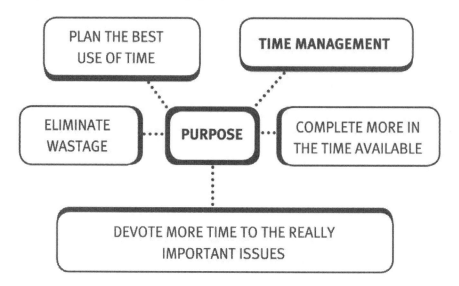

This will allow you to:

- refuse excessive workloads
- monitor the progress of key projects
- allocate your time to more important tasks first
- plan each day efficiently, so you get as much done as possible.

Time is a scarce resource – failure to manage it properly will lead to:

- low productivity
- wasted time spent on non-essential tasks
- missed deadlines
- poor quality work being produced – perhaps due to work being rushed to meet deadlines.

1.2 Time management techniques

- **Spend time planning and organising**

  Using time to think and plan is essential for good time management. Not only should you plan what tasks you wish to accomplish each day or week, you should also spend time reviewing your schedules to check for problems or changes to your workload that require re-scheduling.

 Remember the old saying – 'failing to plan is planning to fail!'

  Obviously, be sensible with the amount of time you spend planning. Clearly you do not want to spend so long planning that you no longer have time to complete your work!

- **Produce an activity log**

  This could include a breakdown of the time spent in a typical week, divided between different activities such as work, home, study, leisure and travel. Consider what proportion of your time is important to you, important to you others and what can be delegated to others or avoided completely.

- **Cost your time**

  Every occasion when you 'save' an hour, or put it to better use, you become more cost-effective.

Test your understanding 1

We will assume you earn $50,000 per annum basic pay. On top of this the direct and indirect costs of your employment are $25,000. You work 37.5 hours per week for 44 weeks of the year.

What is the cost of your time per hour?

A $30.30

B $45.45

C $1,333.33

D $2,000.00

- **Make lists**

  Plan the whole of the coming week in advance, then make a list every day before you start work. Refuse to do anything that is not on the list for each day.

- **Prioritise**

  Look at the list and assess tasks based on their **importance** (if the consequences of failure are significant or it comes from a powerful stakeholder, such as a manager) and **urgency** (whether the deadline for the accomplishment of the task is near).

  Once these two factors have been analysed, the approach to the task can be formulated, as shown below:

	Low Urgency	High Urgency
Importance – High	Some of these tasks may be delegated for now. Will become urgent as the deadline approaches.	You need to deal with these tasks now and devote plenty of time to them.
Importance – Low	These tasks can be delegated to others or simply cancelled.	These tasks can be delegated or removed from your job, as they have low importance to you.

Urgency

1.3 Barriers to effective time management

The main influences on a person's use of time are outlined in the diagram below:

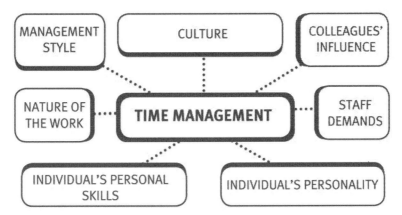

Influences include:

- Established jobs with routine and predictable work have fewer barriers than new or developing work.

- Jobs involving contact with others are more prone to interruptions than those with no near contacts.

- People with offices of their own can operate an 'open door' policy for staff communications but a 'closed door' policy when a physical barrier is needed.

- The location of colleagues, customers and suppliers can contribute to time wasted in travelling.

- Some organisational cultures favour strict adherence to protocol and procedures, discouraging informal contacts. Others encourage an open access communications policy that can be stimulating but time wasting.

- An individual's personal work standards are going to be influenced by the type of decision making (slow and deliberate or quick) in the firm.

- The attributes and style of the job-holder depend on personality and preferences, e.g. some are more assertive and find it easier to deal with colleagues who waste their time.

Barriers to effective time management may be internal or external.

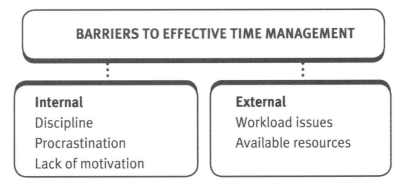

Overcome the internal barriers	Overcome the external barriers
• Be assertive – identify your time wasters and resolve to deal with them, learn to say NO, delegate. • Identify and make use of your personal biorhythms, or 'up' time and 'down' time. • Conquer procrastination – find out what causes you to put off doing something and remedy it, e.g. a feeling of inadequacy could be due to lack of information, lack of a particular skill or lack of training.	• Do the right thing right – doing the right thing is effectiveness; doing things right is efficiency. Focus first on effectiveness (identifying what is the right thing to do), then concentrate on efficiency (doing it right). • Eliminate the urgent – urgent tasks with short-term consequences often get done to the detriment of the important tasks – those with long-term, goal-related implications. • Break big jobs into little steps. • Use negotiation to improve the use of time.

Test your understanding 2

Which of the following would tend to act as a barrier to effective time management for an employee?

A   The employee's job requires little or no contact with other people

B   The employee has their own office

C   The employee needs to regularly visit employees who are located in another town

D   The employee's job is routine and predictable

1.4 The role of information technology in improving personal effectiveness

Information technology (IT) can be extremely useful when improving an individual's time management and general effectiveness in their work.

There are a wide range of different IT tools that individuals and businesses may use, including:

• **Email** – this allows for individuals to electronically send messages and attachments, such as documents and pictures, quickly and efficiently. Email can be sent to large numbers of recipients across the world at the touch of a button, significantly speeding up communication within an organisation.

- **Video conferencing** – this is an IT solution that aids in conducting meetings. Attendees do not need to spend time travelling to the same location to have a meeting – instead the video conference enables them to hold a virtual meeting over their computers from wherever they are in the world. This significantly reduces the costs and travelling time required to attend a meeting. Systems such as Skype™ and WebEx™ help to facilitate this.

- EDI – Electronic Data Interchange (EDI) allows information sharing between computers. This removes the need for much data processing. For instance, a customer may electronically place an order with their suppliers. This order will automatically be placed on the supplier's system without the need for physical goods request forms to be printed, posted and then processed. This saves time and increases accuracy.

- **Intranets** – these are internal networks where employees can access a central store of information. This speeds up communication by the company with its employees. Intranets often contain company policies and procedures, as well as training on key issues, such as ethics or health and safety.

- **Office automation** – this includes systems such as word processors, spreadsheets, databases and desktop publishing. These systems, combined, allow for processing of high volumes of transactions at speed, saving the business time and money.

- **Homeworking** – the systems mentioned above have reduced the need for many workers to be present in their workplace. Instead, many employees now work from home. While this may make it harder for the organisation to control their activities, it offers increased motivation for workers, as well as lower overheads (i.e. smaller offices are needed) for employers.

2 Competency frameworks

Competences are the critical skills, knowledge and attitudes that a jobholder must have to perform effectively. A competent individual will be more able to contribute effectively to the business almost as soon as they are appointed.

As such, it is important for an organisation to ensure that all staff are appropriately qualified and trained for their role in the organisation. Competency frameworks can help with this.

 Competency frameworks attempt to identify all the competencies that are required by anyone taking on a particular role within the organisation.

A list of key competences is produced which can be used as a benchmark to either ensure that the correct individual is chosen for the role or as a way of checking that an existing member of staff has all the up to date skills needed for their role.

Most competency frameworks cover the following categories:

- communication skills
- people management
- team skills
- customer service skills
- results-orientation
- problem-solving skills.

Illustration 1 – Competence frameworks

A research analyst working for the government might have the following factors within their competency framework (amongst others):

Delivery skills

- Focus
- Delivery skills
- Learning and improving

Intellectual capacity

- Critical analysis and decision making
- Constructive thinking

Interpersonal skills

- Developing constructive relationships
- Communicating with impact

Each competence will then be supported by a high level description. For example, 'Learning and improving' could be described as:

'Acknowledges own development needs and seeks new skills. Learns from others and adapts to new people and task needs.'

Test your understanding 3

Consider the following list:

(i)   Attention to detail

(ii)   Communication skills

(iii)   Computer skills

(iv)   Numeracy

Which of these competences would be required by a typical accountant?

A   (i) and (ii) only

B   (ii), (iii) and (iv) only

C   (ii) and (iv) only

D   (i), (ii), (iii) and (iv)

Employers should regularly keep the competency frameworks updated for their employees and assess whether they still have the appropriate skills and abilities needed for their jobs. If not, the employer may wish to consider continuing professional development (CPD) which will involve employees attending training courses or reading technical information to update their skills.

Ensuring that employees have up to date skills will:

* minimise employee errors and mistakes

* improve customer service and satisfaction

* increase employee motivation, as they feel valued by the organisation.

3   Coaching, mentoring and counselling

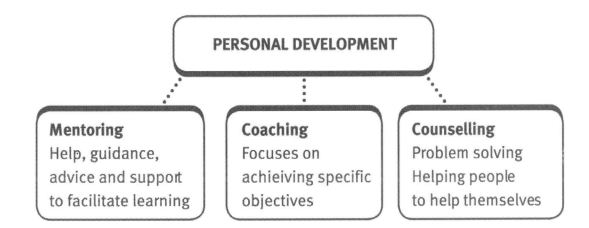

 Make sure that you are able to identify the differences between mentoring, coaching and counselling as you may be tested on this in your exam.

3.1 Mentoring

 Mentoring is the process where one person offers help, guidance, advice and support to facilitate the learning and development of another.

A mentor is usually (although not always) a skilled, senior member of staff who:

- offers practical advice and support

- can give technical, ethical and general guidance

- can help with the development of interpersonal and work skills

- is an impartial sounding board

- is a role model who can help the mentee (the individual being mentored) to improve their career goals.

3.2 Coaching

 Coaching focuses on achieving specific objectives, usually within a defined time period. It is more about improving the performance of someone that is already competent, rather than establishing competency in the first place.

- It is usually on a one-to-one basis, is set in the everyday working situation and is an ongoing activity.

- It involves gently encouraging people to improve their performance, to develop their skills and increase their self-confidence in order to develop their career prospects.

- Most coaching is carried out by a more senior person or manager, however the key issue is that whoever carries out the coaching must have sufficient expertise, experience and judgement to help the person being coached.

3.3 Counselling

 Counselling involves an individual helping another to identify and deal with a problem or problems. It involves the counsellor helping someone else to explore his or her thoughts, feelings and behaviour with the intention of reaching a clearer understanding of the issues he or she is facing.

The counsellor needs to be:

- **Observant** – there is a need to note behaviour, which may be symptomatic of a problem.

- **Sensitive** – there is a need to acknowledge and understand that another person's beliefs and values may be different from their own (for example religious beliefs).

- **Empathetic** – there is a need to appreciate that the problem may seem overwhelming to the individual.

- **Impartial** – there is a need to remain impartial and refrain from giving advice.

- **Discreet** – there will be situations when an employee cannot be completely open unless they are sure that the comments they make will be treated with confidentiality.

Through active listening, the use of open questions and clarifications, the counsellor encourages reflection and helps the client identify issues and solutions. Counselling does not involve giving advice or making suggestions.

Test your understanding 4

JHU plc is a manufacturing company. One of its new employees, K, is fully trained but is not as productive as some of the other workers. The management of JHU have therefore asked a more experienced employee, M, to give K advice on how to improve her productivity.

Would M be classed as K's mentor, counsellor or coach?

4 Personal development plan

A personal development plan is a 'clear developmental action plan for an individual that incorporates a wide set of developmental opportunities including formal training'.

During their career, employees are increasingly encouraged to manage their own development. In consultation with management, they might be asked to set up personal development plans whereby they set targets and propose actions/activities to achieve them.

Development is more general than training, is more forward-looking and orientated towards the individual, and is concerned with enabling the individual to fulfil his or her potential.

Training	Development
• Immediately practical • Connected to job performance	• No immediate practical application • Over time it enables a person to deal with wider problems

4.1 Preparing a personal development plan

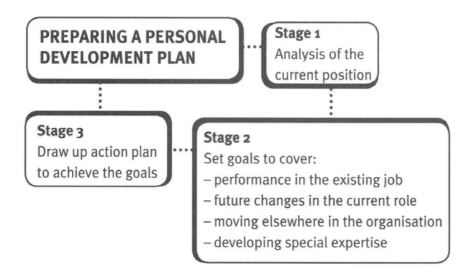

Stage 1 Analysis of current position – requires the individual, with their manager, to carry out a personal SWOT (strengths, weaknesses, opportunities, threats) analysis.

- This can be as simple as assessing what an individual does by referring to the job description, evaluating which aspects of a job an individual likes and dislikes on the one hand, and those aspects that an individual does well and not so well in on the other.

	Strengths	Weaknesses
Opportunities	Tasks the person likes and does well	Tasks the person likes but does not do well
Threats	Tasks the person dislikes but does well	Tasks the person dislikes and does not do well

Stage 2 Set goals – following the above analysis, personal goals should be set for the individual.

- The tasks the person does not do well are examined and reasons are established.

- This can take the form of an alternative and more traditional type of SWOT analysis by examining the person's strengths and weaknesses.

- Particular weaknesses should be identified as being the cause of failure to carry out certain tasks well. This should then inform a personal set of objectives in order to overcome these weaknesses.

Illustration 2 – SWOT

Strengths	Weaknesses
What advantages do you have?	What could you improve?
What do you do well?	What do you do badly?
What resources do you have access to?	What should you avoid?
What do other people see as your strengths?	
Opportunities	**Threats**
Where are the good opportunities facing you?	What obstacles do you face?
What are the interesting trends you are aware of?	Are the required specifications for your job or products changing?
	Is changing technology threatening your position?
	Could any of your weaknesses seriously threaten your job/business?

Goals should have the characteristic of **SMART** objectives:

Specific – it is clear what is meant by the objective.

Measurable – it will be possible to assess the extent to which the objective has been met.

Achievable – the objective represents something that can be implemented in the real world and can be met by the resources available.

Relevant – the objective is linked to the organisation's overall work outcomes.

Timely – delivery of the objective is linked to a specific date.

Stage 3 Draw up action plan – an action plan and training programme should be based on addressing the identified weaknesses and trying to move more of the tasks of the current role into the 'do well' side of the matrix on the left-hand side. It is easier to improve the performance of individuals in tasks that they like performing than in those that they don't.

When drawing up and implementing an action plan, some degree of control is necessary to monitor the extent to which the programme is achieving the goals and stated objectives.

Control processes give people structure, define methods and indicate how their performance will be measured. It is reassuring to know what you are required to do and how the outcome will be measured.

Test your understanding 5

Y works in a call centre for GFD plc. Her role is to attempt to convince customers who are planning to leave GFD that they should remain as customers of the company. Her supervisor has recently set her the following objective:

'Y must retain 100% of the customers that she speaks to over the course of the next year.'

Which of the following SMART criteria is missing from Y's objectives?

A   Specific

B   Measurable

C   Time bounded

D   Achievable

4.2 The importance of continuous monitoring and feedback

Once the goals and personal ambitions have been defined and the person has begun the development plan, the monitoring must begin. Monitoring in simple terms means watching over something that is happening.

Control processes give people timely, relevant feedback on their performance – this is information about how they did in the light of some goal and that can be used to improve performance. Feedback will usually be provided by the manager or supervisor, and should be concurrent – or certainly not long delayed. People naturally want to know how well they are doing on a particular task and need the reassurance that they are on the right track and are achieving what is expected of them.

- Feedback should be clear and frequent and this can only be achieved if there is continuous monitoring of the task.

- Feedback can also have a motivating effect by providing recognition of work done which in turn provides the incentive to sustain and improve performance levels.

- Recognition, praise and encouragement create feelings of confidence, competence, development and progress that enhance the motivation to learn.

Illustration 3 – Personal development plans

How am I doing? Just imagine being completely denied any feedback whatsoever – no guidance, no praise, and no constructive criticism for the things you do. If you received no input at all, how much initiative would you demonstrate? Would your productivity be high, or low? What would your morale be like as time went on? And if you experienced this kind of treatment in the workplace, how likely would you be to look for a job somewhere else?

The sad fact is that most of us take feedback for granted. But interpersonal feedback is a critical nutrient for everyone – it is the psychological equivalent of food and water. Without strong, clear feedback to use as a reference point, people are incapable of functioning fully and productively.

Test your understanding 6

Feedback should occur throughout the year as it provides useful information for the employee which will help them to adjust their activities on an ongoing basis.

Is this statement:

A   True

B   False

5   Conflict

5.1 What is conflict?

Most jobs involve coming into contact with other people on a regular basis. To work effectively, we need to therefore be aware of potential sources of conflict that could damage our working relationship with others, as well as how we can deal with conflict when it arises.

 Conflict is defined as **any personal divergence of interests between groups and individuals**.

While some conflict can be positive within the organisation – leading to existing ways of working and ideas being challenged – conflict is often destructive, harming the relationship between individuals and groups by creating hostility and bad feeling. Such destructive conflict will, in turn, normally damage the interests of the organisation as a whole.

5.2 Types of conflict

There are two main types of conflict:

- **Vertical** – this is conflict that occurs between individuals and groups at different levels of the organisation's hierarchy. For example, this could be the conflict between a junior employee and his or her manager. There may be many causes, including:

  - lack of communication, leading to junior workers feeling alienated or unimportant

  - disagreements over remuneration or working conditions

  - disagreements over employee workloads, due to poor coordination

  - personality clashes.

- **Horizontal** – this is conflict that occurs between individuals and groups at the same level of the organisation's hierarchy. For instance, this could be conflict between individual directors on the Board of Directors. Again, there may be many reasons for such conflict, including:

  - personality clashes

  - role ambiguity, where individuals' authority overlaps – conflicting objectives or priorities

  - a lack of available resources.

Illustration 4 – Conflict

Within a business, the Director of Human Resources (HRD) and the Finance Director (FD) may find themselves in conflict over the hiring of new members of staff.

The HRD will be keen to offer competitive rates of pay for employees in order to attract the very best possible staff, thereby maximising business effectiveness and profitability. The FD may have the same goal of maximising company profit, but may feel that this is best accomplished by offering lower levels of pay, thereby lowering costs.

This would be an example of horizontal conflict. Both of these individuals are at the same level in the business hierarchy, but they disagree about the way that the organisation's goals should be achieved and the allocation of resources. Conflict will also arise if it is unclear which of the directors' approaches should be followed.

This could lead to several problems for the company itself. The relationship between the two directors could be damaged, making it difficult for them to co-operate in the future. In addition, the conflict, if unresolved, could mean that the company finds itself lacking key new members of staff for the immediate future.

5.3 How to avoid conflict

Where possible, then, we can see that destructive conflict should be avoided. This can be accomplished through:

- **Good communication** – Conflict can be caused by simple misunderstandings. Making sure that managers and staff freely and regularly communicate with each other about issues that arise is therefore important.

- **Rules and procedures** – Having clearly defined rules can help to avoid conflict. If all employees know what they are responsible for within the organisation, they are less likely to conflict with each other.

- **Avoiding a 'blame culture'** – Managers need to lead by example here. If a manager is in regular conflict with other employees, this is likely to be imitated by other, more junior members of staff.

- **Ensuring a fair allocation of resources** – Managers should ensure that staff, cash and other resources are fairly allocated between departments and individuals. This should help to reduce disagreements and conflict.

5.4 Conflict management strategies

If conflict cannot be avoided, managers need to know how best to resolve it. There are numerous possible approaches, including:

- **Denial** – this involves the manager ignoring the conflict and hoping that it blows over without needing any intervention. This may well work for minor conflicts between employees.

- **Suppression** – the manager can threaten the conflicting parties with punishment if they fail to overcome their problems. This is likely to be a short-term solution only and will not be successful for major conflicts.

- **Reduction/negotiation** – the manager can act as a neutral third party and negotiate a compromise agreement between the conflicting parties. This tends to be the most common approach, with both parties getting some (but not all) of what they want.

- **Resolution** – the manager seeks to find the root cause of the conflict and solve it. This will hopefully produce a 'win-win' solution where both parties end up satisfied. It is often time-consuming and complex, though it may provide a lasting solution to the conflict.

Ultimately, the strategy used will depend on the situation and the manager themselves.

Test your understanding 7

Two managers are currently working on separate projects. They both need the help of the same skilled employee in order to complete these projects. This has led to conflict between the two managers, who both want access to the employee before the other manager.

A director has decided to try and deal with this conflict. However, he is unsure which of the following four approaches to take:

(1) Do nothing and assume the managers will be able to deal with the problem by themselves.

(2) Talk with the managers and see if an agreement can be reached to share the expert's time between them.

(3) Investigate to see if any other workers within the company have the same, specialist skills. There would then be enough skilled employees for both projects.

(4) Order the two managers to sort out the problem quickly, or they will lose their bonus for the year.

For each of the four approaches, state which conflict management strategy the director would be taking.

6 Consequences of ineffectiveness at work

So far we have looked at ways of improving performance and effectiveness in a work-based context. However, what happens when individuals are **ineffective**? This can occur in a number of ways, including:

- poor quality work produced
- missing deadlines and targets
- lack of communication with others
- having a poor attitude at work
- failing to maintain appropriate levels of key skills.

This can have significant effects on the organisation itself, such as:

- loss of reputation and customers, due to poor quality products and services
- poor productivity and motivation
- lack of information from staff about key issues, making it harder to make key business decisions and solve problems.

It is therefore in the organisation's best interests to encourage its staff to develop themselves and continually improve their performance using the techniques outlined in this chapter.

7 Chapter summary

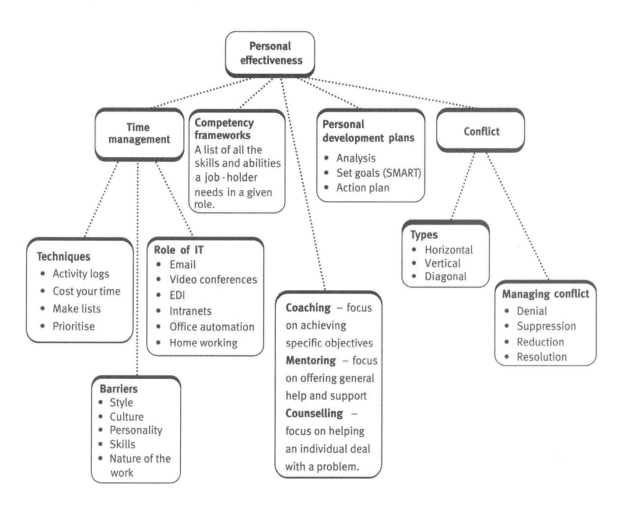

8 Practice questions

Test your understanding 8

Conflict between individuals always damages the operations of an organisation and should be avoided where possible.

Is this statement:

A   True

B   False

Test your understanding 9

Two employees are currently in conflict with each other. They only have to work together for a short period on a mutual project, but the conflict has progressed to the point where they have stated that they are no longer willing to work with one another. Their manager is currently very busy, but is aware that it will be impossible to reach a compromise between the two workers.

Which approach to conflict management would the manager find most appropriate?

A   Suppression

B   Resolution

C   Reduction

D   Denial

Test your understanding 10

Which of the following is one of the SMART criteria for objectives?

A   Suitable

B   Reliable

C   Mandatory

D   Relevant

Test your understanding 11

Competency frameworks list the qualifications that a job-holder needs in order to perform effectively in a given role.

Is this statement:

A   True

B   False

Test your understanding 12

There are a number of ways of dealing with staff on a one-to-one basis within an organisation, including coaching, mentoring, counselling and appraising.

Required:

(a) **For each type of development below, which work situation is most appropriate?**

    A   A one-off discussion between a manager and employee that looks at, amongst other issues, the employee's potential for promotion.

    B   An ongoing working relationship between an experienced worker and a newer member of staff, with the goal of improving the less experienced worker's skills.

    C   A one-off discussion to try and help a worker deal with a problem they are having at work.

    D   An ongoing working relationship where a senior member of staff helps a more junior employee to develop themselves personally and in their careers.

For each of the following, select ONE from A, B, C or D.

    (i)   **Mentoring**

    (ii)   **Coaching**

    (iii) **Counselling**

    (iv)   **Appraising**

(0.5 marks each, total = 2 marks)

An organisation may choose to use counselling as way of developing its staff.

A   Seniority

B   Sensitivity

C   Experience

D   Discretion

E   Firmness

F   Judgemental

G   Talkative

Required:

(b)   **Which TWO of the above are typical features of a successful counsellor?**

(1 mark each, total = 2 marks)

(Total: 4 marks)

Test your understanding answers

Test your understanding 1

The correct answer is B

You work 37.5 hours per week for 44 weeks of the year = 1,650 hours.

$75,000 ÷ 1,650 = $45.45 per hour.

Test your understanding 2

The correct answer is C

Having to travel regularly is likely to waste time, making it harder to have effective time management. Note that the other three options are likely to make it easier for the individual to make best use of their time.

Test your understanding 3

The correct answer is D

The competences an accountant needs include the following:

- Skills
    - Numeracy
    - Literacy
    - IT Literacy
    - Bookkeeping
- Knowledge
    - FRS, IAS, etc.
    - Group accounts preparation
    - Hedging
- Attitude
    - Conscientious
    - Dynamic
    - Attention to detail

Test your understanding 4

M would be classified as K's **coach**.

Coaching focuses on achieving a specific objective (in this case improving productivity). Mentoring is a broader process, involving the provision of general support and impartial advice.

Counselling helps individuals to learn how to overcome problems or issues they are facing. There is no evidence that this is the case with K.

Test your understanding 5

The correct answer is D

It seems highly unlikely that Y will be able to retain 100% of all the people she speaks to and this is likely to be outside her control. The objective given is, however, specific, time bounded and measurable.

Test your understanding 6

The correct answer is A – true

Feedback is information about what has happened, the result or effect of our actions. The environment or other people 'feedback' to us the impact of our behaviour, whether this impact is intended or unintended. Concurrent feedback is information that is 'fed back' to us as we perform and serves as the basis for learning and intelligent self-adjustment en-route. Delayed feedback comes after the task is completed and can only be used to affect future performance.

Test your understanding 7

(1) Doing nothing would be an example of the '**denial**' strategy where the conflict is ignored by management.

(2) Negotiation and compromise would be an example of conflict '**reduction**' which tries to find a solution that satisfies both parties.

(3) This involves the director actually solving the root cause of the conflict, making this a '**resolution**' strategy.

(4) Here the director is simply trying to force a temporary solution between the two managers, making this a '**suppression**' strategy.

KAPLAN PUBLISHING

Test your understanding 8

The correct answer is B – False

Remember that conflict is any divergence of interests between groups or individuals. It can therefore be a way of workers challenging the existing ways of working and suggesting innovations and improvements, which may be beneficial to the organisation.

Test your understanding 9

The correct answer is A

Resolution is unlikely to be adopted by the manager as this would be too time-consuming and the manager is currently very busy. Conflict reduction involves negotiation, which the manager has identified as an inappropriate solution. Denial is also not an option, as the workers have stated that they will not work with one another.

Therefore, the manager should choose suppression. This involves the threat of punishments if the employees do not deal with their differences. It will often work well as a short-term solution, which is all that is required in this case.

Test your understanding 10

The correct answer is D

The criteria are: specific, measurable, achievable, relevant and timely.

Test your understanding 11

The correct answer is B – False

Competency frameworks list the skills, attributes and knowledge required in a particular role, rather than simply the qualifications.

Test your understanding 12

(a) The correct answers are (by definition):

    (i)   D

    (ii)   B

    (iii) C

    (iv) A

(b) The correct answers are: **B** and **D**.

    Note that seniority is not required to be an effective counsellor, nor is past experience. In most cases, counselling is about helping another individual to explore their own problems and decide how to deal with them. Being firm, judgemental and talkative would therefore often be unhelpful.

Communicating in business

Chapter learning objectives

Upon completion of this chapter you will be able to:

- define communications

- identify methods of communication used in the organisation and how they are used

- explain a simple communication model: sender, message, receiver, feedback, noise

- explain formal and informal communication and their importance in the workplace

- identify the consequences of ineffective communication

- describe the attributes of effective communication

- describe the barriers to effective communication and identify practical steps that can be taken to overcome them

- describe the main methods and patterns of communication.

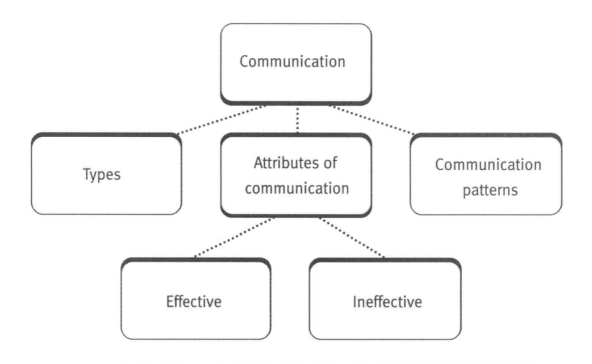

1 What is communication?

 Communication is the two-way interchange of information, ideas, facts and emotions by one or more persons. It establishes relationships and allows for direction and co-ordination of tasks.

Non-verbal communication

Not all communication is verbal – a great deal of communication can take place without any words at all. The raised eyebrow, the curled lip, the frown and the glare all say a great deal; so also can more obvious physical gestures such as the pat on the back or an arm around the shoulders. Body language is about:

- eye contact – looking people in the eye with a relaxed and friendly gaze
- facial expressions
- posture and distance.

In an organisation, communication takes many forms, including:

- giving or receiving information and instructions
- exchanging ideas
- announcing plans and strategies
- laying down rules or procedures
- comparing actual results against a plan
- manuals, organisation charts and job descriptions.

2 The communication process

The process of communication involves the following elements:

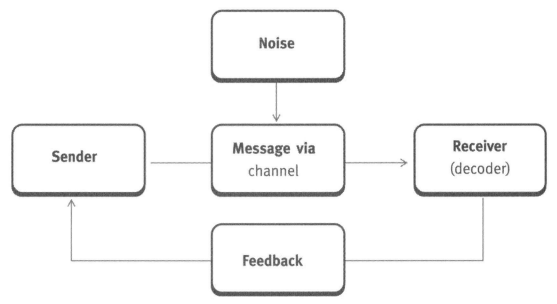

📖 The communication process – further detail

The communication process involves the following stages/elements:

- **Sender (encoder)** – initiates the communication process. To encode is to put the message into words or images.

- **Message** – the information that the sender wants to transmit.

- **Channel** (the words channel and medium are often used interchangeably) – is the means of communication. It can be thought of as a sense, e.g. smelling, tasting, feeling, hearing and seeing. Sometimes it is preferable to think of the channel as the method over which the message will be transmitted: telecommunications, newspaper, radio, letter, poster or other media.

- **Receiver (decoder)** – the person or group for whom the communication effort is intended. The receiver decodes or interprets the message. Thus, in the feedback loop, the receiver becomes the sender and the sender becomes the receiver.

- **Noise** – anything that interferes with the communication or makes it difficult to understand. Noise can arise from many sources, for example:

  - **Environmental noise** – noise that physically disrupts communication, such as noise from machinery or loud music.

  - **Organisational noise** – this could include poorly written instructions, poorly chosen words or grammatical errors – all of which can make it difficult for the receiver to interpret the message.

> - **Psychological noise** – if the receiver is upset or under pressure at work, it may be harder for them to interpret the message accurately.
>
> - **Social noise** – differences in culture or status differentials between the receiver and the sender can lead to misunderstandings or misinterpretation of the message.
>
> - **Feedback** – ensures that mutual understanding has taken place in a communication and makes the communication a two-way process. It indicates to the sender that the message has been successfully received, understood and interpreted.

Illustration 1 – Communication process

We can step through the process using a particular example. Imagine an information clerk in a tourist office answering a query from a traveller about where a particular building is. In communicating the reply there will be the following steps:

- The clerk having heard the query thinks about the wide range of data relevant to the information requested and decides what information, in what language, and how the information is to be communicated.

- The clerk mentally decides on the actual content or wording of verbal and other messages to be given and any other forms of communication to be used.

- The message is transmitted by speech and perhaps also by gesture. The clerk may reinforce the verbal message by giving the inquirer some written information, a street plan in this case. The route to be taken may be shown on a map.

- The traveller receives the message by listening and perhaps looking.

- The message is decoded. The language, pronunciation and words used may be difficult to understand.

- The decoding should lead to the complete understanding of the reply given to the original query, or the reply may not be fully understood.

- The understanding of the reply may lead to action. The traveller may be satisfied with the answer to the query and exit the office. There may, however, be only partial understanding and the query may be restated.

3 Types of communication

Most communication within an organisation can be classified as either formal or informal.

- **Formal communication**

    This helps to provide management structure, so that individuals know what is expected of them and how they have actually performed. It could include plans, procedures, policies and performance reports and meetings, as well as the formal communication of management decisions.

- **Informal communication**

    This is communicated informally by means of face-to-face conversations, telephone conversations, emails and text messages. It does not follow the lines of authority, instead being a feature of cooperation between individuals.

Illustration 2 – Communications in the workplace
Both types of communication are essential in an efficient and effective business organisation. The management of a company makes a formal announcement to the press about a possible acquisition on Thursday. However, most people had already heard about it, because the news had been 'leaked' on Tuesday and passed from person to person within the company and the media.

3.1 Formal communication

As mentioned earlier, this follows the formal channels that are present within the organisation. It can therefore be:

- **Vertical** – downwards, from superior to subordinate, or upwards, from subordinate to superior.

- **Horizontal or lateral** – communication between people at a similar level in the organisation's hierarchy, whether they are in the same peer group or not.

- **Diagonal** – interdepartmental communication between people of different ranks.

Upwards, downwards and lateral communication

- **Downward communication** provides a basis for giving specific job instructions, policy decisions, guidance and resolution of queries. Such information can help clarify operational goals, provide a sense of direction and give subordinates data related to their performance. It also helps link levels of the hierarchy by providing a basis for co-ordinated activity.

  However, too much emphasis on downward communication can create problems. People will become reluctant to come forward with their suggestions and problems and may be averse to taking on new responsibilities. There is also a risk of management getting out of touch with their subordinates. For these reasons it is important to stress upward communication.

- **Upward communication** provides management with feedback from employees on results achieved and problems encountered. It creates a channel from which management can gauge organisational climate and deal with problem areas, such as grievances or low productivity, before they become major issues.

- **Lateral or horizontal communication** – four of the most important reasons for lateral communication are:

  (1) Task co-ordination – department heads may meet periodically to discuss how each department is contributing to organisational objectives.

  (2) Problem solving – members of a department may meet to discuss how they will handle a threatened budget cut.

  (3) Information sharing – members of one department may meet with the members of another department to explain some new information or study.

  (4) Conflict resolution – members of one department may meet to discuss a problem, e.g. duplication of activities in the department and some other department.

  Co-ordination between departments depends on this form of contact, e.g. line and staff positions rely heavily on advice passing laterally. Managers also communicate with sources outside the organisation, e.g. suppliers and customers.

Test your understanding 1

For each of the following three scenarios, identify whether the communication is horizontal, vertical or diagonal.

(i)   A junior member of the accounts department sends a request for information from a senior sales manager.

(ii)   The head of the marketing department sends a report to the head of the HR department.

(iii) A junior salesperson contacts the sales manager to ask for information.

Test your understanding 2

Very little formal horizontal communication may occur in organisations that are managed in an authoritarian style.

Is this statement:

A   True

B   False

Information also flows into and out of the organisation. Managers communicate with various sources such as suppliers and customers.

*   **Inflows** include market research and surveillance, allowing the organisation to identify and respond to any opportunities or threats in the market.

*   **Outflows** include advertising, marketing and public relations and usually involve the organisation trying to influence key external stakeholders.

3.2 Informal communication

While the organisation will have a designated, formal communications network, it is inevitable (and not necessarily a bad thing) that there will also be a number of informal communication channels.

Informal communication:

*   can move in any direction

*   can skip authority levels

*   is as likely to satisfy social needs as facilitate task accomplishments.

A **grapevine** refers to the network of social relationships that arise spontaneously as people associate with one another. It often carries more current information than the formal communication network and may be used by employees to bypass secretive management. The grapevine often carries:

- **Rumour** – this is a message transmitted on the grapevine that is not based on official information. As such is may be true or false, or have elements of both.

- **Gossip** – tends to be idle talk, often of little consequence. However, it may be malicious and cause hurt to individuals, which can damage professional relationships between individuals within the organisation. Conversely, it can also be a morale booster which spells out group norms and allows employees to discuss employment worries.

The grapevine tends to flourish when:

- there is a lack of information provided to employees, meaning they try to fill the gap themselves

- employees feel insecure about their positions

- there is personal animosity or interest in a situation, such as when a friend is disciplined by a supervisor

- there is new information that people wish to spread quickly.

Management may make use of the grapevine by using it to distribute information that they would not usually want to transmit formally. For instance, managers could use the grapevine to prepare staff for the formal announcement of some bad news.

Test your understanding 3

State whether each of the following statements are **true** or **false**.

(1) Informal communications in the workplace should not exist.

(2) Over-reliance on informal communication networks can arise from the failure of formal communication systems.

(3) Informal communications can be used by management to its advantage.

(4) Gossip can have a positive side in that it is a morale booster and can be beneficial to the individual in the workplace.

4 Effective and ineffective communication

The effectiveness of an organisation depends to a large extent on the effectiveness of communication by its management and employees.

4.1 The attributes of effective communication

Effective communication involves ensuring that the right person receives the right information at the rights time. It should therefore be:

- **Timely** – the speed of communication must be linked to the urgency of the issue being communicated. A report that a machine is out of action is of little use if it is delayed for hours or days, as it will increase the amount of production time lost.

- **Accurate and complete** – any information in the communication should be factually correct and all relevant facts should be stated to avoid wrong conclusions being drawn.

- **Relevant** – the message should not be excessive in volume as this will overload the receiver.

- **Directed to the right people** – care must be taken not to send information to the wrong people. This could cause confusion or even loss of confidentiality of sensitive information.

- **Understandable** – care must be taken with the presentation of the information, so that all recipients will be able to comprehend its meaning.

- **Cost effective** – as far as possible, the communication must be achieved at a reasonable cost to the organisation.

Effective communication is essential for the organisation as is ensures that:

- instructions, rules and procedures are properly understood by all employees

- individuals know what is expected of them

- there is better co-ordination between individuals, groups and departments

- it is easier for managers to plan and control operations more efficiently

- forming, swapping and testing of ideas is encouraged, improving innovation

- increased trust and reduced conflict within the organisation.

4.2 Barriers to effective communication

Despite the need for effective communication, there are a number of barriers and breakdowns that can occur, causing problems within the organisation.

A barrier to communication is anything that stops information from:

- getting to its intended recipient(s)
- being understood by the recipient(s) and/or
- being acted on in the manner intended.

Typical communication barriers include:

Status differences between receiver and sender can mean that more junior members of staff can be reluctant to pass information upwards for fear of criticism.

Language differences or the use of technical or professional jargon can prevent understanding of communications.

Conflict between individuals within the organisation may lead to communication being limited or withdrawn between them.

Overload – if too much information is communicated at once, the receiver may become overwhelmed and fail to understand what is expected of them.

Distance between communicators can be a problem. Typically, individuals will respond more promptly to those near-by!

Personal differences between the receiver and sender, such as age, education or priorities may mean that they interpret the information in different ways, causing confusion.

Test your understanding 4

X is a junior manager in his early 40s who joined his company at the age of 16. He sticks to a strict routine, arriving and leaving work punctually. He is married with two children at school. He has always worked in the functional section that he now manages and is the most experienced employee in his particular field. However, he is not familiar with latest developments in information technology and feels swamped by an excess of useless information. He claims that he is, in any case, aware of the information he needs, but his subordinates worry because they notice that he ignores information that does not agree with his opinions.

Y is a young accounting graduate who works in the management information department. She has been promoted quickly to supervisor level, having joined the company a few years ago straight from university. She is single and lives close to the office and often works late because she loves computers and is fascinated by their potential. She frequently and fluently tells anyone willing to listen that the company is old-fashioned and needs to be dragged into the twenty-first century. X hears this, disapproves but does not comment, and carries on in his usual way.

Although Y and X are located in different buildings on the same site, their work requires them to co-operate regularly. Their relations are getting more and more strained and their work is suffering.

Required:

Identify and describe the barriers to communication between the two colleagues.

4.3 Consequences of ineffective communication

If the organisation fails to deal with the barriers to communication, its internal and external communications may become significantly less useful.

Lack of downward communication is likely to result in:

- poor awareness of corporate objectives at lower management levels

- poor understanding of working instructions and responsibilities

- poor morale of junior managers because they are not consulted about changes which affect them or their working conditions.

Lack of upward communication, including 'feedback', has the following undesirable consequences for management:

- early warning of troubled areas is not received

- benefit of creative ability in subordinates is lost

- participation of subordinates is limited

- need for change is not appreciated because management is isolated from the operation areas

- control becomes difficult

- introduction of change is difficult.

Lack of lateral communication often leads to:

- divisions in management teams

- lack of co-ordination

- rivalry between sections and departments

- lack of advice and involvement by staff specialists.

Illustration 3 – Communications in the workplace

Perhaps the best way to think about the way in which communication can go wrong is to consider what good communication would be like:

- It would use appropriate language (e.g. no jargon; written so that the intended recipient can understand it).

- It would go only to who should receive it – not to everyone.

- It would use the right medium to communicate the information.

- The information would get to the recipient in good time for it to be used.

Taking the above list, it is easy to produce a list of how communications go wrong:

- Information is omitted or distorted by the sender.

- Information is misunderstood due to the use of inappropriate jargon or lack of clarity.

- Information is presented using an inappropriate medium (e.g. via email rather than in a proper report, or via telephone when face-to-face is better).

- Information arrives too late, or is incomplete.

4.4 Overcoming barriers to communication

In order to avoid these problems, management should first identify any barriers to communication within their organisation and then consider practical ways of dealing with them.

These could include:

- agree and confirm priorities and deadlines for the receipt of information

- spend sufficient time ensuring that the information is sent to all the right people

- keep communication as simple as possible, avoiding jargon

- confirm that the information sent has been received and understood

- avoid inconsistent verbal/non-verbal communication, as this tends to confuse the receivers.

Illustration 4 – Communications in the workplace

A manager is frequently accused of upsetting his staff by the tone of his memos. How can this situation be resolved?

The manager concerned could spend time reading memos sent by other managers then compare and contrast both the content and tone with that of his own memos. He can call more meetings or speak to staff individually rather than sending memos all the time. He can ask staff, informally, what they dislike about his memos. He can make it clear to staff that the memos are not intended to cause offence. He can ask to, be asked to, or arrange to, attend a short course on communication skills.

Although anticipating is preferable to reacting to problems when they occur, this is not always possible. Unexpected difficulties will invariably arise. Example of these include:

- Unexpected breakdowns of equipment may occur.

- A communication method may be inappropriate for a particular message.

- Receiver(s) may not be in the correct frame of mind to accept a message.

- Messages may be delayed causing mistrust and suspicion.

- An official message may be received before a manager has the opportunity to discuss an issue informally with his staff.

- People may not be available to receive important messages.

Ultimately, successful communication depends on continuous feedback and monitoring of existing communication systems. Information received from monitoring should be evaluated and findings acted on swiftly. If difficulties are identified these need to be corrected before further damage can occur.

Test your understanding 5

Five possible barriers to communication are as follows.

(a) The persons communicating might come from very different backgrounds, in terms of work experience and expertise, or socially. Substantial age differences, and lifestyles, can also create barriers to communication.

(b) The message might be distorted in transmission, e.g. if it has to be transmitted to several people before it reaches the end user.

(c) In a multi-national organisation employees might have to overcome a language barrier to communicate with each other.

(d) If there is information overload, an individual might be given too much information, and be unable to understand the message.

(e) Where there is conflict within the organisation, and two individuals or departments are hostile towards each other, communications from one to the other will be treated with suspicion or disbelief.

Required:

Suggest how these five barriers could be overcome.

5 Communication patterns

A communication pattern illustrates how individuals communicate with each other within a group or organisation.

Leavitt identified five major patterns of communication: wheel (or star), circle, all-channel, chain and 'Y'.

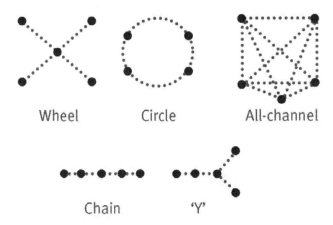

Wheel   Circle   All-channel

Chain   'Y'

These five can be grouped into two main types:

- **centralised networks** – chain, wheel and 'Y' – group members have to go through a central person in order to communicate with others. This leads to unequal access to information within the group.

- **decentralised networks** – circle and all-channel – information flows freely between members without having to go through a central person.

Leavitt's main conclusions were that:

- The wheel is always the fastest way to reach a conclusion, making it ideal for problem-solving. The circle is the slowest.

- For complex problems, the all-channel is the most likely to reach the best decision.

- The level of satisfaction for individuals was highest in the circle, fairly high in the all-channel and relatively low in the other, centralised networks. The centralised networks saw high job satisfaction for the central figure, with the remaining members feeling isolated.

6 Chapter summary

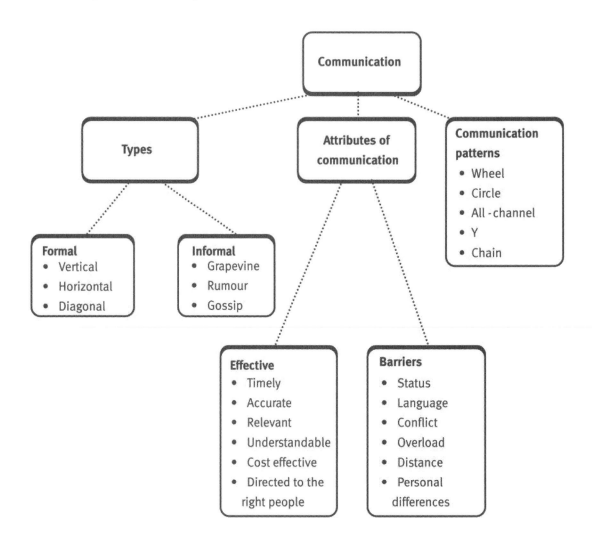

7 Practice questions

Test your understanding 6

Misha, on office junior, is asked to send a message to the head of another department. What type of communication is this?

A   Diagonal

B   Horizontal

C   Lateral

D   Vertical

Test your understanding 7

Which of the following is not usually a purpose of lateral or horizontal communication?

A   Task co-ordination

B   Problem solving

C   Giving instructions

D   Conflict resolution

Test your understanding 8

Which of the following patterns of communication would be best if a quick decision is needed?

A   Chain

B   Y

C   All-channel

D   Wheel

Test your understanding 9

Which of the following is a likely consequence of a lack of downward communication within an organisation?

A   Rivalry between sections and departments

B   Difficulty when introducing change

C   Poor awareness of corporate objectives at lower levels

D   Early warning of problems is not received

Test your understanding 10

Communication can be structured in many different ways within organisations, including wheel, circle, all-channel and Y patterns.

Required:

(a) **Identify which pattern of communication relates to each of the following statements.**

    A   This is the fastest way of reaching a conclusion.

    B   This is the best pattern for dealing with a complex decision.

    C   This produces the highest overall level of satisfaction for participants.

    D   Along with the wheel, this is an example of a centralised network.

    For each of the following, select ONE of A, B, C or D.

    (i)   **All-channel**

    (ii)   **Circle**

    (iii) **Wheel**

    (iv) **Y**

                                     (0.5 marks each, total = 2 marks)

(b) Communication is made up of several key elements. These include:

    A   Encoder

    B   Noise

    C   Receiver

    D   Channel

    The following sentences contain gaps which specify the appropriate element of communication.

    When producing feedback, the 1 will send a message which signals that they have understood and/or acted upon the information they have been provided.

    Required:

    (i)   **Select the correct element of communication which appropriately fills gap 1 above (i.e. select A, B, C or D).**

    The message may not be fully understood upon receipt, due to interference in the transmission channel, known as 2.

    (ii)   **Select the correct element of communication which appropriately fills gap 2 above (i.e. select A, B, C or D).**

                                        (1 mark each, total = 2 marks)

                                              (Total: 4 marks)

Test your understanding answers

Test your understanding 1

The correct answers are:

(i)   Diagonal

(ii)   Horizontal

(iii)   Vertical

Test your understanding 2

The correct answer is A – True

Vertical and lateral (horizontal) communication flows are associated with hierarchical organisations. Vertical communication flows up and down the scalar chain, from boss to subordinate and from subordinate to boss. Lateral communication flows between colleagues or between different sections and departments.

Very little formal horizontal communication may occur in an organisation that is managed in an authoritarian style. This is because the manager 'at the top' wants to know everything that is happening, and wants to be involved in all decision making. Information must therefore be passed up to the top manager so that decisions can be passed back down to someone else.

Test your understanding 3

1   **False** – informal communications in the workplace are inevitable and management should recognise it and use it to their advantage.

2   **True** – in the absence of a formal communication system, rumour and gossip will receive too much employee attention and belief.

3   **True** – there are circumstances when management can effectively harness the informal system.

4   **True**.

Test your understanding 4

Analysis of the case reveals that there are a variety of reasons for the barriers in communication that exist between X and D. The major reasons are:

Differences in social background; for instance, age, education, marital status, etc. These might result in:

- failure to understand each other's point of view, values and priorities

- failure to listen to the information the other person is giving

- lack of shared 'vocabulary', which might lead to lack of understanding of the message

- stereotyping each other into specific classes with similar traits and characteristics, e.g. 'stick-in-the-mud'.

X and D are located in different departments and buildings which may mean they do not share the same departmental objectives and may not have the opportunity to meet and discuss their differences face-to-face. Communication which is limited to telephone calls prevents access to non-verbal messages, which could provide additional information about each other.

Personal barriers may exist which will hinder effective communication. These may be due to:

- Distrust and feeling threatened by and fearing the computerised systems, which can result in any information provided by the system being viewed with scepticism.

- D seeing X as an older person who has failed to advance his career, having reached only junior manager, which may result in her talking down to him. On the other hand X may resent D being promoted to supervisor at a relatively young age.

- D resenting X working 9 to 5, and exhibiting a reluctance to become familiar with the computerised system. X may feel that his family commitments do not allow him to give the extra time required to the organisation, in order that he may learn more about the new computer system.

- D's attitude leading her to make comments which imply criticism of people like X and this could lead to a degree of resentment on the part of X which may also restrict communication.

If the situation described in the question causes personal conflict or antagonism between X and D, then further communication problems can occur:

- emotions (anger, fear, frustration) will creep into communications and further hinder the transmission of clear information

- the receiver of the information will tend to hear what they want to hear in any message and ignore anything they do not want to accept.

Test your understanding 5

(a) When individuals communicating with each other come from different backgrounds, they should be encouraged by management to show consideration for the other person. When an engineer communicates with an accountant, the engineer must be wary of using engineering jargon without explaining it, just as accountants must be careful of using accounting and finance terms that non-accountants are unlikely to know. A highly-educated person, when communicating with someone less educated, should choose his words carefully, so that his message is clear and understandable.

(b) Communication flows should be organised so that there are as few links in the communication chain as possible between the sender of the message and its eventual recipient. Lateral communications should replace unnecessary upward and downward communication flows. Electronic communication systems should contribute towards this aim.

(c) Language difficulties can be reduced in two ways. First, employees should be given language training as appropriate in another language. Secondly, the organisation should select an official language for all its meetings at a certain level of management and above. In many global corporations, English is the official language.

(d) Information overload can be reduced by improvements in reporting systems. For long reports, there should be a much briefer summary containing all the essential points and recommendations. Control reports should use reporting by exception, and draw attention to performance of an unusual or unexpected nature (such as large variances). Narrative can be summarised into tables and diagrams.

(e) Attempts to resolve conflict between individuals or departments should be made by the management in charge of them both. A solution to the problem of conflict is partly an improvement in communications. Management should arrange for more direct contact between individuals in different departments, and should use their interpersonal skills to try to overcome misunderstandings and disagreements.

Test your understanding 6

The correct answer is A

Misha is communicating with someone who is in a different department AND at a different level of the hierarchy to her.

Note that horizontal and lateral communication are the same.

Test your understanding 7

The correct answer is C

Lateral communication refers to communication between individuals at the same level of the organisation's hierarchy. This means that they will be unlikely to have the authority to give each other orders.

The other main purpose of lateral communication is information sharing.

Test your understanding 8

The correct answer is D

The wheel is always seen as the fastest approach to reaching a conclusion.

Test your understanding 9

The correct answer is C

A tends to be a problem without lateral communication, when different sections of the organisation do not communicate with each other. B and D are problems caused by a lack of upward communication, with managers failing to listen to more junior workers.

C is caused by poor downwards communication, where management fail to communicate with junior staff, leading to a lack of awareness of corporate objectives among the workers.

Test your understanding 10

(a)   The correct answers are:

   (i)   **B**

   (ii)   **C**

   (iii)   **A**

   (iv)   **D**

(b)   The correct terms were:

   (i)   **C** – remember that when the feedback is sent, the receiver becomes a sender!

   (ii)   **B** – by definition.

A

B

C

KAPLAN PUBLISHING